THE REPRESENTATION OF
MEANING IN MEMORY

THE EXPERIMENTAL PSYCHOLOGY SERIES

Arthur W. Melton · Consulting Editor

MELTON AND MARTIN · *Coding Processes in Human Memory*, 1972
MCGUIGAN AND LUMSDEN · *Contemporary Approaches to Conditioning and Learning*, 1973
ANDERSON AND BOWER · *Human Associative Memory*, 1973
GARNER · *The Processing of Information and Structure*, 1974
MURDOCK · *Human Memory: Theory and Data*, 1974
KINTSCH · *The Representation of Meaning in Memory*, 1974

THE REPRESENTATION OF MEANING IN MEMORY

BY WALTER KINTSCH

UNIVERSITY OF COLORADO

with the collaboration of:
Edward J. Crothers, Gregory Glass, Janice M. Keenan,
Gail McKoon, and Dorothy Monk

LEA **LAWRENCE ERLBAUM ASSOCIATES, PUBLISHERS**
HILLSDALE, NEW JERSEY
1974

DISTRIBUTED BY THE HALSTED PRESS DIVISION OF

JOHN WILEY & SONS
New York   Toronto   London   Sydney

Lawrence Erlbaum Associates, Publishers
62 Maria Drive
Hillsdale, New Jersey 07642

Distributed solely by Halsted Press Division
John Wiley & Sons, Inc., New York

Library of Congress Cataloging in Publication Data

Kintsch, Walter, 1932–
    The representation of meaning in memory.

    (The Experimental psychology series)
    Bibliography: p.
    1. Memory. 2. Meaning (Psychology) I. Title.
II. Series. [DNLM: 1. Memory. BF371 K56r]
BF371.K477   153.1'2   74–17331
ISBN 0–470–48074–2

Printed in the United States of America

CONTENTS

Preface

1 ORIENTING ATTITUDES 1

PART I   THEORY 7

2 A PROPOSITIONAL THEORY FOR THE REPRESENTATION OF
   MEANING IN KNOWLEDGE AND MEMORY 9
   1. Propositions   13
   2. The Text Base   15
   3. The Structure of Semantic Memory   23
   4. Acceptability and Metaphors   36
   5. Psychological Process Models   39

3 ON THE ADEQUACY OF PROPOSITIONAL TEXT BASES FOR THE
   REPRESENTATION OF MEANING 45
   1. Definite and Indefinite Description   47
   2. Quantification   50
   3. Modality   53
   4. Implication and Presupposition   56
   5. Location, Time, and Tense   62
   6. Conclusion   70

**4   A PROCESS MODEL FOR EPISODIC MEMORY: THE ENCODING
AND RETRIEVAL OF EXPERIENCES** 73
1. Critical Issues   74
2. A General Theory of Storage, Organization, and Retrieval
in Episodic Memory   82
3. Applications   92
4. Discussion   100

PART II   EXPERIMENTAL INVESTIGATIONS 103

**5   ON THE ABSTRACT NATURE OF THE MEMORY
REPRESENTATIONS FOR TEXTS (with D. Monk)** 107
1. Drawing Inferences from Syntactically Simple and Complex
Paragraphs   108
2. Inference Latencies and Paragraph Length   117

**6   THE PSYCHOLOGICAL REALITY OF TEXT BASES I:
READING RATE AND COMPREHENSION (with J. M. Keenan)** 123

**7   THE PSYCHOLOGICAL REALITY OF TEXT BASES II:
SENTENCE MEMORY** 137
1. Recall of Propositions as a Function of their Position in
the Hierarchical Structure (with J. M. Keenan)   137
2. Effects of Propositional Structure upon Sentence
Recall (with G. Glass)   140

8   MEMORY FOR INFORMATION INFERRED DURING READING 153
1. The Identification of Explicitly and Implicitly Presented
Information (with J. M. Keenan)   153
2. Response Latencies to Explicit and Implicit Statements as a
Function of the Delay Between Reading and Test (with
G. McKoon and J. M. Keenan)   166

**9   MEMORY SEARCH I: PARAGRAPH MEMORY AND THE
RETRIEVAL OF INFORMATION** 177
1. Experiment I: Latencies of True-False Judgments as a
Function of the Length of Paragraphs (with D. Monk)   179
2. Experiment II: Recognition Latencies as a Function of
Paragraph Length (with D. Monk)   184
3. Discussion   188

10   MEMORY SEARCH II: THE USE OF KNOWLEDGE IN THE
      VERIFICATION OF STATEMENTS 195
           1. Review   195
           2. Judgments of Semantic Acceptability (with
               E. J. Crothers)   203
           3. Theoretical Implications   210

11   LEXICAL DECOMPOSITION: COMPRESSION AND MEMORY 219
           1. The Problem   219
           2. Experiments on Processing Difficulty   225
           3. Memory Experiments   233
           Conclusion   240

12   INTERIM CONCLUSIONS 243

      REFERENCES 263
      AUTHOR INDEX 273
      SUBJECT INDEX 277

1
ORIENTING ATTITUDES

In recent years cognitive psychology has shaken off the artificial limitations of its subject matter and methodology that had impaired its progress. In focussing their attention once more on the truly important and interesting problems in the field, psychologists are now being forced to disregard the traditional borders of their discipline. Indeed, it is impossible to restrict the study of memory, thought, and language to psychology proper. To do so means cutting off one's investigation from rich bases of knowledge that have been accumulated by linguists and philosophers throughout history. To be sure, linguistics and, even more so, philosophy have their own methods and their own problems, and their results cannot simply be incorporated into psychology. But though these disciplines will certainly remain separate, the cognitive psychologist can neglect the knowledge that is available from neighboring disciplines only at the risk of letting his own work become provincial and trivial.

It is not enough to describe behavior in certain well-controlled laboratory situations; such descriptions must be powerful and general enough to deal with a much broader range of observations about cognition and language derived from other disciplines. Chomsky (1957) was entirely right when he claimed that, on the basis of purely linguistic considerations, certain requirements can be set up which a psychological theory must be able to meet. One could debate about the exact nature of these requirements, but there can be no doubt about the reality of these constraints. Attempts to begin the psychological study of language without inquiring what others have to say about the topic from their own, nonpsychological standpoints are doomed to failure. The neglect with which Skinner's *Verbal Behavior* is treated today attests to this point. Indeed, the constraints that sister sciences impose upon psychological theory should not be viewed as foreign intrusions into psychological territory, but welcomed as a tool to reduce significantly the all too numerous alternative hypotheses

1

that are usually available to the psychologist. When we know as little about cognitive processes as we do now, we have every reason to grasp at every straw that is offered.

Psycholinguistics is a relatively new subarea of cognitive psychology and has developed rather curiously. It is probably fair to say that during the 1960's, a period of rapid growth for psycholinguistics, experimental psychology proper and psycholinguistics managed to avoid almost all interaction. Fillenbaum (1973) claims that "As a matter of historical fact, the concerns of the student of verbal learning and memory and those of the psychologist of language have been, and are different [p. 79]." In support he cites, among others, the almost complete lack of overlap in the references of two representative review articles, "Memory and Verbal Learning" by Tulving and Madigan (1970) and "Psycholinguistics" by Fillenbaum (1971). Fillenbaum is, of course, correct historically; students of verbal learning and memory have for a long time disregarded the new psycholinguistics, and the psycholinguists themselves were often merely interested in testing in the psychological laboratory certain linguistic theses (as for example the psychological reality of sentence transformation), with little regard for such mundane matters as short- and long-term memory. Neither party profited from this mutual neglect, and I believe that times are changing in this respect, too. Psycholinguistics is changing its character, and the memory and learning fraternity is beginning to realize the fascinating possibilities of the new subject matter. The recent publication of Anderson and Bower's *Human Associative Memory* must be a milestone in the integration of psycholinguistics into cognitive experimental psychology. That this is a broadly based development, and not a passing fashion, can be appreciated by thumbing through recent issues of the *Journal of Verbal Learning and Verbal Behavior*. There is a definite trend there in terms of the preferred experimental material: The 1950's were still dominated by the nonsense syllables (with paired-associate learning as the most suitable experimental design), the 1960's were characterized by the use of word lists (with free recall replacing paired-associate learning in the psychologists' favor), while the present decade is witnessing a shift to even more complex learning materials. At present, we have reached the point where lists of sentences are being substituted for word lists in studies of recall and recognition. Hopefully, this will not be the endpoint of this development, and we shall soon see psychologists handle effectively the problems posed by the analysis of connected texts.

The research reported in the present volume is a product of this time of transition. The theory aims at generality and at encompassing as broad a range as possible of phenomena relevant to problems of language processing and memory. In formulating psychological explanations of language and thinking, a conscious attempt has been made to keep in mind the constraints imposed by other disciplines, while at the same time maintaining the traditional standards of experimental psychology. Linguistic and logical scholarship, as well as computer programs, have their uses in guiding the psychologist's thinking, but in the final analysis experimentation under controlled circumstances is necessary to sort out the bewildering array of observations we are faced with. Even if we cannot tell at this particular stage of investigation which particular experiment might be the best and the most fruitful one in the long run, it is nevertheless possible to perform informative and useful experiments.

The point we have just made, that one should not conceive psychological theories so narrow as to exclude linguistic observations about language, can also be turned around: The new theories must be able to deal with the old facts. It would be ill advised to forget that cognitive psychology has available a very solid body of experimental data, the list-learning research of the last decades. Whatever the limitations of this research, it is well-established experimentally and provides a valuable proving ground for any theory of learning and memory.

The approach advocated here conflicts with several widely held views in both psychology and linguistics. It has no use at all for the competence-performance distinction which, in my opinion, is merely an excuse for both the linguist and psychologist to justify the neglect of each others' findings. Chomsky (1965) makes a ". . . fundamental distinction bewteen competence (the speaker-hearer's knowledge of his language) and performance (the actual use of the language in concrete situations) [p. 4]." Competence is ". . . unaffected by such grammatically irrelevant conditions as memory limitations, distractions, shifts of attention and interest, and errors in applying knowledge [p. 3]." Performance reflects competence only in indirect ways: Knowing the linguistic rules to generate a sentence will tell us very little about how people actually generate a sentence. This strict separation permits the linguist to deal with convenient abstractions, uninhibited by psychological reality, and it provides the psychologist with the facetious argument that linguistic theories have nothing to do with processes anyway. As long as a linguistic theory is strictly a competence theory, it is of no interest to the psychologist. Indeed I doubt that it should be of much interest to linguists either, but that is for them to decide. The linguistic theories discussed below are not of that type, and process notions, appeals to a person's beliefs, or to memory processes, are inextricable parts of many of them. Equally to be rejected is the neat separation between structure and process, upon which many psychologists insist today. Such a separation is both impossible and misleading. There is no structure apart from psychological processes; structure is the result of processes. Two examples must do for the moment to illustrate the close interconnection between process and structure in the present approach. In Chapter 2, the set of all semantically acceptable sentences is discussed; this set is not something fixed, something that exists separately from process considerations. It is the result of psychological processing, of applying production rules to information stored in memory. The set of all acceptable sentences is a potential set that could be generated from a given semantic memory, if certain processes take place. Thus, what is a semantically acceptable sentence will differ for different individuals as well as for the same individual at different times. Similarly, in Chapter 3, (psychological) implication is discussed not as a fixed structural relationship that holds between sentences, independent of the beholder, but as the consequence of certain psychological processes performed by a given individual. Thus, whether sentence A implies sentence B is not something fixed for all time, but depends upon the occurrence of specifiable psychological processes; indeed, it is possible that for a given individual at a given time there would be no implicational relationship between two sentences, while under somewhat different circumstances, for the same individual, such a relationship might be constructed between the same two sentences. Structures are what is being generated, but they have no existence of their own.

The distinction between episodic and semantic memory, on the other hand, has proven very valuable in the present context. Semantic memory refers to a person's knowledge; episodic memory, to his store of experiences. Obviously, most or all knowledge is derived in some way from personal experiences at one time or another, but these experiences have become depersonalized, at least in part, separated from their original context, and are thus much more broadly useful than specific, personal, context-bound experiences. This distinction was introduced by Tulving (1972), and the reader is referred to the original discussion for a more detailed treatment, as well as to some complementary remarks in the following Chapters. No sharp line can be drawn between episodic memory and semantic memory, but nevertheless the two separate terms come in handy in sorting out various aspects of memory. If for no other reason, Tulving's distinction is valuable because it helps to focus attention on some problems that have been traditionally neglected in both verbal learning research and psycholinguistics. These are the problems concerned with the processing, retention, and retrieval of knowledge, as distinguished from personal, context-bound memories. Surely, this is one of the reasons why psychological research (as distinguished from programmatic theories without appreciable bases in experimental cognitive psychology) has been so notoriously ineffective in directing educational practice. Most of the experimental research concerning memory has never really dealt with problems of the acquisition and retention of knowledge, but with episodic memory, which is not at all the problem of interest in education. Simply replacing the words with sentences in our experiments will make the research no more relevant to education than it was before (or only very little so). An educational technology squarely based upon psychological research needs research concerned with problems of knowledge. Even the most sophisticated understanding of episodic memory phenomena would be of little use in itself.

Historically, knowledge was considered an important topic for psychologists until the last few decades. What is called semantic memory today was at one time referred to as the apperceptive mass. The term is from Leibniz, but was brought into prominence in psychology by Herbart (1816). Herbart's fundamental insight was that new learning presupposes the availability of memory structures with which the new information can be connected. Learning does not consist in the passive recording of new information, but in apperception: The new information is connected in a meaningful way with a person's background of experience and knowledge. Apperception and apperceptive mass were enormously influential concepts in education and psychology throughout the 19th century. Today they are relegated to the history of psychology.

There is no reason to try to reintroduce these terms (partly because apperception underwent some subtle but confusing changes in meaning between Leibniz and

Wundt, who used it more in the sense of the present-day term "attention"). But it is important that we study the subject matter and the problems that were at one time designated with these terms. In order to do so, we need some sort of a language to talk about "knowledge." The approach taken here is to represent knowledge in terms of propositions. A proposition is a k-tuple of word concepts, one serving as a predicator and the others as arguments. Word concepts are abstract entities to be defined below; words are used to express word concepts verbally. Thus, a distinction is made between different levels of representation. Memory may refer to any of these levels, or to a combination thereof. For example, a sentence may be represented physically as an acoustic pattern, graphically as a string of letters, linguistically as a sequence of words, and conceptually in terms of its meaning. The last representation is the propositional one, and the study of the properties of this level of representation in memory, both theoretically and empirically, is the main concern of this book.

The question arises whether propositional representations as conceived here are indeed at the proper level of analysis for the study of language and thought. The problem is an old one, but it still resists satisfactory solution. None can be provided here either, but it is necessary to point out where and how the present approach fits into the range of solutions proposed by others. The problem can be formulated as "What is an idea?" or, more precisely, "How is an idea to be represented?" It is suggested here that propositions represent ideas, and that language (or imagery) expresses propositions, and hence ideas. Thinking occurs at the propositional level; language is the expression of thought. This is a squarely anti-behaviorist position; arguments against this position have been frequently made, with especial brilliance by Kantor (1936). There is no need to refute these arguments again, since this discussion has left many well-known public records (see, for instance, Humphrey, 1963). A more acute problem is posed today by attacks upon propositional theories from the opposite camp. It is sometimes claimed that propositions do not represent ideas, but that ideas are at a deeper level of analysis than propositions. Ideas are claimed to be unarticulated, pre-propositional schemes of thought; propositions specify ideas, express them in some sense, but rob them of their all-encompassing nature. It is difficult to state this problem clearly because of its very nature, but it has been a recurring question in the study of thinking. Humphrey (1963, p. 260) presents a good historical discussion of the early work concerning this question. He distinguishes various levels of representation of a sentence: the actual choice of words (today we would call this the surface form of the sentence), the sentence schema (a Jamesian term, which has found a contemporary parallel in today's linguistic deep structure), the well-articulated sentence meaning (which is what the propositional representation is concerned with), and finally a state of consciousness from which all the other representations are ultimately derived.

What is the evidence (other than introspection, which might as well be neglected here) for the existence of pre-propositional schemes of thought? Consider, for example, any sufficiently complex event and the propositional representation of its description. Several propositional paraphrases that are all representations of the same event can be devised. In Chapter 2, in the section on discourse analysis, such problems are treated in some detail. A given propositional representation may be complete and sufficient to the extent that everything else about the event in question may be deduced from it, but it is not unique: There may be another way of representing the same state of affairs, just as complete and just as sufficient as the one chosen. Hence, some psychologists have assumed a deeper, more basic, level of representation underlying the propositional one.

The argument just presented is, of course, not very precise. Indeed, if it could be stated with precision, we would probably be able to decide the issue one way or another. As it is, it is difficult to argue on principle against the existence of pre-propositional, unarticulated thoughts. One may maintain, however, that no matter how this problem is eventually decided, it makes little difference for all practical purposes. No one has clear enough notions to permit a serious, scientific investigation of such thought schemes at the present time. We can, and should, do something about the study of propositional representation, on the other hand. If they are not the deepest, most basic elements of thought, it appears almost certain that they are the proper units of analysis for *one* level of representation. Clearly, thoughts do not stay unarticulated forever and must be formulated precisely during some stage of processing. Thus, whatever we find out about the characteristics of the propositional representations would not be wasted, even if that representation is not the most basic one. At this time so little is known about pre-propositional thought schemas that it seems quite defensible to disregard them altogether and to assume, as a working hypothesis, that ideas are represented propositionally.

Before leaving this discussion, one possible misunderstanding must be anticipated. Whatever pre-propositional thought schemas might be, they are not images. Images pose the same problem as propositions: Suppose a person has an image of an object which is sufficient to specify the object in all relevant detail (such an image would be more like a map or a plan than a photograph, presumably). The problem is that there may be alternative maps or plans that would be just as good as the original one. There are as many imagery paraphrases for a scene as propositional paraphrases. Imagery and propositional representations are probably more similar than is commonly admitted. There is good evidence (Pylyshyn, 1973) that imagery is based upon propositional representations, much as verbal expressions are, the differences between the two lying primarily in the way these representations can be processed and accessed in memory.

PART I
THEORY

Understanding a sentence means
understanding a language.

Ludwig Wittgenstein

2

A PROPOSITIONAL THEORY FOR THE REPRESENTATION OF MEANING IN KNOWLEDGE AND MEMORY

The theory to be outlined here is intended to serve as basis for the development of psychological process models. These models should, eventually, provide an account of such topics as the use and acquisition of knowledge and the comprehension and memorization of text, even though only small steps toward the development of such models can be undertaken at the present time. As a consequence of these goals, the formalism for the representation of meaning that is used in the theory must be general enough to be usefully employed in all these different situations. The formalism itself is motivated by various linguistic and logical considerations, which will be detailed in this and the following chapter.

Whenever the term meaning is used here it is used in a psychological sense; we are only concerned with the psychological representation of meaning, that is, the meaning of a concept is defined only with respect to a particular semantic memory. A concept is defined through its relationship with other concepts in semantic memory, but each semantic memory is subjective. Each person's knowledge consists of only a (small) subset of the culturally shared knowledge. We shall neglect these individual differences whenever possible and talk about semantic memory in general terms, though it must be remembered that this is merely an idealization, useful for our purposes, but not to be confused with reality. The theory of meaning advocated here is, therefore, a purely psychological one; broader philosophical issues are of no concern. Specifically, the theory remains neutral with respect to the claim of Frege (1892) that purely psychological theories of meaning are inadequate philosophically. Many philosophers today, following Frege, claim that a semantic analysis must be free of psychology, and that semantics should be concerned with abstract entities called *meanings*, which are independent of any mind or minds (e.g. Quine, 1960). The present theory is not concerned with this issue; instead it focuses exclusively upon the representation of meaning in the mind. It would have been possible to avoid philosophical ambiguity if the term *meaning* had always been replaced by *representation of meaning*, but as long as the reader is aware of our intentions, not much damage can result from a freer use of the term.

The term *semantic memory* as used here is synonymous with personal knowledge (as distinguished from culturally shared knowledge). An important subset of semantic memory is the lexicon. The entries of the lexicon are word concepts. Word concepts are abstract entities that may be expressed in the surface structure as words or phrases. For the sake of clarity and convenience, a word concept will be denoted by the word (in capital letters) usually used to express it, but it must be remembered that word concepts and words have a completely different theoretical status. For each word concept there is a lexical description that specifies its meaning and use. Homographs and homophones are separate lexical entries. Lexical descriptions may contain sensory information (e.g., as part of the lexical entry RED), or motor programs (WALK), as well as linguistic information (the relationship of RED or WALK to other words). However, we shall concentrate entirely upon the semantic component of lexical descriptions. Semantic descriptions are not in terms of semantic primitives, but in terms of other lexical items. Each word is thus defined by reference to other words. The sensory and motor parts of the lexical descriptions permit an escape from the inherent circularity of such descriptions: They provide the interface between the real world and the semantic structure.

Semantic memory also contains entries that do not correspond to words but to concepts for which there is no special word in the language, as well as to broad topics of knowledge. There is no difference in principle between the way single words and general topics of knowledge are defined in semantic memory.

Word concepts appear in semantic memory in two ways: as lexical entries (word-concept types) and as descriptors of other terms in semantic memory (word-concept tokens). Thus, there will be a lexical entry PIANO, describing what a person knows about this word concept (note the importance of sensorimotor information in such a description!), but PIANO will also be used as a token, that is, as a descriptor in many other lexical entries, such as MUSICAL INSTRUMENTS, MUSICIANS, and BARTOK, to name but a few. The token PIANO will also appear as a component of other items in both semantic and episodic memory, not just the lexicon, whenever a memory unit involves PIANO. A token is understood by relating it to its type, which makes available all the information about its meaning and use that is stored with the word-concept type.

The question of how ambitious a lexicon should be, that is, in how much detail the meaning of a word concept should be represented in the lexicon, can not be answered simply. In general, it appears that fine nuances of meaning are not so much the property of a word itself, but are something that is given to the word by its use in a particular context. Therefore, it may not be necessary to specify each word precisely in the lexicon, if one can show how a particular meaning could be elaborated on the basis of a given context.

The same formalism that is used for lexical descriptions can be applied to any kind of description whatever, whether it is a part of semantic memory or not. That is, any text may be represented in this manner. Texts are represented by word-concept tokens. Understanding a text involves understanding the word-concept tokens (by accessing the word-concept types) and their interrelations (by analyzing the structure of the text). Understanding a text, therefore, consists in assimilating it with one's general store of knowledge which is not the same, of course, as making it a permanent part thereof). Since every person's knowledge and experience is somewhat different from every other's, it follows as a corrolary of this claim that the way in which different people understand the same text may not always be the same, just as it may not be quite what the transmitter of the message had originally intended.

In principle, a text T may be derived from a base structure S (for speaker) and may yield as a result of comprehension by two listeners the base structures L_1 and L_2 with $S \neq L_1 \neq L_2$. The differences may be due to omissions on the part of the listeners or misinterpretations, but there also may be more subtle differences: The tokens in L_1 and L_2 may be alike, but the word concepts to which they refer may differ in significant ways. Finally, the possibility must be considered that the text T itself is an incomplete or misleading expression of the speaker's base S. The speaker may have deleted part of the text base S in constructing T (because it was obvious to him from context, or for stylistic reasons, or perhaps merely because he wanted to be obscure). Obviously, such discrepancies must be limited; otherwise communication breaks down.

A text base completely expresses the ideas that a speaker or writer has in mind. The idea itself may, of course, be confused or contradictory, but no noise is introduced in representing an idea in a text base. This is a crucial assumption made here, and it has profound effects on the details of the model that will be developed below. Ideas, whatever they might be, are unambiguously represented by the text base; as they are expressed, they undergo various transformations, but as a rule the message is still unambiguous. Surface expressions (spoken or written text), when complete and in their actual context, both verbal and nonverbal, are usually not ambiguous. Ambiguity arises when sentences are taken from their text and context. The concern with ambiguity that characterizes so much current work in semantics is in part misguided. It arises because linguists write sentence grammars instead of text grammars, philosophers analyze isolated sentence examples, and little psychological work has as yet been done with complete texts and proper contexts. Obviously, no claim is made that ambiguity presents no problems for semantic theory, but only that these problems are greatly exaggerated by focussing upon arbitrary units, such as isolated sentences.

In addition to problems of ambiguity and discrepancies between the representations of a text on the part of speaker and listener, there is another feature of text comprehension which must not be overlooked. That is the familiar fact that text comprehension proceeds at several levels. We are concerned here primarily with the idea level, that is, the text base, but in addition there is the linguistic level (the words and sentences used together with their syntactic description), and finally the actual phonemic or graphemic expressions. The fact that several different levels of text need to be distinguished is of great significance for psychological processing models. Psychological processes may operate on any one of these levels. Sentence comparisons, for instance, may be made at the acoustic level, at a linguistic surface level, at various depths of transformation, or at the idea level. Experimental results will depend upon the level at which subjects are operating.

In the next sections of this chapter a theory for the psychological representation of meaning will be presented. The basic theoretical terms used are word concept, proposition, and text base. Word concepts have already been introduced above. Essentially, they are lexical entries, usually expressed linguistically through a word. Word concepts are joined together according to certain rules to form propositions. Propositions are n-tuples of word concepts, one of which serves as a predicator and the others as arguments. Section 1 will explain the construction of propositions. An ordered list of propositions forms a text base. Text bases are discussed in Section 2. Note that word concept, proposition, and text base are theoretical terms and that their definitions have the status of axioms. In what follows the implications of these axioms will be explored, though not in a formal manner. Whether the theory based upon these axioms is valid or not will be decided on the basis of how well it accounts for various linguistic, logical, and especially psychological observations. As with any other theory, however, the axioms are not directly testable. The only question one could ask about them is why they were chosen in this particular way, rather than in some other manner. Specifically, there are two alternatives that are sometimes preferred by semantic theorists, so that it appears worthwhile to outline here our reasoning for the choices made, even though these matters will be discussed more fully elsewhere. The first concerns the definition of propositions as multi-element units rather than restricting them to binary units. The only reason for assuming binary units appears to be that binary propositions are more convenient in some computer simulations, which is not a consideration that should receive much weight. Their linguistic artificiality speaks against binary units (see the discussion of case relations in Section 3.1), as do some psychological data reported in Chapter 7 which indicate that multi-element propositions indeed correspond to natural language units. The second, and more far reaching decision, concerns our choice not to decompose word concepts into semantic primitives. Three good reasons can be advanced for this decision, even though few semantic theorists favor this alternative. The first reason is logical: If one starts to decompose, it is hard to see where to stop. No one has provided a list of semantic primitives from which every other concept can be reconstructed. In the absence of such a list, decomposition is usually practiced in an arbitrary and inconsistent way. As a randomly chosen example, consider the decomposition of CRY by Anderson and Bower (1973, p. 194) as "Some animal sheds tears": This is just one aspect of CRY, and there is no compelling reason why it should figure so prominently in the decomposition of CRY (Webster's, in fact, does not use this aspect in the definition at all and instead concentrates upon the emotional state implied!). The second reason is simply an *a priori* consideration: It seems to be a poor hypothesis to assume that in memory and comprehension processes all concepts are decomposed into some small set of features, given that language has evolved to where we use complex word concepts. The final and decisive reason, however, consists of the data reported in Chapter 11, which do not support the notion of decomposition.

1. PROPOSITIONS

The semantic base of a text consists of ordered lists of propositions. The elements of a proposition are word concepts, that is, lexical items. A proposition contains a predicator and n arguments ($n \geqslant 1$). Word concepts may be used either as arguments or as predicators. It is the task of the lexicon to specify which combinations of arguments and predicators are permissible. The following conventions are observed: Propositions are enclosed by parentheses; the predicator is always written first; and all terms are separated by commas. Some examples are given below:

John sleeps.	(SLEEP,JOHN)	(1)
Mary bakes a cake.	(BAKE,MARY,CAKE)	(2)
A robin is a bird.	(BIRD,ROBIN)	(3)
A bird has feathers.	(HAVE,BIRD,FEATHERS)	(4)
The man is sick.	(SICK,MAN)	(5)
If Mary trusts John she is a fool.	(IF,(TRUST,MARY,JOHN),(FOOL,MARY))	(6)

In (1) and (2) the predicator is a verb. Sentence (3) is a special case, where a noun appears as the predicator. It would be possible to use a predicator such as IS-A and write (3) as (IS-A,ROBIN,BIRD), but it appears to be more consistent to omit the copula in the base expression of (3), just as it is omitted in (5). Sentence (5) illustrates the use of an adjective as a predicator, while in (6) a conjunction is used in this role. Sentence (6) also shows that propositions may be embedded within other propositions as their arguments. If such embeddings occur, there is an alternative notation that will be used frequently. There are three different propositions involved in (6), and it is sometimes preferable to separate these propositions notationally. This can be done by giving arbitrary names to the embedded propositions (we shall use Greek letters for this purpose). Thus, an alternative way of writing (6) is

$$(IF,\alpha,\beta)\&((TRUST,MARY,JOHN)=\alpha)\&((FOOL,MARY)=\beta). \qquad (6')$$

Many sentences are based upon more than one proposition, like (6). The following sentences provide further examples of compounds:

The old man smiled and left the room. (7)
(OLD,MAN)&(SMILE,MAN)&(LEAVE,MAN,ROOM)

Mary claimed that the old man smiled and left the room. (8)
(CLAIM,MARY,α)&((OLD,MAN)&(SMILE,MAN)&
(LEAVE,MAN,ROOM)=α)

The snow melts slowly. (MELT,SNOW)&(SLOW,MELT) (9)

Note the convention adopted here of connecting propositions by &. The order of propositions in (7) is significant: The first proposition established that there was an old man, and the remainder of the expression makes certain statements about this old man.

Isolated sentences are often ambiguous, but never base structures. It is, for instance, possible to interpret (8) as asserting that Mary claimed something and then left the room, which would correspond to the base structure

$$(\mathrm{CLAIM,MARY},\alpha)\&((\mathrm{OLD,MAN})\&(\mathrm{SMILE,MAN})=\alpha)\&$$
$$(\mathrm{LEAVE,MARY,ROOM}). \tag{8'}$$

The difference between the base structures (8) and (8′) is in the scope of *claim*. But note that both are entirely unambiguous, while at the same time (8) may be an ambiguous expression that could be derived from either base (though normally a speaker would express (8′) as . . . . . *and she left the room*, or at least by a hesitation pause or comma before the *and*).

The rules that turn a proposition into a sentence are complex ones. They include not only syntactic transformation rules, which linguists have explored at least to some extent, but also pragmatic rules about which we know as yet very little. Consider, for instance, that (BAKE,MARY,CAKE), which was example (2) above, may appear in the surface structure as any one of the following expressions, depending upon context:

Mary bakes a cake. (2′)

Mary is baking a cake.

A cake is being baked by Mary.

The baking of a cake by Mary.

Mary's baking of a cake.

Furthermore, in each of these expressions either *Mary* or *cake* may be omitted, creating several new versions. Which of these versions a speaker will use to express (2) depends upon factors that characterize the particular communication situation. What does the speaker want to communicate? What is already known to both speaker and receiver? What does the speaker want to stress? What is the theme of his communication? The propositional expression (BAKE,MARY,CAKE) merely specifies the logical structure of the sentence, with MARY as its logical subject and CAKE as its logical object. What the grammatical structure of the sentence will be, what the grammatical subject and object will be, may differ from case to case. The pragmatic structure of the sentence will vary similarly. Depending upon what the speaker wants to communicate, he may choose either MARY or CAKE as the theme of the sentence and choose a suitable surface form (including stress assignment) accordingly. Halliday (1970) has discussed these problems in a very lucid way. For present purposes it must be understood that for the most part we are working at the logical or ideational level, in Halliday's terminology. It is quite true that the prag-matic factors are of great significance in psychological research on language behavior, as Olson (1972), among others, has stressed so forcefully. Nevertheless, the extreme claim that *only* the pragmatic level is of psychological importance must be rejected.[1] The study of the logical-semantic structure of language and memory appears to be sufficiently rich and promising in itself. It is surely complex enough, and if any simplification can be gained by disregarding further complexities this appears to be a sound research strategy. Certainly, an understanding of both semantic and pragmatic factors will eventually be necessary, but for the moment, concentration upon one or the other seems quite appropriate. The two levels of description are closely intertwined, and though one can emphasize semantic factors, pragmatic considerations can never be neglected for long, as will be seen both in the theoretical treatment to follow and in the psychological experiments of Part II.

It is unlikely that all knowledge can be represented in the same way. Propositional knowledge, which will be our sole concern, is primarily verbal, though it is possible to represent nonverbal information by such means as well, as in some pattern recognition programs that use feature representations of images. On the other hand, analog representations of knowledge may underlie sensorimotor memory. The decision to neglect non-propositional knowledge here by no means implies a judgment that only verbal sources of knowledge are worth considering for the psychologist. It merely reflects the state of the art today: As yet there has been too little work on nonverbal memory, or on the possible analog representations of memory. The psychological research on verbal processes is much richer by comparison, and it is furthermore supported by the well-developed sister science of linguistics.

2. THE TEXT BASE

Propositions do not normally stand alone but together form a text base. A text base must be so constructed that it contains all the necessary information for the derivation of a natural language discourse. The actual rules of derivation are of no concern here; the reader is referred to linguistic work, especially work on generative semantics, e.g., Fillmore (1968), or to artificial intelligence projects, e.g., Simmons (1973), which involve the generation of discourse from abstract text bases not unlike the present propositional base. The converse problem, that of parsing English discourse, that is, of abstracting a text base from a given discourse, is even more formidable, though some limited successes have already been achieved, as illustrated by the work of Winograd (1972) and Simmons (1973). In the present paper, both of these questions are by-passed for a more modest but also more general objective: to investigate some formal properties of text bases, without the restrictions in scope and subject matter that characterize artificial intelligence projects.

Propositions are connected to create a text base by the symbol &. When two or more propositions are connected, recurrent terms (i.e., word concepts) are assumed

---

[1]In the discussion with Bever following the presentation of his paper, Olson goes so far as to deny that sentences have meaning out of context. Bever points out the untenability of such a position (Carroll & Freedle, 1972, Pp. 164 – 165).

to have identical reference. For example, the second appearance of the argument HOUSE in a text base always refers to the HOUSE previously introduced. If such identity of reference is not desired, some special notation such as primes or index numbers must be used to distinguish lexical items, e.g., $HOUSE_1$ and $HOUSE_2$. Note that the repetition refers to word concepts, that is, lexical items, not to words in the surface structure. The lexical entry HOUSE is usually realized as *house* in English text, though under certain circumstances, words such as *structure, dwelling*, or *it* may be used.

The claim that identity of reference in the text base is established through repetition is a very important one. Continuity in a text base depends upon it, as well as the internal structure of a text base. Propositions containing repeated arguments are said to be subordinated to the proposition where the argument originally appeared. Thus, by repetition, a complex net of subordination relationships is established.

The repetition rule has been used to derive the internal structure of a text by various authors (e.g. Kintsch, 1972a; van Dijk, 1972, 1973). The same rule can also be used to establish identity of reference. An alternative approach to the problem of identity of reference in a text is that of McCawley (1970). McCawley separates propositions that contain variables as arguments from identity constituents that identify the variables. The present approach has the apparent advantage that an argument is always introduced in the context of a particular proposition, rather than by itself. Alternative ways of determining the structure of a text base have been suggested by Crothers (1972) and by Frederiksen (1972). Crothers and Frederiksen conceive of structure as something that exists in addition to the propositional content of a paragraph and that can be separated from it. For instance, Frederiksen distinguishes two separate levels of text bases, one corresponding more or less to a propositional base as used here, and the other a level of logical relations, which is used to explicate the structure of the text. The present notion is different in that the internal paragraph structure is merely something implied by and derivable from an ordered proposition list.

While the internal structure of a paragraph can be developed from the content of that paragraph, and is neither superimposed upon it nor prior to it, the organization of paragraphs within a larger text, say the chapters of a book and the sections within the chapters, requires the introduction of units of a higher order than the single proposition. It has already been shown how one proposition may be embedded in another or conjoined with another [sentences (7) and (8)]. As a notational device, the use of names (Greek letters) for embedded propositions was introduced. All that is necessary at this point is to extend the practice of naming propositions to lists of propositions, following van Dijk (1972). Whole lists of propositions may be given arbitrary names, and these names can likewise be linked by the symbol &. Each name can be expanded as a list of other names and eventually propositions. Thus, the macro-structure of a text can be recursively defined simply by combining propositions into ordered lists and then constructing lists of lists, until the desired level of organization has been achieved. In the present notation, then, a text T may be somewhat informally defined as

$$T=\alpha\&\beta\&\gamma\&\delta\& \ldots \ldots \tag{10}$$

$$\alpha=\alpha_1\&\alpha_2\&\alpha_3\&\alpha_4\& \ldots \ldots$$

$$\dot{\alpha}_1=\alpha_{11}\&\alpha_{12}\&\alpha_{13}\& \ldots \ldots$$

$$\alpha_1\ldots\ldots_i=(P,A_1,A_2,\ldots\ldots)$$

Lists α, β, γ, etc. are defined in terms of other lists, until at the lowest level each symbol is identified with a proposition. Thus, the macro-structure of a text is given by the hierarchical structure (10). The macro-structure of a text is implicit in the proposition lists that constitute the text base, in the same sense that the internal structure of a paragraph is implicit in the ordered list of propositions. The repetition rule again indicates subordination. If the list α contains α_1, the latter is subordinated to α; since α is equal to α_1 plus other sublists, α may be considered a first (implicit) appearance of α_1, so that the explicit appearance of α_1 constitutes in fact a repetition, assigning it to a subordinate position.

An example of how these ideas can be applied to an actual text is given by Tables 1 and 2 and Fig. 1. The example is sufficiently complex to be nontrivial, but that makes it fairly hard to follow upon first reading. The example demonstrates how a typical, though fairly cryptic, research report in a psychological journal can be represented as a list of propositions (Table 1) and how this text base can be expressed in English (Table 2). Figure 1 indicates some of the structure of this text. Since psychological research reports usually have subheadings, a convention introducing subheadings had to be adopted. Note, further, that the way in which Table 1 is typed is not theoretically motivated and was done merely for the reader's convenience. Also, the convention of using Greek letters as names for propositions and proposition lists was changed in Table 1 because too many names were needed. Each proposition is typed on a separate line in Table 1 and when it is necessary to refer to a proposition, this is done via the line number. Thus, the third proposition in Table 1 is to be read as the STUDY is CONCERNed with the proposition on line 4, that is, whether PROPOSITIONs are REAL.

Table 1 starts with a title, *Reading time*, and four proposition list names. The rest of the Table breaks these lists down into their constituents. List 2 is called *Introduction* and consists quite simply of four propositions. The first one is deictic in nature and introduces *this study*; the remaining propositions say what this study is about.

List 6 receives the title *Method* and is expanded into three separate subsections: *Subjects, Design,* and *Procedure*. The *Subjects* section is quite self-explanatory, but in the *Design* section some fairly complex material is introduced. The section starts out by introducing the concept of an independent, experimental variable. There are two such variables, which the experimenter investigates and combines factorially. Next, the fact that there were 40 sentences is introduced, and two sentence types, one

TABLE 1

A Sample Text Base

1	Reading Time(2&6&39&54)
2	Introduction(THIS,STUDY)
3	(CONCERN,STUDY,4)
4	(REAL,PROPOSITION)
5	(PSYCHOLOGICAL,REAL)
6	Method(7&11&29)
7	Subjects(STUDENT,SUBJECT)
8	(FEMALE,STUDENT)
9	(VOLUNTEER,STUDENT)
10	(NUMBER,SUBJECT,TWENTY)
11	Design(INVESTIGATE,EXPERIMENTER,VARIABLE)
12	(INDEPENDENT,VARIABLE)
13	(NUMBER,VARIABLE,TWO)
14	(COMBINE,EXPERIMENTER,VARIABLE)
15	(FACTORIAL,COMBINE)
16	(USE,EXPERIMENTER,SENTENCE)
17	(NUMBER,SENTENCE,FORTY)
18	(SOME,SENTENCE)
19	(LENGTH,SENTENCE,20)
20	(NUMBER,WORD,EIGHT)
21	(LENGTH,SENTENCE,22)
22	(NUMBER WORD,SIXTEEN)
23	(HALF OF,SENTENCES)
24	(BASE UPON,23,25)
25	(NUMBER,PROPOSITION,THREE)
26	(OTHER,23)
27	(BASE UPON,26,28)
28	(NUMBER,PROPOSITION,SIX)
29	Procedure(READ,SUBJECT,SENTENCE)
30	(EACH,SENTENCE)
31	(SEPARATE,29)
32	(RECALL,SUBJECT,SENTENCE)
33	(IMMEDIATE,32)
34	(MANNER:IN,32,WRITE)
35	(INSTRUCT,EXPERIMENTER,SUBJECT,36)
36	(NOT,37)
37	(NECESSARY,38)
38	(VERBATIM,RECALL)
39	Results(REQUIRE,SUBJECT,TIME1)
40	(READ,SUBJECT,SENTENCE1)
41	(IN ORDER TO,40,39)
42	(LENGTH,SENTENCE1,43)
43	(OR,20,22)
44	(BASE UPON,SENTENCE1,25)
45	(REQUIRE,SUBJECT,TIME2)
46	(READ,SUBJECT,SENTENCE2)
47	(IN ORDER TO,46,45)
48	(LENGTH,SENTENCE2,43)
49	(BASE UPON,SENTENCE2, 28)

Table 1 (*continued*)

50	(LONGER,TIME2,TIME1)
51	(EQUAL,TIME2,52)
52	(PLUS,TIME1,SECOND)
53	(NUMBER,SECOND,FIVE)
54	Discussion(DEMONSTRATE,55,4)
55	(DEPEND,TIME,NUMBER)
56	(READ,TIME)
57	(HAVE,PROPOSITION,NUMBER)
58	(BASE UPON,PROPOSITION,SENTENCE)
59	(CONCLUDE,EXPERIMENTER,60)
60	(PROCESS,SUBJECT',PROPOSITION)
61	(READ,SUBJECT')
62	(WHEN,60,61)

8-words long and the other 16-words long, are distinguished. The next block of propositions introduces and defines the second experimental variable. Note that this portion of the text base is in fact an explanation of what is meant by factorial combination, though this equivalence is not made explicit here. It could have been, of course, but in the present text base this equivalence can only be established on the basis of the reader's knowledge about experimental design.

The *Procedure* section is comparatively easy to follow. The *Result* section says that subjects took longer to read 6-proposition sentences than 3-proposition sentences.

TABLE 2

An English Version of the Sample Text Base

Reading Time

Introduction

This study concerns the psychological reality of propositions.

Method

Subjects. The subjects were 20 female students. All subjects were volunteers.

Design. Two independent variables were investigated in this experiment. The two variables were combined factorially. Forty sentences were used, some of which were 8 words long and some were 16 words long. Half of the sentences of each length were based upon three propositions and the other half was based upon six propositions.

Procedure. Subjects read each sentence separately and recalled it immediately in writing. They were instructed that recall need not be verbatim.

Results

The time which subjects took to read the 8- and 16-word sentences which were based upon six propositions was 5 sec longer than the time for the 8- and 16-word sentences based upon three propositions.

Discussion

The dependence of reading times upon the number of propositions upon which a sentence was based demonstrates the psychological reality of propositions. It may be concluded that subjects process propositions when reading.

The *Discussion* excells through brevity. It merely states the conclusion of the experiment, relating reading time to the number of propositions upon which a sentence is based, and claims that subjects process propositions during reading.

A surface version of this text base is shown in Table 2. It is instructive to consider some possible alternative versions of this text. A text base may undergo certain transformations before it is expressed in words. Quite commonly, certain propositions that are explicit in the text base may be deleted, if it is possible to infer them on the basis of the remainder of the text, or from one's knowledge about the topic of discussion, in this case about psychological experiments. Consider, for instance, the following alternative version of the *Results* section in Table 2: "Subjects took 5 sec longer to read 6-proposition sentences than 3-proposition sentences, irrespective of sentence length." In order to obtain this version from Table 1, one cannot directly transform the propositional expressions into words and sentences. What is required here is some inferential work at the propositional level, which must precede the syntactic transformations. The speaker or writer must first of all use his knowledge of semantic relationships. More specifically, the lexical definition of the term IRRESPECTIVE OF must be used to infer from the fact expressed in Table 1 that half of the 3-proposition sentences were 8 words long and half were 16 words long, and that the same was true for 6-proposition sentences, that the differences in reading time were obtained *irrespective of* sentence length. The derivation of English text from the base can start only after a proposition expressing this relationship has been inferred from the original text base.

There is nothing very surprising in the claim that a particular surface form, such as the one in Table 2, is neither unique nor necessary. For any text of even moderate complexity there exist several possible paraphrases. Which form will be selected is an interesting psychological problem: Clearly this decision depends upon the speaker's intentions, the assumptions he makes about the hearer, and the nature of the communication situation itself, just to mention a few obvious factors.

Each text base is unique, but by no means necessary. There is no need to use this particular list of propositions in this particular order in order to communicate this message. Several equivalent text bases are conceivable. Some of the changes that are possible are trivial, e.g., it makes no difference for the over-all message in which order the propositions in the *Subject* section are written. Other changes are more consequential; it is, for instance, possible to use the IRRESPECTIVE OF predicate in describing the design of the experiment. Furthermore, the inclusion of the propositions (COMBINE,EXPERIMENTER,VARIABLE)&(FACTORIAL,COMBINE) is quite fortuitous; they are obviously redundant because the experimental design is completely specified without them. Alternatively, the experimental design could simply be described as a factorial design with two variables, letting the reader figure out what this implies about the nature of the experimental sentences. Needless to say, such a text base would be satisfactory only for a reader familiar with the relevant terminology.

Figure 1 partially illustrates the structure of the text base. In order to keep the complexity of the graph within tolerable limits, the text is analyzed only through the

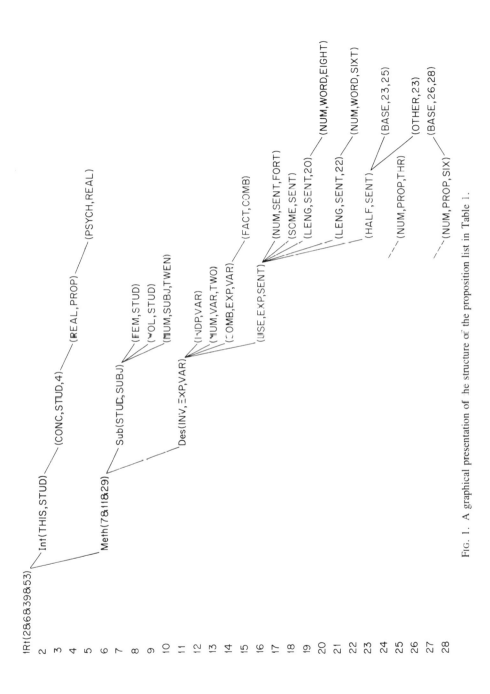

FIG. 1. A graphical presentation of the structure of the proposition list in Table 1.

Design section. Each proposition list is indicated by its number, and each word concept is reduced to the first four letters. The *Introduction* is organized quite simply: First STUDY is repeated, then the whole proposition 4, then the term REAL, resulting in a linear sequence of dependencies. In contrast, the *Subject* section has one superordinate proposition, which introduces the arguments SUBJECT and STU-DENT, and three subordinate propositions in which these arguments are repeated.

The structure of the *Design* section is much more complex. The reader should note, however, that all that was done here was to connect propositions with a repeated argument with the proposition in which the argument appeared originally. Figure 1 merely explicates the structure inherent in Table 1; it adds nothing. The branching is implicit in the ordered proposition list in Table 1: A line connecting two propositions in Fig. 1 merely makes explicit that the left-hand proposition preceded the right-hand one in the proposition list, and that the two propositions share a common argument. Note also the connection between the PROPOSITION introduced in the *Introduction* and the reappearance of this argument in propositions 25 and 28 at the bottom of the table (the connecting lines have been omitted where they would interfere with the rest of the table).

To follow Fig. 1 is a confusing but entirely mechanical exercise: Graphic representations are simply not very suitable for material of this complexity, though they are most useful pedagogically in that they permit the reader to appreciate the implications of the repetition rule. Note that if the *Procedure* section were added to Fig. 1, the graph would become completely unreadable. The very first proposition in that section is subordinated both to SUBJECT in the *Introduction* section and to SENTENCE in the *Design* section. It is obvious that a graphic representation of such dependencies is impossible in a really long and complex text.

In a long text, many word concepts will be used over and over again as arguments, without implying identity with a previous term. Such a case occurs in propositions 60 and 61 of the text base of Table 1. Previously SUBJECT referred to a certain set of people described in the beginning of the text base. Here, however, SUBJECT is used in a different way. It refers to subjects in general, not just to the 20 persons who participated in the experiment. Hence a prime is used to indicate that the term is used in a new way, still to be specified.

The description given above of how one can represent the meaning of a passage of text in fairly simple propositional language quite obviously leaves many questions unanswered, and in fact never touches on some significant problems. It does, however, show how one can go about dealing with these problems. Once one has a way of representing meaning, one can go on to ask questions about psychological processing within this theoretical system. It is not necessary to specify all details of the theory (as you must do when you are trying to make a computer understand language). Many of these details are of more interest to the linguist and philosopher than to the psychologist, at least until psychologists find much more sensitive experimental designs for the study of language processing than are available now. However, in order to take seriously an analysis such as the one shown in Table 1, one must show that it is possible to treat the omitted details within the proposed framework. This will be the topic for Chapter 3, while in the remainder of this chapter we shall turn to some of the more pressing psychological problems.

3. THE STRUCTURE OF SEMANTIC MEMORY

When one talks about the structure of memory, one tends to think about it as something given, something fixed, erected inside the brain in all its complexity, like a Gothic cathedral sitting in a town square. Alternatively, one may think of structure not as something existing physically but as a potential to be generated upon demand on the basis of implicit information and according to certain rules. This is the way we treated the structure of a text in the preceding section. Similarly, the relationships among nouns in semantic memory may either be represented by a network of one kind or another, or they may be specified implicitly by production rules that can generate such networks, as is done below. Actually, these two ways of specifying are not formally incompatible: Given a semantic network, one can easily write down some equivalent rewrite rules, and given a rule system, one can replace it with the structures generated by it. Nevertheless, there are considerable advantages to the rule representation of structure over a static, "structural" model, as several writers have pointed out (e.g. Frijda, 1972). One advantage of the generative viewpoint is that it provides ready means for talking about potential structure as well as actual structure. Propositions may be structurally related, though they may not even exist as actual memory traces, but only as the potential products of inference rules. A proper rule system will account for such potential structure as well as for relations among propositions actually stored in memory, while it would be awkward to talk about a network of potential propositions. The advantages of a rule-based approach over a network approach are nicely illustrated by some contemporary artificial intelligence systems, where rules are expressed as computer programs (e.g. Norman, 1973; Winograd, 1972).

3.1 The Classification of Predicators: Cases

In principle any lexical entry may be used as a predicator of some proposition, and in actual fact there are in the semantic memory of a fluent speaker of English a very large number of lexical entries that are so used, and usually in more ways than one. Can these predicators be organized, that is, classified in some way, so that one does not have to deal with an amorphous set of propositions, but with some orderly structure? For the application of any kind of rules, be it inference rules within semantic memory or grammatical rules to generate text from propositions, it would be of tremendous benefit if such a structure could be identified and rules could be stated not merely for individual propositions but for higher order units.

Let us postpone discussion of nominal predicates (that is, sentences of the form *A robin is a bird*, or *Fritz is a scoundrel*) until the next section and concentrate here on cases where a verb or adjective is used as a predicator. There are several useful ways in which such predicators can be classified. For instance, they may be classified according to whether they imply something positive or negative, something strong or weak, something active or passive. There exists a large literature concerned with this problem, using the semantic differential as an instrument (Osgood, Suci, & Tannenbaum, 1957), and there are numerous demonstrations that such classification is relevant to performance on several tasks. Semantic structure as determined by the semantic differential has many important psychological consequences, say, for instance, in tasks of information integration. The classification used here is of a different nature, however. Its origin lies in recent developments in the field of linguistics, notably the case grammar of Fillmore (1968, 1969, 1971). Although research on its implications is still in its infancy, it is of great significance for theories of semantic memory and deserves closer consideration.

According to case grammar, each argument of a proposition stands in a certain case relationship to its predicator. Thus, *Mary* in *Mary opened the door with a key* is the instigator of an action, while *door* is the object of that action and *key* the instrument by means of which the action is performed. Each of the arguments in (OPEN, MARY, KEY, DOOR) plays a different semantic role, designated by its case. Fillmore (1971) distinguishes the following cases:

agent (A)   — the instigator of an action

experiencer (E) — the experiencer of a psychological event

instrument (I)   — the psychological stimulus of an experience or action elicitor

object (O)   — the object of an action which undergoes change or movement

source (S)   — the source of an action in time, space, or a transfer event

goal (G)   — the goal or result of an action

In addition, Fillmore also includes locative and time as cases; however, a discussion of these rather special cases will be deferred until Section 5.1 of the next chapter.

The following sentences provide illustrations of different cases:

The man broke the window.   (BREAK, A:MAN, O:WINDOW)   (11)

The stone broke the window.   (BREAK, I:STONE, O:WINDOW)   (12)

The man broke the window with a stone.   (13)
      (BREAK, A:MAN, I:STONE, O:WINDOW)

John was sad.   (SAD, E:JOHN)   (14)

The book was sad.   (SAD, I:BOOK)   (15)

Mary cried from morning to night.   (16)
      (CRY, A:MARY, S:MORNING, G:NIGHT)

Mary made Fred unhappy by refusing to come.   (17)
      (CAUSE, A:MARY, O:(UNHAPPY, E:FRED), I:(REFUSE,
      A:MARY, O:(COME, A:MARY)))

Sentence (17) is an example of propositions appearing in some of the case roles.

There are several general comments to be made about Fillmore's case analysis. Fillmore assigns cases in such a way that each proposition has not more than one case of the same kind. In order to uphold this principle, he either reanalyzes apparent counterexamples into more than one proposition, as was done in (17), or attempts to show that superficially similar arguments play different roles after all. He argues, for instance, that *John* and *Fred* are not quite interchangeable in *John resembles Fred*, and on that basis assigns them different case roles. The order of cases within a proposition is determined by a case hierarchy A, E, I, O, S, G. Which argument becomes the syntactic subject is dependent upon this order. Cases may be obligatory or optional; for instance, the verb BREAK requires an object, while agent and instrument are optional, as examples (11)–(13) illustrate. Furthermore, there may be constraints upon the deletion of cases; for instance, DRIVE requires either an agent or locative or both if it has an object, though neither agent nor locative are obligatory in the absence of an object for DRIVE, as is shown by *John drives* and *The truck is driven on the road*, but **The truck is driven*. The original work of Fillmore (1968, 1969, 1971) should be consulted for a more detailed discussion of case grammar and in particular for the syntactic rules that transform propositions into text. It should also be noted that case grammar is still in a state of flux: Fillmore (1968) differs in several respects from the present statement of case grammar, which is based upon Fillmore (1971).

Fillmore's cases do not cover all types of predicators used here. We shall discuss shortly the special case of nominal predicates, but there are others, such as sentence (6), where a conjunction is used as the predicator, sentence (9), in which a verb is modified by an adverb, as well as various other examples that can be culled from Table 1. For most of these, possible classification schemes, say for purposes of grammatical transformations, are readily available. Linguistic necessities, that is, the nature of grammatical rules, will determine the precise nature of such further classification schemes.

3.2 Noun Categories

Propositions of the form (A, B) where both A and B are nouns are usually expressed verbally as *"B is an A."* They will be referred to as nominal propositions. The structure of nominal propositions and the way such propositions are processed in various psychological tasks have received considerable attention in recent years, partly because of the relative simplicity of the noun structure.

We shall say that noun B is *subordinated* to noun A if there exists a proposition (A, B). Let η be the set of nouns in semantic memory. The subordination relationship defines an order relationship upon the set η. Some mathematical properties of this relationship have been explored in Kintsch (1972a). The important point is that the noun structure can not be represented either as a tree or as a lattice, because associativity is violated. What this means in nontechnical language is that there exist cross classifications in the noun hierarchy (e.g., DOG may be subordinated both to MAMMAL and PET), and that certain nouns may be subclassified in more than one way (e.g., ANIMAL may be subclassified into PETS– FARM ANIMALS– WILD

ANIMALS, as well as MAMMAL-BIRD-INSECT-REPTILE, or HUMAN-NONHUMAN).

The structure of nouns in semantic memory is not something fixed once and for all (like a table constructed by some omniscient linguist showing all possible subordination relationships among nouns), but may be modified extensively through the operation of production and deletion rules. Such rules exploit the transitivity of the subordination relationship. A noun-hierarchy production operator permits one to infer a subordination relationship between two nouns N_1 and N_3, given the information that N_1 *is a* N_2 and N_2 *is a* N_3. More formally,

$$\text{NHP}\left[(N_2,N_1), (N_3,N_2)\right] = (N_2,N_1), (N_3,N_2), (N_3,N_1), \tag{18}$$

where commas are used between propositions instead of ampersands because it is not implied that the propositions are joined in a list, but merely that they are stored in semantic memory. Thus, *A robin is an animal* because *A robin is a bird* and *A bird is an animal.* [2]

A noun-hierarchy deletion operator deletes redundant propositions from semantic memory. It takes as an input the right side of (18) and erases from it the inferable (N_3,N_1):

$$\text{NHD}\left[(N_2,N_1), (N_3,N_2), (N_3,N_1)\right] = (N_2,N_1), (N_3,N_2). \tag{19}$$

This is not to say that all redundant nominal propositions are deleted from semantic memory via (19); such propositions can be deleted from memory in the interest of storage economy and re-inferred upon demand via (18), but it may very well be more efficient to retain certain redundant information in memory in some circumstances than to have to regenerate it repeatedly.

The questions of when nominal propositions are inferred and when they are stored directly in semantic memory are, however, much more complex than that. It is instructive to look at the logical alternatives that are available to define set membership, because this is what nominal propositions do; they assert that some noun belongs to a set named by the other noun. One can state a rule that determines whether a certain object is or is not a member of a set, or one can explicitly list all the members of a set. The former is called a *description* of the set, and the latter is a *listing* of the set. For example, we can define a set of two countries by *(a)* stating that they are situated in North America, or *(b)* listing {Canada, USA}. Both these definitions are satisfactory, in that there remains not the slightest doubt whether a given country is or is not a member of the set.

Unlike their mathematical counterparts, many sets that the psychologist has to deal with are not defined as unambiguously. Instead, they are defined by one or more typical members and other members are assigned to it on the basis of similarity. Consider, for instance, the concept of "University of Colorado student" that an

---

[2]It is somewhat misleading to study production rules out of their lexical context; there may be additional lexical information that may block a production. For instance, *chicken* are *fowl*, and *springers* are *chicken*, but *springers* are not *fowl*; this production is blocked by the lexical constraint on *fowl* which restricts it to *mature chicken* (example by J. Keenan).

average inhabitant of Boulder might have. It may be defined by two or three students whom he knows personally, or perhaps by some abstract type derived from several encounters with students: long hair, jeans, sandals, hiking boots, sneakers or barefoot, age, location, etc. How does such a person classify an examplar as a student or nonstudent? He judges whether or not it comes sufficiently close to his idealized type. Thus, for this particular semantic memory, the set of students is not well-defined (though it is in the dean's office, both by rule and listing). With varying degrees of confidence he will judge certain persons to be students. There can be little question about the people streaming out of a lecture hall, and those two in front of the ice cream parlor are probably also students, but the one peddling candles on 13th Street is probably not. Note that this rule is anything but infallible, and the person who operates with it knows that and would hardly be surprised if he were shown some glaring exceptions (there probably is even right now a student running around here somewhere in a tie and jacket, with polished shoes). None of the characteristics contained in this rule is a strict criterion for set membership in the sense that the situation in North America is the criterion for membership in the set mentioned above. The relationship between the characteristics and set membership is entirely probabilistic. Moreover, just as the class itself is defined only vaguely, it is usually not the case that semantic memory contains nominal propositions A is a B which express explicitly to which set A does or does not belong. For the most part, this must be inferred on the basis of probabilistic and ambiguous criteria, as in the example above.

The trouble with semantic categories is that they may be defined in any of the three ways described here. Take the noun *bird* as an example. It is quite possible that there may be a semantic memory in which bird is defined precisely by whatever the relevant criteria are for bird—a biology teacher might operate with such a concept of bird. On the other hand, there may be some experienced bird watcher who has stored with the concept bird a long list of instances together with the appropriate imagery and other relevant information, which comes close to a listing of the category. For most of us, however, the category BIRD is quite fuzzy, and we have neither an exhaustive listing of birds available nor a strict criterion for determining set membership. Instead, we are operating like the Boulderite with the concept of "University student." The concept is described for us by some typical examples for which we have the names, imagery, and properties stored, and these define for us a fuzzy set BIRD. If someone asks us to name all the birds we know, we can respond quickly with the typical birds that we have stored in semantic memory as part of the concept BIRD, and then we have to search semantic memory for other likely candidates for the category BIRD. How this can be done will be discussed below. Conversely, if someone asks us whether the sentence *A swallow is a bird* is true or false, we first try to arrive at a decision by checking semantic memory for a proposition (BIRD, SWALLOW). There must be tremendous individual differences in this respect: Someone who grew up in a country where swallows were among the most frequent and most striking birds may quite likely have this proposition stored as part of his semantic memory, while someone who only learned about swallows from pictures and songs probably does not. In the latter case, he somehow must decide on the basis of what he knows about birds and swallows whether the sentence is true or not. Again, the question of how this may be done must be deferred for the moment.

What has been said above about how categories are defined in semantic memory differs from Kintsch (1972a) and most other models of semantic memory, which rely upon precise definitions of sets. Surely the world would be cleaner and easier to handle for theories of semantic memory if one would not have to worry about fuzzy sets and vague definitions. What, then, is the evidence that forces semantic memory models to deal with fuzzy sets? Most important are the demonstrations of Rosch-Heider (Heider, 1972, 1973; Heider & Olivier, 1972; Rosch, 1973) that both perceptual and conceptual categories may be defined only ambiguously by typical members and that well-defined degrees of "categoriness" exist, and Lakoff's work on hedges (Lakoff, 1973), which arrives at similar conclusions via linguistic analyses.

Rosch's most relevant result was obtained in an experiment where she asked subjects to rank category members as to the degree of their membership in the category. The data were quite orderly, clearly indicating that for these subjects category membership was not merely a yes-no affair, but that it was essentially continuous, from the most typical members of a category to lesser degrees of category membership, down to borderline cases. For the category *birds*, Rosch's subjects named *robins* and *eagles* as the most typical birds, *chickens* and *ducks* as less typical, *penguins* as even less so, and *bats* as hardly birds at all. Similar results were obtained for *vegetables*, where *carrots* and *asparagus* were described as typical members, and *parsley* and *pickle* as peripheral members. In a further study (Rosch, 1973), using a standard concept identification paradigm, it was found that categories composed of typical instances could be learned faster than categories composed of peripheral members. Thus, not only the judgment of experimental subjects, but also their learning rate reflects differences in the degree of category membership.

Lakoff (1973) approached the problem of degrees of category membership from a linguistic standpoint, through an examination of how statements may be hedged. His conclusions are entirely in agreement with the experimental data discussed above. The way hedges are used in English clearly indicates that category membership is not considered by the speaker as an all-or-none affair, but admits to rather fine distinctions as to the nature and degree of membership. Let us use again our University of Colorado student to illustrate Lakoff's points. If one says

    John is technically a CU student.   (20)

one means something like this: John is a student in the sense that his name appears on the proper piece of computer print-out in Admissions and Records, but that he does not qualify as a student in most other ways; perhaps he has not attended classes in months.

If *strictly speaking* is used as a hedge, a quite similar meaning is intended, though not quite as strong:

    Strictly speaking, John is a CU student.   (21)

In this case, John does so many other things that one just does not think of him as a CU student, though he still is one. Quite the opposite meaning is conveyed by

Loosely speaking, John is a student.   (22)

This John is not really a student according to Admissions and Records, but he goes to class and looks like and behaves like a bona fide category member.

John is a regular CU student.   (23)

would be said of someone who expresses the typical student characteristics.

The point of these examples is that they demonstrate quite clearly that category membership is a matter of degree. What does all this imply about the way in which categories are defined in semantic memory? What seems to be necessary is for different characteristics of a category to be weighted differently in semantic memory. This can be done explicitly by specifying certain propositions as NECESSARY or SOMETIMES, or implicitly, in that a certain characteristic may be true for all examples that define the categories, or for some, and there may even be contradictory information present in other instances. Returning to the CU student again, a possible definition of this category in semantic memory may be as follows. For ease of exposition a verbal description will be given, rather than a formal propositional one. A necessary condition is specified, namely that the person is officially enrolled; but note that this criterion is useless in most cases, since one does not normally have access to this information. Other criteria must be specified as generally true: goes to classes, studies on occasion, visits campus, etc. Finally, there are characteristics that are only frequently true: a certain age range, a certain style of dress, and the like.

Given such a category definition in semantic memory, one can determine not only that someone is or is not a member of the set of CU students, but one can also assign a measure of degree to his membership, with the typical student who fulfils all criteria given a measure of 1, say, and the nonstudent who fulfils none of the criteria a measure of 0. Mathematical tools to deal with fuzzy sets have been developed by Zadeh (1965), and their use and logical implications have been explored (Lakoff, 1973; Zadeh, 1965, 1970, 1972). Note that in the present model it is not claimed that every set-membership statement has a measure of degree associated with it in semantic memory, such as *Robin is a bird* (1.0), *Duck is a bird* (.5), but that these measures can be derived from the way in which categories are defined and set membership is determined.

As Lakoff (1973) has pointed out, the fuzziness of categories is particularly important for understanding the use of adjectives. Consider the categories designated by *large ant, large man, large tree.* In none of these cases are there any exact standards for when an *ant*, a *man*, or a *tree* is large. Rather it seems that words like *large, many*, or *fast* are specified in the lexicon as picking out a particular range of size, number, or speed, not in any absolute sense but relative to typical size, number, or speed of the object named. Furthermore, the range specified is imprecise. Thus, *large* picks out the upper ranges of the variation in size that is possible for *ants, men*,

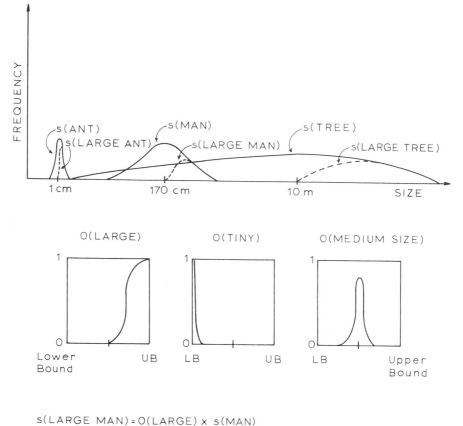

s(LARGE MAN) = O(LARGE) x s(MAN)

s(LARGE TREE) = O(LARGE) x s(TREE)

FIG. 2. Illustrative size distributions and operators.

or *trees*. This implies that semantic memory must contain information about the usual size of *ants, men*, and *trees*, and about the size range possible.[3] The lexicon must specify the comparative and fuzzy character of *large* and, in addition, must specify for each object that has the property *size* a mean size and range, so that one can talk about both *large ants* and *large trees* without ambiguity, but at the same time without precision. Lakoff assumes that such characteristics as size are stored in the form of continuous distributions, as in Fig. 2. Predicators like LARGE, TINY, MEDIUM SIZE, ... modify these distributions in that they operate upon them in a certain way as shown by the inserts in Fig. 2. Note that the scale for the size distributions is in

[3]There is some experimental evidence for this claim. Moyer (1973) observed that reaction times to decide which of two animals is larger depend monotonically upon the difference in size between the animals. He concluded that subjects have stored in memory representations of the actual sizes of animals and operate upon these in much the same way as they do upon perceptual representations.

terms of physical measurements, but that operators are scaled only relatively, specifying only lower and upper bounds, so that they can be stretched and fitted both to s(ANT) and to s(TREE). Lakoff (1973) and Zadeh (1972) have developed these ideas formally and in detail, and the interested reader is referred to their work. Zadeh has also shown how the operator VERY may act upon the operator LARGE and how such operations may be characterized mathematically. For the present, the important point is that adjectives specifying physical dimensions presuppose distributions along these dimensions, and that very similar distributions must be assumed which specify degree of membership in semantic categories. The first claim has long been universally accepted, but the second one is only beginning to be appreciated. However, it seems just as necessary to talk about degrees of category membership as to talk about degrees of size, although only the latter can be scaled physically. *John is very much a CU student* and *John is a regular CU student,* pick out parts of the distribution "being a CU student" in just the same way that *The tree is large* and *The tree is tiny* pick out parts of the size distribution for trees. The analogy is not a complete one because size is a unique physical dimension, while being a CU student is a matter of several different attributes, varying in importance. It may not be very helpful to collapse all of these into a single measure of "categoriness," because such a measure tends to conceal the multidimensionality involved, yet it is crucial to think of category membership not as an all-or-none matter, but as a matter of degree, with frequently vague and indeterminate borders.

3.3 Inferences

A distinction must be made between inferences that operate on the basis of the propositional knowledge stored in memory and inferences that involve different representations of knowledge. Only the former are within the reach of the present model, but a few words will be said later about non-propositional inferences, just to bring the problem into better focus.

There is a great amount of research in psychology that is concerned with inductive reasoning and that goes under the label of "concept identification." There is no need to review this work here as it is widely known, and fairly up-to-date reviews already exist (e.g., Kintsch 1970b, Chapter 7). It must be pointed out, however, that the work on concept identification, or concept formation, as it is also called, does not do full justice to all aspects of inductive reasoning. Laboratory studies have simplified the problem considerably by dealing almost exclusively with well-defined questions (Hunt, Marin, & Stone, 1966) and artificial, discrete yes-no categories (Rosch, 1973).

The experimental work concerned with deductive reasoning is much less extensive than that concerned with inductive reasoning. Traditionally, psychologists have left this area to logicians and designers of artificial intelligence programs. The question of interest in the present context is how to conceive of deductive reasoning in a semantic memory model. What is the nature of the information base from which deductions are made? The answer is simple in principle but will require much further research to be worked out in detail. Inferences require the propositional information that constitutes semantic memory plus rules for operating upon these propositions. What needs to be done, then, is to investigate the nature of these rules. An example has already been given: the noun-hierarchy production and deletion operators (18) and (19). It is possible to write operators in propositional form, e.g., instead of an IMPLY operator one could simply write out (IMPLY, A,B). The operator notation is convenient, though it must be stressed that no new elements are thereby introduced into the theory. Similar operators can be devised for any transitive relationship—for example, a part-hierarchy production operator

$$\text{PHP} \left[(\text{HAS PART, } N_1, N_2), (\text{HAS PART, } N_2, N_3) \right] = \qquad (24)$$
$$= (\text{HAS PART, } N_1, N_2), (\text{HAS PART, } N_2, N_3), (\text{HAS PART, } N_1, N_3),$$

and a corresponding part-hierarchy deletion operator. The operator (24) permits such inferences as *arm is a part of the body, elbow is a part of the arm*; therefore, *elbow is a part of the body*. Note, however, that there are interesting differences in the structures generated by (18) and (24): The noun hierarchy is one single, connected net, with a unique upper bound, while there are many different, unconnected part hierarchies. (Parts of the body, parts of a house, parts of a tree, etc.)

Examples of some operators that do not depend upon transitivity are IMPLY $\left[P \right]$ and CONSEQUENCE $\left[P \right]$, where P may be any proposition. The output of these operators depends entirely upon the information stored in semantic memory.

A few examples will illustrate the hypothetical process. Suppose someone is given the following text: *Melanie opened the window. Soon the room was full of mosquitoes*, and the question *Where did the mosquitoes come from?* The predicator OPEN is stored in the lexicon as (OPEN,A,I,$\underline{O}$), that is, as a frame that requires some kind of object, optional agent, and instrument; *Melanie* fits the agent slot, and *window* the object slot. Also, in the lexicon are implications and consequences of OPEN, so that the IMPLICATION operator will produce the information that the window was closed before Melanie opened it, and the CONSEQUENCE operator will determine that it was open thereafter. The latter proposition, together with other information in semantic memory about how one can enter rooms, will be sufficient to deduce that the mosquitoes came in through the window.

Another example of a different kind is a PART $\left[N \right]$ operator which gives the parts of a noun N, if that noun has parts according to its lexical description. Thus, *Melanie's car stalled, The battery was dead*, is a continuous text because PART $\left[CAR \right]$ will provide the necessary link between the two sentences.

An example of a more psychological nature would be a purpose operator that, when applied to a proposition containing an agent, searches for the purpose behind this action. This search is much more complicated than the rather simple lexical processes considered so far. Both general knowledge about acts and motivation, and specific situational knowledge that might explain the motivation for a particular action, must be taken into account.

The examples given above were chosen unsystematically. What they have in common is that they all exploit in some way the redundancy of the information stored in memory. The production operators do not generate new information; they only make explicit implications that are already in the lexicon and memory. In that sense, they are rules for deductive inference, or lexical redundancy rules.

Another type of inference rule that will need to be explored is concerned with negative inferences. Several cases can be distinguished. First, a question or problem may be meaningless; that is, it may be semantically unacceptable in the sense described in Section 4, following. If a question is interpretable, it may receive as an answer either "No" or "Don't know." A "No" answer is appropriate if a proposition that contradicts the question can be derived from the information held in memory. Contradictions to a given proposition P can be found by a contradiction operator CONTRADICTION [P], which determines all implications and consequences that are incompatible with P. If neither the truth nor falsity of a proposition can be determined, it is left undecided.

Finding implications, parts, superconcepts, and contradictions are formal operations within semantic memory. The question of interest to the psychologist is how these operations are used in psychological processes. But the answers to that question are still quite incomplete. It will require considerable further research before we know how operators are acquired, what contribution is made by innate factors, or how operators select the relevant pieces of knowledge from semantic memory and ignore irrelevant ones. Some suggestions will be made in the discussion of specific psychological experiments in Part II of this book. At present, however, we cannot leave this topic without at least mentioning the importance of inference rules that operate upon nonpropositional information. Nowhere, perhaps, are the limitations of a proposition-based approach to memory more serious than in this respect.

Much reasoning is, without doubt, nonverbal and nonpropositional. Sloman (1971) has distinguished two kinds of reasoning: reasoning based upon what he calls a Fregean representation of knowledge, of which the predicate calculus or various programming languages as well as the propositional language of the present model would be examples, and reasoning based upon analogical representations of knowledge. Examples of the latter kind would be found in the realm of sensorimotor behavior, e.g., in reaching for a moving object. Both types of reasoning are important for human thinking, because memory representations are both propositional and analogical. Purely propositional representations of concepts like *triangular* or *ladder*, or actions like *swim*, would surely be impossible. Our knowledge of *swim* is primarily a motor knowledge, the propositional representation of which is quite secondary. Norman (1973) has emphasized this fact and discussed some of its implications. Propositional representations have the advantage of greater generality and hence are the basis for the almost limitless richness of human thought processes. Analogical thinking, however, has advantages of its own. For instance, an operator CONSEQUENCE has been introduced above which generates the consequences of a proposition (or text) to which it is applied in terms of other propositions that are derivable from the information stored in semantic memory. There must, however, also be an analogical consequence operator, which permits one to infer the consequences of some event or action analogically, rather than via propositional reasoning.

Such analogical reasoning is important not only for sensorimotor behavior, but also for many abstract problems that can be represented analogically by means of maps or physical models. The advantage of such reasoning is that it is easier to avoid senseless hypotheses. Changes in the input and output are continuous and it is possible to see where a certain line of reasoning will lead, which is not generally the case in propositional reasoning.

3.4 The Role of Verb Frames in the Lexicon

The subjective lexicon specifies for each word its meaning and use. It is an important subset of semantic memory, which, in addition, contains various kinds of inference rules, as discussed above, and topics of knowledge that are indexed by word combinations (such as *"How to enter a house," "The economy of Britain," "Climbing on Long's Peak"*). Lexical entries for nouns specify their properties, their class membership (as described in Section 3.2), and the kind of verb frames that the noun may enter as an argument. Verbs, and other predicators, are specified primarily through verb frames, that is, a listing of the cases that the predicator may take, and various implications, presuppositions, and consequences. Verb frames provide a basis for the classification of propositions, in that all verbs with the same frame can be grouped together. This classification scheme is hierarchical. Arguments can be specified in increasingly more general terms. Thus, at one level the verb *sauté* may be specified as requiring a *heavy iron skillet*; that, however, belongs to the class of *cooking utensils* so that at a more general level *sauté* can be grouped together with other verbs requiring *cooking utensils*. Finally, *sauté* may be included in an even more general class by noting that *utensils* has the semantic function of an *instrument*, so that *sauté* can be assigned to the class of verbs that take an *instrument* case. A similar hierarchical classification of verbs can be obtained by looking at their implications and consequences, which also can be expressed in more and more general terms. To stay with the cooking example (after Lehrer, 1969) *sauté* has certain consequences (and requires certain procedures) that contrast, for example, with *deep-fry*; both of these terms, however, can be subsumed under *fry*, which has implications and consequences that are true for both *sauté* and *deep-fry*. At a more general level, *fry*, together with *boil, broil*, and *bake*, can be combined as *cook*, and implications and consequences can be formulated that are true for all methods of cooking. *Cook* in turn may be combined with other household activities to form a higher order class, until finally one arrives at a class of verbs that all have the same case structure as *cook*. Note, that in this view, cases are not like semantic primitives: They are merely a rather general way of classifying verb frames that captures important semantic information and is needed for the operation of syntactic transformation rules.

An example of how verb frames may help to specify the use of a verb is given in Table 3. The verb selected is *feel*, after a suggestion of McNamara (1971). In Webster's New Collegiate Dictionary there are five entries for *feel* as a transitive verb, five as an intransitive verb, and three as a noun. Table 3 shows only two different verb frames, one requiring an agent and one an experiencer, plus a subclas-

TABLE 3

A Sample Lexical Entry *Feel*
Cases in the Examples Are Shown Only for the Main Propositions

(FEEL,$\underline{A}$,O)		implies that the agent is also the experiencer of a sensation.
		e.g. *John feels the cloth* (FEEL,A:JOHN,O:CLOTH)
		John feels (along the edge) (FEEL,A:JOHN)
(FEEL,E,I)	(1)	where I is physical object. Implies that the experiencer perceives the object.
		e.g. *John feels the needle entering his arm.*
		(FEEL,E:JOHN,I:(ENTER,NEEDLE,ARM))
		John feels (FEEL,E:JOHN)
		The water feels warm (FEEL,I:(WARM,WATER))
	(2)	where I is an emotional object. Implies that the experiencer has an emotion.
		e.g. *John feels the horror of her situation.*
		(FEEL,E:JOHN,I:((HORRIBLE,SITUATION)&(HER,SITUATION))
		John feels sad (FEEL,E:JOHN,I:(SAD,JOHN))
		John feels (FEEL,E:JOHN)
		Happiness feels unbearable (FEEL,I:(UNBEARABLE,HAPPINESS))
	(3)	where I is an intellectual object. Implies that experiencer thinks, believes.
		e.g. *John feels the validity of the reproach.*
		(FEEL,E:JOHN,I:(VALID,REPROACH))
		John feels that he had acted like a fool
		(FEEL,E:JOHN,I:α)&((LIKE,β,γ)=α)&((ACT,JOHN)=β)&((ACT,
		FOOL)=γ)
		Lexical Transformation Rule: (FEEL,X) $\rightarrow X$'s *feel.*

sification of the instrument case, depending upon whether the source of the experience is a physical stimulus, an emotion, or an intellectual object. This subclassification is necessary because the implications of *feel* are different in these three cases. The use of *feel* as a noun is given quite parsimoniously by a lexical transformation rule. Idioms in which *feel* appears *(feel for, feel a person out, feel like, feel oneself, feel up to)* must be handled separately, just a they are in Webster's.

Not all implications, consequences, etc. of *feel* are stated in Table 3, but only a few are included as illustrations, and the notation has been kept informal to facilitate reading. Obligatory cases are underlined. The method of stating implications as propositions which was adopted here is only one possible representation, of course, but somehow it seems much more natural and simpler than feature representations. The latter frequently require rather forced "features," such as +*lid* for *braise*, or +*preserve shape* for *poach* in Lehrer's semantic cuisine (Lehrer, 1969). Compared with Webster's entry for *feel*, Table 3 is quite simple, and elucidates the interrelationships among the various uses of *feel* more clearly. Note the absence of the transitive-intransitive classification, which is handled simply as optional arguments. In Table 3 the uses of *feel* as a noun are derived naturally from the various verb frames into which *feel* enters and do not require independent listing.

The claim that the lexicon specifies the meaning and use of words is, of course, terribly vague. How much detail must be supplied? Presumably, such gross characteristics as the two different case frames in Table 3 must be specified, but what about inferential and metaphorical uses of a word? Bolinger (1971), in a most interesting study of the verb *remind*, argues that the referential meaning of a word (*make think* in the case of *remind*) must be carefully distinguished from inferential meanings (*resemble*, in this case). A lexicon should not be too ambitious. It should deal only with the established referential meaning of words. When a word is used differently, its precise meaning must be inferred from the context in which it appears. The richness of meaning and the subtle shadings of words in use contrast quite sharply with the lack of differentiation in lexical descriptions. It is the interaction among words that produces richness, not something inherent in each word separately.

4. ACCEPTABILITY AND METAPHORS

The decision made above to restrict the lexicon to referential meaning has important consequences. Primarily, it follows that a distinction must be made between semantically acceptable sentences and semantically unacceptable sentences. Semantically acceptable sentences are derived from propositions that are either stored in semantic memory or may be generated from stored propositions through the recursive applications of the redundancy rules, which are also part of the memory system. A sentence is semantically unacceptable if it is based upon a proposition that is not part of semantic memory and cannot be generated in semantic memory. A more formal definition of semantic acceptability has been given in Kintsch (1972a, Pp. 278–280) and also in Chapter 10. However, for present purposes an informal verbal statement is quite sufficient. Note that semantic acceptability is not synonymous with truth: A proposition that is semantically acceptable may be either true or false, depending upon the state of the world, but it makes no sense to talk about the truth or falsity of unacceptable propositions.

Semantically acceptable sentences that, in all likelihood, are stored in the semantic memory of at least some people would be *A shark is a fish*, or *A shark can swim*, or *Sharks are vicious*. Semantically acceptable sentences that, presumably, are not directly stored in memory but have been generated on the basis of stored information, general knowledge about the use of words, and given perceptual information might be, for example, *The trophy on the basement wall is a shark that Roy caught in Puerto Rico*. It implies that a shark may be a trophy, that such a trophy can be hung on a basement wall, that people catch fish, and that there are sharks off Puerto Rico—to mention just a few components of this sentence. Each one of these components is either stored in memory directly or can be generated (e.g., we know what sort of things can be used as trophies, and though most people have never seen a shark in that role, we know that any sufficiently large animal might be used in that way). On the other hand, *The shark is a telephone pole* is a semantically unacceptable sentence: The categories to which *shark* and *telephone pole* belong are incompatible.

It is, of course, true that given enough time and ingenuity, people will interpret almost any sentence, however unacceptable it may be. It is easy to imagine, for example, a person comparing a certain shark with a telephone pole (*long black thing floating in the water*) and uttering the sentence just deemed unacceptable semantically. While this is certainly true, one must not let this fact obscure the distinction between acceptable and unacceptable sentences, as some authors have done (Collins & Quillian, 1972b). People know when they are interpreting a sentence metaphorically and when they are not. A semantic memory model must be able to account for this distinction. Surely, there are degrees of unacceptability (as there are degrees of acceptability, see Chapter 10), but this must not obscure the basic dichotomy between the two types of propositions. A further factor that adds to the difficulty of distinguishing between literal and metaphorical interpretations of a sentence is that for every language, expressions, which were at one point clearly metaphorical, become idiomatic and accepted in general use. An example familiar to every student of psycholinguistics is Chomsky's famous semantically unacceptable sentence, *Colorless green ideas sleep furiously*, which can be quoted by quite a number of people by now and has acquired its own peculiar meaning through use and overuse.

Any model of semantic memory must, of course, be able to provide a mechanism for the nonliteral interpretation of semantically unacceptable sentences. This was done in Kintsch (1972a, Pp. 280–284) by describing a set of inference rules, called analogy rules. Analogy rules were formulated for both the production and acceptance of metaphors and were stated formally. The analogy rules were supplemented by syntactic transformation rules, which, for want of a better expression, were called compression rules. I shall only present here a brief informal summary of that work.

First of all, as was pointed out above, all semantically unacceptable sentences may be interpreted as metaphors. This, of course, does not imply that such sentences always, or even regularly, will receive a metaphorical interpretation. A metaphor in this view is, therefore, a semantically unacceptable sentence that has been inferentially interpreted. The interpretation consists of elaborating the metaphor in such a way that an explicit comparison is being made, involving only semantically acceptable sentences and replacing the original unacceptable sentences. Suppose someone is given the sentence

> The volcano burps,   (25)

one of Matthews' (1971) examples. The sentence is unacceptable because the lexical specification of BURP demands an agent, and *volcano* cannot assume this role. The hearer of the sentence then begins to search his semantic memory for implications of the two acceptable sentences that can be formed from the original input sentence: *Someone burps*, and *The volcano does something*. According to the lexicon, burps are caused by gaseous pressure, are abrupt, involve an emission of air, etc. Also according to the lexicon volcanos can erupt, which has some of the same lexical implications as burp. Hence, a comparison can be constructed

> The volcano erupts like a man burps.   (26)

Sentence (26) is the meaning of (25). It involves only semantically acceptable propositions.

The production of metaphors begins with a description: the abrupt, pressure-produced emissions that characterize some volcanic eruptions. For stylistic reasons, the speaker decides not to express this information directly but via a comparison. A man's burping offers itself for that purpose because of the common implications of the particular type of volcanic eruption to be described and the act of burping. Thus the comparison statement (26) is formed, involving only semantically acceptable sentences. Compression rules, which are a special kind of syntactic transformation rule, then take the explicit comparison (26) into the metaphor (25).

The reader who requires more information about the processing of metaphors according to this theory is referred to the original report, as well as to some extensions of this work by Abraham (1973). The question that needs to be raised here concerns the generality and adequacy of this approach. Are all metaphors compressed comparisons? Black (1962) has argued that they are not, but his examples are not convincing. Sentences like *The poor are the blacks of Europe*, which according to Black cannot be explained by the comparison theory, can, in fact, easily be treated as comparisons. Abraham has pointed out that the underlying comparison in this case might be *The poor in Europe are like the black in America*. Certainly, whether or not all metaphors involve comparisons, the class of metaphors that does is a very large one.

According to the present theory, only semantically unacceptable sentences can be metaphors. I agree with Matthews (1971) that *The old rock is becoming brittle* is not in itself a metaphor at all, unless it refers to, say, a professor emeritus. In that case, there is an underlying proposition that identifies the professor with the rock, and that total statement is semantically unacceptable and metaphorical. Other examples sometimes offered as metaphors, such as *At night all cats are black*, may also be regarded as nonmetaphorical by themselves. That something is black at night is perfectly acceptable semantically, and hence cats may be black, too, at night. It is possible, however, to use this sentence in a metaphorical way — but in that case the whole text, not just the single sentence, is deviant and metaphorical.

Among alternative theories of metaphor, one by Matthews (1971), who develops some ideas of Chomsky (1965), seems to be the most explicit one today. However, Matthews uses a feature analysis, and his theory suffers from the general difficulties associated with a feature approach. Features like + *gaseous pressure* always seem to be quite *ad hoc*. Also, as Abraham (1973) points out, Matthews' treatment of metaphors in terms of violations of selection restrictions is too narrow, as illustrated by his own example *The man is a wolf*, where one can hardly talk about violation of selection restrictions. However, in one respect, Matthews' theory is just like the present one, in that it emphasizes that sentences (or their underlying propositions) are deviant, and not single words (lexemes). The latter view, in which metaphorization is regarded as a process of substitution of similar words, goes back to Aristotle and has been the traditional one.

The greatest weakness of the present theory of metaphor is that it does not distinguish between good metaphors and bad metaphors. Why is *bachelor girl* a good metaphor, but *spinster boy* not? It is not that the latter is harder to interpret, because the inferences that one has to go through in arriving at an interpretation are quite parallel in the two cases. Nevertheless, some authors (Bickerton, 1969) go so far as claiming that *spinster boy* is simply unacceptable and not a metaphor at all. Unfortunately, such problems of style are poorly understood.

When do people interpret an unacceptable sentence metaphorically, and when will it be called simply unacceptable? Though there is no satisfactory answer to this question, task demands play an obvious role here. If the preacher says strange things, his parishioners will do their best to impute a metaphorical sense to it, and so will the reader of poetry from baroque times to modern days. In numerous other situations, however, deviant sentences are simply regarded as deviant, and not as metaphors. One must also remember that semantic memory is not something fixed, but fluid and continuously changing in response to new experiences. The set of semantically unacceptable sentences is not identical for all individuals, and not necessarily the same for the same individual at different times.

5. PSYCHOLOGICAL PROCESS MODELS

An attempt has been made in this chapter to outline a model of the structure of semantic memory that can provide a framework within which human intellectual functioning can be understood. The model is essentially an educated guess, based upon insights from various disciplines, primarily psychology and linguistics. In order to subject this model to empirical test in the experimental psychology laboratory, it must be further supplemented by psychological process assumptions. If the assumptions about the structure of memory are right, or even approximately right, what additional mechanisms are needed to understand behavior in specific experimental situations? Clearly, process models must be to some extent task specific, and such broad, general assumptions as have been made concerning the structure of memory are difficult to make with regard to processes. Nevertheless, what is of real interest in processing models are precisely the general statements that can be made, the commonality in behavior rather than its task-specific components. Cognitive psychology must be more than a collection of various isolated processing models for some specialized, artificial laboratory paradigms, even though these may be quite detailed and perhaps even correct. Such models have their uses, and we shall add to their number in Part II, but it is necessary to inquire, in addition, about the basic cognitive operations and general characteristics of human information-processing activities.

The only significant and well-developed general theory of cognitive processes has been associationism. In over 2000 years of development, associationism has gained almost complete ascendancy over competitive notions, so that it today dominates the thinking of friend and foe alike to the extent that neither can avoid thinking in its categories and employing its terminology. This is not the place to review the history of associationism [Anderson & Bower (1973) have recently done so in a similar context], but we should discuss briefly its major tenets. Associationism as a cognitive psychological theory (to distinguish it from its later, debased version as conditioning theory) reached its highest and purest development in the work of William James and G. E. Müller, around the year 1900. Its only law is a sort of attraction among psychical elements (ideas, usually, but "things" for James, *Vorstellungen*, which is more like images, for Müller): the law of contiguity. The memory traces of temporally contiguous psychic events are interconnected or associated, so that the recurrence of one of them elicits the others. The result of the repeated contiguity of events in different patterns is an associative net, which is both a record of past experience and a prediction for the future. Given any one node of the net, the probability that another node will be elicited is proportional to the associative strengths of the links between the stimulus node and its neighbors. Not all neighbors will be elicited, but only one, since the reproductive tendencies compete and inhibit each other. Just as opposing tendencies inhibit each other, it is also possible for associations to summate in producing a response. Therefore, elements that are associated with more than one stimulus are especially likely to be reproduced. The interplay of inhibitory and facilitative tendencies is the only determining factor in psychological processes, according to classical associationist doctrine. It accounts for the facts very well, as long as, in James's words, "the train of imagery wanders at its own sweet will." The real problem for associationism is to account for directed, purposeful thought. This problem has found an elegant solution in the constellation theory of James (1890) and Müller (1911). It retains the assumption that all associations arise independently, without direction. The task or purpose that appears to direct a psychological process is simply one more association, which adds its weight to pertinent associations and thereby inhibits the rest. In Müller's terminology, the task functions as a directional image that amplifies thematic images and inhibits irrelevant images. For example, in a lecture the particular topics discussed are not only connected by temporal contiguity, but each one is also connected to the theme of the lecture. Therefore, it is possible to reproduce the lecture topic by topic, avoiding the associations that each topic may have with different themes. As ingenious as this explanation is, it is nevertheless unsatisfactory. Let me quote from Selz, one of the most brilliant critics of associationism. The quote will be fairly extensive because of the unavailability of Selz's work in English (and its virtual unavailability in German, too). It is taken from lectures that Selz gave in Holland in the winter and spring of 1940 (Lecture No. 7, reprinted in Seebohm, 1970).

> The explanation which the constellation theory offers for the orderly course of thinking may sound convincing, were it not for the facts. This explanation fails first of all in all those cases where a solution of a task from memory is impossible, that is, where prior association between a goal and a solution cannot exist. Even worse, it can not explain reproductive thinking either. Suppose, for example, that we ask a subject to respond to a stimulus word with its superordinate. The stimulus "farmer" is presented and promptly and usually without any conscious meditation the response "occupation" is given. G. E. Müller suggested the following explanation for such problem solutions. The task to respond with a superordinate produces a state of heightened availability for all superordinate terms in memory. Among those is the superordinate "occupation." Thus, the pertinent association "farmer" – "occupation" is strengthened beyond the many other associations which "farmer" has, in accordance with the experimental instructions, and the correct solution occurs.
>
> This explanation would be valid only if the constellation produced by the task of generating superordinates would not also facilitate task irrelevant reproductive tendencies to the same extent. The task of naming a superordinate will make available not only the superordinate term "occupation," but any other terms which are superordinates, several of which are also associated with "farmer." For instance, "artisan" is a superordinate in its own right, and it is associated with farmer as a coordinate term. The constellation facilitates the reproduction of "artisan" no less than it does that of "occupation." The constellation theory is, therefore,

unable to explain why the coordinate "artisan" does not occur erroneously with substantial frequency in response to the stimulus term "farmer" when the subject is asked to name a superordinate.

The basic mistake of the constellation theory of thinking was that it regarded cognitive processes as a system of diffuse reactions. It was forced thereby to postulate the mutual facilitation of associations as the directional principle in thought.

Selz goes on to describe the historical origins of associationism and its roots in an analogy with the laws of physics, in particular, Newton's law of gravitation. Early associationists, such as Hobbes and Hume, were quite explicit about this analogy, which was still cited with approval by James (1890, p. 597). Selz argues, however, that the proper analogy for psychological processes should not have been with Newtonian mechanics and its diffuse forces, but with biology. It is not the momentarily strongest response tendency that decides what reaction will occur, but rather the specific nature of the stimulus. Responses in a biological system are unambiguously coordinated to specific releasing stimuli. There is indeed a network, but the relations among nodes are not all of the same type, differing only in degree; instead, these relations differ in kind. Selz (1970) says

The reason why cognitive processes have for so long been treated as a system of diffuse associative reproductions is that the essential difference has not been appreciated between an associative system and the specific reaction systems which characterize biological processes. Both systems have in common the idea of connection between analytic elements (association in Latin). Memory traces of stimuli are thought to be interconnected by specific nerve pathways just like sensory excitations and motor reactions. These individual reactions are conjoint in chains of responses. Thus, the fertile idea which was inherent in associationism, namely the fixed coordination of elements, is retained in the theory of specific reactions, and merely developed more successfully [from Lecture No. 8].

Selz rejects the concept of diffuse associations and replaces it with a system of specific interconnections, which might be called labeled or marked links, or simply relations. However, a relational system shares one very important property with an associational system: Both attempt to reconstruct meaningful wholes from analytic elements. In this respect, both disagree with the claim made by Gestalt psychologists that such synthesis is impossible. Selz maintains that this impossibility only characterized the inadequate attempts to construct meaningful wholes from meaningless associations, but that an analytic psychology is not inherently impossible. However, the elements that are to be synthesized must be meaningful units in their own right. Selz called such a unit *Sachverhältnis*, which translates as "relation among objects." These relations among objects constitute the meaningful units with which cognitive psychology must be concerned. Analysis into elements is not wrong in itself, only analysis into meaningless elements.

Such ideas are not, of course, the exclusive property of Selz, though I find Selz's discussion particularly lucid and insightful. To mention just one important example, Wundt's *Gesamtvorstellung* (total idea) is a closely related concept. It too is a unit of memory and thought that consists of elements (objects, concepts) that stand in a meaningful relationship to each other (Wundt, 1880; see also the excerpts translated from Wundt's writing in Blumenthal, 1970). In the present work, the term proposition has been used for the same purpose, though proposition may not be completely equivalent to either Selz's or Wundt's term. The important point is that the units of the system are not diffuse associations, but specific relations among elements. As stated once before, though *melon-fruit, nose-head*, and *bread-butter* are equally strongly associated, in the sense that the likelihood of eliciting the response word with the stimulus word is about the same for the three word pairs, the most characteristic property of each pair, the specific kind of relationship that exists between stimulus and response term, is neglected by an associational analysis (Kintsch, 1970a).

Associations are simply unmarked links among elements, which vary only in strength. Relations, on the other hand, are specific, marked links among elements, and in that sense fundamentally different from associations. Modern cognitive psychology should concern itself with relations, not associations. There have been attempts recently to update associationism by making relations out of associations while still retaining the term association. Anderson and Bower (1973) have chosen such a terminology, thereby turning the concept of an association into the opposite of what it has stood for in the last 2000 years. The title of their book is "Human Associative Memory," but associationists from Aristotle to James would have to disavow their efforts: Instead of diffuse associations, Anderson and Bower deal with specific relations much like the propositions of the present theory (except for a restriction to binary relations). This is good for their psychology, but bad for their history. Perhaps, it would be better to coin a new term for a new concept rather than to muddy historical waters.

If associationism (in the traditional sense) must be rejected, what are the basic cognitive operations out of which one might put together psychological processing models? How can one operate upon a relational structure, specifically the propositional structure described earlier? As a result of his extensive experimental investigations of cognitive processes, Selz (1913) proposed four basic intellectual operations. I shall merely list and describe these here without justifying their selection. There is no way today to decide whether Selz's list is correct, but the examples he cites are interesting, and in constructing actual processing models for particular experimental situations we shall repeatedly have recourse to Selz's basic operations.

1. *Pattern matching*. A given input unit is matched with a corresponding memory trace. (Pattern is my translation of the German term *Komplex*.)

2. *Pattern completion*. An input unit is matched with a memory trace that contains not only the representation of the input itself but also additional information. Two special cases must be distinguished. The first involves a part-whole match, that is, a part leads to the redintegration of the whole memory trace. Hamilton's law of redintegration and Höffding's law of totality are previous formulations of this kind of pattern completion (Hamilton, 1859; Höffding, 1891). As an example, the word fragment *strawb-* will elicit the complete word *strawberry* by means of a process of pattern completion. The second case involves pattern completion on the basis of a schema. An anticipatory schema is used to retrieve information. For example, a

proposition with an argument missing might be used to interrogate memory: (SUPERORDINATE,FARMER,$). By the process of pattern completion this schematic proposition will be matched with (SUPERORDINATE,FARMER, OCCUPATION) and thereby complete the pattern.

3. The modification of an existing memory unit, which may be either *abstration* or *differentiation*.

4. The *generation* of a new memory unit from elements that previously had not been connected as a unit.

Pattern matching and pattern completion will appear frequently throughout this volume. The problem of how new memory traces are formed and interrogated will be the main topic of Chapter 4. Very little will be said, however, about abstraction and differentiation, in spite of the obvious significance of these processes for semantic memory.

The term "unit of memory" which has been used above needs some clarification. The appropriate unit of analysis in memory is not something fixed for all times and all occasions, but something that is highly flexible and task dependent: a phoneme cluster in a short-term memory experiment, a word in a list-learning study, a proposition in comprehending a text or in making inferences about it, a sentence "chunk" for verbatim reproduction of a text, or perhaps the theme of a paragraph in long-term recall. Any one of these may under appropriate experimental conditions become the unit of processing. Processing may occur at any one of these levels of analysis, and in fact usually at more than one level, though only one may be reflected in the performance of subjects. What appears as a unit at one level may be an element at another level. The important characteristic of memory units is that when they enter into relations with other units these relations are not relations among their elements, but relations between the units as wholes. This is a property that some associationist theories share with the present approach. For instance, Müller (1911) held that patterns may be associated, but not their elements directly, and Estes (1972) has introduced control elements, which allows connections to exist between units in the absence of connections between their elements.

The level of analysis that will concern us most in the present work, though by no means exclusively, is the propositional one. Indeed, the motivation for the experiments reported in Part II has been, at least in part, to demonstrate the psychological reality of the propositional level of representation. Various psychological process models will be discussed in the context of these experiments. These models are highly task specific, but they fit quite well into the framework of the theory of cognitive processes which has been outlined above. In particular, the notions of specific (rather than diffuse associative) relationships among units and the operation of pattern completion are central to practically all processing models. Thus, we may finally perceive at least the outline, though certainly not the details, of a general theory of information processing to replace associationism.

3

ON THE ADEQUACY OF
PROPOSITIONAL TEXT BASES FOR
THE REPRESENTATION OF MEANING

The study of semantic memory has come into its own in psychology and artificial intelligence only within recent years, but closely related problems have traditionally been investigated by philosophers and linguists. In the present chapter the adequacy of semantic memory models will be examined with respect to some of these problems.

Linguists, philosophers, psychologists, and computer programmers all share an interest in the structure of knowledge and in the operations that are permissible within that structure, that is, the natural logic of thought processes. Given that very little is known about this "natural logic," it is surely not surprising that the investigator almost invariably turns to logic proper for guidance. Standard logic has reached an extremely high stage of development and initially, at least, it seems to be a close relative of the sought after natural logic. Thus, most discussions in the philosophical literature involve in some way or another attempts to translate language and cognition into standard logic. This literature is quite extensive but seems to have had relatively little influence on either linguistics or psychology, though there are some attempts in the linguistic literature to make use of standard logic. What is surprising, however, is how unsystematic these attempts usually have been. It is a widespread practice in linguistic discussions to use a formula from the predicate calculus here and there when it comes in handy and to conveniently forget about it otherwise. Notable examples of a systematic use of a modified modal predicate calculus for the description of natural language are the presuppositional logic of Keenan (1970, 1971) and the text logic of van Dijk (1973). Among psychologists only very few have been concerned with modelling thought processes, and standard logic has hardly ever been considered as a base for such an endeavor. The significant exceptions are Piaget, who studied the development of thinking with explicit reference to logical models (Inhelder & Piaget, 1964; Piaget, 1949), and Suppes' recent work on language acquisition where a modal predicate calculus is being used in psycholinguistic research (Suppes, 1973). Many earlier researchers in artificial intelligence made serious efforts to translate language and knowledge into a standard logical language in order to employ the deductive capacities of that language. Indeed, the translation of text into the predicate calculus has been quite useful for the purpose of theorem proving, as long as a program deals only with a relatively narrow topic (e.g., Green & Raphael, 1968). Recently, however, a trend has appeared in artificial intelligence work towards the development of special purpose, quasi-logical languages in place of standard logic.

Most of the work on semantic models that has come out of computer science and psychology in recent years has not used standard logic as a model. Instead, new formalisms have been proposed for the study of semantic memory and natural logic. One does not lightly exchange the tried and powerful methods of standard logic for some as yet vague and incomplete ideas, but there are some very strong arguments that may make any attempt to model the natural logic after standard logic appear fundamentally misguided. Standard logic is normative, not descriptive of actual human thinking. It was developed as an alternative to the natural logic, in order to permit unambiguous, correct inferences. This goal was achieved in standard logic by cleanly separating logical syntax and semantics. The former is prior, and what are acceptable expressions and proofs is determined by syntactic rules. What is a well-formed formula (wff), how wff's may be combined into compounds, and what constitutes a valid proof are purely syntactic-formal questions; the semantics of standard logic is concerned with truth values in possible worlds. Syntactic-formal rules have no such priority in natural language and natural logic, and it is never possible to separate them from semantic considerations. What is an acceptable proposition, what is an acceptable sentence, and what can be inferred from them can not be decided on purely formal grounds. The meaning of an expression is its most decisive aspect. To comprehend a sentence is to compute its meaning, for which its syntax must be taken into account, but it can not be separated from semantic and pragmatic considerations. Even the simplest inference in semantic memory involves world knowledge and attention to special situational factors. Truth value alone is by no means an overriding concern in semantic memory.

The arguments made above can be extended. For an especially clear statement of the issues involved see van Dijk (1973), who lists a number of specific divergences between standard logic and natural language, such as the treatment of quantification, the nature of truth functional connectives versus natural language conjunctions, and others which will play a significant role in the body of this paper. Whether these considerations justify the complete emancipation of natural logic from standard logic, or whether some modification of standard logic will eventually prove more successful after all, is probably impossible to tell at this point. Nevertheless, the fact remains that several investigators in psychology and artificial intelligence have at least tried to make fresh starts and to construct semantic memory models with a more or less explicit disregard for standard logic. Representative examples for this kind of approach are Anderson and Bower (1973), Collins and Quillian (1972), Rumelhart,

Lindsay, and Norman (1972), Quillian (1968, 1969), Schank (1972), Simmons (1972), and Winograd (1972), as well as the present work. There seems to be no way of relating these studies to a common denominator beyond saying that they are all concerned in some way or another with the development of natural logic. All of the models, except for the present one, are realized as computer programs, and the fact that these programs function proves their feasibility.

The model of semantic memory presented in the previous chapter is based upon the notion that propositions are the basic elements of the semantic structure. Similar assumptions about the role of propositions (or equivalent graphical representations) have been made in some of the other models mentioned above, especially Rumelhart et al. (1972), Schank (1972), and Simmons (1972). Furthermore, propositional representations have frequently been employed in linguistics, e.g., Bierwisch (1969), and Weinreich (1963). The seminal work in this area appears to be that of Schmidt (1962).

One of the main problems that nonstandard approaches to natural logic (specifically, propositional models) face is to determine the adequacy of the proposed formalism as a base for natural language. Whatever base is proposed, it must be able to carry all the necessary information that is expressed in the surface structure. Linguists and philosophers have explored this problem extensively, frequently by translating sentences into the predicate calculus. The resulting expressions can be extremely complex and awesomely subtle. No wonder there is a widespread belief that any formalism weaker than the predicate calculus would be hopelessly inadequate to represent what needs to be represented in a semantic base. None of the users of propositional models have as yet investigated in a systematic way whether or not propositional models are indeed adequate for the problems at hand. To initiate this kind of investigation will be the purpose of this chapter.

In the following sections, problems such as quantification, definite and indefinite noun-phrases, modality and tense, and implication and presupposition will be explored within the framework of the propositional model. It will be shown that the model is sufficiently powerful and explicit to account for at least some aspects of these classic topics in the logical description of language.

1. DEFINITE AND INDEFINITE DESCRIPTION

A text base must contain information about whether a noun phrase is used as a definite or indefinite term. Such information is needed to represent adequately the meaning of sentences, as well as for the operation of many syntactic rules, e.g., those of pronominalization. The propositional model contains no explicit apparatus to represent the definite-indefinite distinction. Nevertheless, the distinction is implicitly present in the model.

1.1

It is assumed that a lexical noun-entry by itself is always singular, unique, but unspecified. Thus, the lexical entry HOUSE appears in the surface structure as *a house*, meaning one, nonspecified house. The original meaning of the indefinite article *a* is therefore the numeral *one*. Linguistic arguments for the derivation of *a* from *one* have been given by Perlmutter (1970). Thus, when a lexical entry for a noun first appears in a text base, it is unique and indefinite. Repetition makes it definite. It is assumed by the repetition rule (or the principle of coherent progression of van Dijk, 1973) that a repeated term in a text base is always identical with its prior appearance, unless the contrary is specifically indicated. The repeated term becomes definite, i.e., specified with respect to another term in the text base. In the surface structure the definite article *the* can be used for a repeated noun. The function of this article is to point to the previous appearance of the noun or to its presence in the nonlinguistic context. *The* may therefore be regarded as the reduced form of *that*, as was argued by Thorne (1972).

The model outlined in Section 2 thus accounts for definite and indefinite descriptions in a very straightforward and intuitive way. It is done by considering a text as a whole; sentences taken out of context can not be disambiguated in the present system. Sentences taken out of a context have, however, been the main concern of traditional logics, and a powerful but complex apparatus has been developed for their description. Consider

A woman bought steak yesterday. $\qquad\qquad$ (1)

An ϵ-operator, appropriately defined in terms of the standard existential and universal quantifiers,[1] is used to indicate the uniqueness and indefiniteness of *woman*:

$$(\epsilon x)\{\text{woman}(x) \wedge \text{steak}(y) \wedge \text{buy}(x,y)\}, \qquad\qquad (2)$$

where only the details concerned with the representation of *woman* are of interest. Similarly, to represent

The woman bought steak yesterday. $\qquad\qquad$ (3)

an ι-operator for the description of unique, definite terms is employed:

$$(\iota x)\{\text{woman}(x) \wedge \text{steak}(y) \wedge \text{buy}(x,y)\}. \qquad\qquad (4)$$

On the other hand,

(BUY,WOMAN,STEAK) $\qquad\qquad$ (5)

does not distinguish between (1) and (3). There is no need to do so, however. Single sentences are just as artificial and inappropriate units as the single words with which experimental psychologists have had such a long-lasting love affair. What is needed is to represent text unambiguously. Consider

#A woman bought steak yesterday. The woman was shocked by the price. $\qquad$ (6)

---

[1] By defining such operators in terms of existential and universal quantifiers and the identity relation, Whitehead and Russell (1927) made a similar point, namely, that such operators are not basic terms in the system but must be expressed by means of other, simpler terms. What differs is the nature of the proposed reduction.

where the symbol # is used to indicate the beginning of the text. In terms of the present notation we have

$$\#(BUY, WOMAN, STEAK) \& (SHOCKED, WOMAN, BY PRICE) \qquad (7)$$

which is quite unambiguous. In the first proposition WOMAN is introduced as a singular, unspecified term; but the repetition in the second sentence is definite, since by the repetition rule it must refer to the woman who bought the steak.

There are of course many occasions where a text might begin with sentences such as (3), that is, where a definite description is used without a previous introduction of the term, in apparent contradiction to the present model. Two explanations for such usage can be given. First, it may be the case that the text base actually contains an unspecified introduction, as required by the model, but that this proposition has been deleted during the base-to-surface transformations. Thus, a narrative may begin with (3), with the narrator having a perfectly well-specified person in mind but choosing for stylistic reasons not yet to reveal this to the reader. A more important reason for initial sentences with definite descriptions is that terms may be introduced not merely through previous text, but also through nonlinguistic context.[2] In any communication situation a certain number of terms are considered given by the participants. These include not only objects present in the physical environment, but also objects only psychologically present, such as habitual topics of discourse in particular situations. Indeed, nonlinguistic context is just as natural and just as important as linguistic context: *That* can point to a physical object or event as well as to a lexical item.

For the repetition rule to apply, a lexical item must be repeated in the semantic base of a text. It is not necessary that a particular word be repeated. Synonyms, partial synonyms, related words, and most importantly pronouns may be substituted for the original word. Thus, the propositions

$$\#(START, MINER, (SPEAK, MINER)) \& $$
$$(TALL, MINER) \& (STRONG, MINER) \qquad (8)$$

may be realized as

A miner started to speak. The miner was tall and strong. (9i)

He . . . . (9ii)

The man . . . . (9iii)

The miner who started to speak was tall and strong. (9iv)

Man is used in (9iii) not as a synonym of *miner*, but in order to attract attention to one particular feature of *miner*, his maleness, when we talk about the size and strength of his body. Note that the sentence with the restrictive relative clause begins with a

[2]Gross violations in this regard simply make a text incomprehensible. For instance, Bransford and Johnson (1972) have shown that a story in which terms such as *the sound, the balloons* occur without identification were poorly understood and poorly remembered. However, when these terms were properly identified (by providing the reader with a picture of the scene involved) the difficulties disappeared.

definite article. This is not a violation of the repetition rule: This rule merely claims that a noun is indefinite when it is first introduced in a text base, that is in (8), but syntactic transformation rules may reverse this order as in (9iv).

1.2

Considering sentences in context also helps to understand how one can account for particular and nonparticular descriptions in a system without quantifiers. As is well known, indefinite noun phrases may refer to a particular individual, identified in the speaker's mind, or to some nonparticular individual whose identity is unknown to the speaker and perhaps not even of concern. Thus, *A shopper complained about the price of steak* may mean that a particular shopper, say my wife, complained, or merely that someone whose identity was not established was overheard to complain. A similar distinction exists for definite descriptions. *The general who lost this battle . . . .* may refer to a well-known national hero or just to anyone who fits the description. Logicians use special quantifiers to make these distinctions; linguists assign the feature $[\pm \text{PARTICULAR}]$ to noun phrases. However, within a text base it is always possible to decide whether or not a noun phrase is particular, without any special notation. Just as definiteness can be decided by looking at the prior text (and finding out whether a term has been previously introduced or not), the consecutive text either identifies a noun phrase or does not. A noun phrase is particular if, somewhere in the text base, it is identified. The identification may only be in the speaker's mind and never be expressed in the text itself. But, as has been said before, we stipulate that every relevant thought content must be represented in the semantic base, even if it is later deleted. Thus, a propositional base implicitly contains information about definiteness and particularity; if such information is needed (say, in a syntactic transformation), it can be determined and made explicit. However, there is no need to burden the model with a complex apparatus merely to represent these distinctions explicitly in each separate sentence.

2. QUANTIFICATION

Attempts to account for quantification in natural languages by taking the existential and universal quantifiers as primitives have not been impressively successful and at best result in quite clumsy expressions. It will be argued here that it is not necessary to imitate logical practice. An explicit account of quantification in natural language can be obtained within a propositional system as proposed here.

2.1

Quantifiers will be treated as predicators. Thus, *All men die* will be represented as[3]

$$(DIE,MAN)\&(ALL,MAN). \tag{1}$$

There are, of course, differences in syntactic treatment between quantifiers and other, more familiar types of propositions, but these can be neglected here. A more

---

[3]We shall disregard mass nouns for the purpose of this discussion.

significant characteristic of propositions containing a quantifier as their first term is that such propositions never stand alone. By itself #(OLD,MAN)# is a meaningful though cryptic text, but #(ALL,MAN)# is not. Something else must be predicated of *men* before it can be transformed into a meaningful English sentence.[4] Since quantifier propositions never occur alone, questions of scope become particularly important, though one must bear in mind that considerations of scope are crucial not only for quantifiers but for all propositional expressions. The scope of *strange* in *Nancy has a strange lover* and *It is strange that Nancy has a lover* is just as important for the interpretation of these sentences as the scope of the quantifiers in *Every man likes a pretty girl* and *This man likes every pretty girl.*

Lexical entries for quantifiers must contain statements about how the term is to be used, and what its implications are. In this respect quantifiers are treated exactly like other lexical entries (see the example for FEEL in Chapter 2). In order to be able to state the meaning postulates of English quantifiers, scales of numerosity must be postulated as part of semantic memory. Numbers, as well as arithmetical operations, must also be part of the semantic base. Every set that is defined in semantic memory has a number n associated with it, which is the number of elements in the set. Obviously, n cannot always be a precise number and may frequently be quite vague, e.g., merely an order of magnitude. How n is determined is easy to understand for sets that are defined in semantic memory by enumeration (e.g., *the countries of Europe, the mammalian species*). Most sets, of course, are defined implicitly by some property (*pretty girls, Nancy's lovers*), and it is often impossible to enumerate the members of the set. However, the semantic base must contain the necessary world knowledge to specify set size either directly (I might know all about Nancy) or to permit one to infer set size. Thus, there must be millions of pretty girls around, but whoever Nancy might be, the number of her lovers can not be very large. How such inferences are made in the present system is an important problem, but one that can not be considered now.

Given a semantic memory in which for each set a (fuzzy) set size n is defined, we can now consider the various quantifiers of English separately.[5]

2.2

All, as in *All citizens complained*, is represented as (COMPLAIN,CITIZEN)& (ALL,CITIZEN). The (partial) lexical entry for ALL is

$$(R,N)\&(ALL,N) \equiv (R,N)\&(NUMBER\ OF,N,n)$$

where N is a noun, R is an arbitrary predicate, and n is the size of the set N, as discussed above.

Half of, one, two, ... each carry with them precise implications about the number of terms under consideration:

---

[4]Utterances such as *All men* in answer to the question *How many men must die?* or *The men were few (in number)* appear to be cases of elliptic speech; in the propositional base the first example would in fact be something like (1), while in the second example the base contains a surpressed reference to some location or time.

[5]Mass nouns will again be neglected here.

$$(R,N)\&(HALF\ OF,N)\ \equiv\ (R,N)\&(NUMBER\ OF,N,n/2)$$

$$(R,N)\&(ONE,N)\ \equiv\ (R,N)\&(NUMBER\ OF,N,1)$$

$$(R,N)\&(TWO,N)\ \equiv\ (R,N)\&(NUMBER\ OF,N,2).$$

Some, as in *Some citizens complained*, (COMPLAIN,CITIZEN)&(SOME, CITIZEN), has the lexical entry

$$(R,N)\&(SOME,N)\ \equiv\ (R,N)\&(NUMBER\ OF,N,k)$$

where $0 < k < n$.

Examples like *Not all dogs bark (but some do), Not all girls are pretty*, etc. suggest a second part of the lexical entry:

$$(NOT,(R,N)\&(ALL,N))\ \equiv\ (R,N)\&(SOME,N).$$

Note that *Not all trees fly* would receive a correct interpretation because the first component of (FLY,TREE)&(SOME,TREE) would be rejected by the semantic system.

Many as in *Many citizens complained* would be represented as (COMPLAIN, CITIZEN)&(MANY,CITIZEN), with the lexical entry

$$(R,N)\&(MANY,N)\ \equiv\ (R,N)\&(NUMBER\ OF,N,k)\&(LARGE,k).$$

The relativity of *many* is captured by the fact that LARGE is relative, too: Whatever value of k is large depends upon the size of n.

Few is handled similarly, except that it is stipulated that k must be small.

Several implies that k is between 2 and a dozen or so, but it is not defined relatively as are *few* and *many*.[6]

Comparative quantifiers such as *more, less*, and *as many* presuppose the previous introduction into the text base of some (not necessarily precise) reference quantity. An appropriate k-value can then be defined with respect to the reference quantity. Frequently the reference quantity is not given explicitly in the text itself but determined by the nonlinguistic context or through common knowledge (*No general won more battles than Napoleon*). Other quantifiers do not refer to a predetermined reference quantity, but indicate a procedure by means of which such a quantity can be calculated on the basis of the given text and situational knowledge. Thus, the quantity referred to in *Use as little flour as possible* is determined by the objective to be achieved, as described in the rest of the text.

2.3

The surface representation of the quantifiers introduced above is quite complex and presents many thorny problems for linguists to worry about. ALL may be expressed in English as *all*, but *every* and *each* may also be used as surface variations. When the

---

[6]Recently an experimental study of quantifier usage has been reported by Borges and Sawyers (1974). Their data indicate that the term *several* is more complex than assumed here. In general, however, the results of Borges and Sawyers are in excellent agreement with the intuitive definitions proposed here and could be used to refine and empirically substantiate these definitions..

indefinite article *a* is used generically, it also must be represented in the base as ALL, as in *A grizzly bear is huge*. The surface form *any* may sometimes also derive from a base structure ALL, as in *Anyone can break his leg*. But this is not always the case. In a sentence such as *Paul does not like anyone*, *any* can not possibly be a surface form of ALL, because by a rule given above NOT ALL is equal to SOME, which would make *Paul likes someone* a paraphrase of *Paul does not like anyone*, which is clearly false. Furthermore, the surface form *all* itself is not always used in its universal meaning, as in *All kinds of wines were served at the dinner*.

The problems alluded to above are certainly nontrivial, and no solution is offered here. But it must be remembered that the model merely aims for an unambiguous semantic base. Ambiguities in the surface structure derived from that base are of less concern here, just as the rules that permit surface structure derivations are neglected.

2.4

A number of other English quantifiers can be considered within the framework developed above. The lexical description of *other* presupposes that some noun phrase N' has previously been introduced:

$$(R,N)\&(OTHER,N) \equiv (R,N)\&(DIFFERENT,N',N)$$

Similarly, we have as part of the lexical entry for *only*

$$(R,N)\&(ONLY,N) \equiv (R,N)\&(NOT,(R,N'))\&(DIFFERENT,N',N)$$

All but is closely related to *only* as is shown by *Only John kissed Nancy* and *Everyone but John did not kiss Nancy*:

$$(R,N)\&(ALL\ BUT,N) \equiv (NOT,(R,N))\&(ONLY,N).$$

Temporal quantifiers such as *always, usually, occasionally, rarely, never, sometimes, . . .* must also be treated as predicators. That is, the base expression for *Citizens always complain* should be (ALWAYS,COMPLAIN)&(COMPLAIN, CITIZENS). Meaning postulates can be stated in terms of TIME, e.g., ALWAYS $\equiv$ ALL TIME, RARELY $\equiv$ FEW TIME, but detailed discussion must await a better understanding of the role of time and space in the semantic structure in general. The same problems arise with spatial quantifiers *(everywhere, somewhere)*.

Iterated quantifiers present no special problems in the present system. *Most of the four dogs bark* is represented as (BARK,DOG)&(4,DOG)&(MOST,DOG), where the DOG of the second proposition, by the repetition rule, refers to the barking dog introduced earlier, and the final DOG refers to the previously specified four barking dogs.

3. MODALITY

Several proposals for a semantic base distinguish two separate sentence constituents: modality and propositions. A proposition, to quote Fillmore (1968), is a "tenseless set of relationships involving verbs and nouns," while the modality component specifies information concerning the sentence as a whole. Negation, tense, mood, and aspect, as well as sentence adverbials, are often thought to be part of this modality component. In this section it will be shown that negation as well as sentence adverbials can be treated more parsimoniously as proposition modifiers (Rivero, 1972), while a discussion of tense will be postponed for Section 5.

3.1

In several previous examples negation was treated as a predicate NOT with a propositional argument. Negation can always be treated this way; what is negated are always propositions. This claim needs justification in view of the many sentences in which a particular argument is negated. However, it is not necessary to require negation of arguments in the base structure. Thus, *No guests came to the party* has the base structure (COME,(NONE,GUEST),PARTY), which involves the quantifier NONE rather than negation. In other cases where specific arguments appear to be negated, the base structure is more complex. Suppose one wants to negate *baby* in *The baby spilled the milk*. A possible sentence expressing this negation might be, with the proper stress *Not the báby spilled the milk*, or more adequately *It was not the baby who spilled the milk*. The base structure for these sentences is not, however

*(SPILL,(NOT,BABY),MILK)

but rather involves three propositions:

(NOT,(SPILL,BABY,MILK))&(SPILL,$,MILK).

What is expressed by such a sentence is not just a negation, but also some additional information that the milk was indeed spilled, but by someone unsuspected, other than the baby. Without special stress, negation of a sentence is usually ambiguous. *The baby did not spill the milk* may mean several things: that nothing was spilled, that the cat spilled the milk, or that the baby spilled the coffee. If any of these further possibilities are being asserted, this must be done in the base structure through a separate proposition, even though it may not be explicit in the surface structure and indicated only by the stress assignment.

3.2

Sentence adverbials can also be treated as proposition modifiers. *Unfortunately Myrna came to the party* is represented by two propositions

((COME,MYRNA,PARTY) = α)&(UNFORTUNATE,α)

Either proposition can be negated separately:

((COME,MYRNA,PARTY) = α)&((NOT,α) = β)&(UNFORTUNATE,β)

can be expressed as *Unfortunately Myrna did not come to the party*, and

((COME,MYRNA,PARTY) = α)&((UNFORTUNATE,α) = β)&(NOT,β)

leads to *It was not unfortunate that Myrna came to the party.* I believe this is true for all sentence adverbials, though this claim is not generally accepted. Keenan (1971) maintains that *also* and *even* can not be regarded as predicates. In *The book was also dull* the *also* does not make a separate statement about the book which could be negated separately. Rather, negating *The book was also dull* implies that the book was not dull. *Also* seems to do two things: It implies that something else happened, in addition to whatever we are told by the proposition in which *also* appears, and it serves to deemphasize the latter information. Thus, *The book was also dull* implies something else, perhaps that the book was badly written, or that the reader was tired, and it indicates that the dullness of the book is of secondary importance in the communicative event relative to the "something else." While agreeing with Keenan's analysis as far as the meaning of *also* is concerned, his claim that *also* can not be negated separately is false. Negating the *also* separately in *The book was also dull* may be rare and perhaps odd, but by no means impossible. Someone may very well say *The book was not also dull — it was first of all and primarily dull, whatever else might have been wrong with it.* Thus, ALSO may be regarded as a predicate just as other sentence adverbials, defined in the subjective lexicon by meaning postulates as indicated by Keenan's analysis.

A similar argument can be made about *even*. Negating *Even John read the book* normally denies *John read the book*, but under certain circumstances one could explicitly negate the *even* alone. This is admittedly unusual in English, and clumsy, but there is nothing to keep one from saying *It is not right to say "Even John read the book," because he was in fact the first one to do so and the implication of "even," that John's reading of the book is in any way surprising, is unfair to poor John.* Thus, the suggested base structure for *Even John read the book* is ((READ,JOHN, BOOK)=α)&(EVEN,α). The lexical definition for EVEN must include not only the proper implications of the term, but also rules for its use: to stress a particular piece of information.

While this is not the place to provide lexical definitions for the many sentence adverbials that need to be considered, some remarks can nevertheless be made concerning adverbs of possibility and probability. As has long been known to logicians, these adverbs may be defined in terms of the quantifiers *all, some*, and *many/most*. Thus, the base of *All bears bite* is (BITE,BEAR)&(ALL,BEAR) which is equivalent to (NECESSARY,(BITE,BEAR)) = (IMPOSSIBLE,(NOT,(BITE, BEAR))). *Some bears bite* is derived from (BITE,BEAR)&(SOME,BEAR) = (POSSIBLE,(BITE,BEAR)). It is assumed here that (POSSIBLE,α) = (NOT, (NECESSARY,α))&(NOT,(IMPOSSIBLE,α)).[7] *Many bears bite* can be similarly related to *probably:* (BITE,BEAR)&(MANY,BEAR) = (PROBABLE, (BITE,BEAR)). The surface realizations of these terms are interesting and notoriously complex. NECESSARY may often be represented by *must;* POSSIBLE, by *can* or *may;* PROBABLE, by *should* or ought. However, *must, can,* etc. are by

---

[7]This definition is somewhat controversial, as some logicians prefer to use *possible* simply as the negation of *impossible.*

no means reliable indicators of base structure NECESSARY or POSSIBLE. While retaining their relation to quantifiers as described above, these words may also refer to a dimension of obligation rather than possibility. Thus, *must* may be derived from a base structure OBLIGATORY; *can,* from PERMISSIBLE; and *must not,* from FORBIDDEN.

3.3

It is not clear whether performatives need or even can be treated within a semantic system, since a full account necessarily involves pragmatic factors. Performatives are used to specify certain aspects of the speaker-listener interaction. The presence of a performative is, in part, what turns a proposition into an utterance. Thus, a consideration of performatives is probably beyond the bounds of semantic models. Nevertheless, it seems worthwhile to point to the possibility of treating performatives as proposition modifiers, just like other modals. Linguists (e.g., Rivero, 1972; Ross, 1970) have made similar suggestions, and Russell has pointed out that such constructions provide a solution to a long-standing logical paradox. The sentence *I am lying* need no longer trouble philosophers once it is embedded in a performative proposition: "The man who says *I am lying* is really asserting *There is a proposition which I am asserting and which is false.* That is presumably what you mean by lying [Russell, 1956, p. 263]." Thus, *I am lying* becomes (DECLARATIVE,α)& ((LIE,I)=α) = (ASSERT,I,α)&((LIE,I)=α), and *Close the door!* will be (IMPERATIVE,α)&((CLOSE,YOU,DOOR)=α) = (ORDER,I,YOU,α)& ((CLOSE,YOU,DOOR)=α). Questions can be handled similarly. A narrative may be represented in the base by (NARRATIVE,α) plus a list of propositions which is named α. Other texts could similarly be identified as FAIRY TALE, SCIENTIFIC REPORT, etc., with important consequences both for the style of the verbal expression of the text base thus labeled and for the way in which the listener will process the material. Thus, (SCIENTIFIC REPORT,α) means that a certain set of inference rules and attitudes on the part of the reader must be used in interpreting the text α. While (FAIRY TALE,α) asks the reader to be ready to suspend certain normally used semantic restrictions, so that bean stalks can grow into the sky and frogs may talk.

4. IMPLICATION AND PRESUPPOSITION

4.1

Among the many possible relations among propositions, implication and presupposition have received special attention in recent years. Implication in natural language (which shall be denoted by an arrow: $\rightarrow$) is not identical with logical implication. Logical implication ($\supset$) is defined in terms of the truth or falsity of propositions; furthermore, it is defined in a counterintuitive way. P materially implies Q, P $\supset$ Q, if either P and Q are both true, or if P is false; P $\supset$ Q is false only if P is true but Q is false. Thus, we have (example from Rescher, 1964) *Napoleon lost at*

Waterloo ⊃ *Caesar crossed the Rubicon,* but also *Napoleon won at Waterloo* ⊃ *Caesar crossed (did not cross) the Rubicon.* As has been frequently noted, material implication is too strong a concept for the representation of natural language. Thus, weaker uses of "imply" have been advocated. Karttunen (1970) defines "imply" as

> P implies Q iff   (1)
> whenever P is asserted,
> the speaker ought to believe that Q.

Leaving implication up to what the speaker ought to do is altogether too vague. In a propositional system such as the one envisaged here, a more objective definition is possible.

> P implies Q iff   (2)
> given a semantic memory S, which contains a set of inference rules J,
> and given a proposition P, Q is derivable from P.

This definition should be generalized, in that implication should be stated for a text base T (that is, a list of propositions), and not necessarily for a single proposition P. Note that implication as defined by (2) is a far cry from material implication, but that it is closely related to (1): Indeed one could regard it as a specification of the conditions necessary for (1). It is important to realize what has happened here. Attention has been shifted away from logical considerations to a psychological pro cess explanation. Implication in logic is a relation between sentences; deriving one sentence from another is a psychological process. Implication as defined by (2) depends upon whose semantic memory and whose inference rules one is talking about. If a person does not have the necessary information or the required inference rules to derive A from B, then for that person B does not imply A, even though it might for someone else. Furthermore, if in some rapid conversation a person fails to make the inference that B implies A, then for that person and that moment in time B and A are in fact unrelated, even though the same person may be quite able to make the necessary inference under other circumstances. Structure is not something finished and immutable, but something that must be continually generated psycholog- ically. There is no way of separating semantic structure from psychological proces- sing.

In order for (2) to have substance, the semantic memory S and the set of infer- ence rules J must be known, because otherwise the notion of "derivability" is empty. Although our understanding of S and J is far from adequate at present, some special cases of how inferences are made in S have been explored. Consider

> *All dogs bark* implies *Collies bark*   (3)
> (BARK,DOG)&(ALL,DOG)→(BARK,COLLIE)

> *His whole body was covered with soot*   (4)
>   implies *His arms were covered with soot,*
> (COVER,SOOT,BODY)&(WHOLE,BODY)→(COVER,SOOT,ARM)

We have already explored how such inferences can be made in a propositional system. It is necessary to assume certain structural relations among lexical items defining an IS-A and HAS-PART hierarchy, as well as the existence of certain hierarchy-deletion and hierarchy-production operators.

Implication relationships between main sentences and their complements have been studied by Karttunen (1970). Karttunen distinguishes eight types of complement constructions; sentences 5–10 are quoted from his paper:

John manages to kiss Mary. $\qquad\qquad$ (5)
$(\mathrm{MANAGE,JOHN},\alpha)\&((\mathrm{KISS,JOHN,MARY})=\alpha)\mapsto\alpha$
John did not manage to kiss Mary.
$(\mathrm{NOT,(MANAGE,JOHN},\alpha))\&((\mathrm{KISS,JOHN,MARY})=\alpha)\mapsto(\mathrm{NOT},\alpha)$

John avoided getting caught in the traffic. $\qquad\qquad$ (6)
$(\mathrm{AVOID,JOHN},\alpha)\&((\mathrm{GET\ CAUGHT,JOHN,\ IN\ TRAFFIC})=\alpha)\mapsto$
(NOT,α)
John did not avoid getting caught in the traffic.
$(\mathrm{NOT,(AVOID,JOHN},\alpha)\&((\mathrm{GET\ CAUGHT,JOHN,IN\ TRAFFIC})=$
$\alpha)\mapsto\alpha$

John killed Harry. $\qquad\qquad$ (7)
$(\mathrm{CAUSE,JOHN},\alpha)\&((\mathrm{DEAD,HARRY})=\alpha)\mapsto\alpha$

John prevented Mary from leaving. $\qquad\qquad$ (8)
$(\mathrm{PREVENT,JOHN},\alpha)\&((\mathrm{LEAVE,MARY})=\alpha)\mapsto(\mathrm{NOT},\alpha)$

Sebastian was unable to leave the country. $\qquad\qquad$ (9)
$(\mathrm{NOT,(ABLE,SEBASTIAN},\alpha)\&$
$((\mathrm{LEAVE,SEBASTIAN,COUNTRY})=\alpha)\mapsto(\mathrm{NOT},\alpha)$

Bill did not hesitate to call him a liar. $\qquad\qquad$ (10)
$(\mathrm{NOT,(HESITATE,BILL},\alpha))\&((\mathrm{CALL,BILL,\$,LIAR})=\alpha)\mapsto\alpha$

It is (not) surprising that Peter came to the party. $\qquad\qquad$ (11)
$(\mathrm{SURPRISE},\alpha)\&((\mathrm{COME,PETER,PARTY})=\alpha)\mapsto\alpha$
$(\mathrm{NOT,(SURPRISE},\alpha))\&((\mathrm{COME,PETER,PARTY})=\alpha)\mapsto\alpha$

It is likely that Peter came to the party. $\qquad\qquad$ (12)
$(\mathrm{LIKELY},\alpha)\&((\mathrm{COME,PETER,PARTY})=\alpha)\mapsto\emptyset$

As Karttunen has pointed out, the implication relationships in (5) – (12) can be summarized in a simple table:

		Complement		
		Assert	Negate	None
Main Sentence	Assert	(5), (7), (11)	(6), (8)	(9), (10), (12)
	Negate	(6), (10), (11)	(5), (9)	(7), (8), (12)

In other words, there are eight types of verbs that take sentence complements. If the lexical entry for each such verb specifies which type it belongs to, a simple production rule can be stated that permits one to infer whether a sentence complement is asserted (or negated). Note that the second proposition in $(CAUSE,JOHN,\alpha)\&$ $((DEAD,HARRY)=\alpha)$ does not by itself assert $(DEAD,HARRY)$. In order to do that, $(DEAD,HARRY)$ would have to precede $(CAUSE,JOHN,\alpha)$, in which case a possible surface rendering might be *Harry is dead. John killed him.* In this case it would not matter if we take back the normal implication of *John killed Harry* by a *perhaps*. We still would know that Harry is dead, although we no longer can infer it from *Perhaps John killed him.*

The reason for reporting Karttunen's work so fully is that it is an excellent example of the kind of study that is badly needed, but which is as yet all too rare. A few references to other studies of how inference rules operate in semantic memory were given in Chapter 2. Needless to say, all of this together falls far short of an adequate understanding of semantic inferences, but it does provide a few examples of possible approaches and gives some substance to the claim that implication can be defined in terms of derivability.

4.2

Sentence (11) is an example of a presupposition. A definition of "presuppose" can easily be given in terms of "imply," and hence ultimately in terms of derivability, via (2):

P presupposes Q iff   (13)
$P \rightarrow Q$ and $(NOT,P) \rightarrow Q$.

Alternatively, presupposition can be defined in terms of truth values, but such definitions are the source of great difficulties. The definition of presupposition in standard logic is much too narrow to be useful for linguistic purposes, and extended definitions are required. This means that an entire nonstandard presuppositional logic must be developed. The work of Keenan (1970) represents the most serious development of such a nature.

Most linguists use "presupposition" without a definition, or only with the very vaguest one. This creates problems, because although the definition given in (13) may be adequate for certain cases, e.g., (11), it can not be extended to cover everything for which the term presupposition has been employed in the literature. Consider the following examples, most of which are taken verbatim from the literature.[8] No further examples of predicate complement constructions will be given. The symbol ⇒ will be used for "presupposes":

John is (not) a bachelor.   John is male.   (14)
$(BACHELOR,JOHN) \Rightarrow (MALE,JOHN)$

[8]Sentences (15) and (18)–(23) are from Keenan (1970); sentences (16) and (24) are from Kiparsky and Kiparsky (1971).

That arithmetic is incomplete surprised (did not surprise) Magrid.
Magrid is intelligent. (15)
(SURPRISE,MAGRID,α)&((INCOMPLETE,ARITHMETIC)=α)⇒
(INTELLIGENT,MAGRID)

I ignored (did not ignore) an ant on my plate.   I perceived an ant. (16)
(IGNORE,I,ANT)&(ON PLATE,ANT)⇒(PERCEIVE,I,ANT)

The girl opened (did not open) the door.   The door was closed. (17)
(OPEN,GIRL,DOOR)⇒(CLOSED,DOOR)

John resumed (did not resume) speaking.   John was speaking. (18)
(RESUME,JOHN,SPEAK)⇒(SPEAK,JOHN)

Fred ate (did not eat) another hot dog.   Fred ate at least one hot dog. (19)
(EAT,FRED,HOTDOG)&(OTHER,HOTDOG)⇒
(EAT,FRED,HOTDOG)&(SEVERAL,HOTDOG)

The presuppositions shown for (14)–(19) appear to be at least in principle derivable in a semantic system, as required by definition (2), though not all the necessary inference rules have as yet been spelled out. The presupposition *John is male* in (14) follows directly from *bachelor*, presumably through a lexical search. Examples (16) – (19) can be treated similarly. In each case the lexical entry for the verb contains the necessary information for the required inferences. Thus, for the lexical entry IG-NORE one must assume a production rule that expands (IGNORE,X) into (PERCEIVE,X)&(IGNORE,X), neglecting the temporal aspects involved. The inference rule used in (17) is a very general one. For all process-action verbs (the terminology is Chafe's, 1970), it must be true that (VERB,AGENT,PATIENT) can be expanded as (NOT,(VERB,PATIENT))&(VERB,AGENT,PATIENT). Similar rules are conceivable for aspectuals such as *resume* in (18) and the iterative in (19).

While the inferences treated so far appear feasible within the present system, at least upon an optimistic assessment of the problems involved, (15) presents a much tougher task. A good deal of knowledge must be involved in the inference that *Magrid is intelligent* (and *well-educated*, etc.) because the incompleteness of arithmetic did or did not surprise her. To formulate the necessary inference rules within the present system is quite beyond anyone's power at present, but there appear to be no reasons why such a formulation should be impossible in principle in a more fully developed model of semantic memory.

Now consider a second set of examples of what are also sometimes called presuppositions.

John called.   Something is known about "John." (20)
($,JOHN)&(CALL,JOHN)

Marvin married Joe's sister.   Joe has a sister. (21)
(HAVE,JOE,SISTER)&(MARRY,MARVIN,SISTER)

Mary loves the puppy she found.   Mary found a puppy.   (22)
(FIND,MARY,PUPPY)&(LOVE,MARY,PUPPY)

The Tiv, who respected Bohannon, are a generous people.
    The Tiv respected Bohannon.   (23)
(RESPECT,TIV,BOHANNON)&(GENEROUS,TIV)

Two languages are spoken by everyone.
    Two specific languages.   (24)
($,(2,LANGUAGE))&(SPEAK,(ALL,PERSON),(2,LANGUAGE))

Examples (20)–(24) are obviously very different from the previous set of examples. Nothing could be gained here by using the $\Rightarrow$ notation: In every case what would follow the double arrow would be simply a proposition already stated on its left side. The notation (FIND,MARY,PUPPY)&(LOVE,MARY,PUPPY) $\Rightarrow$ (FIND,MARY,PUPPY) is totally redundant, which was not at all the case in examples (14)–(19). One might want to call *Mary loves the puppy she found* a case of textual presupposition, in contrast to the lexical presuppositions discussed earlier; and one might wonder whether such textual presuppositions should be called presuppositions at all. Certainly definition (2) can not be applied to such cases. There is no way to derive (FIND,MARY,PUPPY) from (LOVE,MARY,PUPPY) on the basis of lexical properties and inference rules, while to claim that the derivation is based upon both propositions of (22) is, at best, a misuse of the term "derive."

Sentences (20)–(24) do not presuppose anything (at least not what is claimed), but simply assert two propositions. In each case one (or more) arguments of the first proposition are repeated in the second proposition, and thus becomes definite by the repetition rule of Section 1. It is meaningless to say that the first proposition is presupposed in these examples, since it is already asserted. This can be seen most clearly by paraphrasing (21)–(24) in such a way that the propositional bases remain unchanged but a separate sentence is used for each proposition [we shall omit (20) because the $-sign in the first proposition does not sufficiently specify the way in which *John* is identified]:

Joe has a sister.   Marvin married the sister (her).   (21′)

Mary found a puppy.   Mary (she) loves the puppy (it).   (22′)

The Tiv respected Bohannon.   The Tiv (they) are generous people. (23′)

There are two specific languages.   (24′)
    Everyone speaks these languages (them).

Note the contrast of (24′) with *Everyone speaks two languages*, which is derived from a different base (SPEAK,(ALL,PERSON),(2,LANGUAGES)), in which the two languages are not identified by a previous proposition. Actually, *Two languages are spoken by everyone* is ambiguous: It may either be used as in (24) or in the sense of *Everyone speaks two languages*.

It is doubtful that anyone would talk about presupposition in the context of (21')–(24'). But if the claim is accepted that *Mary loves the puppy she found* and *Mary found a puppy — She loves it* are both expressions of the same underlying base (FIND,MARY,PUPPY)&(LOVE,MARY,PUPPY), it makes no sense to talk about presuppositions in the context of (20)–(24) either. Surely, presupposition must be a relation among propositions, not surface structures (sentences).

5. LOCATION, TIME, AND TENSE

5.1 Cases

Of the cases that have something to do with time and space, only Time and Locative will be discussed here; Source and Goal, which are concerned with motion in time and space, are used in the present system exactly as suggested by Fillmore (1971), and I have nothing to add here. The cases Time and Locative, however, appear to be quite special and differ from other cases (Agent, Instrument, Experiencer, and Object) in important ways. Consider the following examples, of which (3), (4), and (5) have been taken from Fillmore (1971):

Boulder is beautiful. (1)

Winter is cold. (2)

The beer was in the garage yesterday. (3)

I lived in Milwaukee in the forties. (4)

Jeffrey spent Tuesday afternoon at the beach. (5)

Jane slept on the sofa after the dance. (6)

According to Fillmore, the first five sentences are examples of verbs that take time and space complements directly. In (6), however, the Time and Locative cases are optional and are introduced through separate higher sentences containing verbs such as *occur* or *happen* to which the cases Time and Locative are attached. The need for such higher order sentences can easily be appreciated because the alternative of writing the base of (6) as

*(SLEEP,JANE,SOFA,DANCE) (6i)

is obviously unsatisfactory. The base (6i) does not specify that the prepositions *on* and *after* should be used. If one only knows that SOFA is a Locative, did Jane sleep *on* the sofa, or *behind, into*, or *via* it? Is the Time supposed to be *before* or *after*, or *during* the dance? Clearly a propositional base must specify these relations, and the most obvious way to do this is through separate spatial and temporal predicates. Therefore, the base structure of (6) must be

$$((SLEEP,JANE)=\alpha)\&(LOC:ON,\alpha,SOFA)\&$$
$$(TIME:AFTER,\alpha,DANCE). \quad (6ii)$$

The syntactic rules that transform (6ii) into (6) need not concern us here. Transformation rules which are as complex, or even more complex, are needed in the grammar anyway for quite different reasons (see Fillmore's, 1971, examples of conflation involving verbs of motion).

The great majority of time and space references in a text can be treated as in (6ii). In order to do so, only a limited number of LOCATION and TIME predicators are needed: the general predicators LOC and TIME, one for each proposition, and tense operators (which, however, will be redefined in terms of temporal primitives in Section 5.3). Thus, we have

$$\text{LOC:}\emptyset/\text{IN}/\text{ON}/\text{AT}/\text{TO}/\text{OVER}/\text{BESIDE}/ \ldots \ldots \qquad (7)$$
$$\text{TIME:}\emptyset/\text{BEFORE}/\text{AFTER}/\text{DURING}/\text{PAST}/\text{FUTURE}/ \ldots \ldots$$

by means of which the time and location of events (propositions) or objects can be specified. For instance,

$$(\text{FIND,I,BOOK})\&(\text{LOC,BOOK,THERE}) \qquad (8)$$
I found the book there
$$((\text{STAND,JOHN})=\alpha)\&(\text{LOC:BEIIIND},\alpha,\text{COUNTER})$$
John stands behind the counter
$$((\text{BREAK,JOHN,LEG})=\alpha)\&(\text{TIME},\alpha,\text{YESTERDAY})$$
John broke his (a) leg yesterday
$$((\text{INVADE,CAESAR,GAUL})=\alpha)\&(\text{TIME:YEAR},\alpha,\text{58B.C.})$$
Caesar invaded Gaul in 58 B.C.

If spatial and temporal information is sometimes introduced into a sentence via separate propositions containing special LOC and TIME predicators, but at other times as direct verb complements as in (1)–(5), the question arises as to which verbs may take Locative or Time cases directly and which require predicates like (7) and (8). The answer to this question is not clear, though one can enumerate special cases, as has been done here and in Fillmore's original paper. There is, however, a more satisfactory solution, namely, to treat (3)–(5) not as Fillmore suggested, but in the same way as (6). In other words, spatial and temporal information can always be represented in a propositional base by special LOC and TIME predicates. Usually propositions containing LOC and TIME are subordinate to some other predicate, as in (6) and (8), but in some cases they stand alone, as in (3)–(5):

$$(\text{TIME,BEER,YESTERDAY})\&(\text{LOC:IN,BEER,GARAGE}) \qquad (3i)$$

$$(\text{TIME,I,FORTIES})\&(\text{LOC:IN,I,MILWAUKEE}) \qquad (4i)$$

$$(\text{TIME,JEFFREY,TUESDAY AFTERNOON})\&$$
$$(\text{LOC:AT,JEFFREY,BEACH}) \qquad (5i)$$

Transformation rules are needed to turn these base structures into surface expressions containing a form of the verb *be*, or some paraphrase thereof as in (4) and (5). [Actually, (4i) and (5i) are the bases for *I was in Milwaukee in the forties*, and *Jeffrey was at the beach Tuesday afternoon*. Sentences (4) and (5) may imply more than that: *Spent* means that Jeffrey was there all afternoon, and *lived* implies some minimum amount of time in Milwaukee. In order to express these qualifications in the base, (4i) and (5i) would have to be interpreted within some suitable context.]

This leaves sentences like (1) and (2) which according to Fillmore (1968) also contain Locative or Time cases. To treat (1) and (2) in a similar way results in rather unnatural constructions. However, *Boulder* in (1) and *winter* in (2) may not be Locative or Time cases at all. In these sentences *Boulder* and *winter* appear to be used in an Instrument role, as the elicitors of the sensations *beautiful* and *cold*.[9] Sentences (1) and (2) can be regarded as parallel constructions to *The town is beautiful* and *The wind is cold*, rather than as sentences containing a Locative or Time case.

5.2 Tense

English sentences are always tensed statements, but the propositions that constitute a text base, and from which the sentences are supposedly derived, are not. How, then, do tenses get into sentences? We shall, as always, disregard the task of actually constructing the linguistic rules that will assign to sentences appropriate tenses. However, a text base must somehow contain the kind of information that will appear in the surface structure as the tenses of verbs, and the nature of this information must be explicated.

The argument used here follows some suggestions by Chafe (1973, 1974), who maintained that tenses are to be derived from other information already available. This may be either in the form of explicit temporal statements that appear in a text base, or it may be contextually given information. Finally, there are temporally neutral propositions for which the present tense is used in English.

If there is an explicit time reference in a text base, tense is chosen in accordance with it. It is assumed that *now, yesterday, in the year 1280, next week*, etc. are specified in the lexicon as to the tense they require. Such explicit specifications of time establish a time reference that is valid for a whole text, not merely for a particular proposition. Thus,

$$\#((\text{FALL},\text{JANE},\text{HORSE})=$$
$$\alpha)\&(\text{TIME},\alpha,\text{YESTERDAY})\&(\text{ANGRY},\text{JANE})\# \tag{9}$$

is expressed as

Jane fell off (her) horse yesterday. She was (very) angry. (9i)

The past tense is used in the second sentence, even though the underlying proposition carries no time reference, because it belongs to the same text for which *yesterday* has already been established as a temporal reference point.

Many texts in memory are specified as past. These include historical knowledge (*Caesar invaded Gaul*) and personally experienced episodes (*I heard the Grieg piano concerto yesterday*). The temporal information may either be contained in the memory code itself (e.g., one may remember that a certain event took place *yesterday evening*, or on *New Year's eve 1956*) or it may be reconstructed relative to other remembered events (e.g., *Caesar lived in the first century B.C.*).

Unlike the past, it is assumed here that the future tense always reflects an explicit time reference in the base (though not necessarily to some specified time). Complex

---

[9] If there is a case *patient* for objects that have a certain property, as suggested by Chafe (1970), *Boulder* and *winter* could be called patients.

propositional expressions containing such higher order predicates as *I plan, I predict* are supposed to be the source of sentences in the future tense, a view which seems acceptable at least to some linguists (Lyons, 1968, Pp. 304–317). These higher order predicates appear in the surface structure only as a future tense:

$$(\text{PLAN},\text{I},\alpha)\&((\text{DRIVE},\text{I},\text{DENVER})=\alpha) \qquad (10)$$

I shall drive to Denver, or *I think I shall drive to Denver.* (10i)

In addition, of course, such sentences may also contain adverbs like *tomorrow*. It must be noted, however, that *shall* and *will* are not always used in English with a future time reference (e.g., *Thou shalt not kill*), and may have to be represented by a different modal in the base (like *must* or *may*), and that other modals beside *shall* and *will* may indicate the future in English *(John may come tomorrow)*.

While many text bases contain explicit time references, as has been discussed above, there are others that clearly do not. In order to assign tenses to such statements, information that is essentially of a psychological nature must be considered. When a proposition is transformed into a sentence, the proposition is present in a person's consciousness. In fact, not only is the proposition itself present, but information about its processing history as well. That is, the person knows that a certain proposition was retrieved from memory, while another entered consciousness as the result of a perceptual experience, and a third one had yet a different origin in that it was newly constructed. People know whether they perceive, remember, or make something up. This kind of given information about a proposition can be used to determine tenses.

Information just entering consciousness from the environment as a result of perceptual processing carries with it the temporal characteristic *now*. If it is conceptualized as a proposition and expressed as a sentence, the present tense will be used. If the perceptual stimulus is no longer present in the environment, information is characterized as *past*, and if expressed in a sentence the past tense will be used. This use of the past tense can be called a short-term memory past, for it implies that an event has just been perceived and the speaker is still conscious of it. As Chafe (1973, 1974) has pointed out, this particular kind of past tense may be expressed in English without temporal adverbs (or perhaps a *just*). In Chafe's example,

Steve fell into the swimming pool (11)

the past tense implies that the event took place recently and is still present in the speaker's consciousness. This use of the past tense contrasts with the past tense that indicates that a certain proposition has been retrieved from memory, in which case temporal adverbs would have to be used to indicate the time involved. Thus, if the speaker refers not to something in his short-term memory, but to events retrieved from long-term memory, he might say

Steve fell into the swimming pool yesterday. (12)

Chafe (1973, 1974) has discussed in some detail the kind of inferences that a hearer can make, and is expected to make, about the speaker's memory processes from the speaker's use of temporal adverbs.

The term consciousness and short-term memory which have been employed here deserve some comment. A short-term memory store has been postulated not on the basis of psychological data, but because such a concept proved to be necessary to explain a linguistic phenomenon, namely, the use of the past tense in English. In psychology, the term short-term memory is used in several different ways, and it has by no means always been equated with a kind of continuing consciousness. Such a conception of short-term memory is, however, not foreign to psychology. It is the Jamesian notion of primary memory: "An object of primary memory is not brought back; it was never lost; its date was never cut off in consciousness from that of the immediately present moment. In fact it comes to us as belonging to the rearward portion of the present space of time, and not to the genuine past [James, 1890, p. 647, Vol. I]." In recent years the term primary memory has sometimes been used without James' emphasis on consciousness (Waugh & Norman, 1965). However, the reevaluation of much of the psychological research on short-term memory that has recently been offered by Craik (1973) includes an essentially Jamesian primary memory, and the general model of organization and retrieval in episodic memory which has been developed in Chapter 4 has as one of its most important components a short-term store that is defined as the active, conscious subset of memory. Thus, modern psychological research has found here a meeting ground with James' intuitions and Chafe's linguistic arguments.

Information that does not enter consciousness from the environment, but rather is retrieved from memory, may or may not be temporally specified. If it is, the tense assignment is made in accordance with the temporal specification, as has been discussed at the beginning of this section. Propositions that are temporally neutral are assigned the present tense in English. Two broad classes of such propositions need to be distinguished, as exemplified by

Two points define a straight line.   (13)

It always snows on the 4th of March.   (14)

Sentence (13) is a timeless statement, while (14) is a proposition that is supposed to be realized at all times, without regard to the time of assertion.

What has been said here about tense assignment surely can not explain all of the linguistic problems involved, but it demonstrates how tense can be approached in a propositional system, and it permits some interesting generalizations. Three cases have been discussed. First, there are text bases that are temporally specified; the resulting sentences will be assigned tenses in accordance with this temporal specification. Such propositions may either be retrieved from memory or may be newly constructed, and depending upon their temporal specification, either the past, present, or future tense may be used. It was claimed that the future tense always requires an explicit temporal specification in the base. Secondly, the tense assignment to propositions that entered short-term memory from the environment was discussed, which includes the present and an immediate past. Finally, temporally neutral propositions retrieved from memory have been considered. In all three cases the "tenses never carry anything but given information, new information regarding temporal orientation being conveyed by adverbs [Chafe, 1974, p. 22]." In Case I, the tense merely duplicates the adverb; in Case III the present is used in a temporally neutral sense [see also (15) below]; in Case II the tense again expresses only what is already given to the speaker and addressee in a communication situation. If some event is taking place now in the communication environment, or has just occurred, this information is given in the speaker's consciousness, and the use of the present or past tense is merely a reflection of this given information. Of course, more than merely temporal information must be considered in order to understand a communication. Tenses are only one example of a much broader phenomenon. Information such as the characteristics of the speaker and listener (e.g., in order to understand the use of performatives), the identity and characteristics of the place of communication, including the objects and events present in the environment (e.g., for the definitivization of noun phrases), and the prior content of the communication itself must all be taken into account. In other words, all kinds of given information are important for the comprehension of a text base. Just as a single proposition remains ambiguous unless it is embedded in a text, so too the text itself cannot stand alone. In order to understand what at first appear to be purely linguistic phenomena (tense, definitivization) the psychological characteristics of the communication act and its environment must be considered.

5.3 Modality and Temporal Reasoning

Inferences about temporal relationships must be possible within a semantic system. Precise temporal information must be available in the subjective lexicon, and the information must be in such a format that it can be readily processed.

The lexicon must contain information about the temporal characteristics of various predicates. At a minimum, a distinction must be made between the following three modals of time: permanent properties, enduring states, and transient characteristics. The sentence *Bronze is an alloy* can be specified lexically as implying

$$(TIME,(ALLOY,BRONZE),ALWAYS) \equiv$$
$$(NECESSARY,(ALLOY,BRONZE)). \tag{15}$$

Fritz is a scoundrel, on the other hand, specifies an enduring characteristic of Fritz, but not a necessary one:

$$(TIME,(SCOUNDREL,FRITZ),MOST\ TIME) \equiv$$
$$(PROBABLE,(SCOUNDREL,FRITZ)). \tag{16}$$

A third class of predicates merely indicate transient states, as in *Fritz is tired*:

$$(TIME,(TIRED,FRITZ),SOMETIME) \equiv$$
$$(POSSIBLE,(TIRED,FRITZ)). \tag{17}$$

Just like properties, processes also have their own temporal characteristics which must be indicated in the lexicon. Rescher and Urquhart (1971) suggest the following distinctions, which in the present notation become

> (PROCESS:HOMOGENEOUS,α) is required by *driving a car*   (18)
> (PROCESS:MAJORITATIVE,α) is required by *reading a book*
> (PROCESS:OCCASIONAL,α) is required by *drinking wine*
> (PROCESS:WHOLISTIC,α) is required by *baking a cake*.

A homogeneous process is performed continuously during some interval of time, while a majoritative process does not take up all of the time, and an occasional process requires only that small fraction of the time during which a person is engaged in it. A wholistic process is one that requires completion and hence a certain minimum time: One does not really bake a cake unless one goes through the whole process, while one can drive a car for any length of time.

It is clear that all these temporal specifications make heavy demands upon the lexicon: A bewildering array of TIME operators seems to be needed. Propositions must be classified as past-present-future, with a forever changing reference point, the *now* of consciousness. At the same time, there are the fixed temporal relations defined by *before* and *after*. How are inferences possible in such a confusing system? It is probably necessary to transform many of the TIME operators used here into more basic expressions. Rescher and Urquhart in their *Temporal Logic* (1971) have shown how tense operators can be derived from the temporal primitive *before*. Some of their ideas can be extended to the present system, thereby making it much more tractable for the operation of inference rules.

We want to express tense operators, say (TIME:PAST,α), in terms of the fixed temporal relationship (BEFORE,X,Y),[10] where X and Y are times, either specified by dates *(March 4, 1972)* or pseudo-dates *(yesterday)*, or unspecified *(some time)*. For the latter, the \$-sign notation will be used to denote an unspecified time case. Thus, (TIME:\$,α) means that the proposition α is realized at some unspecified time. With this notation the three elementary tense operators, present, past, and future, can be defined:

$$(TIME:PRESENT,\alpha) = (TIME:NOW,\alpha) \tag{19}$$

$$(TIME:PAST,\alpha) = (TIME:\$,\alpha)\&(BEFORE,TIME:\$,NOW) \tag{20}$$

$$(TIME:FUTURE,\alpha) = (TIME:\$,\alpha)\&(BEFORE,NOW,TIME:\$) \tag{21}$$

In addition, continuous past and continuous future can be obtained by adding the proposition (ALL,TIME:\$) to (20) and (21), respectively.

More complex tenses can be obtained through a combination of the elementary tense operators. However, before this subject can be further explored, some ques-

---

[10]To simplify notation, prepositions are used here as predicators without indicating the TIME, e.g., (BEFORE,X,Y) instead of (TIME:BEFORE,X,Y) as required by (7).

tions concerning the iteration of tense operators must be clarified. Consider the expression: *It is the case at TIME:$2 that α is the case at TIME:$1*. Rescher and Urquhart claim that such iteration of time operators is vacuous:

$$(TIME:\$2,(TIME:\$1,\alpha)) = (TIME:\$1,\alpha). \tag{22}$$

If, however, one of the times involved is NOW, a shift in the reference point will occur. Rescher and Urquhart have called this the transparency of NOW:

$$(TIME:\$,(TIME:NOW,\alpha)) = (TIME:\$,\alpha). \tag{23}$$

In words, *It is the case at TIME:$ that α is the case NOW* means that α is the case at TIME:$.

With the tense operators (19)–(21) and the definitions (22) and (23), compound operators such as future perfect may be obtained:

$$(TIME:FUTURE,(TIME:PAST,\alpha)) = \tag{24}$$
$$(TIME:FUTURE,((TIME:\$1,\alpha)\&(BEFORE,TIME:\$1,NOW))=$$
$$(TIME:\$2,((TIME:\$1,\alpha)\&(BEFORE,TIME:\$1,NOW))\&$$
$$(BEFORE,NOW,TIME:\$2) =$$
$$(TIME:\$2,(TIME:\$1,\alpha))\&(TIME:\$2,(BEFORE,TIME:\$1,NOW))\&$$
$$(BEFORE,NOW,TIME:\$2) =$$
$$(TIME:\$1,\alpha)\&(BEFORE,TIME:\$1,TIME:\$2)\&(BEFORE,NOW,$$
$$TIME:\$2).$$

The first three lines of (24) simply state the double operator future-past and its definition in terms of elementary temporal predicates; in the fourth line the double brackets are distributed, and in the last line definitions (22) and (23) have been applied to the time iterations. The final expressions say that α is realized at some time before some other unspecified future event takes place, as in *He will have gone*. A similar derivation is possible for the past perfect *He had gone*.

Precise temporal specification of propositions is crucial for the correct functioning of a semantic system. Even when time specifications do not appear in the surface structure, one must assume that they were available in the propositional base, for otherwise certain pathologies of reasoning and linguistic behavior would occur which are not normally observed. Problems arise when propositions are used in reasoning which are true only for certain times rather than permanently, e.g., sentences (16) and (17). Consider the following example:

> *The Chinese invented porcelain.* (25)
> *The Chinese are communists.*
> *Communists invented porcelain.*

The conclusion is wrong because time specifications have been omitted in the premises; therefore the base structure of (25) must contain the information that the time at which porcelain was invented is not included in the period during which the Chinese or anyone else were communists. Inappropriate time specifications may not only block inferences as in (25), but also certain linguistic processes. Fillmore (1971) has analyzed

I hit the ball over the fence. (26)

as two separate events: *I hit the ball* and *The ball went over the fence*. If these two propositions are causally related, they will be conflated and (26) results. However, conflation will be blocked if *hitting the ball* and *going over the fence* have different time specifications: The relation CAUSE requires temporal contiguity.

The last example brings us to a much more general problem, namely, that of the representation of processes in semantic memory. A process is a programmed temporal sequence of repeatable states. Any kind of performance model of language and reasoning must involve the specification of numerous processes, including some very complex ones. Since processes are defined as state sequences they must be characterized through the interstate transitions. Chomsky (1957) has pointed out that such simple process models as finite automata and Markov chains are not sufficiently powerful for language processing and reasoning. His arguments are well-known and generally accepted today. A more satisfactory process representation available for psychological theorizing is Woods' (1970) augmented transition network. An augmented transition network is an extremely powerful mechanism, yet one that is quite simple in principle. In essence, it is a finite transition network with two additions. The network is recursive, that is, it has the capability of calling subroutines at any point in the process. Once the subroutine computation is finished, control is shifted back to where the original process was interrupted. Secondly, in an augmented transition network, arbitrary conditions can be added to the transition arcs, which must be met in order for the arc to be followed. Making the network recursive gives it the power of a context-free grammar; placing conditions on the arcs makes the transitions context dependent. The power of a Turing machine is thereby achieved in a very natural way, well-suited for purposes of psychological modelling.

6. CONCLUSION

At least a few of the problems encountered in the semantic description of language, which at first glance may seem quite intractable for propositional models of semantic memory, have been discussed here. The propositional model was shown to be sufficiently specific and explicit to serve as a basis for language. There are, of course, many questions that have not been explored, but the topics that have been touched upon are significant ones, recurring over and over again in the literature.

The methods used here were not those of linguistics. Linguists try to infer properties of the base structure inductively, on the basis of a careful analysis of sentence materials. The present chapter proceeded, more crudely, in a deductive manner. Some simple, parsimonious assumptions were made about how particular pieces of information can be represented in the base structure, and the adequacy of this representation was then explored by means of linguistic examples. Many relevant problems have not yet been treated, and others only superficially. The two most important gaps in the theory are the absence of a parser (to translate a text into a text base) and a grammar (to derive a text from a base). Obviously, neither of these problems is in any way insignificant or trivial, quite the contrary. But both present immense problems, and no general solution appears to be in sight for either, in spite of the fine work by linguists and computer scientists. In the meantime, psychological research can commence on many interesting problems, without waiting for the solution to these questions. The theory postulates text bases of certain kinds, and one can experimentally investigate their properties, even though the rules that relate text and base are not explicitly available. To borrow an example from Quine (1960), the fact that the phrase *poor violinist* has three rather different meanings is important here only in so far as the three meanings must be unambiguously represented in the text base.

$$(POOR_1,PERSON)\&(PLAY,PERSON,VIOLIN) \qquad (1)$$
$$\text{where } (POOR_1,SOMEONE) =$$
$$(NOT,(HAVE,SOMEONE,MONEY))$$

$$(POOR_2,PERSON)\&(PLAY,PERSON,VIOLIN) \qquad (2)$$
$$\text{where } (POOR_2,SOMEONE) = (FEEL\ SORRY,I,FOR\ SOMEONE)$$

$$(PLAY,PERSON,VIOLIN)\&(BAD,PLAY) \qquad (3)$$

The meanings of *poor violinist* that Quine distinguishes appear in the base structure as (1), (2), or (3). There are no ambiguities about these expressions. On the other hand, how *poor violinist* is to be derived from (1), (2), or (3) is a problem for transformational grammar, which is not considered here. It does not appear to be an insoluble problem, however, in view of much recent work in linguistics. The second problem mentioned above, how to obtain either (1), (2), or (3) from *poor violinist*, appears much more difficult. But it, too, is beyond the scope of the present investigation.

In fact, no parser can obtain either (1), (2), or (3) from *poor violinist* by itself. The phrase in isolation is completely ambiguous. Only by considering it as part of a text can a specific base structure be assigned to it. Context, however, plays a crucial role not only in parsing a sentence, but even in the interpretation of the base structures themselves. Consider another one of Quine's (1960) sentences: *Ernest is hunting a lion*. In the present theory this is a surface form of (HUNT,ERNEST,LION). Neither sentence nor proposition are unambiguous by themselves. Whether Ernest is scrambling through the bush in the hope of finding a lion to shoot at, or whether he is following a certain lion who has just eaten a native, that is, what the precise meaning of HUNT actually is, is determined only by the context. It is neither necessary to distinguish two separate meanings of HUNT, nor to indicate whether LION is particular or not. Ambiguity in an isolated proposition is of no concern, as long as the text base as a whole clearly specifies how each single proposition is to be interpreted.

The propositional base representation was not developed to solve linguistic or philosophical problems, but as a tool for the psychological investigation of language performance and thinking. As such it must be capable of handling the problems discussed, at least to some degree. But the main criterion by which it will be evaluated is its usefulness in psychological research and artificial intelligence projects. However, if a psychological experiment shows, for instance, that reading time for 16-word sentences is a linear function of the number of propositions in the base structure, each adding 1.5 sec to the reading time (Chapter 6), then such a conclusion would be meaningless, unless the psychologist can be assured that a propositional base structure is indeed a suitable representation of the content of a text.

One final remark needs to be made. All of the previous discussion involves a gross oversimplification. Only literal language use has so far been considered. It is no news, however, that much of language must be understood in a nonliteral sense. Propositional bases will have to be extended to account for such use. Beginnings have been made. A process model for the production and comprehension of metaphors was discussed in Chapter 2. Proverbs can probably be handled similarly. The more general case, where pragmatic factors determine the meaning of an utterance, has as yet received less attention. Bolinger (1971) makes the point that *I'm starved* does not really mean *Serve me dinner*, though a hungry husband may use it for that purpose. Perhaps the hungry husband's *I'm starved* derives from a (STARVE,I)&(WANT, I,DINNER) in the base, where the second proposition has been deleted. But what are the rules governing such deletions? Surely, this is more a psychological than a linguistic problem. Wundt (1880) some time ago pointed out that an emphatic *No!* uttered in the presence of a small child approaching a hot stove is actually a surface expression of the proposition (*Gesamtvorstellung,* in his terminology) which under less urgent circumstances might have been expressed as *Don't touch the stove!* Divergencies between the message and the meaning of an utterance are often used intentionally as a means of artistic expression. Words may say one thing, but something else is meant to be understood. For an especially beautiful example, take the end of the first act of the *Rosenkavalier*, where the Marschallin tells with whom she will have lunch and the rest of her petty plans for that day, but in fact she is saying good-bye forever to her young lover, as the music makes abundantly clear. Nevertheless, instances of nonliteral language use, whether trivial or sublime, do not argue against propositional text bases, though they present a challenge. Regardless of what will be needed to deal with message content as distinct from meaning *per se*, some kind of semantic representation will always play an important role in the analysis of verbal behavior. The propositional model discussed here aspires to such a role.

4

A PROCESS MODEL FOR EPISODIC MEMORY: THE ENCODING AND RETRIEVAL OF EXPERIENCES

In this chapter we shall be concerned exclusively with list-learning experiments. Indeed, Chapter 4 is the only chapter in this book that deals with list-learning paradigms. All the experiments reported in Part II are concerned with problems arising from the general theoretical background presented earlier. However, the inclusion of the present chapter in this book is by no means arbitrary. It has not been possible in the previous chapters to advance a well-developed psychological processing theory for the comprehension and memory of meaningful texts. The experiments to be reported in Part II were in part designed to explore some of the features of such a theory, but so far the available results are not informative enough to support a detailed processing model. The situation with regard to list-learning studies is entirely different. There exists enormous amount of experimental evidence concerning various aspects of theoretically interesting problems, enough to make the formulation of a general theory feasible. I am convinced that such a theory would have consequences for psychological models of text processing: The tasks are different, but the organism is the same, and it is not too much to hope that some of the same cognitive processes that can be identified in laboratory experiments with word lists will reappear in experiments concerned with the processing of meaningful text and with the use of knowledge. Cases where this indeed happens will be pointed out in Part II, but first of all it is necessary to concern ourselves with the nature of these cognitive processes that characterize memory storage and retrieval in list-learning experiments.

Although there is now a considerable accumulation of facts in this area, the clarification of theoretical issues has lagged behind data collection. Knowledge about memory comes today in bits and pieces rather than integrated in some system. It is the purpose of the present work to help systematize this knowledge. A workable theory of long-term memory will be proposed which incorporates a wide range of significant empirical results, all of them, in one way or other, having to do with organization and retrieval in memory. In doing so no effort will be made to define the terms retrieval and organization in any precise way, because it appears hopeless to legislate exact meanings for terms that have been used loosely for such a long time. Instead, what is needed is a precise theory that accounts for the phenomena usually referred to under these labels. Thus, a framework will be outlined within which specific and sometimes formal models can be developed for the treatment of organizational and retrieval phenomena in memory. The emphasis will be on the presentation of the general theory on a conceptual level, rather than the formalization of the theory or the elaboration of submodels.

1. CRITICAL ISSUES

In contrast to short-term memory, there are only a few reasonably formal and specific models of organization and long-term memory processes. Most of these belong to the class of generation-recognition models, though there are exceptions, such as the memory search model of Shiffrin (1970).[1] Important generation-recognition theories are those of Anderson (1972), Anderson and Bower (1972), Bahrick (1970), James (1890), Kintsch (1970a), and Müller (1913). Though these models are by no means identical, they share some significant commonalities. All of them conceive of recall as a two-stage process: an implicit retrieval of the to-be-recalled item followed by a recognition check. Retrieval is seen as a process that operates on a structure, the semantic memory network. Suppose a subject in a free-recall experiment is faced with the task of memorizing a list of words. It is assumed that as the words are presented the subject traces out a path from one word to the next through his memory net, leaving tags as he moves along that will enable him to retrace this path upon retrieval, thus implicitly locating list members along this path. A recognition check can then be used to determine whether a particular item that was retrieved was actually a member of the word list that he was to remember, or whether it was merely a mediating link in the path.

It is one of the most salient facts about memory that organized material is easier to remember than unorganized material, and that subjects actively strive to detect how to-be-learned material is organized, and impose their own subjective organization if none other can be found. The ability of the models of Anderson and Bower (1972) and Kintsch (1970a) to account for these phenomena, at least in part, is an important and nontrivial achievement that must be maintained by any new model in this area. The theory proposed here incorporates a notion of retrieval quite similar to the one just outlined, but it differs from previous models in attempting to incorporate several important insights and research findings that pose problems for the earlier models. Some of these critical issues are discussed below.

---

[1]Search models constitute an alternative approach to the one taken here, and their respective advantages and difficulties will not be discussed.

1.1 Recall and Recognition

The experimental evidence upon which generation-recognition models are based is primarily of two kinds. First, there are Bahrick's demonstrations that the effects of extralist cuing can be adequately accounted for by such a theory (Bahrick, 1969, 1970). Bahrick's subjects partially learned a paired-associate list and were then given a prompted recall test. Extralist prompts were used, and the likelihood that they would produce the target word was known from previous work. The likelihood that each target word would be recognized as correct was also determined independently. Cued recall performance could be predicted quite well on the basis of these two statistics. The probability of recall of the target word in response to the extralist cue was approximately equal to the probability of the generation of that word in response to the cue multiplied by the probability of correct recognition.

The second kind of evidence for the two-stage theory of recall comes from studies that show that even with identical learning conditions recognition and recall tests may yield quite different results. The important observation is not that recognition is usually better than recall, but that some experimental variables, which are very effective if memory is assessed with a recall test, have little or no effect upon recognition. There is, by now, a large literature concerned with this problem. Fortunately, up-to-date reviews are available (Kintsch, 1970a; McCormack, 1972) so that a brief summary of the main results will suffice here. Though many experimental variables affect recognition and recall in the same way, an important class of experimental variables, which apparently all have to do with organization, has large and consistent effects on recall but either no, or only small, effects upon recognition. Characteristic experimental prototypes are, on the one hand, studies that use highly structured learning materials (e.g., words from different conceptual classes), and studies in which the subjects' organizing activity during learning is manipulated (through various kinds of incidental and intentional learning instructions, for instance). If the subject organizes, either because the material is well-structured or because of other experimental manipulations, recall is strongly facilitated, though not recognition, which frequently is totally unaffected by organization, or at best shows small effects that are peculiar to particular experimental conditions. The evidence for this generalization is discussed in the two reviews mentioned. In addition, several recent reports have made important additions to the list of differences between recall and recognition. Thomson (1972) noted how context effects differ between recognition and recall if a new context is introduced at the time of testing. Recognition is impaired in that case, but recall is facilitated if the contextual cue is related to the to-be-remembered item. Hogan and Kintsch (1971) reported some striking differential effects of test trials on long-term recall and recognition. Test trials during training, which encourage organization and retrieval, facilitated recall, while study trials, which ensure greater item exposure, yielded better recognition. Finally, there are a number of studies where a directed forgetting paradigm was used (reviewed by Bjork, 1972) in which no differences were observed in the subject's ability to recognize items that were to be forgotten and items that were to be rehearsed, while at the same time recall of the to-be-forgotten items was gravely impaired.

These experimental differences are real and can not be questioned. The problem, of course, is how to account for them. The traditional view has been that recognition and recall involve essentially the same processes, but that one is simply more of it than the other: Recall requires a greater response strength than recognition, because the recall threshold is higher. How a threshold theory could account for the data referred to above is completely unclear, and it is doubtful that it can be done without a bevy of *ad hoc* assumptions. The retrieval theory (e.g., Tulving & Thomson, 1971, who maintain that there is nothing "inherently different about processes of recall and recognition") is just as unsatisfactory in this respect. First of all, their use of the concepts of retrieval and retrieval cue is entirely too vague; secondly, no systematic attempt has ever been made to show how such a theory could account for the differences that have been observed between recall and recognition.

Alternatively, instead of claiming recognition and recall to be essentially identical, two different processes can be postulated, with recall being sensitive to organizational variables and recognition not. In that case the occasional small effects of organization on recognition must be explained. Such effects are easy to understand if one remembers that what is assumed to be distinct are the psychological processes of recall and recognition. This does not imply that a subject in a recognition experiment can not use recall strategies. If experimental conditions are right, a subject's recognition process may lead to an answer about which he is ambiguous (or the task may be excessively difficult); under these conditions he may try to determine whether a given test item can also be recalled, in order to increase his certainty about it. In fact, Mandler (1972) has described several instances where such recall checks were used by subjects in recognition tasks. To the extent that recall checks are employed in recognition experiments, organizational variables should be effective in recognition. There is no way to prove that this was, indeed, the mechanism responsible for the occasional organizational effects that have been reported, but given their sporadic nature and relatively small magnitude, this explanation is plausible.

The two-stage theory is an attempt to specify the manner in which recognition and recall differ. The basic idea is that successful recognition is possible, given only a relatively raw record of experience. Recall, other than from short-term memory, requires a more elaborate memory trace which must be integrated into some kind of network. On the basis of that network a target item is retrieved implicitly and recalled overtly if it passes a recognition check. In terms of retrieval cues, the item itself is its own retrieval cue on a recognition test. On the other hand, for recall to take place some other, specific retrieval cue is required to provide access to the target item. A recognition check then assures that the target item, but not extralist retrieval cues, will be recalled. In this sense recognition and recall must be regarded as essentially different processes, recognition involving only the target item and its memory representation, while recall requires that the memory representation of a to-be-recalled item be connected with other items that may serve as retrieval cues for it. Although recognition is based only upon a comparison of the target item and its memory representation, the context of the other items on the list may still be a powerful determinant of recognition performance. How an item will be encoded, and therefore whether it will match or fail to match a previously encoded target stimulus, is largely determined by context. Previous generation-recognition theories have failed to take account of context effects in recognition, with the exception of Anderson and Bower (1972) who used list tags to mark items as old, thereby incorporating context effects into their theory. Mere familiarity tags that are not context specific, on the other hand, are not sufficient to account for context effects in recognition. In the past few years a considerable amount of research has been devoted to the exploration of such effects, and it is now clear that except, perhaps, when an input list consists of single, unrelated words, context effects in recognition memory seem to be ubiquitous. Briefly, if the context is changed between the presentation of an item and its test, recognition will be impaired. Several investigators have studied this phenomenon, but the Thomson (1972) dissertation may be considered representative. In the theory to be developed below, context effects will be handled by means of the encoding variability hypothesis in the manner of Thomson.

1.2 Encoding Specificity and the Distinction Between Episodic and Semantic Memory

Some serious deficiencies in contemporary generation-recognition models have been pointed out by Tulving and Thomson (1973). Tulving and Thomson have shown that under certain conditions subjects can not recognize an item, though they are able to recall it, in decided contradiction to generation-recognition models. Schematically, their experiment is as follows. Subjects were first shown a word pair like *ground* COLD. They were told to remember the capitalized word, but also to look at the accompanying cue since it might help them. Later, subjects were asked to free associate to stimulus words like *hot*. Quite frequently the to-be-remembered word COLD was given as an associate to *hot*. Then subjects were asked to circle among the associates that they had just produced all words that were to-be-remembered items from the earlier list. Recognition performance was extremely poor: Only 24% of the words were recognized! To make their demonstration even more impressive, Tulving and Thomson gave their subjects a final cued recall test: When given *ground* as a cue, subjects' recall of COLD was up to 63%! Thus, given its proper retrieval cue, subjects could recall COLD quite well, while just moments before they were able to recognize COLD only very poorly in a different context.

On the basis of these data and earlier results by Tulving and Osler (1968) and Thomson and Tulving (1970), Tulving has formulated the encoding specificity principle. The principle states "that a retrieval cue can provide access to information available about an event in the memory store if and only if it has been stored as part of the specific memory trace of the event [Tulving & Thomson, 1973, p. 16]." Thus, given the retrieval cue *ground* in the experiment described above, subjects could recall COLD very well, but they could not recognize the COLD produced in the free association phase of the experiment as a to-be-recalled word because that COLD did not contain any information about list membership.

The principle of encoding specificity will be incorporated as a basic assumption in the model presented below. The model will thus be a generation-recognition theory

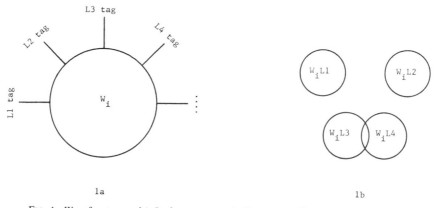

FIG. 1. W_i refers to word i; L_i denotes a certain list context. For explanation see text.

based upon the encoding specificity principle. Tulving and Thomson (1973) have argued that their data contradict generation-recognition models, but they are right only in so far as they criticize previous generation-recognition models. As will be shown, the issues of encoding specificity and generation-recognition are quite independent in principle, though historically generation-recognition models have included assumptions that brought them into conflict with the encoding specificity principle.

The trouble with present generation-recognition models is that they are tagging models. Figure 1a illustrates the problem. Once the word node i has been accessed,[2] all the information stored there is available. It is merely a matter of checking all the tags. The encoding specificity principle implies a quite different situation, as is shown in Fig. 1b. Word i is stored in memory not just in one central place with tags, but as several separate copies. Thus, there is a code for word i in the context of List 1, List 2, etc. Some of these memory codes may be interrelated (as L3 and L4 are in the present example), but others are not. What this means is that access to the memory code W_iL1 does not in itself make available the information that the same word i has also been experienced in contexts $L2$, 3, and 4.

Figure 1b is incomplete in that it is only concerned with the memory for a particular word i in certain experimental contexts. This is what Tulving (1972) has called episodic memory. However, if the recent work on organizational factors in memory has made anything clear at all, it is that one can not understand memory in terms of isolated episodes apart from the total memory structure. A person's memory structure, his knowledge of the meaning and use of a word, determine whether and how a memory episode will be encoded. Material that is well-organized, that is, whose structure corresponds to some previously acquired structure in the learner's memory, is easier to remember than unorganized material. This general store of knowledge is a

[2]What constitutes a word has often been misunderstood, but at least some of the models have clearly specified that the criterion for a word is a meaning unit, so that homographs must be regarded as separate words.

person's semantic memory. A crucial problem for any model of memory is therefore the nature of the interaction between semantic and episodic memory. On the one hand, there is the problem of how general knowledge (semantic memory) develops on the basis of particular experiences (episodic memory), though this question need not concern us here. Instead, we propose to investigate how the formation of episodic memory codes depends upon the nature of semantic memory. It should be noted that this is a very old question. It played a large role in educational theory and practice at one time, when one of the main problems of pedagogy was how the apperceptive mass influences (and makes possible) new learning (Herbart, 1816). The generation-recognition models discussed above are also addressed to that question. As the modern counterpart of the apperceptive mass, Anderson and Bower (1972) embedded their word nodes into an associative network, and Kintsch (1970a, 1972a) has postulated a propositional structure for semantic memory. In both cases, access to particular word nodes could be obtained via the network of interrelations among words in semantic memory. Once access was gained, episodic memory tags could be checked off. However, this solution appears to be inadequate because it involves the tagging notion schematized in Fig. 1a. Instead, a solution along the lines of Fig. 1b, which does not violate the encoding specificity principle, must be attempted.

1.3 List-Learning Data and Models of Memory

The only solid body of experimental evidence that students of memory have available today comes from list-learning experiments. The experimental study of memory for prose, comprehension, inferential processes, and semantic memory is just beginning. Thus, memory theorists have shown an unfortunate tendency to rely solely upon list-learning data, to neglect other problems, and finally to construct not models of memory, but models of memory for word lists.

As long as one is concerned only with memory for separate words, tagging models are very simple, but beyond this tagging models lose much of their appeal. One may assume a lexical structure, or an associative network, if you will, which can be used for tagging purposes. But when words are strung together in sentences it becomes inconceivable to suggest a preexisting network with sentences as the nodes to be tagged. Most sentences that one encounters have never been experienced before in quite the same way. Identical problems must be faced when nonverbal memory is considered — memory for sensations, perceptions, for simple as well as complex experiences of all kinds. Too little is known today about that kind of memory, but a model should be able to account in principle for more than word lists, though list-learning experiments will undoubtedly remain the proving ground for memory models for a while to come.

One can extend tagging models so that, for instance, the internal representation of a sentence is first constructed before it is tagged with a list marker. However, once the necessity of constructing structures *de novo* is admitted, the notion of tagging appears superfluous. Each construction occurs in a certain context and is context specific. Thus, these context specific aspects of a memory code play the same role as a list tag.

1.4 Towards a Theory of Episodic Memory

The alternative to tagging models is a conceptualization of learning as the formation and storage of new traces, rather than the tagging of preexisting structures. Such models, however, must be constructed in a way that preserves the main achievement of tagging models, the ability to account for organizational effects. In the proposed theory this will be done by choosing a format for information storage — sets of complex elements — upon which an operation of pattern completion can naturally be defined, which permits an interaction between semantic structures and the encoding of to-be-memorized materials. Thus, the facilitating effects of organization can be accounted for without restricting the theory to list-learning data and without violating the encoding specificity principle. The episodic network, though a partial copy of semantic memory, is operationally distinct from it. Episodic memory will be made context specific by letting the construction of episodic memory codes be subject to an encoding bias. Context, as represented by the contents of short-term memory, guides the selection of information to be included in a memory code. At the same time the proposed theory will be a generation-recognition theory, which provides a satisfactory way of accounting for the empirically observed recognition-recall differences. Two conceptually, though not empirically, distinct mechanisms will be described. Recognition will be based upon an item by item encoding of the learning material, while recall will require, in addition, the formation of explicit interitem connections.

The theoretical mechanisms that are needed to achieve these goals are relatively simple, though a certain flexibility in their use must be permitted, given the undeniable complexity of human memory processes. The basic assumption to be made will be that memory codes can be represented as sets of complex elements. For instance, semantic information is represented in human memory through (partially ordered) sets of propositions. Propositions, however, are complex elements, because they in turn can be broken down into predicators and arguments. Other elements of memory codes, which may also possess some internal structure of their own, though this structure will remain unspecified, are phonemic elements, imagery elements, and other sensory elements. Related notions have been used previously, especially the multicomponent and stimulus-sampling theories of Bower (1967, 1972), and the vectors of features in Norman and Rumelhart's model for short-term memory (1970), as well as Kintsch (1970a, 1972a). The different types of elements that may comprise a memory code have been listed more systematically by Underwood (1969), who used the term attributes of memory.

A distinction will be made between semantic memory and episodic memory, as illustrated in Fig. 2. The subset of semantic memory that is of greatest interest here is lexical memory. It is assumed that each word i is represented in lexical memory by a semantic memory code, S_i, composed of phonemic, graphemic, syntactic, semantic, imaginal, and other sensory elements. In addition, the lexical representation may also contain a certain number of personal experiences connected with that word.[3] Thus, a person's lexical entry for BEAR may contain some memory episodes, such as "the

---

[3]Note that this conception of semantic memory is somewhat different from that of Tulving (1972).

night the bear visited our tent'' or ''how I met my first dancing bear when I was still a little child.'' However, there may be many other memory episodes involving BEAR which are not part of the lexical entry BEAR, as shown in Fig. 2, and which therefore can not be automatically accessed from it. In Fig. 2 the convention of designating semantic memory codes by S and episodes by M is introduced. Thus we have

$$S_i = S_{ph} \cup S_{gr} \cup S_{syn} \cup S_{sem} \cup S_{im} \cup S_{sens} \cup M_1 \cup M_2 \cup \ldots \cup M_k.$$

$S = \{S_i\}$ is semantic memory (more precisely, the subjective lexicon, or lexical memory, which is a subset of semantic memory), and $M = \{M_i\}$ is episodic memory.

Once the format of information storage has been indicated, the operations permissible in this system can be specified. They are of two kinds: operations of pattern matching and selection operations. The fundamental operation is pattern matching, or more precisely, pattern completion. In this respect the theory follows closely the classic work of Selz (1922), who pointed out the significance of pattern completion (Komplexergänzung) for the actualization of knowledge as well as memory episodes. Some set of elements X may be matched with another set Y if most of the elements of X are also members of Y. Pattern completion makes available the union of the two sets, $X \cup Y$. Biased selection of elements from this completed set may then occur, or the members of this set may be used for further matching operations.

The foregoing remarks were intended to clarify what problems the present model proposes to deal with and to indicate how this will be done. The next section of this chapter contains a detailed presentation of the theoretical framework. This will be

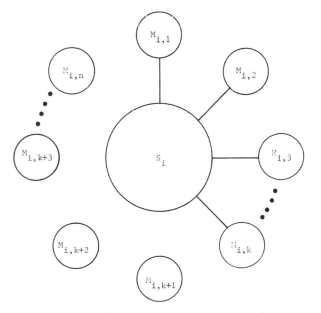

FIG. 2. Schematic representation of the relation between memory codes for the word i. S_i is the lexical entry, $M_1 - M_n$ are episodic codes; only the first k episodes are connected with S_i.

followed by a discussion of some important problems in contemporary memory research in the context of the proposed theory.

2. A GENERAL THEORY OF STORAGE, ORGANIZATION, AND RETRIEVAL IN EPISODIC MEMORY

2.1. Assumptions

The following boundary conditions will be assumed for the theory: In order to facilitate the exposition, the problem shall be the retention of spoken words. Extensions to other presentation modalities are obvious; possible extensions to sentence and paragraph memory will be indicated later. It is also assumed that the subject knows how to parse appropriately his stream of experiences during the experiment. The subject is told that the experiment is concerned with memory for a list of separate words, and it is assumed that he parses environmental events according to instructions so that the experiment can be represented by the following temporal sequence of events: $E_1 - E_2 - E_3 - \ldots - E_i - \ldots$, where E_i is a set of elements, the perceptual representation of the *ith* stimulus word. How the subject arrives at this parsing is one of the great neglected problems of psychology and is beyond the scope of this discussion (but see Becker, 1973, for a possible approach).

The principal assumptions of the model are three: (1) Information is stored as sets of phonemic, semantic, and imagery elements; (2) the basic operation is one of pattern completion; and (3) the contents of short-term memory bias encoding processes both in perception and memory.

2.1.1. The format of information storage. Perceptual as well as memory traces will be represented as sets of complex elements, in particular phonemic, semantic, imaginal, as well as other sensory elements. Although the terms phonemic, semantic, and imagery specify important types of elements, such a list is obviously not exhaustive. At this time, not much can be said about the nature of these elements, nor is it necessary to do so for present purposes. It is assumed that these elements, which are the elements of the sets that constitute the memory representations in the present theory, are themselves complex, that is, that they have some internal structure. This assumption is made because the only type of elements—the semantic elements—that have, as yet, been studied in detail, have a complex internal structure. Semantic elements are propositions, and the propositional nature of semantic elements will be of great significance in the discussion that follows. Note also that the propositions that form the definition of a lexical entry are weakly structured, i.e., they are partially ordered sets. An analogous study of the nature of phonemic elements would be possible today, since there exists a rich literature in this area, but is beyond the scope of this work. In the case of imagery elements, on the other hand, present knowledge is so poor that not even educated guesses would be feasible as to their nature (but see Pylyshyn, 1973). Thus, for present purposes, semantic elements will be interpreted as propositions in the sense of Chapter 2, while nothing will be said about imagery and phonemic elements, except that they are assumed to have some internal structure analogous to semantic elements.

The set of all S_i's constitutes the subjective lexicon, a subset of semantic memory, and the set of all M_i's is a subset of episodic memory: $S \supset \{S_i\}$, and $M \supset \{M_i\}$. The set representation just described will be used in three ways: for perceptual events, E; semantic memory traces, S; and for episodic memory traces, M.

The formation of a memory code is outlined schematically in Fig. 3. The perceptual parser is of interest in the present context only in so far as its output is concerned. Environmental stimuli, by instructions primarily the sound of the spoken words, but also other contextual stimuli from various sensory modalities, as well as interoceptive stimuli, are processed perceptually and result in a set of elements E_i, which will be called the perceptual representation of the ith word, and which is the input to the memory system. E_i, by assumption, consists largely of a set of phonemic elements $E_{i,ph}$ plus some contextual elements $E_{i,cx}$.[4] If $N(X)$ is a function that assigns to a set X the number of its elements, we have therefore $N(E_{i,ph}) > N(E_{i,cx})$.

In addition to the perceptual representations of the to-be-learned words, there is another perceptual event that is of interest here. The subject in a psychological experiment perceives (and remembers) not only the to-be-remembered words, but also the laboratory context as such, including the experimental instructions. Let E_{CTXT} be the representation of the experimental context. Note also that $E_{cx} \subset E_{CTXT}$.

The semantic memory representation for the ith word, S_i, is composed of subsets of elements, $S_i = S_{ph} \cup S_{sem} \cup S_{im} \cup \ldots \cup M_{i,j} \cup M_{i,k} \cup \ldots$. The set S_{ph} is the result of many experiences with previous episodes involving the ith word and includes everything there is to know about this particular speech sound. How S_{ph} is developed is unknown, but it is assumed here that S_{ph} is approximately equal to the union of previous experiences, such that $E_{ph} \subset S_{ph}$.[5]

The memory code M_i is formed by taking a nonrandom sample from $S_i \cup E_i$, as explained below. Thus, $M_i \subset S_i \cup E_{cx}$. It is assumed that $N(M_i) < N(E_i) < N(S_i)$.

2.1.2. *Pattern completion.* Storage, organization, and retrieval processes in memory all involve the operation of pattern completion. It is assumed that when a subject understands a spoken word, he matches the set of phonemic elements E_{ph} with the phonemic representation of that word in semantic memory S_{ph} on the basis of common elements, thereby retrieving the whole set of cues S_i. The likelihood of successfully completing a set in this way depends upon how many elements of the input stimulus can be matched up with elements of the memory representation, but not on the total number of elements in the memory representation. Furthermore, given an input set Y, the problem is not to match this to some set X, but to find the best matching set X in some set $\mathcal{X}$. A maximum selector is needed to pick out the best possible match of Y and the elements of $\mathcal{X}$. Thus, the following pattern completion rule is assumed here

$$\Pr(match\ Y\ to\ \mathcal{X}) = \max \frac{N(X_j \wedge Y)}{N(Y)}, \quad X_j \epsilon \mathcal{X}. \tag{1}$$

[4]In order to improve readability, the subscript i will be dropped wherever this can be done without causing confusion.

[5]Note that we can always construct E_{ph} such that $E_{ph} \subset S_{ph}$ is true by assigning ideosyncratic phonemic cues that are not members of S_{ph} to the context set E_{cx}.

Note that Eq. (1) does not imply that if Y is a Chinese word it will be matched to the best possible X in the lexicon of some person who does not speak Chinese: A best fit will be picked out, but the actual probability of a match would still be very small. The fact that once in a while a Chinese word may be mistaken for some English word is also in agreement with Eq. (1). Equation (1) is merely the simplest possible version of a pattern matching rule on the basis of common elements. Various refinements are possible (some are mentioned in Section 4), but in a general presentation their consideration would only distract from the conceptually important issues.

2.1.3. Encoding biases. All encoding operations are subject to short-term memory biases in the present model, as shown in Fig. 3. Perceptual encoding biases are used to avoid problems due to lexical ambiguity. Given a homonym, such as *bank*, which would match two or more lexical representations equally well, the contents of short-term memory decide which lexical entry is to be selected. If, for instance, *money* (the *a* in Fig. 3) is held in short-term memory, a different lexical entry will be selected for *bank* (namely, the one containing the element MONEY) than if *river* were in short-term memory. Secondly, memory encoding biases ensure that elements that are already present in short-term memory will be included in the memory code. More specifically, if an item E_i is presented, a memory code M_i is formed by selection from the complete set $E_i \cup S_i$. This selection is not random: Elements of $E_i \cup S_i$ that are at the same time also represented in short-term memory are assumed to be activated, or especially available, and such elements are always sampled preferentially.

What is implied here is easier to understand by an example, rather than a general discussion. Suppose the input is the word *fox*, and suppose that among the items in short-term memory is the code for the word *bear*, containing among its elements the proposition *bear is an animal*, which may be written as (ANIMAL,BEAR). Also assume thet (ANIMAL,FOX) is part of the semantic notion of fox. Since (ANIMAL,FOX) shares an argument with a proposition already in short-term memory, namely (ANIMAL,BEAR), it is selected for inclusion in M_{fox}.

Contextual elements are favored by this selection process, since they are likely to be already represented in short-term memory. If all contextual elements are included in M_i (as presumably would happen if context is constant), $N(M_i) = \theta N(S_i) + N(E_{cx})$. Since $N(M_i)$ is small relative to $N(S_i)$ the fraction θ of semantic memory elements included in the episodic code must, in general, also be small. Its actual size would, of course, depend upon such factors as task demands, study time, number of repetitions, and available processing capacity.

2.2. The Initial Encoding of Events in Episodic Memory

A stimulus word gives rise to the perceptual representation E_i. The match of E_i to S_i will be successful because, by assumption, the majority of elements in E_i are the phonemic elements E_{ph}, which can be matched up with members of S_i. Only the E_{cx} elements cannot be matched up, but since $N(E_{cx}) < N(E_{ph})$, the probability of a successful match is high and could, in actual modeling work, be further increased to a desired value through the choice of an appropriate threshold function. Thus, the

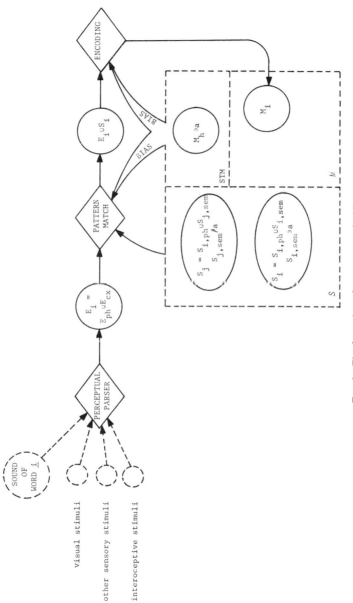

FIG. 3. The formation of a memory code M_i.

perceptual event E_i is identified, and through pattern completion the set $S_i \cup E_i$ now becomes available. M_i is constructed from this set in the manner already discussed.

Once a memory code is formed it becomes a member of episodic memory. More specifically, it becomes a member of a special subset of episodic memory, called short-term memory. The short-term store assumed here corresponds to James' (1890) notion of primary memory. It comprises a set of items that have just been processed and are still held in consciousness. Such items are privileged in the sense that they are readily available. Recognition and recall is perfect for them, and recoding is possible without requiring another rematch with the corresponding semantic memory representation. In other words, the theory assumes that memory codes held in short-term memory have a special active status, but that at the same time they are still flexible and easily changed. Thus, a change in context may cause items in short-term memory to be recoded. As long as items are held in short-term memory they are still being processed: Their make-up influences the comprehension of new input words as well as their encoding; at the same time the new inputs may change the composition of the short-term memory items themselves. Items are lost from short-term memory by distracting attention away from them, which in the kind of experiments discussed here normally means that new input items displace items held in short-term memory. When items leave short-term memory they lose their specially privileged, active status but are still members of the nonconscious portion of episodic memory. They are no longer immediately accessible, and how and whether they will be retrieved depends upon testing conditions. Three important cases will be discussed below: recognition, free recall, and cued recall.

Episodic memory at the end of a study period contains the memory codes $M_1, M_2, M_3, \ldots$, one for each word presented (assuming equal division of attention), plus a code M_{CTXT}, which is a representation of the experimental context but not, except as noted in Section 2.3, of specific words. Given an encoding process as just described, some quite specific predictions can be derived for performance in recognition and recall experiments. In a recognition experiment the subject is presented with a nominally identical copy of a previously presented stimulus, or with a distractor item, and asked whether the test stimulus was a member of the study list. The original stimulus is E_i in the present notation, and the subject's memory code for it is M_i; the test stimulus is either E_i^*, that is, a repetition of the original word, or a distractor item E_d^*. How does the subject recognize E_i^* as "old" and E_d^* as "new"?

A framework for a performance model is outlined in Fig. 4. E_i^* is identified, that is, matched with its corresponding lexical representation S_i. From the product of this match a new memory code M_i^* is formed, and M_i^* is compared with all episodes in $\mathcal{M}$. If a match is successful, the subject responds "old"; if not, "new." The likelihood of a successful match will depend strongly upon context effects. If M_i and M_i^* are formed under identical circumstances, they will share the same set of contextual cues E_{cx}, as well as most of the cues selected from S_i. Encoding biases ensure that the same elements of S_i will be selected in the two cases as long as context and hence the contents of short-term memory remain the same. As context changes, recognition of M_i* deteriorates because both the contextual cues themselves as well as the selections made from S_i will differ for M_i and M_i*.

Given a distractor item E_d* recognition will again depend upon context, and in addition upon the similarity of E_i and E_d*. If context is constant M_i and M_d* share the common set of contextual elements E_{cx} and hence a discrimination problem exists. However, a suitably chosen threshold function would still permit good performance. To the extent that the distractor item is similar to the learning item, i.e., S_d and S_i share common elements, recognition performance becomes more difficult, since these common elements increase the probability of a false recognition response according to Eq. (1).

The recognition procedures outlined above are stronger than logically required. Subjects do not really have to identify a test stimulus with some particular memory representation; they only have to say whether the test stimulus is "old" or "new." In matching the test pattern M_i* to the memory episodes in $\mathcal{M}$, intersections of the form $M_j \wedge M_i*$ must be formed. It would be sufficient to calculate the magnitude of these intersections, and for subjects to respond "old" if any exceeds some threshold value c. The value of c could be adjusted to the demands of the experimental situation (a priori probabilities, pay-offs, instructions), as has been observed in many recognition experiments. In Section 3 it will be argued that subjects employ both recognition procedures, depending upon task demands.

Now consider what happens when the subject is given a free-recall test. The stimulus situation is represented by the context only, E_{CTXT}. Again, just as a word is identified by the subject, there must be some semantic representation S_{CTXT} (say, of "laboratory rooms") that can be used to identify $E*_{CTXT}$ (subjects know where they are). After this process of pattern completion a code $M*_{CTXT}$ is constructed, subject to the usual biases, and matched with $\mathcal{M}$. Most likely, the best match is obtained for M_{CTXT}, the memory representation of the experimental context at the time of study.

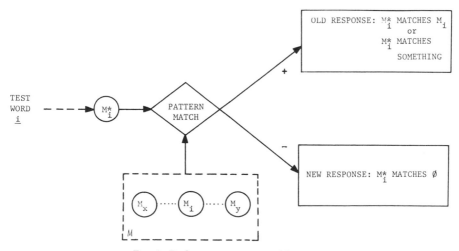

FIG. 4. Performance on a recognition test.

Thus, the subject can respond, "Yes, I have been here before," but he has no access to the to-be-recalled words. The only words that can be recalled are those still available in short-term memory. Organizational processes, as described in the next section, are a prerequisite for recall.

The prediction that after the initial recording of events in episodic memory, recall, except from the short-term store, is impossible should not be held against the theory. The initial recording process is merely an idealization probably never realized in real experimental situations. The experimenter can suppress the organizing activity of subjects during learning, but he can not entirely prevent it, and to the extent that subjects build interitem relations into the memory codes that they form, recall will succeed. The important point is that recognition can operate with no more than has been described up to now, while recall can not, even if the zero-organization case assumed here can only be approximated in experimental work.

2.3 The Formation of Interrelationships Among Episodes and Recall

2.3.1. Encoding. Organizing activity according to the present model consists in the formation of explicit interepisode relationships. How some interitem dependencies are introduced through the short-term memory biasing of the encoding process has already been discussed. In this section, organizational processes will be described that ensure that memory codes contain explicit references to other episodes. During recall, these references serve as retrieval cues: Given one episode, they provide access to others, and a recognition check then assures the list membership of the accessed item.

Instead of a general treatment, four illustrative cases will be discussed. These are not meant to be exhaustive, but representative of the principles involved. The same principles are applied in each case. The theory itself is completely general and it is broken down here into four examples only because such a presentation is easier to follow than an abstract general one. It should also be noted that the encoding strategies described here (and others not mentioned) may be used in various combinations in list learning.

Case I: Class membership. Suppose short-term memory contains the code M_{bear} with the element (ANIMAL,BEAR), and the input E_{fox} is presented. It has already been shown how the proposition (ANIMAL,FOX) will be selected for inclusion in the memory code M_{fox} on the basis of a common argument. Now a more elaborate coding scheme is proposed. Instead of merely including (ANIMAL,FOX) among the elements of M_{fox}, (ANIMAL,BEAR) and (ANIMAL,FOX) will be combined into (AND,(ANIMAL,BEAR),(ANIMAL,FOX)), and this compound proposition will be stored as a member of both M_{fox} and M_{bear}. More precisely, references will be made to episodes, rather than to lexical items. Usually in a proposition such as (ANIMAL,FOX) both ANIMAL and FOX are references to items in semantic memory (addresses in computer terminology), so that the proposition really could be written as (S_{animal}, S_{fox}). If, on the other hand, interitem relationships are to be formed in episodic memory, reference must be made not to semantic memory representations such as S_{fox} and S_{bear}, but to the episodes M_{fox} and M_{bear} themselves. Thus, what gets stored in episodic memory are propositions with arguments that refer to specific list items, not to lexical entries. In the present example one would have entries like (S_{animal}, M_{fox}) — assuming that *fox*, but not *animal* is among the to-be-remembered items.

Case II: Other semantic relationships among words. Suppose M_{hunter} is in short-term memory and the input stimulus is E_{fox}. The task is to relate the two words. Both E_{fox} and M_{hunter} can be identified so that the complete patterns $E_{fox} \cup S_{fox}$ and $M_{hunter} \cup S_{hunter}$ are available. If these sets include a proposition that explicitly relates *hunter* and *fox*, perhaps (SHOOT,HUNTER,FOX), this proposition will be included in both M_{fox} and M_{hunter} in the form $(S_{shoot}, M_{hunter}, M_{fox})$. If a suitable proposition can not be found, an attempt is made to infer one on the basis of the available propositions. In the present example such an inference must surely be possible. Kintsch (1972a) has discussed some operations for the evaluation of propositions such as (SHOOT,HUNTER,FOX) as true or false. But how one would generate that proposition from the lexical entries for *hunter* and *fox* is yet another problem. For present purposes this is, however, a side issue that can be neglected. All that needs to be assumed here is that such an inference is indeed possible.

Case III: The method of places. The precondition for this well-known mnemonic device is that a subject has as a part of his general knowledge a fixed scheme of locations, something like

$$S_{loc} = \{(\text{IS AT},\$,\text{LOC}_A) \to (\text{IS AT},\$,\text{LOC}_B) \to$$
$$(\text{IS AT},\$,\text{LOC}_C) \to \ldots\ldots\},$$

where the arrow is merely a notational convenience to be interpreted as "followed by," and the $-sign denotes a free variable. Learning consists in replacing the variable sign $ in each proposition by some episode that is to be remembered. Thus, at the end of learning we have

$$M_{loc/cx} = \{(\text{IS AT},M_1,\text{LOC}_A) \to (\text{IS AT},M_2,\text{LOC}_B) \to \ldots\ldots\},$$

which is now an episode, specific to some particular context cx. Since it contains all the M's in fixed order, it can serve as their retrieval cue. Note also that S_{loc} is reusable: A different set of episodes can be stored in this scheme in some other context, cx', without interference from $M_{loc/cx}$, because what is reused is a semantic memory structure, not an episode.

Again, as in Case II, an important problem has been glossed over: How is the $-sign replaced by M_1? Imagery is involved, obviously, and some of the conditions necessary for successful use of this method—properties of both the location scheme and the code for the episode to be stored there—have been explored. But until much more is known about the general format of storage of images and the permissible operations with image codes, no answer can be given to this question.

Case IV: Rote learning. In the first three cases, some preexisting structure in semantic memory was employed in the coding process. Rote learning, by definition, consists in the arbitrary connection of input stimuli. Given the memory representation of the experimental context M_{CTXT} and the episode M_i, the proposition (PART OF,

M_i, M_{CTXT}) will be included in M_{CTXT}. Thus, M_{CTXT} may contain an explicit listing of to-be-remembered words.

If it is as simple as that, why is rote learning not the generally preferred strategy? The *ad hoc* assumption can be made that the formation of new associations is more difficult than the mere copying of preexisting structures from semantic memory. Perhaps a more profound reason has to do with the nature of the M_{CTXT} code. If M_{CTXT} has been retrieved, all rote associations become available, but how accessible is M_{CTXT}? It depends entirely upon how closely the original learning context can be reinstated. If one memorizes the Gettysburg Address the proper retrieval cue should not be one's study environment, but some context-independent cue "The Gettysburg Address." That, however, means storage in semantic memory, which presumably requires generalization and abstraction from many episodes, something that can hardly be achieved in a session in an experimental laboratory.

2.3.2. Free recall. It remains to be explained how the explicit interitem relations that are formed during learning help retrieval during recall. The principle is a very simple one and entirely in accordance with the two-stage theory of James and Müller. Given a particular memory representation of an item, all of its elements (which are, as noted above, in essence addresses to other items) become accessible, and a recognition check determines whether they were list members or not.

Figure 5 outlines performance on a recall test. Suppose item M_j has already been recalled (from short-term memory, rote recall, or some interitem relationship) and is held in short-term memory. The elements of M_j are now accessible. Suppose M_j contains the proposition (S_c, M_a, M_b, S_d). To continue a previous example, this might for instance be $(S_{shoot}, M_{hunter}, M_{fox}, S_{gun})$. The model assumes that the elements of M_j, such as M_a, M_b, S_c, and S_d, will be matched against the implicitly retrieved memory code M_{CTXT} in order to determine which of them are to-be-remembered items from the list experienced in context $CTXT$, and which are merely mediating links used in the construction of the retrieval scheme. If the number of common elements between M_{CTXT} and the implicitly retrieved memory codes $M_a, M_b, S_c, S_d, \ldots$ exceeds a threshold value c the item is classified as a list member.

It is not possible to recall a list item such as M_a directly, because M_a does not necessarily contain all the information needed for the pronunciation of that word. Therefore, the implicitly retrieved M_a must be matched with its corresponding lexical representation S_a before overt recall can occur. Failure of this match may be an additional source of recall failures. Confusion errors may occur in recall when an episode M_a is mistakenly matched with a similar lexical representation S_x rather than with S_a during the process of generation.

2.3.3. Cued recall. Two cases must be distinguished, depending upon whether or not the cue has been properly encoded together with the to-be-recalled word. If a cue and a recall word are encoded together as a unit, the cued recall task becomes essentially a recognition task. The cue is recognized, and by a process of pattern completion the whole memory unit containing the to-be-recalled word becomes available. For instance, if a memory episode $M_{smart fox}$ is formed during learning, the stimulus word *smart* will be encoded on a test as M_{smart}, match $M_{smart fox}$, and recall of

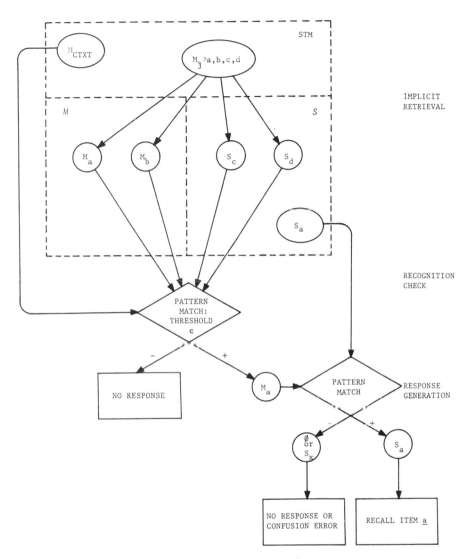

FIG. 5. Performance on a recall test.

fox occurs. Another possibility is that during learning separate memory episodes may have been formed for *smart* and *fox*, M_{smart} and M_{fox}, but that M_{smart} contained a reference to M_{fox}. In this case, the test word *smart* would produce a match with M_{smart} only, but M_{fox} can then be obtained through a recognition check as in a free-recall task.

If a cue and a to-be-recalled word are not encoded as a unit, the situation is entirely different. Suppose *fox* is to be recalled given the cue *smart*, but they are not encoded as a unit. The lexical entry S_{smart} may contain a reference to *fox*, perhaps the proposition (S_{smart}, S_{fox}). However, a recognition check on S_{fox} will be negative, because none of the proper context elements will be detected. What has been accessed is the lexical entry *fox*, not the elusive episodic *fox*!

3. APPLICATIONS

Without going into detail it will be shown how some important experimental results in recognition and recall can be explained within the general framework of the present theory. For several of the topics to be discussed here formal models could in principle be derived from the theory, and for others connections to existing formal and informal models will be pointed out.

3.1. Recognition

3.1.1. Response biases. If recognition is based upon the identification of a stimulus, a low-threshold model along the lines of Luce's work can be constructed (Luce, 1963). The probability of a successful match for any item is given by Eq. (1), and it merely must be assumed that subjects change their responses in accordance with task demands, as hypothesized by Luce.

If, on the other hand, recognition is based upon less than a complete identification, a signal detection model can easily be derived. An "old" response occurs if the number of identical elements in the memory representation and in the representation of the test stimulus exceeds some threshold value c. Under quite reasonable assumptions the number of identical elements between memory episodes and test stimuli would be distributed normally, with some mean μ (from context elements and other similarities) for distractors and a mean $\mu + \delta$ for repetitions of old items.

3.1.2. False recognition as a function of the similarity of distractors. The more similar (on any dimension) a distractor is to a study item, the more likely that a match will be successful. However, this probability can never be very high, because even in extreme cases many differentiating elements remain (the phonetic cues for synonyms, semantic cues for homonyms, plus contextual cues). There is, however, another basis for false recognition responses. If a subject encodes a study item together with a related nonlist item, e.g., the implicit associative responses of Underwood (1965), that nonlist item should be mistakenly recognized as "old" if it is presented as a distractor item on a recognition test. Such a test item will match the episode that includes it, and hence permits pattern completion. This prediction of the model appears to be correct (e.g., Cramer, 1970).

3.1.3. Context effects. As soon as context changes, the representation of a test stimulus and the corresponding memory episode begin to differ, and recognition performance declines. In the extreme case, different meanings of homographs may be elicited on study and test trials, so that two different lexical items will be used for the encoding. An "old" response under these circumstances is quite unlikely.

There are other kinds of context effects in recognition which are extremely powerful. Given a study list of nouns, no subject will respond "old" to items that are not nouns. The noun-ness of the items will, of course, be a part of all the memory codes, because short-term memory biases ensure that such common information will be encoded. However, such class recognition may involve more complex decision procedures. It is conceivable that a subject encodes as part of the contextual episode M_{CTXT} the proposition "all items are nouns." At the time of testing, this proposition may be retrieved and used to monitor output.

3.1.4. Study time, frequency, and recency.

The longer the study time, the more cues can be included in a memory code, and the more resistant recognition becomes to encoding variability.

Frequency judgments may be based upon a count of the number of times a recognition threshold c is exceeded by a given test stimulus. Thus, recognition and frequency judgments derive from the same kind of information, and a high correlation should be expected. Underwood (1972) has reported just such a correlation.

Recency judgments, on the other hand, require a temporal organization of episodes. No such extension of the model will be attempted here.[6] But note that frequency and recency judgments involve quite different theoretical processes. Data that show that the two are relatively unrelated are in general agreement with the theory in this respect (e.g., Peterson, 1967).

3.1.5. Recognition latencies.

The relationship between response probabilities and latencies in recognition tests is complex and probably strategy dependent. A frequently used strategy is that described by the models of Atkinson and Juola (1974) and Murdock (1974), which can easily be related to the present theory. In these models, recognition depends upon the familiarity of an item. If familiarity is high (or low) enough, a response ("old" or "new," respectively) occurs with a short latency; if it is in an intermediate zone of uncertainty, further processing is required, which lengthens response times. In the present model, the common element count provides a ready substitute for the concept of familiarity, and two kinds of further processing may occur. A response may be based upon full identification of the item, or a recall check may be used. If an episode can be retrieved, it must be related to other list members, and hence the likelihood that it too was part of the study list is increased. Thus, an "old" response is made, even though the recognition check itself is not decisive. Mandler (1972) as well as Hogan and Kintsch (1971) have provided evidence not based upon latency data that subjects engage in such recall checks during recognition tests.

3.1.6. Organization and recognition.

According to the theory, recognition could work in the absence of any organizational structures. In fact, however, recognition experiments always involve organization in some way and to some extent. The match upon which a recognition response is based is not facilitated through organization; on the contrary, elaborately encoded interitem relationships may not be duplicated on test trials and could depress performance. On the other hand, the possibility exists that subjects may use recall checks in doubtful recognition cases as explained above. Subjects can turn a recognition test into a recall task, and

[6]This is not to deny the importance of temporal organization in memory. One way in which material *could* be organized temporally would be by including explicit temporal information as elements of the memory representations, such as the proposition (AFTER,M_i,M_k).

given a stable organization of the list members, performance might be improved appreciably. However, with two opposing effects general predictions are difficult to make. On balance one should probably expect organizational effects to be small and inconsistent in recognition experiments, which is quite clearly the actual state of affairs (Kintsch, 1970a; McCormack, 1972).

3.2. Recall

3.2.1. Learning. Two steps are necessary before recall is possible, according to the present theory: the initial recording of experiences, upon which recognition is based, and the organization of these experiences into memory nets. The free-recall model of Kintsch and Morris (1965) can be regarded as a bare-bones version of these processes: Each state is approximated by an all-or-none process. Current two-stage models of paired-associate learning (e.g., Greeno, 1970) are based upon a related notion. Greeno distinguishes a storage and retrieval phase of learning, and one may consider the present theory as an attempt to describe in information-processing terms what goes on during these two phases.

The repetition of an item in a learning experiment may have complex effects on episodic memory. Assume that for a given item a memory code M_1 has been formed on Trial 1. A memory code M_2 on Trial 2 may retrieve M_1 via a pattern matching procedure, and the two codes may then be combined into M_{1+2}. Thus, at the end of learning a memory code for a given item may represent the sum of various experiences with that item. The effects of later trials may be quite small, because with constant context later encodings probably add very few new elements to the already formed code. However, learning may take a different course when a memory code, say M_2 on Trial 2, does not make contact with an earlier representation, say M_1. The pattern match M_2-M_1 may be negative for various reasons, e.g., changes in context, or M_1 may simply be a very poor code. Thus, multiple representations will be formed during learning for the same item. In the most extreme case, a separate memory episode might be formed for a particular item on each trial of a learning experiment.

Whether a subject encodes a repeated identical or similar stimulus with respect to its earlier memory representation, or whether a new, independent memory episode is formed, also plays a crucial role in transfer experiments. Positive or negative transfer occurs to the extent that memory codes strengthen or interfere with each other, which depends upon the subject's encoding operations. Martin (1968, 1972) has used the notion of encoding variability to develop a detailed theory of transfer which is quite compatible, at least at a general level, with the present theoretical framework.

3.2.2. Spacing of repetition effects. It is well-known that the effects of item repetition in both recall (Melton, 1970; Peterson et al., 1963) and recognition (Kintsch, 1966) depend upon the spacing of the repetition, that is, upon the number of trials with other list items that intervene between the repetitions of a given item. When repetitions are massed they are much less effective than when they are spaced, with the optimal spacing somewhat dependent upon experimental conditions, but generally between 10 or 20 items. The most plausible explanation for these effects is in terms of encoding variability (Melton, 1970). If two presentations of an item are massed, context is likely to be the same, and hence the two encodings will be largely identical and redundant. Little is learned. On the other hand, if two presentations are spaced sufficiently far apart, context may differ and the code formed on the second trial may add some new cues to those of the first trial. In this way a more general episode will be obtained, which will be easier to recognize and to recall. Note that this explanation of the effects of massing and spacing of trials asserts that spacing effects occur because of correlated context changes. It is therefore implied that if context can be changed without manipulating the spacing of repetitions, similar effects should be observable. Gartman and Johnson (1972) report an experiment that confirms this prediction. By biasing different encodings of homonyms on two trials these authors observed strong context effects, and at the same time could eliminate spacing effects for other items that were encoded in the same way on both trials. It should be obvious that encoding variability explanations of spacing effects are in complete agreement with predictions from the present theory. Indeed, the biased encoding processes described here provide a process explanation of encoding variability.

3.2.3. Organizational effects. Any kind of relationship among items in semantic memory can be used to interconnect episodes and will therefore facilitate recall. Interitem relations are easiest to use if items occupy the short-term memory buffer together. Thus, categorized lists are easier to recall when the related items are presented in blocks (e.g., Cofer, Bruce, & Reicher, 1966), and the closer two related items are in an input list, the more likely it is that they will be recalled (Glanzer, 1969).

However, adjacency on an input list is by no means a necessary condition for the interconnection of items in episodic memory. As Atkinson and Shiffrin (1969) have shown, a given item may survive in the buffer for quite some time, and thus be paired with input items that appeared much later on the list. More importantly, a memory code may at any time be brought back into the buffer from episodic memory, in order to interrelate it with other items in the buffer. During learning, items already in episodic memory but still accessible because they are related to some item in the buffer may be implicitly recalled, returned to the buffer, and interconnected with more recently presented items. Obviously, such a rehearsal process requires time and effort, and the extent to which it is employed will vary with experimental conditions. Data by Weist (1972) show that subjects do indeed use fairly complex rehearsal schemes. Weist obtained rehearsal protocols from his subjects in several multitrial free-recall experiments. An initial dependence of rehearsal upon input order was quickly overcome in Weist's protocols, and subjects began to rehearse semantically related sets together. Just as Rundus (1971) had observed earlier, what was rehearsed more was recalled better, and what was rehearsed together was recalled together.

3.2.4. Output order in free recall. For reasons already discussed, items that are presented together are most likely to be interconnected in episodic memory and hence recalled together. Mandler and Dean (1969) have provided ample evidence that this is indeed generally the case. However, in line with previous arguments, the presence of any kind of structure in the input list can override input order effects. Items that appear to be related in semantic memory (as judged from the performance of subjects in other tasks, such as sorting and problem solving) tend to cluster in the output, as was demonstrated by Kintsch, Miller, and Hogan (1970).

The present theory also clarifies some less obvious output order phenomena in recall. Hogan (1972) has shown that where recall starts in a list determines to some extent which items will be recalled. If in a 20-word list subjects are induced to start recall with an item from the early part of the list, that part is recalled better, but there is a compensating loss in the middle and final sections of the lists. Hogan could predict recall quantitatively very well by estimating the interrelationships among items in episodic memory from rehearsal protocols obtained during learning. The nature of the episodic network explained the experimental results. Given a starting point, a certain set of connections among the list items becomes available, but some parts of the network could simply never be reached from that starting point. A related phenomenon which was first reported by Slamecka (1968) may be explained in a similar way. If part of a list is presented as a retrieval cue, recall of the remaining items may be poorer than when no cues are provided. Giving the subject a portion of the list forces him into a retrieval scheme based upon that part, while in free recall the subject is allowed to follow his own design, and he may trace out a path among items that includes more of the list.

3.3 Cued Recall

The predictions of the model for cued recall experiments have already been outlined in Section 2.3. Briefly, cued recall presupposes encoding of the recall cue and the to-be-recalled item as a unit. Thus, the model is in good agreement with those paired-associate studies that stress the importance of encoding the stimulus-response pair as a unit (e.g., Greeno, 1970) and the cued recall studies by Tulving and his associates upon which the notion of encoding specificity has been based (Thomson & Tulving, 1970; Tulving & Osler, 1968; Tulving & Thomson, 1973). To recapitulate the argument, suppose M_i is a to-be-recalled word, S_i is the corresponding lexical representation, and X is an extralist recall cue. Even though S_x may be related to S_i and thus make available S_i, recall will not occur, because the necessary contextual elements that characterize the list membership of M_i are lacking in S_i. Thus, if the to-be-recalled word is *fox* and the retrieval cue is *smart*, the cue might produce the semantic memory element S_{fox}, but without prior encoding it can not produce what is really needed for recall, namely, the episode M_{fox}.

There is no easy way out of this dilemma. Suppose the subject tries a different strategy. S_{fox} is not matched against M_{CTXT} in an effort to detect contextual elements, but against all memory episodes in $\mathcal{M}$ in the hope of locating some episode containing *fox*, which then can be checked for the proper kind of contextual elements. This strategy will not work, because S_{fox} contains many more elements than episodes such as M_{fox}, and therefore it will not be possible to match up most of the elements in S_{fox} with counterparts in M_{fox}. Thus, the probability of a successful match of this kind must remain low according to Eq. (1).

However, even more complex retrieval strategies can be devised that may be more successful. Suppose a very determined subject tries the following. Given S_{fox}, he pronounces the word implicitly, producing a set of cues E_{fox} in the proper experimental context. From $E_{fox} \cup S_{fox}$ a memory code M^*_{fox} can be selected and matched against $\mathcal{M}$. It may very well be that M^*_{fox} succeeds where S_{fox} had failed, and that a match will be produced with M_{fox}. There are fewer cues in an episode than in lexical entries, and there are some context elements that may be partly identical with those included earlier in M_{fox}. Therefore, the overlap between the two episodes may be sufficient for a match.

One might object that the arguments just presented allow too much flexibility for the model and make it very difficult to generate really specific predictions. However, no new *ad hoc* mechanisms have been introduced here: It is merely that the basic operations of the theory (pattern matching, encoding operations, the use of interitem relationships among memory codes for searching memory) have been used in a rather complex strategy. There are at least some data that suggest that subjects are able to use extralist cues effectively, in spite of the lack of specific encoding. Bahrick (1969, 1970) has shown that subjects could recall words given associates as cues, approximately in the proportion that would be expected from associative norms. There may be other explanations for Bahrick's data. It may have been possible, for instance, that implicit associative responses occurred to the to-be-recalled words during learning, so that at least some of the time the future recall cue was, indeed, encoded together with the to-be-recalled word. This kind of an explanation is, however, less likely for data recently reported by Pellegrino and Salzberg (1973), who found evidence both for and against encoding specificity. Recall cues that were different from those used during learning were indeed less effective than specifically encoded cues, but if subjects were forced to respond their performance became equally good under both cuing conditions. Therefore it seems that if one can get subjects to try very hard, they can somehow overcome disadvantageous encoding conditions. The complex strategy outlined above may be a possible explanation for how this could be done. An additional observation of Pellegrino and Salzberg (1973) lends it at least some credibility. They gave their subjects a final recognition test in which items that were associatively related to the recall cues were employed as distractors. After forced response instructions an elevated false recognition rate for these items was noticed. It appears that when forced to respond in the recall task, subjects were making many implicit associative responses, something clearly required if the retrieval strategy outlined above is to work. On the subsequent recognition test these associates tended to be falsely recognized.

3.4. Short-Term Memory

Once a code for a memory episode M is formed it remains for a while in an activated state, during which it is readily accessible, and the intermediary computations that were performed in its construction are still recoverable. Thus, the composition of the memory code can be changed, if required by a change in context. Memory episodes in this activated state comprise the short-term store which is therefore a special subset of episodic memory.

The short-term store is viewed here as a working memory that makes possible the context sensitive encoding and recoding of memory episodes. Episodes displaced from the short-term store through shifts in attention are not lost but remain members of episodic memory, though without the special access privileges that characterized them before.

Traditionally, theorists have assumed two characteristic properties of the short-term stores: limited capacity and acoustic encoding (Kintsch, 1970b). The first presents no problem for the present theory; a limited-capacity assumption can easily be added to the model. However, the hypothesis that items held in the short-term store are encoded acoustically can not be incorporated into the present model. Items in short-term memory are memory episodes and their composition is in no way different from other elements of episodic memory. Actually, the viewpoint that items in the short-term store must be exclusively acoustic is no longer tenable today. Recent experiments (e.g., Raser, 1972; Shulman, 1970) have demonstrated that primary memory may contain nonacoustic information, but it is nevertheless necessary to look at this problem more closely. Primary memory may not be exclusively acoustic, but undeniably there is a strong preference for acoustic encoding under a variety of experimental conditions. This observation suggests an interesting modification of the encoding assumptions of the present model.

The selection of a memory code M from the pool of cues $E \cup S$ has up to now been regarded as random, except for context biases. The data on acoustic coding in short-term memory suggest, however, that the cue selection may be at least partly under the control of the subject as well as dependent upon task demands. It appears likely that in some experimental situations subjects form memory episodes consisting largely of phonemic cues, while in other situations semantic and imagery cues may be preferred. If this additional assumption is made in the model, a good many observations about short-term retention become interpretable. However, instead of a general review, only two representative studies will be discussed here.

Consider first Conrad's observation that confusion errors in short-term memory for visually presented letters were quite similar to confusion matrices obtained in auditory perception experiments (Conrad, 1964). Given the visual stimulus i, perceptual processing makes available the set of cues $E_i \cup S_i$, where E_i consists primarily of visual cues, and S_i contains the subset of phonemic cues that characterize the letter i. Assume that in Conrad's experiment a memory code M_i was formed consisting primarily of phonemic cues. Thus, for instance, if the stimulus was the letter b, but a code was formed in which the crucial feature that distinguishes b and v was not included, confusion between b and v would occur at the time of recall: The memory code M_b matches both S_b and S_v, i.e., it does not specify the response unambiguously. Conrad's results follow from such a model. It is only necessary to assume that phonemic cues are favored in the construction of memory codes, without actually assuming that subjects translate the visual stimulus into phonemic form by "speaking the letter to themselves." In the present model, memory codes are never based directly on the stimulus, but always on an enriched cue set, in which, through the operation of pattern completion, perceptual and memory elements have been combined.

The second experiment to be discussed here is that of Kintsch and Buschke (1969). Brief lists of words, containing either homophones or synonyms, were presented visually to subjects for immediate probed recall. By means of an analytic procedure suggested by Waugh and Norman (1965), total recall was separated into a stable secondary memory component and a primary memory component, which accounted for the improved recall of the last few list items. In the homophone lists primary memory was reduced, but the secondary memory component remained unchanged. Synonyms had exactly the opposite effect, that is, recall was reduced only for secondary memory. These results were originally explained in terms of the then prevalent box model of short-term memory: In primary memory information is encoded acoustically, whereas secondary memory employs a semantic code. This view must be reconsidered. The primary memory component of the Waugh and Norman model can be equated with the short-term store of the present theory, while secondary memory corresponds to the remainder of episodic memory. Since the short-term store is defined as merely a temporarily active subset of episodic memory, there can be no differences in encoding modality between primary and secondary memory. But suppose that subjects in experiments like those of Kintsch and Buschke have a strong preference for using phonemic cues in the construction of memory episodes and that the resulting episodes contain no (or few) interitem relationships that could be used to retrieve an item given another one on a recall test. In spite of that, recall will be perfect as long as these predominantly phonemic episodes remain in the short-term store. Once they leave, however, recall will be impossible for lack of retrieval cues. Assume, in addition, that on a certain proportion of items, encoding is not merely phonemic, but that semantic cues are included, and interitem relationships are formed among the semantic cues, permitting later retrieval; those will be the only items that can be recalled, once they have left short-term memory. It should be clear that such a system would mimic an acoustically encoded primary memory and a semantically encoded secondary memory. In actual fact, however, no such separate stores exist at all; it is just that those episodes that use only phonemic cues can only be recalled while they are still retained in the short-term store, and only the relatively few codes containing explicit semantic retrieval cues can be recalled otherwise.

Only a speculative answer can be given to the question of why subjects prefer phonemic encoding in many short-term memory experiments. For short-term retention it may simply be easier to encode words phonemically, to concentrate upon holding them in consciousness, and to forget about the construction of elaborate retrieval cues based upon semantic relationships or imagery. It is quite plausible that this would be an efficient strategy for subjects in certain experiments. However, if the experimental task demands a different approach, subjects are quite able to change their encoding strategy. If long-term retention is demanded, retrieval cues must be built into the memory codes. Even in some short-term memory experiments predominantly phonemic encoding may not be appropriate and is not used (e.g., Raser, 1972; Shulman, 1970).

The impression has been given above that retrieval cues (as described in Section 2.3.1.) are necessarily semantic, or imaginal. Yet this is not the case, since phonemic cues may serve the same purpose. Subjects do use rhymes and other phonemic relations among words as retrieval cues. As with semantic or imagery cues, such interitem phonemic relationships must be specifically encoded in a memory episode if it is to serve its purpose. However, even if encoding is otherwise primarily phonemic, semantic or imaginal relationships between words are apparently easier to come by, in general, than rhymes and alliterations.

4. DISCUSSION

The purpose of this chapter was to present the general framework for a theory of encoding and retrieval in episodic memory. Structures and operations have been specified which are presumed to underlie what psychologists call organization and retrieval, but no attempt has been made to define these terms in any precise way. To do so, that is, to restrict these terms to some specific meaning, has had little success historically, and probably would produce only further terminological confusion. Retrieval and organization are terms that we know in our hearts; we need them to communicate, but scientific arguments should be directed to the substantive assumptions of a theory, not to the labels used.

At the beginning of this chapter several critical issues for memory models were discussed. Various reasons were adduced why a memory model has to be a two-stage generation-recognition type model, but at the same time must incorporate the encoding specificity principle. The distinction between semantic and episodic memory was of great help in working out the necessary characteristics of such a model. Indeed, one can regard encoding specificity as a corollary of the semantic-episodic memory distinction: If there are multiple representations of items in memory it is not the case that given one of these representations all others must be automatically accessible. Relations that connect memory codes must be specifically built into the codes, even when these codes are based upon the same distal stimulus experienced at different times and in different contexts. Nevertheless, one must guard against taking too literally the semantic-episodic memory distinction; it is no more than a convenient heuristic. It simplifies the presentation to have a separate symbol S for a lexical representation and M for some context-specific experience. But, as long as one remembers the compositions of these memory codes, it is not at all necessary to use distinct notations. By no means do I wish to imply that semantic and episodic memory are separate boxes in which codes may be deposited. All M's and S's in this work could be replaced by the same symbol, simply for memory, without affecting the mechanisms described!

One of the chief advantages of the present theory is that it is not restricted to list-learning data but can be extended to memory for natural language material. How this extension can be done is easy to see in principle, but it is not yet feasible, given the present status of knowledge in psycholinguistics. Not enough is known about the sentence encoding strategies that people use. A sentence may be stored in exactly the same format as was used here for words. Indeed, there is nothing in the general theory that singles out the word as a basic unit. Information stored in memory at one location constitutes a memory unit (location must not be understood in neurophysiological terms — it may very well be that these units are stored in the brain in a distributive fashion), and it may as well be a proposition, or a complex propositional structure, as a word. Thus, all the recognition and recall mechanisms described apply to propositional memory as well as to word memory. The difficulty is this. It was reasonable to assume that all words are available in semantic memory and that the incoming stimulus contacts this lexical information. All sentences, on the other hand, are clearly not available as units in semantic memory, though some evidently are. In Chapter 9, a study will be reported which demonstrates that definitional sentences, that is, sentences that may be expected to occur in memory as part of the definition of a lexical item, are recognized as meaningful more rapidly than sentences that presumably have to be generated on the basis of available knowledge but are not stored directly in memory. Other sentence evaluation data reviewed in Chapter 9 also support this contention. There are also some memory data that show that what has been called here definitional sentences behave as units in free-recall experiments. Rosenberg (1968) found that sentences with highly interassociated words were learned in an all-or-none manner, presumably because such input sentences can make contact with stored representations in semantic memory. On the other hand, the matter is very different for sentences encountered *de novo*. Recall is not all-or-none, but a characteristic pattern of errors is observed which depends upon structural properties of the sentences. New sentences cannot simply be matched with an entry in semantic memory; they must be analyzed, and their meaning must be constructed from information about words and phrases that is available in semantic memory. How this is done is quite beyond the scope of this chapter, and until one understands reasonably well the nature of this encoding process, detailed models of sentence memory can not be considered. Parenthetically it should be noted that an understanding of encoding strategies is required not only for sentence memory, but for any kind of memory involving materials that find no correspondence with existing memory units. In this sense, models for memory of nonsense materials and models for sentence memory face quite similar problems (e.g., Prytulak, 1971).

Pattern matching and pattern completion were assumed to be the basic operations of the memory system. It must be pointed out once more that Eq. (1) is merely the simplest, most obvious expression available for a pattern completion mechanism. Hopefully, none of the psychologically significant features of that operation have been overlooked in its formulation, but it cannot be assumed that Eq. (1) is the best possible candidate for actual formal model work. Various improvements are possible, and some are probably necessary. Since the present work is not concerned with quantitative predictions but rather with the conceptual outlines of the theory, such improvements might have been more distracting than informative. Nilsson (1965) and Minsky and Papert (1969) provide excellent descriptions of pattern matching devices more powerful than the one proposed. In addition, there is no reason why one should be restricted to pattern classification on the basis of discriminant functions. Holographic procedures for pattern completion might be more suitable (Gabor, 1969). The point here is to argue for pattern completion as a basic operation in memory, not about particular implementations of that operation. There is one problem, however, that may be raised in objection to any kind of pattern-matching device. That is the impossibility of distinguishing crucial features. Features may be weighted, but there is no natural way to make a feature an absolutely necessary precondition for a match. This may be a serious problem for artificial intelligence devices that need to operate as efficiently as possible, but it may not be disastrous in a model of human behavior. Indeed, there appears to be no evidence that people use critical features, and there are at least some experimental results that argue against this possibility. For instance, it is well-known (Anisfeld, 1970; Fillenbaum, 1969; Grossman & Eagle, 1970) that subjects frequently make false recognition responses to words that are in fact antonyms of those actually presented. Presumably, a mechanism with critical features could not be trapped into such errors. At the very least, then, pattern-matching models for human memory should not be discounted on *a priori* grounds. Also, it is possible that supplementary decision procedures may override the outcome of the pattern-matching process, as was indicated in Section 3.1 in the discussion of context effects in recognition-learning experiments.

Whatever the eventual modifications and extensions of the theoretical framework presented here may be, it serves at least one function at this point: It allows one to talk with consistency and relative specificity about a large body of experimental research on organization and retrieval in memory.

PART II
EXPERIMENTAL INVESTIGATIONS

Just as the outer form of the language can only appear as an actually existing language, so the inner form implies only the actual psychological characteristics and relations that bring about specific outer forms by their effects.

Wilhelm Wundt

The experimental investigations reported here represent the outcome of several years work in our laboratory at the University of Colorado. Needless to say, at the beginning of this work there was no grand plan in existence that dictated the design of this series of experiments. But as the work developed, the common theme and the common concerns that underlie it became more and more noticeable, and the whole enterprise revealed a structure of its own. First of all, none of the studies reported here is concerned with list learning; thus, none is directly related to the theory of episodic memory in the previous chapter. We believe there exists enough work relevant to that theory to evaluate its general usefulness, while the specific submodels that are needed in order to perform strict tests of that theory have not yet been developed. All of the work reported here is concerned with the processing of meaningful verbal materials, sentences, or even larger text units.

Our main concern was, of course, to be able to find empirical tests for the propositional theory that has formed the background for all of this work. To some extent, we have succeeded in devising fairly direct tests of this theory. Chapter 6 reports a study in which the rate of reading paragraphs of varying lengths is shown to be directly related to the number of propositions in the base structure of the texts. This study is presented both as a demonstration of the psychological reality of propositions and as a contribution to the analysis of the reading process. If one looks at the propositions in the base structure of a text rather than at the surface characteristics of the text, it becomes possible to study directly the acquisition of information during reading, and that is, after all, what reading is all about. In the succeeding chapter (7), the nature of propositions is further analyzed. The question raised there is whether we can obtain experimental evidence about the unitary character of multi-argument propositions. According to the theory, propositions with several arguments (say, Agent, Object, Instrument, and Goal) should be processed as units, while alternative theories treat such expressions as complexes consisting of several binary propositions, in the manner of phrase structure grammars. We argued that free recall could provide such a test. One can compare the tendency to recall sentences as wholes, when each sentence is based upon a single (multi-argument) proposition, with the recall of sentences equal in length, but based upon more than one proposition. Since we found that subjects recalled as units only what the theory claimed was a unit, namely propositions, we took this as good support for the present formulation of the theory. Another series of studies that we believe is crucial for the theory are the decomposition experiments reported in Chapter 11. These studies provide the much needed justification for one of the main features of the theory: Concepts that enter propositions in the present theory may be lexically simple or they may be complex. We do not decompose lexically complex word concepts into semantic primitives as some linguistic and many artificial intelligence theories do. As an example, we take as a proposition (KILL,HUNTER,DEER), and do not decompose KILL into CAUSE-BECOME-DEAD, or HUNTER into SOMEONE WHO HUNTS. There are good *a priori* reasons for decomposition, but the issue for the psychologist is an empirical one, and the comprehension and memory data of Chapter 11 totally fail to support the idea of decomposition.

Other studies in this series are less directly related to the theory of Part I. They are addressed to various questions about text comprehension and memory, but they are not so much deductions from an explicit processing theory as they are experiments in search of a theory. In Chapter 8, for instance, we explore further the process of comprehension during reading, as well as memory for what has been read. According to the view espoused here, comprehension consists in constructing a propositional text base from whatever surface cues are available. We tried to find out how subjects comprehend propositions that have no directly corresponding verbal expressions. It appeared that such propositions are inferred during reading, just as other propositions that are directly represented in the text. At the same time, we noted some curious interaction effects, which we interpreted as evidence for different levels of memory: memory for the surface form of a text, in addition to the propositional memory for its meaning.

Chapters 9 and 10 are entitled Memory Search and devoted to the exploration of how information is retrieved from memory. The first chapter deals with the retrieval of sentences from episodic memory, as an addendum to the rich literature on retrieval in list-learning experiments. Somewhat to our surprise, the results with sentences and paragraphs parallel those obtained with words and word lists in important ways. Perhaps the extensive literature on list learning may, after all, be quite directly relevant to problems of text memory. In the next chapter, we take up the question of retrieval from semantic memory, but only in the limited context of sentence verification studies. Our data make two main points: They demand a two-stage model in which a semantic similarity check precedes the detailed evaluation of the sentence, and they emphasize the need for an active, inference-making memory system.

It will be obvious to the reader, by now, that the topics we have selected for experimental tests are somewhat accidental choices from the large set of problems that could have been attempted. At the same time, the choices are clearly not random, and the results of these experiments, taken together, have some fairly definitive implications for the development of a true processing theory. Most importantly, they show that as far as the theory has been developed in Part I, it appears to hold up all right, and they do give some hints how to go on. But before we begin our discussion of these experiments, we would like to report in Chapter 5 a series of studies that is still pretheoretical. By examining the speed with which inferences can be made after reading various paragraphs, these studies argue for the essential precondition for all this work: that there is, indeed, an abstract representation of meaning in memory, apart from the actual verbal input.

5
ON THE ABSTRACT NATURE OF
THE MEMORY REPRESENTATION
FOR TEXTS

When a subject reads a paragraph of text and stores the information in memory for further use, he must, according to the model of Part I, code the information in propositional form. Such coding is required both for the comprehension of the text and for its further processing, such as nonverbatim recall or the generation of inferences. In the present chapter, some experiments are reported that bear upon these coding assumptions. The experiments are not full tests of the model, since the model is much too complex to be testable in a single experiment, but their outcomes have direct consequences for the model. What is being tested is a more general hypothesis than the one actually made in the model, namely, that content is represented abstractly at a deeper level than the linguistic surface structure of a text. One possible abstract representation is, of course, the propositional representation developed here, but the present experiments are not concerned with the particular form that such abstract representations may take (that is, they do not discriminate between the propositional model and other similar models). We are merely concerned here with the hypothesis that the memory representation of a text is a function of the content of the text, but not of the way in which it is expressed. That is, identical memory representations may be formed for paragraphs that are all members of the same paraphrase set.

The last statement must be immediately qualified. It is obvious, of course, that people can and under certain circumstances do remember verbatim a story, a conversation, or a poem. Memory for surface structures has in fact been investigated quite extensively in the psychological laboratory, and quite a bit is known about variables affecting verbatim recall (e.g., syntactic factors), ease of learning, and the course of forgetting (for a review see, for instance, Kintsch, 1970b). Memory for text (or for anything else, as Craik and Lockhart, 1972, argue) may involve more than one level of analysis. People may remember the sound of a sentence that was spoken by someone, or the way it was printed on a page, or at a more abstract level of analysis, the exact words used (that is, the linguistic surface structure), or merely the meaning of the sentence (that is, a propositional representation) or some combination thereof. The present experiments were designed to demonstrate the psychological reality of the last named memory representation and its independence from the other levels.

1. DRAWING INFERENCES FROM SYNTACTICALLY SIMPLE AND COMPLEX PARAGRAPHS[1]

Two versions of a paragraph were prepared. In one, the simplest possible syntax was used, generating a string of simple sentences which expressed in as straightforward a manner as possible the underlying propositions of the paragraph. In the second version, all conceivable syntactic and semantic transformations were used to generate one long, complex sentence, which, however, still expressed the same propositions. In this way, the complex version of the paragraph differed from the simple version not only in surface structure, but also in deep structure (semantic transformations involved such changes as substituting THE OCEAN IS WEST OF THE HIGHWAY for THE HIGHWAY IS EAST OF THE OCEAN, or A BUYS X FROM B for B SELLS X TO A). It seems likely that when subjects are given these two versions to read, they will take longer with the complex version than with the simpler version. However, if they are then asked to make an inference, the speed with which the inference can be made should be the same for the two versions if the information is stored in a logical form, while if storage is verbatim the complex version should again require more processing time. It is not necessary to assume that all subjects represent the paragraphs in the same form; certainly, the meanings that individual subjects extract from the input paragraph will not always be exactly the same. The experimental hypothesis is merely that the simple and complex versions of each paragraph share the same meaning and that what is stored in memory is a representation of that common meaning which is not systematically influenced by the way chosen to express that meaning.

Thus, one may predict that if subjects are allowed to read a paragraph at their own rates, they will have available in memory a representation of this paragraph which is independent of the actual choice of words, as long as that choice leaves unchanged the underlying logical propositions. However, it should take more time to encode into this abstract logical form a paragraph with an involved syntax than a syntactically simple paragraph. On the other hand, if reading time is limited, one would expect the likelihood of a complete and correct encoding to be smaller for the complex version than for the simple version. If, nevertheless, an encoding is achieved during the time allotted, the time needed to infer the answer to a subsequent question should again be identical for the two versions.

[1]This study has been published as ''Storage of complex information in memory: Some implications of the speed with which inferences can be made'' by W. Kintsch and D. Monk, *Journal of Experimental Psychology,* 1972, **94**, 25 – 32. It is reprinted here with permission of the American Psychological Association.

Three experiments were conducted, differing in the nature of the paragraphs used, in which subjects read paragraphs under conditions of either unlimited self-paced reading time or restricted reading time and then answered inferential questions. In presenting these results, Exp. I will be emphasized and Exp. II and III will be treated more briefly. These experiments were performed in the reverse order, but the early experiments suffer from some methodological weaknesses which were at least partly resolved in the final effort.

Experiment I

Method. Sixty students recruited from dormitories at the University of Colorado served as subjects in individual sessions. They were paid $1.50 for their participation. Half of the subjects were assigned to the self-paced condition and half to the restricted reading time condition. In each condition, 15 subjects worked with Material Set 1 and 15 subjects with Material Set 2.

Three types of paragraphs were constructed. Each type consisted of four propositions, A, B, C, and D, which were related to each other in three different ways. The structure of Type 1 paragraphs was as follows: A causes B, B and C cause D (or $-$D), assert A and C (or A and $-$C); question: D? In Type 2 paragraphs the four propositions formed a single inference chain: A causes B, B causes C, C causes D, assert A (or $-$A); question: D? Type 3 paragraphs were constructed according to the following outline: A causes B, C is an instance of A, D is an instance of B, assert C (or $-$C); question: D? These three problem types were arbitrarily selected, but care was taken that the number of elementary propositions as well as the total number of propositions was the same for all types, and that the reasoning involved should be simple enough to assure a high percentage of correct responses even under difficult experimental conditions.

The paragraphs used here present informal arguments. These arguments were constructed to be intuitivly compelling, but by renouncing standard logic, a certain vagueness is inevitably introduced. Certainly not everyone will interpret these arguments in precisely the same way they were interpreted in these experiments (particularly not a logician). The subjects were instructed to answer the questions only on the basis of the information actually contained in the paragraphs, i.e., without assuming logically possible extraneous factors.

For each problem type, four paragraphs were constructed; for instance, the Type 1 structure was expressed once as a problem concerning smog, once as a problem concerning the price of soap, once crime was the topic, and once it dealt with an explorer in a mythical land. Each of these paragraphs was written in two versions: a simple version in which the sentences followed as closely as possible the propositional outline, and a complex version in which the whole paragraph was made into one long sentence. Every syntactic transformation available was employed, and an attempt was made to substitute semantically equivalent expressions wherever possible. Thus, the two versions of each paragraph were equal only at the level of their propositional base. The length of each paragraph in all its versions was 46 words. All questions were 6 words long. As an example, a problem of Type 1 is given below in its two versions:

Simple: The council of elders in the land of Syndra meets whenever a stranger arrives. If the council meets and if the stranger presents the proper gifts to the council, he is not molested by the natives. The explorer Portmanteau came to Syndra without any valuable gifts.

Complex: The arrival of strangers in the land of Syndra, like the explorer Portmanteau, who did not bring valuable gifts, always resulted in a meeting of the council of elders, which insured that the stranger was not molested by the natives upon receipt of the proper gifts.

Question: Was Portmanteau molested by the natives?

The propositional base structure from which both paragraphs are derived can be expressed as follows, following the conventions of Kintsch (1972): ((COME, STRANGER,TO SYNDRA) = A) & ((MEET,COUNCIL OF ELDERS,IN SYNDRA) = B) & (CAUSE,A,B) & ((PRESENT,STRANGER,GIFTS,TO COUNCIL) = C) & ((MOLEST,NATIVES,STRANGER) = D) & (CAUSE, $B \wedge C$,NOT D) & (COME,EXPLORER PORTMANTEAU,TO SYNDRA) & (NOT C).

In addition to the 24 experimental paragraphs thus obtained, 8 filler problems were used. Paragraphs prepared for Exp. II were employed for this purpose. These filler paragraphs did not follow any definite logical scheme, nor was their length constant.

Two experimental lists, Set 1 and Set 2, were constructed. Each list began with four warm-up problems (filler items), two in the simple and two in the complex version, with the correct response being YES for two and NO for the others. Thereafter, problems were arranged in four blocks of four. Each block contained one problem of Types 1, 2, and 3 plus a filler item. Whether a problem appeared in the simple or complex version, and whether a YES or NO item was used was determined by a counterbalancing scheme following a Latin square. Two different orders were prepared for each set of paragraphs. The filler items were used in order to prevent subjects from noticing that the same schemes kept reoccurring in the experimental problems. Set 2 was simply the complement of Set 1: If a particular paragraph appeared in the simple form in Set 1, the complex form was used for Set 2. Thus, each paragraph was represented exactly once in each set, either in its simple or its complex version. In each set the correct answer was YES for half of the simple problems as well as for half of the complex problems, and NO for the other half. However, only one response form was used for a given paragraph, so that a particular paragraph appeared always as a YES (or NO) item, in both its simple and complex versions.

Slides were made for all paragraphs and questions. The subject was seated about 4 m in front of a screen on which the slides were shown by means of a Kodak Carousel projector. In the self-paced condition, the experimenter, who was seated behind the subject, exposed a paragraph and at the same time started a Hunter timer. In front of the subject, there was a box with three labeled response buttons: a YES and a NO button on top, and an ADVANCE button on the right side of the box. The subject kept two fingers of his left hand on the YES and NO buttons and the index finger of his right hand on the ADVANCE button. When the subject finished reading the paragraph, he pressed the ADVANCE button, which brought on the question slide, stopped the timer, and started a second Hunter timer. Depressing either the YES or NO key stopped the second timer and turned on an indicator light at the experimenter's console. After recording the results of an item, the experimenter gave the subject a "Ready" signal and proceeded to the next item. The subjects were instructed that all questions required an inference rather than a simple answer from memory. They were asked to "work as fast as you can, but remember that the important thing is to be correct, not speed."

The procedure for the restricted reading time condition was identical, except that the subject kept his right hand on the table without touching the ADVANCE button, and the experimenter terminated the reading time for each paragraph slide after 10 sec by advancing the question slide.

Results. The mean reading times for items on which a correct response occurred (shown in Table 1) are longer for the complex versions of the experimental paragraphs than for the simple versions. These differences are quite substantial, except for Type 2 problems.

The data from Problem Sets 1 and 2 were pooled because they did not differ significantly statistically, $F < 1$. Reading times were then analyzed as a two-factor factorial design, with complexity and problem type as main effects. Because of unequal cell frequencies, the approximation suggested by Walker and Lev (1953) was used. Complexity and type were both highly significant, $F(1,276) = 68.54$ and $F(2, 276) = 63.50$, respectively.[2] Mean reading times for complex paragraphs were about 12% longer than for simple paragraphs. Type 2 problems took more time to read than either Type 1 or Type 3 problems, which were quite comparable. However, the interpretation of these main effects is somewhat complicated by a significant interaction effect, $F(2, 276) = 8.07, p < .01$. As can be seen from Table 1, Type 2 problems took only a little longer to read in the complex versions than in their simple versions. Further analysis shows that one of the Type 2 problems was for some reason too easy in its complex version: The mean reading time for that problem was only 21.86 sec, versus 33.94 sec for the complex versions of the other three Type 2 problems. The same problem, however, was of about average difficulty in its simple form. Why this problem was read much faster than the other problems is not clear, but

[2] *Statistical Note.* Whenever possible, we have analyzed our results in such a way as to permit generalizations over both subject and material populations (Clark, 1973), e.g., the sentence research in Chapters 10 and 11. Unfortunately, this type of analysis is not always feasible. It is frequently not possible to treat paragraphs as a random variable in the statistical analysis, because there are too few paragraphs to work with which satisfy the often very strict demands that are made on their construction. Sometimes we can simply not design experiments with enough statistical power to make generalizations over material meaningful; furthermore, it is not always clear what the population of paragraphs might be for which statistical generalizations could be made. The way out of this dilemma, which we take in the present Chapter and also in Chapters 8 and 9, is to repeat the experiment several times with different materials. Each time there are only a few paragraphs involved, but if we obtain similar results in the different replications with different materials, at least some generality is achieved for our conclusions.

if the results for this problem could be disregarded, the results for the remaining Type 2 problems would be quite consistent with the overall pattern. It should also be noted that one of the Type 3 problems was easier than the others, in the sense that it required less reading time, but equally so in its simple and complex versions. The original intent, to construct four equally difficult problems of each type, was fully achieved only for the Type 1 problems.

Reading times on items on which an incorrect response was made revealed no systematic trends. However, only relatively few observations were available. The mean reading time for error trials was 28.44 sec, which is quite close to the overall mean for correct items, 27.47 sec.

In spite of the fact that the problems used were not equated as well as one might wish, the principal conclusion of interest seems well supported: Subjects took longer to read the complex versions of the paragraphs than the simple versions.

Table 1 also shows the mean inference times for the self-paced condition for items on which a correct response occurred. Unlike the reading times, inference times did not differ systematically for the simple and complex versions of the paragraphs. An analysis of variance confirms this impression. An $F < 1$ was obtained for the complexity effect, while problem type yielded $F (2, 276) = 2.81, p > .05$, and the interaction effect was not significant either, $F < 1$. The mean inference times for the experimenter-paced condition are shown in Table 2. Again, the values for simple and complex paragraphs are almost identical.

It is clear that the time subjects needed to make an inference did not depend upon whether they had seen the simple or the complex version of a paragraph. In fact, inference times were independent of reading times for both the simple and complex paragraphs. For each subject, the inference times and the reading times were corre-

TABLE 1

Average Reading Times, Inference Times together with Their Standard Errors, and Percent Correct for the Three Problem Types as a Function of the Complexity of the Paragraphs

Problem type	Reading time	Inference time	Percent correct
1			
Simple	24.07 (1.46)	4.29 (.47)	92
Complex	29.64 (1.88)	4.53 (.41)	82
2			
Simple	29.90 (1.68)	5.64 (.51)	83
Complex	30.87 (1.84)	5.23 (.41)	88
3			
Simple	23.74 (1.55)	4.87 (.63)	90
Complex	26.94 (1.45)	4.74 (.36)	83
Total			
Simple	25.79 (.92)	4.91 (.32)	88
Complex	29.18 (1.00)	4.84 (.23)	84

Note.—Inference times are measured in seconds.

lated over the 12 experimental problems. Of these product-moment correlation coefficients, 18 were positive (1 of them significant at the .01 level) and 12 were negative (none significant), with the average correlation being .123. Thus, there is no reason to question the null hypothesis of independence.

Whether YES or NO was the correct response had very little influence upon inference times. The mean inference time of all (correct) YES responses was 4.91 sec, and the mean inference time for all (correct) NO responses was 4.83 sec.

As Table 3 shows, the likelihood of a correct response was smaller when the reading time was restricted to 10 sec than when subjects were allowed to take as much time as they wanted. This decrease was significant statistically both for the simple and complex paragraphs. On the other hand, simple paragraphs were answered correctly somewhat more often than complex paragraphs (see also Table 1). This difference was not significant statistically, though it approached significance in the paced condition, as is also shown in Table 3.

TABLE 2

Mean Response Times

Problem type	Exp. I		Exp. II		Exp. III	
	Self-paced	10-sec. exposure	Self-paced	One-third exposure	Self-paced	23-sec exposure
			Reading times			
Simple	25.8**	——	33.0**	——	35.9*	——
Complex	29.2**	——	37.8**	——	45.9*	——
			Inference times			
Simple	4.9	4.1	12.3	14.8	21.7	16.0
Complex	4.8	3.9	12.3	15.5	21.3	15.8

Note.—Response times are measured in seconds.
*$p < .025$.
**$p < .01$.

TABLE 3

Proportions of Correct Responses

Exp.	Self-paced		p [a]	Experimenter-paced		p [a]
	Simple	Complex		Simple	Complex	
I	.88	.84	.50	.73	.66	.07
II	.82	.79	.39	.68	.59	.13
III	.71	.65	.50	.63	.59	.30
All			.37			.02

[a]p is the likelihood of observing a difference as large or larger as determined by a sign test.

Experiment II

Experiment II differed from Exp. I mainly in that the paragraphs used were more varied in logical structure as well as length.

Method. Thirty-two students who were paid $1.50 plus a $.05 bonus for each item answered correctly participated in the experiment. Half of the subjects were in the self-paced condition and half in the restricted reading time condition.

Twenty paragraphs differing in subject matter, length (between 24 and 79 units, counting words and punctuation marks), and the type of inference required (e.g., classification, comparison, arithmetic problems, or logical reasoning) were constructed in both simple and complex versions, as in Exp. I. Both versions of a paragraph were of about the same length. Because these paragraphs were of unequal difficulty, and because length seemed to be a major determinant of reading time, the 20 paragraphs were divided into four subsets such that the total number of words in each of the four subsets was about equal. Each subject was administered the four subsets, one under each of the four experimental conditions. A new partition into subsets was constructed for each 4 subjects. A counterbalancing scheme was devised such that over the 16 subjects, each paragraph was represented equally often in all experimental conditions (simple and complex versions, true or false responses). Thus, each subject responded to 20 paragraphs, half of them simple and half complex.

The same procedure as in Exp. I was used, except that subjects responded TRUE or FALSE to the questions and a practice item was discussed in detail before the experiment proper.

In the restricted reading time condition, the time allowed for each paragraph was made proportional to the time taken by the self-paced subjects. The reading time for each paragraph was reduced to about one-third of that used by self-paced subjects. Thus, reading times varied between 5 sec and 16 sec.

Results. As in Exp. I, there was a significant effect of complexity upon reading times, $F(1,15) = 16.6, p < .01$. Table 2 shows that the magnitude of this effect was about the same as observed in Exp. I, with complex paragraphs requiring 14% more reading time. Inference times, on the other hand, were about the same for simple and complex paragraphs. The proportions of correct responses also followed the pattern of Exp. I quite closely (Table 3): More correct responses occurred when reading was self-paced than when reading time was restricted, but there was no statistically reliable difference between simple and complex problems, although the probability of a correct item was again higher for simple than for complex paragraphs, especially in the restricted reading time condition.

Paragraph length was indeed a powerful determinant of both reading time and inference time, which correlated .66 and .50, respectively, with the number of words plus punctuation marks for simple paragraphs.

Experiment III

A third experiment was conducted which was similar in purpose, design, and procedure to the other two, but which differed in the type of materials in that syllogistic arguments were employed in this experiment.

Method. Students from the University of Colorado served as subjects as part of a course requirement. Thirteen subjects were assigned to the self-paced condition and 15 to the restricted reading time condition.

Twelve arguments in the form of classical syllogisms were constructed, each on a different subject. Care was taken that all arguments appeared plausible, or at least conceivable. Arguments consisted of the two premises, plus some logically irrelevant material which was used to conceal the logical structure and to approximately equate length of different problems. The conclusion was always used as the question. Each problem contained three quantifiers from the four used (ALL, NO, SOME, SOME NOT). Half of the arguments were valid and half were invalid. Invalid arguments were obtained by changing a quantifier or the figure of a valid argument. As in Exp. I and II, each argument was constructed in two versions, a syntactically simple one and a complex version.

The same procedure was used as in Exp. II. In the restricted reading time condition, subjects were shown each paragraph for 23 sec (about half of the mean premise exposure time taken by subjects in a pilot study).

Results. The results of Exp. III are also shown in Tables 2 and 3. They agree very well with the results of the earlier experiments. The effect of complexity upon reading times is significant statistically, $F(1, 12) = 8.0, p < .025$, and larger than before (28%). Syllogisms profited even more from a simple syntactic structure than the general problems used earlier. As in the other experiments, the time needed to respond VALID or INVALID to the conclusion of a syllogistic argument was independent of complexity. The proportions of correct responses were always higher for the simple arguments than for the complex ones, but, as before, this difference was not significant statistically.

An incidental but noteworthy result of this study is that the probability of a correct response was not very much above the guessing level. The subjects found correct logical reasoning extremely difficult. Of the four figures of the syllogisms (see, for instance, Hilbert & Ackermann, 1950), the third was significantly easier than the others, and the fourth somewhat harder, $X^2(3) = 9.04, p < .05$. The third figure may have been easier because it is the only one where an argument is repeated in the two premises in such a way that it forms the grammatical subject in both cases.

Discussion

Given the widely different materials used in the three experiments reported here, the agreement of their results permits one to draw conclusions with fair assurance. Paragraphs that are derived from the same logical base, but that differ in the way in which the underlying semantic propositions are expressed linguistically, require less time to read and comprehend if the linguistic structure reflects in a fairly direct way the propositional structure than when a syntactically more complex formulation is used. However, the way in which information is stored in memory appears to be identical in the two cases and independent of the linguistic complexity of the input. This conclusion is based upon the fact that in three different experiments and under both self-paced and experimenter-paced conditions, subjects needed the same amount of time to make inferences from memory, whether the original input paragraphs were simple or complex. Therefore, the information upon which subjects operated to make their inferences must have been available to them in a comparable form for both types of paragraphs. Because of the way the paragraphs were constructed, a representation in memory that is consistent with the experimental results would be a semantic base as suggested in Kintsch (1972a), or something equivalent to it, but it could not be the linguistic surface structure, nor the linguistic deep structure.

If the above interpretation of the observed reading times and inference times is correct, some implications follow for the probability of correct responses under experimental conditions where the reading time is restricted, as was pointed out in the introduction to this report. Restricted reading times should decrease the likelihood of a correct response for complex paragraphs more than for simple paragraphs because the former require more time for comprehension and storage in memory. On the other hand, if reading time is unlimited one might expect no difference in the proportion of correct responses for simple and complex paragraphs because subjects work on a paragraph as long as necessary for complete understanding. As Table 3 shows, these predictions were confirmed only if the evidence from all three experiments is considered together. In none of the separate experiments was the difference between simple and complex paragraphs statistically reliable, though it was always in the expected direction; combining the data from all subjects, though, provides quite convincing evidence in favor of the experimental hypothesis. If reading time was restricted, the likelihood of a correct response was indeed lower for complex than for simple paragraphs, while if reading time was unlimited, this difference was reduced in magnitude and not significant statistically.

The conclusion that information is stored in an abstract semantic form is, of course, restricted to the kind of experimental situation used here. In this experiment, subjects knew that an inference task would be required of them, rather than the recall of the paragraph or something like it. Obviously, subjects can retain verbal and linguistic information in memory if there is some reason to do so. It has only been shown here that subjects can store in memory the logical-semantic content of a paragraph, disregarding the actual form in which it is expressed.

Using quite a different experimental approach Sachs (1967) and Bransford and Franks (1971) have also obtained experimental evidence which indicates that information stored in memory may be independent of its linguistic expression. Furthermore, the present study complements a number of recent reaction time experiments by several authors (e.g., Clark, 1969) which showed that subjects can process simple sentences faster than complex sentences, where complexity was introduced through negation, marked versus unmarked adjectives, changes in prepositions, and the like. In the present case, complexity was entirely a matter of syntactic variation: The semantic transformation did not really add to complexity in any systematic way, it merely made the two paragraph versions different (like saying A IS EAST OF B versus B IS WEST OF A). Thus, the finding that (syntactically) complex paragraphs took longer to read than simple paragraphs is quite in agreement with the observation that (semantically and syntactically) complex sentences require more processing time.

"Reading time" in the present study is somewhat of a misnomer: Much of the processing, probably including the drawing of some obvious inferences, takes place during this "reading." The important point is that when subjects knew that only the logical-semantic information in a paragraph would be needed to make a future inference (and the paragraph was presented visually, so that the load on short-term memory was not unduly great due to the necessity to hold the input), they could and did process the paragraph *on input*, retaining in memory logical-semantic information; this input process took longer for a syntactically complex paragraph than for a simple one, but the end result in memory was apparently the same for both. This finding implies in turn that if subjects are given a complex sentence and then must use this sentence *from memory* in some task, processing times may be quite different, depending upon the exact task requirements. In the experiments of Clark (1969), however, decoding time and inference time were not separated, so that the reaction times reported in these experiments correspond to the reading-plus-inference times of the present study. There is one early study on sentence reaction times as a function of syntactic complexity (McMahon, 1963; see also Slobin, 1966) that is relevant in this connection. McMahon found that reaction time differences due to the grammatical complexity of sentences disappeared if a 10-sec delay was interposed between the reading of a sentence and the presentation of a picture for verification.

Finally, it should be pointed out that Schlesinger (1968) failed to observe effects of syntactic structure upon readability and concluded that what makes reading difficult is, at least in part, a function of content. We believe Schlesinger's conclusion is correct, but the present study provides evidence that even when content is strictly controlled syntactic complexity may retard reading rates.

2. INFERENCE LATENCIES AND PARAGRAPH LENGTH

Experiment IV[3]

Experiment IV followed the design of the earlier studies, but added a new experimental variable: irrelevant information in the paragraph. This information was nontrivial and semantically related to the relevant information in the paragraph, which was logically required to perform the inference task correctly. The irrelevant information increased the number of propositions upon which the text was based, but it was not required for the inference task, nor was it synonymous with any required information. Since the irrelevant information was thematically related to the required information, subjects had no way of knowing beforehand what part of the paragraph, if any, was irrelevant to the subsequent question; they therefore had to process all information with equal care and as well as they could.

There are several questions of interest in this experiment. First, how does the presence of irrelevant information in memory affect response times? If a question based on a paragraph without irrelevant information is answered faster than one based on the paragraph with irrelevant information added, one may assume that subjects had

[3]This experiment is by D. Monk.

to search through the whole memory representation of the paragraph during the inference task. For instance, the paragraph's propositions might be stored as an ordered list and accessed sequentially. On the other hand, if the presence of irrelevant information in a paragraph does not increase inference time, required propositions may be accessed directly, without a search through the whole list. Second, assuming that reading time increases as information is added, to what extent does this increase depend on syntactic complexity? Making syntactically complex paragraphs longer may make reading time disproportionately longer. Finally, the present experiment provides a replication of Exp. I – III, where the syntactic complexity of the input paragraphs had no effects upon inference times.

Method

Design. The unit of irrelevant information defined in this experiment was the clause. Each irrelevant clause embodied a new, plausible, substantive fact which met the following criterion for irrelevancy: The answer to the inference question can be determined easily without such factual information, i.e., it is irrelevant (and not equivalent) to the propositional information that the inference requires. Four conditions, with three observations each, constituted a 2 × 2 within-subjects factorial design in which the variables were complexity and presence of irrelevant information. The two complexity levels were designated simple and complex; the irrelevant information was either absent or contained in two clauses (16 words). The entire within-subjects design was repeated in five different lists of paragraphs which balanced Subject Matter × Condition combinations between subjects. List was the single between-subjects variable. The two conditions in which only relevant information was presented constitute a replication of Exp. I, except for method of administration.

Subjects. Twenty-five undergraduate students at the University of Colorado were recruited with ads posted on campus and in the student newspaper. The sample included 11 males and 14 females. They were each paid $1.50 for participation in the 40-minute experiment.

Materials. Five basic items were constructed from each of three logical skeletons, with an inference statement for each. An item consisted of a sequence of factual statements that implied either the truth or falsity of the inference statement. Each of the 15 basic items was written in five forms, one corresponding to each of the four within-subjects conditions and one having an intermediate syntax level. The latter form was used to collect preliminary data on questions beyond the scope of this report; therefore, items in this fifth form have been treated as unscored fillers in the results reported here. The two forms with no irrelevant information, one grammatically simple and one grammatically complex, contained 46 words relevant to the inference statement. (Most of these paragraphs were used previously in Exp. I.) The two partly irrelevant forms, one simple and one complex, had 62 words each, that is, the 46 relevant words plus two clauses whose contents were irrelevant to the inference question. The two irrelevant clauses were separated, one occurring within each half of the paragraph. The true or false inference statement, the same for all forms of an item, was six words long and grammatically simple.

Three independently randomized 5 × 5 Latin squares, one for each logical skeleton, were used to assign one of the five forms to each basic item for each of five lists. Four practice items and five fillers, which did not conform to the other items in length, complexity, and logical structure, were included in each list to prevent subjects from noticing recurring features of the experimental items. For the order of administration, one restricted random order of the item numbers (subject matter index) was chosen to insure that the practice items came first and that each following group of five paragraphs contained one item in each form and one nonconforming filler. Each list contained three items, one of each logical type, under each of the four conditions; the linguistic form of a given item and Form × Subject Matter combinations varied systematically across lists. There were 24 paragraphs in each list, half of them having correct answer "true," half "false."

Instructions and procedure. The experiment was administered by the Sigma 3 computer operating in the Computer Laboratory for Instruction and Psychological Research of the University of Colorado at Boulder. Each subject was tested individually with one list, and each list was used for five subjects. The subject was taken to a room containing a Xerox Model 7555 typewriter-like keyboard and display screen. Complete instructions for the entire experiment were presented on the screen after the experimenter left the room. The experiment was completely subject-paced. The subject's primary task was to read paragraphs of text and answer a question after each. A small window in the door allowed the experimenter, unseen, to observe the equipment and subject. A paragraph of factual information (with a typing instruction) was displayed until subject typed "r"; the screen was then erased and a true-false statement (with a typing instruction) was displayed until subject typed "t" or "f." If the subject made a typing error, he was asked to respond again. The paragraph and statement exposure times and response for each item were recorded by the computer. After all items in the list were presented, the subject was informed of his score and feedback was presented for missed items.

Results

A summary of the results is given in Table 4. Data from all lists have been pooled, since no significant main effects or interactions involving lists were found in the analyses of number of errors, reading times, or response times. No problems were encountered with the computer program, operation, or interaction with subjects. For comparable conditions the subjects' information-processing times were longer with the computer than with the manual slide presentation of Exp. I.

A total of 300 items, 75 in each condition, were scored. The number of errors was 45 or 15%. Although there were more errors on the complex items than on the simple, neither this difference nor the presence of irrelevant information was significant.

Four means, one for each condition, were computed for each subject from the paragraph exposure times of those items on which his response was correct; each

TABLE 4

Percent Correct, Mean Reading and Inference Times by Condition,
Collapsed Across All Paragraphs

Result	No irrelevant clauses		2 irrelevant clauses	
	Simple	Complex	Simple	Complex
Percent correct	89	83	89	79
Mean paragraph exposure time (sec)	31.6	32.8	38.2	48.9
Mean statement exposure time (sec)	5.7	5.7	7.1	6.1

mean is thus based on from one to three observations. The computed means were treated as the raw data for the statistical analyses, and their means are given in Table 4. A three-way analysis of variance was conducted with list as a between-subjects variable and complexity and number of irrelevant clauses as within-subjects variables.[4] Both the within-subjects variables and their interaction were significant, contributing to paragraph exposure time; list and list interactions were not significant. For complexity, $F(1,19) = 10.90, p < .005$; for irrelevant information, $F(1,19) = 46.87, p < .001$; and for Complexity $\times$ Irrelevant Information, $F(1,19) = 4.67, p < .05$.

Individual subject means of exposure times to the inference statements for items answered correctly were computed for each condition, and a similar analysis of variance was performed. None of the variables had significant main effects or interactions. The obtained F values for complexity and the Complexity $\times$ Length Interaction was less than 1. The length effect resulted in $F(1,19) = 1.18$. Since the nonsignificance of the F values is important for the interpretation of the present results, a power calculation was performed. The reading time for long paragraphs was 35% longer than for short ones. A proportional difference between the inference times would have increased the mean inference time for long paragraphs by about 2 sec. The power of the present experiment to detect such a difference, assuming a 5% significance level, was only about .68.

Discussion

The results of Experiment IV are in complete accord with those of Exp. I–III. Complexity regarding the form in which factual information was presented did not affect the accuracy or speed of its retrieval for use in an inference task, but increased complexity did increase reading time. However, subjects took more time processing computer-presented than slide-presented paragraphs. These data confirm what is quite obvious on inspection of the experimental apparatus: The characters on the slides (made from photographs of typescript prepared on an IBM selectric typewriter)

[4]The number of degrees of freedom for each within-error term was reduced by one to 19 because of the necessity of estimating two individual means for subjects with no correct items in one condition.

were of better quality than those of the computer display screen, which were all capital letters with much poorer resolution. Thus, the increased time was probably used in the perception of the letters themselves.

The significant effect of irrelevant information on reading time in Exp. IV reflects the increased paragraph length due to the irrelevant clauses. Note the strong interaction between complexity and added information. Much more additional reading time was required when irrelevant information was included in the complex version of a paragraph (about 16 sec) than when it was included in the simple version (about 7 sec). The interaction in reading time of length of the paragraph and complexity is consistent with the fact that processing time per proposition recalled increases with the length of the text (Chapter 6) and indicates that some of this increase is normally due to syntactic complexity. However, this relationship needs to be investigated further. In Exp. II, with less well-controlled material but a wider length range, such an interaction was not obtained.

The question of whether the speed of access to a proposition depends upon the total number of other propositions that are stored with it could not be answered conclusively in this experiment. Inference times for paragraphs containing irrelevant information were longer than inference times for paragraphs without the irrelevant information, but the effects observed were not statistically significant, and the power of the test was quite low. Instead of increasing the statistical power of this experiment to acceptable levels, we decided to postpone the problem until Chapter 9, where a more systematic investigation of this question will be made outside the context of inference tasks.

The four experiments reported here have lent substantial support to the conclusion that paragraph memory in these cases consisted of an abstract representation of the content of the paragraph, irrespective of the actual surface form used. We are not asserting that the simple and the complex versions of each paragraph were encoded in precisely the same way, only that there were no systematic differences due to the complexity of the input form. Undoubtedly, there were individual differences between subjects. Indeed, the occasional errors made in evaluating test sentences are an indication that a representation of the paragraph had been formed which differed from the canonical form. The alternative explanation for errors is a failure to make a correct inference, but for the extremely simple materials used here this seems unlikely. It is much more plausible that subjects who made an error worked with an incomplete or erroneous representation of the paragraph.

An important assumption made throughout this work is that subjects made their inferences at the time they were questioned, not during the original reading of the paragraph. We have no conclusive evidence for this claim, but we believe that it is well-founded because of the complexity of the paragraphs used. In general, several different questions could have been asked about each paragraph, and subjects had no way of anticipating any one in particular (except perhaps with the syllogisms in Exp. III). It appears quite unlikely that subjects were trying to form all possible inferences in the 20–30 seconds during which they read a paragraph, and almost impossible when the exposure time was restricted. It would be much easier for subjects to wait for the test sentence, especially since the inferences that were required were all quite trivial and whatever difficulty there was consisted in assimilating correctly and retaining the information presented. The inference statements were not integral parts of the paragraphs. One could read and comprehend each paragraph by itself, without ever considering the inference statement. The inference statement in these paragraphs consisted of an elaboration of the original material, but it was not a necessary component of it that was required for the rest to make sense.

Summary

Given a particular text base, one can construct the corresponding verbal texts in such a way that they will be syntactically simple or complex. For a total of 59 paragraphs, varying in length between 15 and 79 words, both a simple and a complex surface form was given to subjects to read. As expected, subjects took longer to read the complex forms. After reading each paragraph, a test question was given to the subject for a true-false decision. In each case, the truth of the test question could be inferred from the paragraph, but the statement was not directly contained in the paragraph. The main result of the study was that subjects answered the test question equally rapidly after reading simple and complex paragraphs. Since the answer to the test question had to be computed from the memory representation, it was concluded that the memory representation upon which the inferences were based were the same, or at least identical in complexity, for syntactically simple and complex input paragraphs. Thus, memory for meaning appeared to be independent of the actual verbal input, as long as that input was derived from the same text base. This result says little as yet about the nature of the text base—only that a common, abstract base exists. The next chapter will explore some of the postulated characteristics of such text bases.

6

THE PSYCHOLOGICAL REALITY
OF TEXT BASES
I: READING RATE AND
COMPREHENSION[1]

The studies reported in the previous chapter add to the already considerable evidence that sentences and prose material, in general, are not stored in memory verbatim but are coded as to their content. The next question is much more difficult to answer and much more controversial, namely, what, precisely, is the format of encoding for content? Clearly, no one today can give a completely satisfactory answer to this question. The purpose of the present chapter is to provide some experimental evidence in favor of the propositional model advocated here. An attempt will be made to show that the propositional base structure of a sentence has predictable empirical effects upon behavior. Such a demonstration is of crucial importance if the speculations that have been offered about semantic memory are to be taken seriously as a psychological model.

The experiment was designed to determine whether the number of propositions in the base structure of a sentence is an important psychological variable. In particular, sentences that differed in the number of underlying propositions, but which were equal in terms of total number of words, were given to subjects to read and to recall immediately after reading. A second set of sentences and paragraphs, in which number of words and number of propositions covaried, was also used in order to study the number of propositions over a wider range. With the number of words per sentence controlled, propositions varied from 4 to 9; with the second set of sentences, propositions varied from 2 to 23. If number of propositions is an effective psychological variable, reading time should increase as more propositions are processed;

[1]This research has been published as "Reading rate and retention as a function of the number of the propositions in the base structure of sentences," *Cognitive Psychology,* 1973, **5**, 257–274, by W. Kintsch and Janice M. Keenan. It is reproduced here with the permission of Academic Press. Some slight changes have been made. Additional material from this publication is presented in Chapter 7.

likewise, the number of propositions subjects are able to recall should be related to processing time in a lawful way. Of course, by averaging over all kinds of different propositions and looking only at the effect of the total number of propositions, many potentially significant sources of variance are being neglected. In addition to the mere number of propositions, the nature and number of their arguments, their complexity, structural relations among them, lexical factors, and many other properties might be important determinants of reading speed and comprehensibility. In the studies reported here, all of these factors vary unsystematically. Thus, the difficulty that each proposition presents is certainly not a constant, but a random variable with an appreciable variance. Nevertheless, as long as one deals with averages, the number of propositions upon which a text is based should have a strong and significant effect, if the proposition is indeed the proper unit of analysis for studies concerned with the processing and storage of linguistic information.

Some subjects were allowed to study each sentence or paragraph as long as they wanted; their reading time was one of the major dependent variables of interest for the present study. Other subjects, however, were given only a limited reading time. Their recall was compared with that of unrestricted subjects, and a processing model that captures some of the most salient features of both sets of data was developed.

Method

Subjects. In the free reading-time condition, 23 undergraduates from the University of Colorado served as subjects. They were fulfilling part of a course requirement. For the restricted reading-time condition, 44 students were each paid $2.00 for their participation.

Material. Two sets of materials were constructed for this experiment. Set A consisted of 10 sentences 16–17 words long (counting punctuation marks). The sentences were not related to each other; most of them dealt with topics from classical history. This choice of topics was made in an attempt to hold the relative familiarity of the text to a minimum, while avoiding problems of vocabulary concomitant with equally unfamiliar but more technical material.

Although word length in these sentences was fairly strictly controlled, the number of propositions upon which each sentence was based varied between four and nine. Two sample sentences, together with the propositions from which they were constructed and the hierarchical relationships that exist among these propositions, are shown in Table 1. The analysis into propositions was made according to the theory described in Chapter 2. Propositions have been numbered solely for the purpose of identification in the graphs showing the hierarchical relations among them. As described in Chapter 2, these hierarchical relations are implicit in the order in which propositions are written: A proposition β is subordinated to another proposition α if α precedes β in the list of propositions and if α and β have at least one term (relation or argument) in common.

One of the major problems in work of this type is that no algorithmic procedure exists to analyze a given sentence (or paragraph) into its propositional base structure. However, for present purposes the problem can be circumvented in the following

TABLE 1

Two Sample Sentences from Set A (Sentences I and VIII), Together with their Propositional Analyses

	I.	Romulus, the legendary founder of Rome, took the women of the Sabine by force.
1		(TOOK,ROMULUS,WOMEN, BY FORCE)
2		(FOUND,ROMULUS,ROME)
3		(LEGENDARY,ROMULUS)
4		(SABINE,WOMEN)
	VIII.	Cleopatra's downfall lay in her foolish trust in the fickle political figures of the Roman world.
1		(BECAUSE,α,β)
2		(FELL DOWN,CLEOPATRA) = α
3		(TRUST,CLEOPATRA,FIGURES) = β
4		(FOOLISH,TRUST)
5		(FICKLE,FIGURES)
6		(POLITICAL,FIGURES)
7		(PART OF,FIGURES,WORLD)
8		(ROMAN,WORLD)

way: One can start with the propositional expressions themselves and translate these into English text. The rules for doing so are simpler and are somewhat better understood, although they do not really exist in explicit form either. At least very substantial agreement could be obtained that the sentences used are indeed one way to express the meaning of the coordinated propositions.

Set B consisted of 20 sentences or paragraphs in which the number of underlying propositions and the number of words were confounded. The shortest sentence contained seven words in two propositions; the longest paragraphs were based upon 22 propositions, requiring 58 words, and 23 propositions, requiring 45 words. All sentences in Set B were definitions and descriptions of psychological terms, modified from the glossaries of several psychological texts, and thus dealt with relatively unfamiliar topics.

Procedure. Free reading: Slides were made for all sentences and paragraphs. The subject was seated about 3 m in front of a screen on which the slides were shown by means of a Kodak Carousel projector. The experimenter, who was seated behind the subject, exposed a slide and simultaneously started a Hunter Timer. In front of the subject there was a box with two labeled response buttons: an Advance slide button and a Finish button. The subject was instructed to read the sentence carefully and to press the Advance button in front of him when he was finished. This response stopped the timer, started a second timer, and removed the sentence from the screen. The subject then recalled the sentence he had just seen in writing. Each sentence was written on a separate page of a booklet. When the subject finished writing, he pressed the Finish button which stopped the second timer and turned on an indicator light at the experimenter's console. After recording the results, the experimenter made sure that the subject had turned to a new page and had put his finger on the Advance button; the experimenter then gave the subject a "Ready" signal and started the next trial.

One warm-up problem preceded the 30 experimental trials. New random orders of the experimental slides were constructed for every three subjects. The instructions emphasized that exact wording was not as important as the meaning of the sentences, and the subjects were asked to work as fast as possible, keeping in mind that the important thing was how much they remembered, not speed.

Restricted reading time: The procedure was identical to that used in the free reading-time condition, except that the sentence slide was exposed only for a certain predetermined amount of time, and the subjects disregarded the Advance button. The exposure time for each sentence was made proportional to its length in terms of the number of words. In the free-reading condition, the over-all average reading time per word was .97 sec. A third of that, .33 sec, was taken as the exposure time per word for the restricted reading-time condition. The choice of one-third was made because it had been observed in earlier work (Chapter 5) that restrictions of that magnitude still allowed the subjects to read through a text under normal circumstances but were severe enough to produce noticeable behavioral effects. Thus, each sentence of Set A was exposed for 5 sec. For Set B, exposure times increased from 2 sec for the shortest sentences to 19 sec for the longest paragraph.

Results

Sentence Set A. The subjects' recall protocols for the 10 sentences in Set A were scored for propositional recall. For each protocol it was determined which of the propositions were recalled. Paraphrases of the original wording were accepted as correct, as long as the propositional meaning was accurately expressed. If a subject made an error in a superordinate proposition which then reappeared in a subordinate proposition, which was otherwise correct, the subordinate proposition was accepted as correctly recalled, while the superordinate proposition itself was scored as incorrect. For example, suppose a subject recalled Sentence I as *Romulus took the Sabine cities by force.* Proposition 1 was scored as incorrect because of the substitution of *cities* for *women*, but Proposition 4 was scored as correct. Although the subject had made an error in the superordinate proposition, he had recalled correctly that, whatever the superordinate proposition was concerned with, it was *Sabine.* Scoring was done independently by the two authors who agreed in 95.2% of all recall protocols. All disagreements, most of which were simply errors by one or the other scorer, could be resolved in conference.

Mean reading times as a function of the number of propositions in the base structure of the sentences are shown in Fig. 1. A least square line,

$$t = 6.37 + .94 P_{pres} \tag{1}$$

is also shown. For these sentences, which were all of the same length, the subjects took about one additional second reading time per proposition. The subjects did not, however, always recall a sentence perfectly. Since there probably was very little, if any, forgetting with the brief sentences in Set A, one can assume therefore that the subjects did not always process all the propositions in a sentence as they were presented. Thus, a better estimate of the reading time needed by subjects to process propositions can be obtained if reading time is computed as a function of the number of propositions that the subjects were actually able to recall on each trial, irrespective

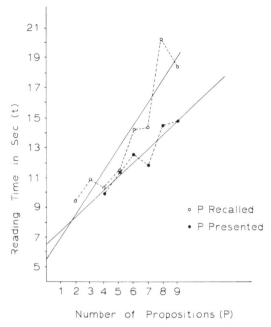

FIG. 1. Mean reading time for the sentences of Set A as a function of the number of propositions in the base structure of the sentences as presented and as a function of the number of propositions recalled by the subjects, together with least square lines.

of how many propositions a sentence contained. These data are also shown in Fig. 1. It is clear that if propositions recalled rather than propositions presented are considered, the dependence of reading time upon number of propositions in a sentence is even more pronounced. The least square line in this case is

$$t = 5.53 + 1.48 P_{rec}, \tag{2}$$

which means that every proposition processed required about 1.5 sec additional reading time. An analysis of variance confirmed this effect to be statistically reliable. The average reading times for each subject were computed, providing the subject recalled 2/3, 4, 5, 6, 7, or 8/9 propositions. The F value for Propositions was $F(5,112) = 10.9, p \leq .01$ (the degrees of freedom for the error term take into account some missing cell entries). A trend analysis revealed most of this effect to be due to deviations from linear trend (87% of the variance associated with propositions, which was highly significant), while quadratic and higher order trends resulted in F values less than one. Estimating the proportion of the total within-subject variance of the reading times that were accounted for by linear regression upon the number of propositions recalled produced est. $\omega^2 = .21$.

Mean reading times were also computed separately for those instances where the subjects recalled a complete sentence correctly, and where they recalled only some of the propositions of a sentence. There was no systematic difference between these two sets of data, which justifies lumping them together as was done in Fig. 1.

Figure 2 allows a comparison between recall after free-reading and limited-reading time. The free-reading data are partly implied by the results already discussed: Equations (1) and (2) can be combined to obtain a relationship between the number of propositions presented and recalled. This relationship is shown as the broken line in Fig. 2. Obviously, it describes the actual data quite well, although its slope (.64) somewhat underestimates the least squares value (.69). Number of propositions presented and mean number recalled correlate $r = .91$ in the data shown. This high value is not quite matched by the data from the restricted reading condition where an $r = .74$ was obtained. When reading time was limited recall was not as good as when reading time was free, and this difference was greatest for the most difficult sentences, that is, those based upon a large number of propositions. However, the same kind of relationship between propositions presented and propositions recalled appears to hold for both conditions.

Sentence Set B. In Fig. 3 the mean reading times for each of the 20 sentences of Set B are shown as a function of the number of propositions actually recalled. Figure 3 thus corresponds to Fig. 1, except that each curve is based upon only one-tenth as much data. Because the sentences of Set B differed in length, the data from different sentences could not be averaged as in Set A. In order to obtain stable data, the functions shown in Fig. 3 have been Vincentized. For each sentence the average reading time was determined separately for those trials on which few propositions were recalled (lower 50%, or as close to that as was possible) and for those trials on which many (upper 50%) propositions were recalled. For 19 of the 20 sentences the reading time is longer when more propositions have been recalled than when few propositions have been recalled. Since each curve is based on only one sentence, the number of words as well as syntax are fixed; what differs is the amount of processing done by a subject, as indexed by his ability to reproduce the content of the sentence immediately after reading it. In almost every case more recall meant longer reading times. There is also an indication that as the sentences and paragraphs became longer, the slope of the functions relating the reading time and the number of propositions recalled increases. For the 16-word sentences of Set A, the subjects needed about 1.5 sec per proposition. For the shortest sentences in Set B, those 10 words or less, 1.3 sec were required per proposition recalled. However, for the longest paragraphs (43–58 words) the subjects needed an average of 4.3 sec extra reading time to process a proposition.

The relationship between the number of propositions upon which a sentence or paragraph was based and the average number of propositions that the subjects recalled from that sentence is shown in Fig. 4. For the free-reading condition, the results look much like those obtained for Sentence Set A; there is a strong positive relationship between number of propositions presented and recalled ($r = .86$). The relationship may not be linear, but at least for the range represented here, the subjects are still able to recall more when they are presented with more. When reading time is restricted, however, this is no longer the case. Except perhaps for the first few points, which are close to perfect recall, there is no noticeable relationship between the number of propositions in a sentence and the amount recalled ($r = .23$, which is not statistically significant). This lack of a relationship occurred in spite of the fact that reading time

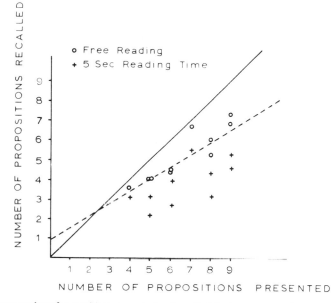

FIG. 2. Mean number of propositions presented and recalled for the sentences of Set A. The predictions for the free-reading data are shown by the broken line (for explanation see text).

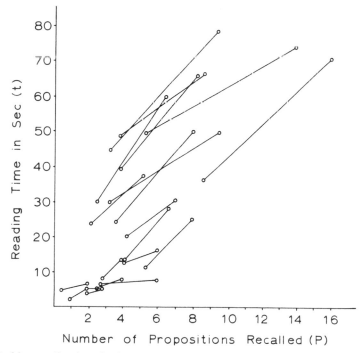

FIG. 3. Mean reading times for the 20 sentences of Set B as a function of the number of propositions recalled. The data for each sentence are shown as Vincent curves.

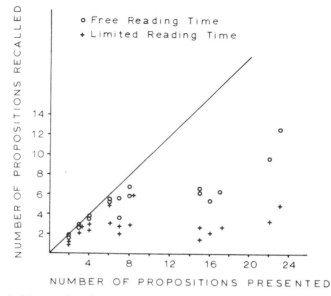

FIG. 4. Mean number of sentences presented and recalled for the sentences of Set B.

was longer for the longer paragraphs in proportion to the number of words. Obviously, proportionality was not enough: Processing rates decrease more rapidly. Such a result is precisely what one would expect from the free reading data shown in Fig. 3. The slopes and intercepts of the functions in Fig. 3 increase quite dramatically as a function of the length of a sentence, so that giving subjects the same amount of time per word irrespective of total length, as was done here, should not be sufficient for effective processing for the longer sentences. A third of a second per word was quite enough for the shortest sentences, but for the longer paragraphs several times as much would have been required per word to achieve an equivalent level of processing.

Discussion

The purpose of this experiment was to determine whether the number of propositions in the semantic base of a sentence affects the time required by subjects to read that sentence and store it in memory. As Figs. 1 and 3 demonstrate, reading time is indeed a monotonically increasing function of the number of propositions being processed. These data extend beyond earlier results, which merely demonstrated the existence and psychological importance of semantic base structures, in that they support a particular type of semantic model, namely, one based upon a propositional analysis. Thus, the interest in the present study was not in the basic empirical finding, namely, the longer the study time for a sentence, the better the recall. On the contrary, this relationship may well be assumed to be true in general. The fact that it was possible to maintain this relationship, using the particular analysis of both the text and the recall protocols into propositional units as postulated by the model, may be taken as support for the model. Of course, there may be alternative models and there may be alternative ways to analyze these data. We shall not explore these possibilities here; it is enough to present one feasible approach, given the current lack of satisfactory methods of analyzing comprehension and recall of natural language text.

Are the present data informative enough to permit some inferences as to how information is processed and stored during reading? The general problem is much too complicated and will require extensive research; but the data do offer a reasonable way of approaching the problem and permit the formulation of some simple hypotheses. A rudimentary information-processing model can be constructed to account for some aspects of the reading process. In presenting this model we shall limit the discussion to the data from Sentence Set A. These sentences have been selected because the assumption of constant processing rates appears to hold for them, according to Fig. 1.

Let us accept Fig. 1 as the basis for building the model. We can represent Fig. 1 by

$$t_i = a + bP_i, \tag{3}$$

where t_i is the mean reading time for Sentence i, P_i is the number of propositions upon which Sentence i is based, and a and b are constants. Equation (3) suggests that reading time may be decomposed into two factors: b sec for each proposition read, plus a constant of a sec mean duration. As a psychological interpretation of this equation, one can hypothesize the following. The a sec are a time during which an overall evaluation of the sentence is made, part of which certainly includes syntactic parsing. During each of the b sec periods, a proposition is being processed. Note that it is not necessary that all of the a sec for general analysis precede the processing of separate propositions.

Now let us assume that the processing times for each proposition are exponentially distributed with rate $1/b = \lambda$. This assumption is chosen merely because it is the simplest one known for workable reaction-time models. The total processing times for Sentence i would then be composed of a constant plus a gamma distribution with parameters λ and P_i. However, since the subjects may, and do, stop reading at any time, the observable reading time distributions are truncated in unknown ways. This problem could be avoided by considering only the reading times for perfectly recalled sentences, but in the present data, the frequency of such events is much too small to permit an analysis of reading time distributions.

A more practical approach may be taken by noting that if a subject reads a sentence based upon P propositions for time $(t - a)$ with rate λ, the likelihood that he will have processed x propositions during this time is a Poisson variable with a parameter $\lambda(t - a)$. But by Eq. (3) and the definition of λ,

$$\lambda(t - a) = \lambda(t - t + bP) = \lambda bP = \lambda\frac{1}{\lambda}P = P,$$

so that

$$\Pr(x;P) = \frac{e^{-P}P^x}{x!} \qquad \text{if } x < P, \tag{4a}$$

$$\Pr(x = P;P) = \sum_{x=P}^{\infty} \frac{e^{-P}P^x}{x!}. \tag{4b}$$

Hence one can calculate the likelihood of recall of 0, 1, 2, . . ., P_i propositions for each sentence simply by referring to tables of the Poisson distribution. Equation (4) is concerned with the performance of the average subject since the mean reading time t_i has been used in place of a distribution with considerable variance. But in spite of this simplifying step, Eq. (4) can be used to predict mean recall. Of course, this model is seriously incomplete: It treats all propositions alike, and thus predicts that all sentences of equal word length and of equal number of propositions should be, on the average, equally well-remembered. This is obviously false, but within the design of the present experiment such variability must be treated as error, to the detriment of goodness-of-fit tests.

In actual fact, this means that the model can be tested only on the basis of data averaged over sentences, so that sentence idiosyncrasies may have a chance to cancel each other out. The problem of how to average over recall distributions differing in the number of propositions has been solved in Fig. 5 in the usual way, namely, by Vincentizing into quartiles. Predicted and observed recall distributions show a reasonable degree of overlap, but the fit is by no means perfect (the Kolmogorov-Smirnov test detects a significant difference at the .01 level). The source of the problem is easy to see: There are not as many instances of perfect (or near perfect) recall as predicted. This is, however, exactly the kind of deviation from predictions that would be obtained on the basis of individual differences in recallability of propositions. Since some propositions are difficult to recall, especially in the longer sentences, perfect recall will be rarer than if all propositions were of equal difficulty.

The extension of the model to the restricted reading-time condition is straightforward. If a person reads for exactly 5 sec the probability that he will have processed exactly x propositions, given a sentence i that consists of a total of P_i propositions, is

$$\text{Pr}_i(x;\tau(5 - c)) = \frac{e^{-\tau(5 - c)}((5 - c)\tau)^x}{x!} \quad \text{if } x < P_i \tag{5a}$$

$$\text{Pr}_i(x = P_i;\tau(5 - c)) = \sum_{x = P_i}^{\infty} \frac{e^{-\tau(5 - c)}((5 - c)\tau)^x}{x!}. \tag{5b}$$

Note that no assumptions about parameter constancy during free reading and restricted reading are made and that new parameters c and τ (corresponding to a and λ) are introduced in Eq. (5). To assume parameter constancy in this case would be quite absurd: Subjects have only 5 sec to read each sentence, but the intercept in Fig. 1 was about that much, so unless the subjects speed up their processing rates they could not read the sentences at all.

Unlike Eq. (4), where the parameters could be predicted from an independent set of data, c and τ must be estimated from the observed distributions of the number of propositions recalled. Before doing so, however, attention should be called to a very striking feature of Eq. (5): It predicts that the likelihood of recalling x propositions, as long as x is less than the total number of propositions in the sentence, is the same for all sentences, independent of the actual total number of propositions. In other words, the probability of correctly recalling 4 propositions from a sentence that contains a

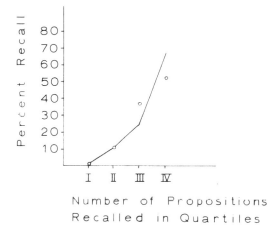

FIG. 5. Predicted (line) and observed (circles) distributions of the number of propositions recalled for the sentences of Set A, free-reading time.

total of 5 propositions is the same as the probability of recalling exactly 4 propositions from a sentence that contains 9 propositions. Unfortunately this strong prediction is not testable because of the incompleteness of the model. As already mentioned, the model deals only with the number of propositions upon which a sentence is based and disregards differences between individual propositions. Hence, if one tests the adequacy of Eq. (5a), deviations from expected values may occur not because the model is wrong, but simply because of its obvious incompleteness.

If the partial recall data from all sentences are pooled, and if Eq. (5a) is fitted to the pooled data by means of a minimum chi-square procedure, the fit obtained is quite good, as is shown in Fig. 6. The minimum chi-square is 14.44, so that for 8 df, $p >$ .05. The estimate for the rate parameter $\tau(5\text{-}c)$ is 4.2. If this estimate is used in Eq. (5b), the proportions of complete recall for each sentence can also be predicted. Both predictions and data are also shown in Fig. 6. Obviously, these predictions are poor. This is because the data are based upon much fewer observations than the partial recall data, and each point was obtained from only one or two sentences, thus again introducing sentence-specific effects. Note, however, that the prediction (and observation) that the likelihood of complete recall decreases as the number of underlying propositions increases in a sentence agrees loosely with the results reported by Perfetti (1969). Perfetti found that sentences with a high lexical density, a statistic correlated with, though not identical to, number of propositions, were recalled more poorly than sentences with low lexical density. There are many other procedural and scoring differences between Perfetti's study and the present experiment, but the consistency of the results should not be overlooked.

From $\tau(5\text{-}c) = 4.2$ one can obtain somewhat speculative estimates of c and τ, if one is willing to assume that the relationship between slope and intercept that was observed in Fig. 1 holds true even if reading time is restricted. Thus, if the intercept is about 4 times the slope, τ becomes 1.64, which compares with $\lambda = .68$ for the free

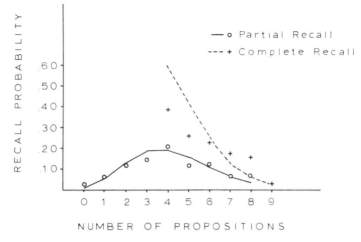

FIG. 6. Predicted (lines) and observed (circles and crosses) recall probabilities for sentence Set A, 5 sec reading time. The partial recall data are averaged over all sentences. The complete recall data are based upon either one or two sentences and have been smoothed by taking running triplet means.

reading data. In other words, while the subjects took about 1.5 sec per proposition if reading time was unlimited, only .61 sec per proposition was needed when each sentence was exposed for 5 sec.

Clearly, no information-processing model will be satisfactory unless differences among propositions are taken into account. However, this limitation, which is inherent not only in the model but in the whole design of the present study, should not detract from the positive accomplishments. Number of propositions, although by no means the whole story, has proven to be a useful independent variable for the analysis of both reading time and recall data. One of the next steps will be to account explicitly for at least some differences among propositions. Indeed, although this experiment was not designed for this purpose, some of the subsidiary results to be discussed in Chapter 7 will provide interesting clues about some characteristics of propositions that are probably important.

The role of the syntactic complexity of the material used in the present study needs to be examined further. It has been shown in an earlier study (Chapter 5) that syntactic complexity may slow down the reading rate, even if propositional content is held constant. One could therefore argue that the results shown in Fig. 1 may be due, at least in part, to a confounding with syntactic complexity. Increasing the number of propositions in a sentence while holding constant the number of words is necessarily accompanied by an increase in syntactic complexity. Thus, syntactic factors may have been partly responsible for the effects shown in Fig. 1. That such factors cannot wholly, or even largely, be responsible is shown by the data in Fig. 3, where reading time is plotted separately for each sentence. Each curve in Fig. 3 is based upon the same material, so that syntax, as well as the number of words, cannot explain the effects shown.

The data suggest that the processing time per proposition depends upon the length of the text being read. For the briefest sentences used in this experiment, the subjects required little more than 1 sec reading time per proposition, while for 50-word paragraphs about three times as much processing time was required per proposition. It may be that as the length of a text increases, each proposition must be related to more and more others in the text, which could produce such an effect. Furthermore, interpretations that correlate the increase in reading difficulty with the length of the text are complicated by the possibility that, for the longer paragraphs, some material that had actually been processed might have been forgotten before it could be written down.

The relationship between the present results and the large literature on readability should also be discussed. Chall (1958) reviewed the somewhat meager results of these studies. Readability, as measured by comprehension tests or simply by subjective judgment, seems to be mainly a question of vocabulary diversity and rarity and sentence length. Attempts to show that "idea density" contributes to reading difficulty have been generally unsuccessful. This has probably been the case because the measures used for "idea density" have been arbitrary and theoretically unfounded (for instance, the most successful index has been the relative number of prepositional phrases in a text). Chall asks, "Can one actually dismiss the entire problem of difficulty as one of hard or long words and long sentences?" He clearly does not want to do so, but he lacks a means for quantifying the relevant aspects of a text. More recently, Schlesinger (1968) has shown that sentence length *per se* is not an important variable if some concomitant factors, such as sentence structure and number of words, are controlled. His attempts to show that syntactic factors are important determinants of readability, however, have been largely negative, and he concludes that complexity is primarily a function of content. If one is willing to accept reading rate as an index of readability, the present results hold some promise that more appropriate quantitative measures of content difficulty can be found. The number of propositions in a text seems to be one such measure, though, as has been mentioned above, the particular type of proposition as well as structural relations among propositions also play important roles which future research will have to specify.

Summary

The most obvious characteristic of a text base that offers itself for measurement is the total number of propositions in the base. Although all propositions do not contribute equally, the number of propositions in a text base may be regarded as a crude measure of the amount of content information in the text. Since in list-learning studies the amount of study time needed to memorize a list is proportional to the length of the list, the amount of time required to read and remember a paragraph should be proportional to the number of propositions in its base. An experiment to test this prediction was performed by giving subjects sentences to read which were all about 16 words long, but varied in the number of underlying propositions from 4 to 9. The number of propositions recalled by the subjects immediately after reading was considered a measure of the amount of comprehension. Reading time was found to be a linear function of this measure: For each proposition processed, subjects required an additional 1.5 sec reading time. Further work revealed that the amount of processing time per proposition was not constant, but depended upon the total length of the text, varying from little more than 1 sec for 10-word sentences up to 4 sec for 50-word paragraphs. By being able to relate an experimental variable, reading time in this case, to one of our key theoretical concepts, the number of propositions in a text base, we have confirmed experimentally a prediction derived from the theory. In addition, the measure of the amount of content in a paragraph may hold some promise for further research on reading.

7
THE PSYCHOLOGICAL REALITY
OF TEXT BASES.
II: SENTENCE MEMORY

Up to now, we have treated propositions as if they were all equal. In this chapter, some investigations of the differences in recallability between various kinds of propositions will be reported. There are two different aspects of that problem: Propositions may be different because of the role they play in a text base, that is, the proposition hierarchy, as such, may determine the recallability of propositions, independent of their properties as individual propositions. Secondly, the number and type of arguments that a proposition has might influence how easy or hard it is to recall, even when its role in the text base as a whole is controlled. As for the first question, it turns out that an analysis of the recall data cited in the previous chapter provides some rather striking insights, in spite of the fact that the experiment had not been designed for this purpose. In order to investigate the second question, two new experiments will be reported below.

1. RECALL OF PROPOSITIONS AS A FUNCTION OF THEIR POSITION IN THE HIERARCHICAL STRUCTURE[1]

In the experiment reported in Chapter 6, subjects recalled 80% of the propositions correctly when reading was self-paced. Given the design of that experiment, one cannot, of course, specify the cause of the errors. It may be a failure of processing, or forgetting, or a combination of both. Therefore, only correct responses will be discussed here. The percentage of propositions recalled of those actually presented was independent of either the total number of propositions in each sentence, the total

---

[1] After "Reading rate and retention as a function of the number of propositions in the base structure of sentences," W. Kintsch and J. Keenan, *Cognitive Psychology*, 1973, **5**, 257 – 274, used with the permission of Academic Press.

number of terms appearing in the propositions for each sentence, or the reading time for that sentence. However, which propositions were recalled was by no means random. The hierarchical relationships among the propositions in each sentence were a powerful determinant of recall. There are two obvious ways to quantify these hierarchies. One is to consider the rank of each proposition in a sentence, with the most superordinate proposition assigned rank 0, the immediately subordinate proposition rank 1, etc. Thus, in Sentence VIII of Table 1 (Ch. 6) Proposition 1 would have rank 0; Propositions 2 and 3 would have rank 1; Propositions 4, 5, and 7 would have rank 2; and Propositions 6 and 8 would be assigned rank 3. The likelihood of an error was computed for all propositions as a function of rank thus defined and is shown in Fig. 1. Of course, propositions of high rank must necessarily come from sentences with many propositions. In order to avoid possible selection effects, the propositions of each sentence were divided into two classes — low and high rank. When rank was Vincentized in this way, the decrease in the likelihood of a correct recall was still correlated with rank: Recall was 86% for the superordinate propositions and 74% for the subordinate propositions.

A second way of quantifying propositional hierarchies is to count the number of descendants for each proposition. For example, in Sentence VIII, Proposition 1 has 7 descendants, Proposition 3 has 5 descendants, Propositions 5 and 7 have 1 descendant each, while Propositions 2, 4, 6, and 8 have no descendants. Calculating recall as a function of number of descendants also reveals a strong tendency for propositions with fewer descendants to be recalled more poorly. Propositions with 0–2 descendants were recalled 76% of the time, while propositions with 3 or more descendants were recalled 90% of the time. The two analyses in terms of rank and descendants were combined as shown in Fig. 1 by computing separately recall of propositions as a function of their rank for propositions with and without descendants (about half of all propositions did not have descendants). While the probability of recall was strongly influenced by rank, the number of descendants had no effect upon recall if rank was controlled.

Several other factors were found to be important determinants of the recall likelihood of a proposition. For instance, many propositions appear in the surface structure as adjectival or adverbial modifiers. The error rate for those propositions is an astounding 30%. On the other hand, proper names were used as modifiers in the experimental sentences quite frequently, and the error rate for such modifiers was a very low 8%. Neither of these effects is due exclusively to rank.

The results from the restricted reading-time condition were quite similar to the free-reading results, as is shown in Fig. 2. In both cases, the likelihood that a proposition would be recalled correctly decreased quite considerably as a function of rank. The over-all likelihood of recall was, of course, much less when the reading time per sentence was restricted to 5 sec than when the reading time was subject controlled, but the decrease in recall probability as a function of rank holds equally for both conditions. Note that the data for both conditions are based upon the same sentence material.

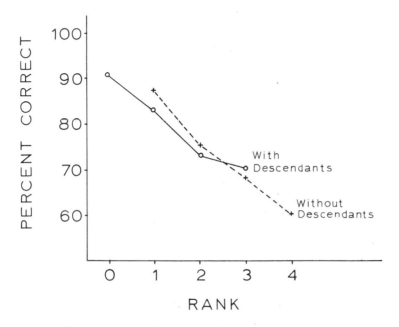

FIG. 1. Recall as a function of rank and number of descendants.

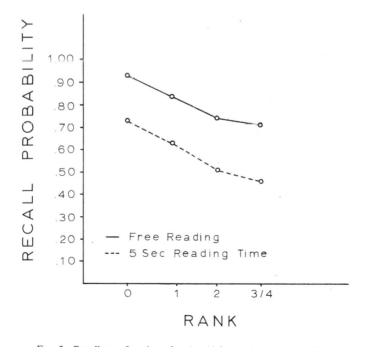

FIG. 2. Recall as a function of rank and free and restricted reading time.

That superordinate propositions were recalled better than propositions that were low in the sentence hierarchies is reminiscent of an observation reported by Johnson (1970). Johnson found that sentence constituents (defined objectively but atheoretically) that were rated as important for the structure of the whole text were also recalled best. However, in the present experiment a theoretically motivated analysis has replaced the judgment of raters.

Crothers (1972) has also investigated recall probability as a function of the hierarchical structure in a paragraph, but in his study, superordinate material was not recalled any better than subordinate material. However, Crothers' analysis of paragraph structure is quite different from a propositional analysis. Superordinate concepts in his analysis tend to be fairly abstract generalizations and are not, as in Johnson (1970) and the present study, chunks of the actual text. Therefore, Crothers' results are probably not comparable with the present data.

What has been reported here is an incidental result, which turned up in a study designed for quite different purposes. It is a surprisingly clean and unambiguous result, and it is certainly worth noting. It is, however, equally certain that this will not be the last word on the question of hierarchical relationships among propositions and recall, if for no other reason than that we dealt here with 16-word sentences, and therefore a level of complexity that is minimal compared to even a paragraph of moderate length.

2. EFFECTS OF PROPOSITIONAL STRUCTURE UPON SENTENCE RECALL[2]

The two experiments reported here have a common procedure, differing only in the type of learning material used. In each experiment, the subject listened to a block of five sentences and then recalled as much as he could about these sentences in writing. The five sentences all have the same structure, but the sentence structure was varied between blocks, in an attempt to explore how this variable affects recall. Structure here does not refer primarily to syntactic structure, though that also varied. Rather, the important variable was propositional structure. Some sentences were generated from one underlying proposition, with both the number of arguments and their nature as variables. As far as the former is concerned, it is quite easy to make predictions: Recall should certainly depend upon the number of arguments. In list-learning studies, recall measured in terms of number of words recalled increases with list length, while at the same time, the percentage of words recalled decreases. One would have every reason to expect analogous results from sentence-learning experiments, with the number of content words in a sentence (that is, arguments plus predicators) corresponding to list length. More interesting questions can be asked about sentences having the same number of content words but differing in structure. Two such structural differences will be explored here. First of all, for sentences based upon one proposition only, the case role of the arguments might affect recall.

[2]By W. Kintsch and G. Glass.

Secondly, it is possible to vary the number of propositions in the sentence base while keeping the number of content words in the sentence the same. The question of greatest interest concerns the possible differential effects of these two types of structural variations. As far as the case role of the arguments is concerned, there is no theoretical reason why it should affect sentence recallability, but neither are such effects precluded: The theory is simply not specific enough concerning this point. But even in the absence of an elaborate psychological process model the theory clearly implies that the number of propositions in the base structure of a sentence should affect recall. It should be easier to store one proposition than two or three, even though the number of content words may be the same. A single proposition with, say, four content words should make a better unit for memory than a sentence based upon two or three propositions with the same number of content words in the surface structure. For example, *The policeman issued the driver a summons* has four content words and is based upon a single proposition, with an agent, a goal, and an object as arguments. On the other hand, *The crowded passengers squirmed uncomfortably* also has four content words but derives from three propositions, *The passengers squirmed, The passengers were crowded,* and *The squirming was uncomfortable.* If this analysis is correct, the second sentence should be harder to recall, and more specifically, should be recalled less frequently as a unit than the earlier example.

Specific experimental predictions can best be described by means of Table 1, which summarizes the design of the experiments. The comparisons of major interest in Exp. I were those between sentences containing three content words based upon one or two propositions (that is, VAO versus $P_1 \& P_2$), and those between sentences containing four content words containing one or three propositions (that is, $VAOG/VAOI$ versus $P_1 \& P_2 \& P_3$). In addition, the experiment also permitted a comparison between sentences varying in number of content words (from two to four) and those varying in number of propositions (from one to three).

Experiment II is an extension of the first study. The major comparison is again between one- and two-proposition sentences, this time all containing four content words ($VAOI$ versus $VAOL/VAOT/P_1 \& P_2$). The $VAOI$ sentences are the same ones as in Exp. I, to ensure comparability between the two studies, but the two-proposition sentences are quite different now: They are sentences containing a locative or time case or sentences based upon two coordinated propositions. To treat locatives and times as separate propositions is, of course, not a generally accepted practice, but arguments in favor of such a procedure were discussed at length in Chapter 3. The present experiment provides an experimental test of the validity of these arguments: Will $VAOL$ and $VAOT$ sentences behave more like one-proposition sentences or more like two-proposition sentences in a free recall experiment?

The final two groups of sentences in Exp. II are both passive sentences. Indeed, the $VAOG$ sentences are simply the passive versions of the corresponding sentences of Exp. I. These sentences were included in order to throw some light on otherwise neglected factors which, however, may be quite important in recall. In particular, the sentences in Exp. I were all constructed in such a way that the agent was also the grammatical subject of the sentence as well as the theme of the sentence (Halliday,

1967). By using some passive sentences, these roles could be at least in part separated: The theme of a passive *VAOG* sentence is no longer its agent but its object. Will the recall pattern be alike for active and passive *VAOG* sentences, or will there be significant changes? Specifically, will the theme of the sentence be preferred in recall, independent of its case role?

Experiment I

Subjects. Twenty-six undergraduates from the University of Colorado participated in this experiment as part of a course requirement.

Materials. The six sentence types used are as shown in Table 1. There were 10 unrelated sentences of each type, divided into two blocks of five. In addition, there were two blocks of warm-up sentences, for a total of 70 sentences. All sentences used the past tense, definite articles wherever possible, concrete rather than abstract nouns, no proper names, and words of at least medium frequency according to the Kučera and Francis word count. In addition, there were semantic constraints imposed on the sentences; only well-integrated sentences were used, but no definitional sentences. By well-integrated we mean, quite informally, that the arguments of a proposition are reasonably typical ones; e.g., our policeman *issues a summons*, rather than *bakes a cake*, which would also be a semantically acceptable sentence, though not a well-integrated one.

TABLE 1

Sample Sentences and their Propositional Structure for Experiments I and II

Number of propositions	Number of content words	Sentence type	Example
Experiment I:			
1	2	*VA*	The sentry yawned.
1	3	*VAO*	The travelers noticed a restaurant.
2	3	$P_1 \& P_2$	The excited audience applauded.
1	4	*VAOG*	The policeman issued the driver a summons.
1	4	*VAOI*	The settler built the cabin by hand.
3	4	$P_1 \& P_2 \& P_3$	The crowded passengers squirmed uncomfortably.
Experiment II:			
1	3	*VOI(pass)*	The entrance was blocked by the chair.
1	4	*VAOI*	The settler built the cabin by hand.
1	4	*VOAG(pass)*	The summons was issued to the driver by the policeman.
2	4	*VAO-L*	The architect finished the project at home.
2	4	*VAO·T*	The lifeguard cleared the beach at dusk.
2	4	$P_1 \& P_2$	The horse stumbled and broke a leg.

Note.—V = verb, A = agent, O = object, I = instrument, G = goal, T = time, L = locative, P = proposition.

Procedure. The subjects were tested individually. After listening to a block of five sentences, a subject was asked to recall in writing whatever he could remember. There was a two-minute recall period for each five-sentence block. The sentences were tape recorded by a male speaker at the rate of approximately 1.5 words per sec. Two-second pauses separated the sentences of each block. A ready signal preceded each block. Six tape recordings of the sentences in different orders were prepared. In each order, exactly one five-sentence block of each sentence type occurred in each half of the presentation sequence. Each order started with the two blocks of warm-up sentences.

Results. Table 2 summarizes the main results of the experiment. Only the recall of content words was scored, and verb tenses were neglected. The first numerical column shows complete sentence recall. The second column shows partial sentence recall. The third column shows partial proposition recall; it differs from the previous column only for those sentences based upon more than one proposition. The final column indicates total recall, which is the sum of the first two columns.

The comparisons of interest are on the one hand between the *VAO* sentences and the $P_1 \& P_2$ sentences, and between the *VAOG* and *VAOI* sentences and the $P_1 \& P_2 \& P_3$ sentences. In terms of total recall, the *VAO* and $P_1 \& P_2$ sentences are almost equal, $F(1,125) < 1$, but there was more partial recall for the two-proposition sentences than for the one-proposition sentences, $F(1,125) = 3.72$, which is marginally significant, $p = .059$. For the sentences with four content words, similar results were obtained, except that the one-proposition sentences were significantly better recalled over-all than the three-proposition sentences, $F(1,125) = 17.50, p < .01$. But, again, partial recall for the three-proposition sentences was considerably greater than partial recall for the one-proposition sentences, $F(1,125) = 41.61, p < .001$.[3]

The data, therefore, confirm the principal experimental hypothesis: With number of content words controlled, sentences based upon two or three propositions are recalled less as a unit than sentences based upon a single proposition. There was about twice as much partial recall from multiproposition sentences as from single-proposition sentences.

The second experimental hypothesis, that multiproposition sentences would be recalled less well than single-proposition sentences when the number of content words in the sentence is controlled, was confirmed only if "recall" means "complete sentence recall." If, on the other hand, partial sentence recall is also considered, there was essentially no difference between the *VAO* and the $P_1 \& P_2$ sentences, while a difference in the predicted direction still remained between the *VAOG/VAOI* sentences and the $P_1 \& P_2 \& P_3$ sentences.

The data in Table 2 present a striking confirmation of the propositional analysis advocated here, in the sense that the sentence recall of the subjects in this experiment reflected the units of the theoretical analysis quite precisely. Independent of the

---

[3]The ANOVA reported here does not include sentences as random effects. Since each block of sentences was always presented in the same order, there are strong serial position effects that prohibit sentence-by-sentence comparisons.

number of arguments, where the theory says that a sentence is based upon one propositional unit, recall of the sentence tends to be as a unit. Where the theory says that a sentence is based upon two or three propositional units, recall as a unit was correspondingly lower. Specifically, if one calculates from Table 2 the percentage of total recall that came from complete sentence recall, one obtains values of .93, .91, .92, and .89 for the one-proposition sentences (*VA, VAO, VAOG,* and *VAOI,* respectively), while only .84 of the recall of two-proposition sentences came from complete sentence recall, and the figure was only .74 with three-proposition sentences. Thus, propositions really behaved as units in this experiment, as claimed by the theory.

TABLE 2

Percent of Content Words Recalled in Experiment I

Sentence type:		Complete sentence recall	Partial sentence recall	Partial proposition recall	Total recall
VA	*V*		3		
	A		9		
	Σ	75	6		81
VAO	*V*		3		
	A		11		
	O		6		
	Σ	65	6		71
$P_1\&P_2$	*V*		12	2	
	A		15	3	
	Mod.		6	3	
	Σ	58	11	3	69
VAOG	*V*		3		
	A		11		
	O		3		
	G		8		
	Σ	72	6		78
VAOI	*V*		7		
	A		12		
	O		6		
	I		7		
	Σ	65	8		73
$P_1\&P_2\&P_3$	*V*		20	0	
	A		22	4	
	Adj.Mod.		12	5	
	Adj.Mod.		14	5	
	Σ	50	17	4	67

Experiment II

Method. Twenty-four subjects from the same subject pool as in Exp. I served in this study. The experimental procedure was identical in every respect with that of the previous experiment. The only difference between the experiments were the six different sentence types used as stimulus material in Exp. II. The six sentence types are described in Table 1, and the motivation for using these particular types of sentences has also been discussed.

Results. The question of primary interest is how far the data from Exp. II support the results of Exp. I. Specifically, are one-proposition sentences again recalled more as a unit than two-proposition sentences? The relevant comparison is between the *VAOI* sentences and the three kinds of two-proposition sentences used here (Locative, Time, and coordinated propositions). In terms of total recall, there were no significant differences, but, as before, partial recall was significantly greater for the two-proposition sentences than for the *VAOI* sentences, $F(1,115) = 7.09, p<.01$. The data are shown in Table 3. The proportion of total recall that came from complete sentence recall for two-proposition sentences was quite comparable to the values observed in Exp. I: .84 for the coordinated propositions (which is exactly the same as for the sentences with adjective modifiers in Exp. I), .84 for the locative sentences, and .74 for the time sentences. On the other hand, for the one-proposition *VAOI* sentences, .87 of the total recall came from complete sentence recall (in Exp. I, a value of .89 was obtained for the same sentences — both are rather low for one-proposition sentences).

The question of whether partial recall is alike for *(a)* two-proposition sentences, where one of the propositions specifies a location or time, and *(b)* for other kinds of two-proposition sentences (the coordinated propositions in the present experiment) can be answered affirmatively, as the relevant F-test yielded a nonsignificant value, $F(1,115) = 2.65, p<.05$. However, there was considerably more partial recall for time sentences than for locative sentences, $F(1,115) = 11.60, p<.01$. This is probably an artifact of the way the test sentences were constructed. For most sentences used, the places are fairly constrained, while times are not. For example, in the sample sentence given in Table 1, the lifeguard may clear the beach at dusk, or equally well at some other time, but there are not many plausible places for the architect to finish his work. Hence, there was much confusion about what time went with what sentence in the five-sentence blocks that subjects had to remember, whereas this kind of confusion was less likely to occur with any other sentence component.

In summary, then, we can say that Exp. II confirmed the principal results of the previous study: Sentences based upon two propositions are recalled less well as a unit than sentences with the same number of content words, but based upon a single proposition.

A comparison of the recall of the *VAOI* sentences in Exp. I and II allows one to evaluate the over-all comparability of the two experiments. A chi-square test comparing the number of subjects who recalled these sentences completely, partially, or not at all, revealed no significant differences, $\chi^2(2) = 2.80$, $.2 < p < .3$. Thus, comparisons across experiments appear to be justified. The interesting comparison involves the *VAOG* sentences, which were active sentences in one experiment and passive sentences in the other. A chi-square test, like the one above, showed that differences

TABLE 3

Percent of Content Words Recalled in Experiment II

Sentence type:		Complete sentence recall	Partial sentence recall	Partial proposition recall	Total recall
VOI	*V*		5		
	O		8		
	I		2		
	Σ	69	5		74
VAOI	*V*		7		
	A		17		
	O		5		
	I		8		
	Σ	60	9		69
VAOG	*V*		14		
	A		10		
	O		13		
	G		10		
	Σ	58	11		69
VOA-L	*V*		11	7	
	A		20	16	
	O		6	3	
	L		8	—	
	Σ	58	11	6	69
VOA-T	*V*		21	6	
	A		28	13	
	O		18	3	
	T		7	—	
	Σ	51	19	6	70
$P_1 \& P_2$	V_1		9	0	
	N_1		21	13	
	V_2		8	5	
	N_2		17	2	
	Σ	60	14	5	74

between the active and passive versions were highly significant, $\chi^2(2) = 9.62$, $p<$ .01. A second chi-square test was performed taking into account only the partial recall data for these sentences. It, too, was highly significant: $\chi^2(6) = 17.66$, $p<.01$. Thus, not only over-all recall, but also the pattern of partial recall was affected by the way the *VAOG* propositions were expressed in the surface structure. What happened can be readily seen from Tables 2 and 3. For all one-proposition sentences, the agent was by far the most frequently recalled word, except for the passive *VAOG* sentences. For these sentences, the object was the argument best recalled. One may conclude, therefore, that the recall preference for the agent, which is so obvious in Exp. I, was not really a genuine preference for the agent case, but rather a preference for the theme and grammatical subject of the sentence.

The passive *VAOG* sentences are curious in one other respect: There was much more partial recall for these sentences than for any other one-proposition sentence in either experiment. This resulted primarily from a tendency to recall these sentences as truncated passives. The most frequent partial recall pattern consisted in the omission of the agent, but correct recall of the rest of the sentence.

Discussion. If one averages the results over Tables 1 and 2 and computes total recall as a function of the number of content words in the sentence, percentages of .81, .72, and .71 are obtained for sentences with 2, 3, and 4 content words. Though these percentages decline, the corresponding total numbers of words recalled increases considerably: 1.62, 2.16, and 2.84 words, respectively. This is, of course, the result anyone would expect. Slightly more interesting is the decline in total recall when the sentences are classified in terms of the number of underlying propositions, 1, 2, or 3. The corresponding recall percentages are .74, .70, and .69. The really significant result of this study, however, is the contrast between the small and frequently nonsignificant differences in total recall scores and the considerable and statistically significant differences in partial recall scores that have been obtained for sentences differing in the number of underlying propositions. Figure 3 summarizes these results. The data are averages over Tables 2 and 3, with the number of content words in the sentences as a control factor. The figure illustrates quite effectively, and the statistical tests discussed above support this conclusion statistically, that *(a)* differences in total recall were small, but that *(b)* partial recall was more than twice as great for sentences that were based upon more than one proposition than for sentences based upon a single proposition, and that, therefore, *(c)* complete sentence recall was substantially better for sentences that were a propositional unit than for sentences that were not. This is strong support for the propositional theory and indirectly also for the case grammar analysis. Multi-argument propositions appear to be the units out of which sentence memory is constituted. Alternative approaches, such as syntactically motivated analyses of sentences into binary units, as advocated by Anderson and Bower (1973), would be hard put to explain the unitary recall of such fairly complex propositions as, for instance, the *VAOG* sentences, in view of the tendency for partial recall of other sentences with equal number of content words. Certainly, the phrase structure of *VAOG* sentences is not more unitary nor simpler than the phrase structure of a *VAO* sentence with a modifier.[4]

What artifacts in the design of these experiments or in the selection of the experimental material might have produced these results? First of all, there are many ways in which two propositions can be combined into one surface structure sentence,

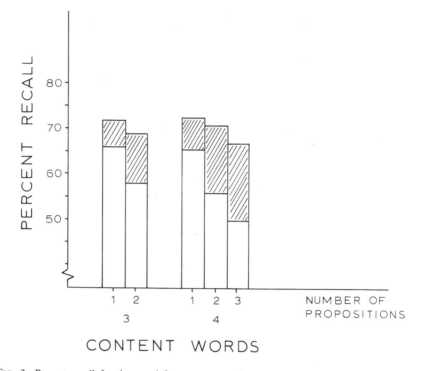

FIG. 3. Percent recall for three and four content word sentences as a function of the number of propositions in the base structure. The unshaded portion of each bar represents recall from instances where the whole sentence was recalled; the shaded portion represents partial sentence recall.

[4]Anderson and Bower (1973, Chapter 11) have presented some experimental data in support of their argument that sentences are stored as networks of independent associations rather than as Gestalt-like units. It is questionable, however, whether their data really support such an argument. The evidence upon which their conclusion is based is quite different from that considered here. Anderson and Bower claim that the mere presence of partial sentence recall contradicts the idea of multi-element units, while we have merely argued that one-proposition sentences will lead to less partial recall than multiproposition sentences. It is unreasonable to restrict theories postulating multi-element units in such a way that only whole sentences as presented by the experimenter can be encoded. Instead, one should permit such theories the same amount of flexibility that associative network theories require to account for partial recall. HAM explains partial recall through partial encoding; in much the same way we claim that the proposition that the subject actually encodes is not necessarily the same as the one upon which the experimenter's sentence was based. A stimulus sentence in an experiment is no more than an invitation to the subject to construct and store in memory certain propositions. There is no guarantee that the propositions actually constructed will be precisely those contained in the sentence. Thus, "The boy hit the girl" may be encoded as "It was about a boy," or "A boy hit someone," and recall of the corresponding propositions will be scored as partial recall.

and we have certainly not investigated all of them. We have, however, tested a fair variety. In Exp. I, multi-proposition sentences were constructed by using modifiers, and one might every well suspect such sentences to be a special case (Clark, 1966). However, in Exp. II, two propositions were coordinated in a sentence, and the results were very similar. In fact, in terms of the proportion of total recall that derived from complete sentence recall, the two-proposition sentences using modifiers and coordinations were exactly equivalent. Further generality was obtained by using two-proposition sentences in which one of the propositions was a Locative or Time, and these did not differ from other kinds of two-proposition sentences in terms of the propensity for partial recall.

A second possible artifact might be that the one-proposition sentences used in these experiments formed images more readily than the two-proposition sentences. In order to investigate this possibility, all sentences were rated on a five-point scale as to the ease with which they aroused an image. A separate group of 60 subjects was used for this rating task. Mean ratings were computed for each of the six different sentence types used in each experiment. There was very little variation in these mean ratings. It appeared that we had selected a group of sentences that was extremely homogeneous in image value. The sentences that were rated highest in imagery value happened to be the two- and three-proposition sentences of Exp. I. The rank order correlation between imagery value and partial recall scores was − .01. Thus, there is no reason at all to suspect that differences in imagery might have been responsible for our results.

The subsidiary result of greatest interest concerns the comparison of the *VAOG* sentences in Exp. I, where they were expressed as active sentences, and in Exp. II, where they were expressed as passive sentences. The recall difference that this change produced was considerable. In the active sentences the most recalled argument was the agent; in the passive sentences the most recalled argument was the object; in both cases the most favored argument was the grammatical subject of the sentence and its theme. Thus, it appears that the great superiority in recall for the agent, which is so obvious in Table 1, was a consequence of the way our sentences were written. In all of these sentences the agent was also the grammatical subject, and hence the theme of the sentence. In the sentences of Exp. II where the agent role and the theme role were unconfounded, agents lost their recall superiority. Thus, our data are in good agreement with the results of Clark and Card (1969), who also concluded that the theme of a sentence is recalled best. The arguments that James (1972) raised against this conclusion, namely, that it was based upon a confounding with imagery, do not apply in the present case. We used the same sentences in both the active and passive versions, and hence the imagery was presumably the same in both instances. The point James makes, that with single sentences it is not necessarily the case that the grammatical subject will also be the theme, is a reasonable one. Surely, context effects will interact with word order in determining what will be considered the theme of a sentence. But in experiments like the present one, where a subject listens to a block of structurally alike sentences in a neutral laboratory context, it may very well be that the subject uses word order as a focus for his attention and as a cue for the thematic structure of the sentence. Apparently, this is what subjects did in the present experiments.

There are a number of reports in the literature that sentence subjects are remembered best, objects next best, and verbs are remembered worst (e.g., Horovitz & Prytulak, 1969, for free and cued recall; James, 1972, also for free recall; and Wearing, 1970, for recognition). The present data replicate these findings but also extend and qualify them. If one looks at the one-proposition sentences in Tables 2 and 3, it is quite obvious that verbs are recalled less well than other sentence components, and that the subject (which usually was the agent, as discussed above) is recalled best. This result extends the findings cited above, in that it was obtained here with more complex sentences (the *VAOI* and *VAOG* sentences) than the simple subject-verb-object constructions used by other investigators. Tables 2 and 3 also show quite clearly, however, that the rule "verbs are recalled worst" is very limited in generality. It certainly does not hold in general for the two- and three-proposition sentences, or for the *VAOG*-passive sentences. This simply goes to show how risky it is to generalize from a limited sample of sentence types.

The results reported in this chapter have some fairly strong implications for theories of sentence memory. They tend to indicate that the multi-argument propositional units postulated by the present theory, as well as the hierarchical relations among them, do have some psychological reality. This means, in the present context, that the data are consistent with the idea that the output of the sentence parser consists of propositions, and that these are ordered as claimed by the theory. These ordered propositions are stored in memory. There is, presumably, also some subsidiary nonpropositional information in memory, which may in part be responsible for the recall of proposition fragments. The nature of this information will concern us in later experiments. For the moment it is enough to be able to conclude that sentence memory may be regarded at least at one level as proposition lists. Note that our research has not been directed at the problem of how this memory is expressed at the time of recall when actual sentences must be reconstructed from the propositional bases stored in memory. Others (notably James, Thompson, & Baldwin, 1973; Perfetti & Goldman, 1974) have shown how context effects and our normal speech habits combine in determining the way in which a particular base will be expressed verbally.

SUMMARY

Text bases are ordered lists of propositions. The order of propositions in the base defines the rank of a proposition, such that the most superordinate propositions receive the lowest rank, with more and more deeply subordinated propositions receiving higher scores. The likelihood of recall of propositions after one reading of a paragraph was shown to depend strongly upon the rank of the proposition, with the superordinate propositions being recalled most frequently, and decreasing recall for propositions of higher rank.

Even if rank differences are controlled by working with unrelated sentences rather than paragraphs, the likelihood of recall of a proposition varies with its number of arguments, as well as with the nature of the arguments. Most importantly, however, it could be shown that subjects tend to recall whole sentences if they are based upon a single proposition, while the tendency to recall sentences in an all-or-none fashion was greatly reduced for sentences based upon two or more propositions, even though the number of content words in the sentences was the same in both cases. This finding was taken to support one of the key assumptions of the theory, namely, that propositions consist of a predicate plus one or more arguments that form a relational unit with the predicate. Thus, in our view, even multi-argument propositions are processed and remembered as units, as opposed to theories that claim that propositions are always binary.

8
MEMORY FOR INFORMATION
INFERRED DURING READING

The relationship between a text base and a text is flexible, and indeed essentially indeterminate. By assumption, text bases are sufficient to express the intended meaning, but not every proposition contained in a text base must be represented explicitly in the text itself. Depending upon the assumptions the speaker or writer makes, he will delete certain redundant propositions from the text base before giving it verbal expression and rely upon his audience to infer the deleted information. This is what makes machine parsing of text so difficult: The surface form of a text is usually incomplete, supplying not more than one cue from which the text base must be reconstructed. Surface structure cues must be supplemented by the comprehender's knowledge of semantics as well as the special topic under discussion, properties of the source, and the particular communication environment. Implied information must be reconstructed. Gaps in the continuity of a text must be filled in by means of suitable inferences about the material at hand. The interesting observation about these inferences is, however, that one is usually not even aware of them. Only upon reflection does one realize the sometimes substantial contributions that one must make in comprehending a text. In the present chapter, some studies are reported that are concerned with the processing of propositions that are not explicitly represented in a text but which, in order to make sense of the text, must be inferred by the reader on the basis of context or general knowledge.

1. THE IDENTIFICATION OF EXPLICITLY AND IMPLICITLY PRESENTED INFORMATION[1]

The hypothesis to be investigated in this experiment is that when subjects read a text, they store in memory a propositional representation of that text which is not

[1]By J. M. Keenan and W. Kintsch.

necessarily a precise copy of the text base from which the text had been generated in the first place. Specifically, if there were some propositions in the original text base that were not expressed explicitly in the text itself, the reader will infer these propositions and store them in memory in the same way as other propositions that were represented explicitly in the text. This assumes, of course, that only propositions that are in some way redundant are deleted in generating a text. Deleted propositions must express facts that can be taken for granted; when other types of propositions are deleted a text simply becomes incomprehensible.

The material for the present experiment consisted of pairs of paragraph surface structures which were both derived from the same propositional base. In one case, the explicit paragraph, all propositions in the text base were expressed in the text; in the implicit version of the paragraph, one or more redundant propositions were deleted before the text base was expressed verbally. Subjects were given these paragraphs to read and afterwards were asked to identify a test sentence as true or false. In either case, the test sentence was a verbal expression of the critical proposition that was deleted in one version of the paragraph but not the other. It was predicted that the likelihood of a correct response (that is, of saying that the test sentence was true) as well as the response latency would be independent of which version of a paragraph had been read. This prediction is based upon two assumptions. First, it is assumed that subjects process and store the critical proposition whether or not it is presented explicitly. If there are surface structure cues from which that proposition can be derived, as is the case for the explicit paragraphs, processing should be easy. If such cues are lacking, as is the case in the implicit paragraphs, processing should be more difficult, because an inference will have to be made. Nevertheless, once the proposition has been processed, whether it was derived directly from the surface structure or via an inference, it will be stored in memory in the same way. The second assumption made concerns the form of the memory representation. It is assumed here, in agreement with the results of Chapters 6 and 7, that the product of reading and comprehension, which is stored in memory, is a propositional representation of the paragraph. In addition, of course, other levels of memory may be also involved, such as memory for the exact words used, or a phonemic string memory, but this possibility will be disregarded for the moment. The experiment, therefore, tests the two assumptions jointly: that the memory for text is propositional, and that necessary nonexplicit textual information is inferred during reading.

Method

Subjects. Forty summer school students from the University of Colorado served as subjects; they were paid $1.50 per session for a total of $3.00 for their participation.

Design. The forty subjects were randomly assigned to two groups. The first group read the explicit version of each paragraph, and the second read the implicit version. Within each group the subjects read both short (Materials Set I) and long (Materials Set II) paragraphs.

Materials. Two sets of paragraphs were constructed in the following manner. A pair of English paragraphs were derived from a given propositional structure. Each pair consisted of an explicit version of the underlying propositions and an implicit version.

Materials Set 1 contains twelve such pairs of two-sentence paragraphs, each pair on a different topic. In each case the underlying structure contained eight propositions. All eight propositions were represented in the surface structure of the explicit version; the implicit versions explicitly represented only seven base propositions. The variation in the number of words is small: 21 to 28 for the explicit versions and 17 to 24 for the implicit versions. By necessity the explicit versions contained 3 to 5 more words than the implicit versions. The following is an example of such a pair of paragraphs.

Explicit: A carelessly discarded burning cigarette started a fire. The fire destroyed many acres of virgin forest.
Implicit: A burning cigarette was carelessly discarded. The fire destroyed many acres of virgin forest.

The propositional structure from which these versions were derived is as follows:

$$((DISCARD,CIGARETTE)=\alpha)\&(CARELESS,DISCARD)\&$$
$$(BURN,CIGARETTE)\&(CAUSE,\alpha,FIRE)\&$$
$$(DESTROY,FIRE,FOREST)\&(SIZE,FOREST,ACRE)\&$$
$$(VIRGIN,FOREST)\&(MANY,ACRE)$$

The implicit, to-be-inferred proposition in the implicit version is $(CAUSE,\alpha, FIRE)$. The test question for both paragraphs was "The discarded cigarette caused the fire."

To infer a proposition is simply to discover part of the underlying base without the aid of an explicit English counterpart. If inferences of this kind are made during reading rather than during question answering, then varying the level of processing necessary to encode the proposition should affect reading time, but not question-answering time. The propositions left unrepresented in the implicit versions were classified according to the amount of information assumed to be involved in processing them, regardless of whether they were explicit or implicit. There are three classes with four paragraphs in each class. Examples of experimental paragraphs from each level are given in Table 1.

Level 1 propositions are representative of a very general property of text processing: A particular lexical item may not always be referred to with the same word. In the example for Level 1, there are two occurrences of DOG in the listing of propositions: first (RESTRAIN,MAN, DOG) and later, (HAS,DOG,INSTINCT). The second appearance of DOG may be realized in the surface structure as *dog* or, equivalently, as *it*; similarly, words such as *animal* or *beast* may be substituted. The reader of the explicit version has the substitution of the word *animal* for *dog* explicitly stated in the text; the reader of the implicit version must assume the substitution. In both cases what is involved in the processing of (ANIMAL,DOG) is a fairly simple use of

TABLE 1

Sample Paragraphs for Three Levels of Inference Difficulty—Experiment I

Level 1

Explicit: *A strong hand was needed to restrain the dog. The dog was an animal whose instincts had been aroused by the sight of the fleeing deer.*

Implicit: *A strong hand was needed to restrain the dog. The animal's instincts had been aroused by the sight of the fleeing deer.*

Implicit Proposition and Test Statement: (ANIMAL, DOG) *The dog was an animal.*

Level 2

Explicit: *A carelessly discarded burning cigarette started a fire. The fire destroyed many acres of virgin forest.*

Implicit: *A burning cigarette was carelessly discarded. The fire destroyed many acres of virgin forest.*

Implicit Proposition and Test Statement: (CAUSE, α, FIRE), where α is (DISCARD, CIGARETTE) *A discarded cigarette started a fire.*

Level 3

Explicit: *Police are hunting a man in hiding. The man is Bob Birch, whose wife disclosed illegal business practices in an interview on Saturday.*

Implicit: *Police are hunting a man in hiding. The wife of Bob Birch disclosed illegal business practices in an interview on Saturday.*

Implicit Proposition and Test Statement: (HIDE, MAN)&(MAN, BOB BIRCH) *Bob Birch is the man who is hiding.*

---

information included in the lexical entry for DOG. It is assumed that the reader of the implicit version has such information available and that he will automatically use it. Motivation to process the implicit proposition is twofold: *(a)* Processing of successive propositions depends upon the implicit proposition, and *(b)* processing reduces the number of lexical items to be held in working memory.

All of the Level-2 propositions involve the notion of causation. For the example in Table 1, it is assumed that when a subject encodes ((DISCARD,CIGARETTE)=α) and (DESTROY,FIRE,FOREST), he will infer (CAUSE,α,FIRE) regardless of whether or not it is explicitly presented in the text. What is involved in processing this proposition is a one-step inference based on information available in semantic memory, namely, the causes of fires and the results of discarding burning cigarettes. Whereas processing a Level-1 proposition involves only a single lexical look-up, processing Level-2 propositions involves the use of information for two lexical entries and requires that a causal relationship between the two be found.

Unlike Level-1 and Level-2 propositions, Level-3 propositions are not directly available in memory but must be constructed on the basis of textual and memorial information. Thus, for the example in Table 1, encoding (HIDE,MAN)&(MAN, BOB BIRCH) must involve the use of information such as: If the police search for a man, the man may be suspected of a crime; people who commit a crime go into hiding; illegal business practices are a crime; the wife of Bob Birch probably did not disclose her own crime but someone else's; the someone else is the husband in this case; therefore, the husband is hiding; then Bob Birch is the husband; and, finally, Bob Birch is hiding.

These are simply the presuppositions of the text. The reader of the explicit version must process these presuppositions in order to make sense out of the surface representation of the Level-3 proposition. The reader of the implicit version must process them in order to *derive* the Level-3 proposition. The processing difference between the two versions is one of motivation to process the presuppositions. While the surface representation of the proposition in the explicit version induces processing of its presuppositions, no such motivation is present in the implicit version. Consequently, experimental instructions emphasized integrating the two sentences as a story.

A question was constructed for each of the 24 paragraphs. The questions were based on the propositions left unrepresented in the implicit versions, and all required a True answer. In order to counterbalance the expected number of True responses, twelve dummy paragraphs were also constructed; the questions for these paragraphs required a False answer. Subjects from each group thus read 24 paragraphs, 12 experimental and 12 dummies, from Materials Set I.

Materials Set II differed from Set I with respect to length of paragraphs and the number of propositions left unrepresented in the surface structure of the implicit version. Ten pairs of paragraphs (explicit and implicit versions) on different topics were constructed as before. The paragraphs dealt with little known facts about familiar people, places, objects from art and political history. The number of propositions in the underlying base structures ranged from 20 to 39. Number of words ranged from 41 to 123 for the explicit versions and from 34 to 108 for implicit versions. Set II left from 2 (for the shorter paragraphs) to 6 (for the longer) propositions unrepresented. Again, the types of implicit propositions were varied, but no attempt was made to categorize them according to levels of processing. An example of one of the experimental pairs is the following:

Explicit: If Shakespeare needs any excuse for the exuberance of his language, it should be remembered that he was doing on the stage of his day what on the pictorial stage of our day is not so much required. It was the stage which influenced Shakespeare's language in that he had to create the setting through dialogue. Shakespeare's dramatic figures stood out on a platform-stage, without background, with the audience on three sides of it. And the whole of his atmosphere and environment had to come from the gestures and language of the actors. When they spoke, they provided their own scenery, which we now provide for them.

Implicit: If Shakespeare needs any excuse for the exuberance of his language, it should be remembered that he was doing on the stage of his own day what on the pictorial stage of our day is not so much required. Shakespeare's dramatic figures stood out on a platform-stage, without background, with the audience on three sides of it. And the whole of his atmosphere and environment had to come from the gestures and language of the actors. When they spoke, they provided their own scenery.

The implicit propositions in the second version and the corresponding test statements are:

(INFLUENCE,STAGE,SHAKESPEARE)   (1)
   The stage influenced Shakespeare.

(CREATE,SHAKESPEARE,SETTING)   (2)
   Shakespeare created his settings.

(PROVIDE,WE,ACTORS,SCENERY)   (3)
   We provide actors with scenery.

As it happens, an increase in paragraph length and number of implicit propositions results in two attendant surface structure differences between the explicit and implicit versions. First of all, the number of words is considerably less for the implicit version than for the explicit version: The greatest difference was 37 words in the case of the paragraphs that differed in the representation of 6 propositions; the smallest difference was 7 words in the case in which only 2 propositions were at issue. Secondly, there is a difference in the complexity of syntax between the two versions. With longer paragraphs it is impossible to realize all the base propositions without affecting the readability of the text. The explicit version is always syntactically more complex than the implicit version, as can be readily seen in the above example paragraphs. This may be precisely why inferences of the type studied here are so prevalent in the language — semantic inferences allow for simpler syntax. As a check on our intuitions, a rating of "readability" was taken for the paragraphs. Each of five judges were given both versions of each of the ten paragraphs and were asked to judge which version was most readable. The implicit version was judged to be better than the explicit in 66% of the cases.

Two types of True-False questions were constructed for each paragraph: inference questions and textual questions. The inference questions were the questions of experimental interest; each question dealt with one of the propositions left unrepresented in the implicit versions, and all required a "true" answer. The number of inference questions for each paragraph depended upon the number of implicit propositions in the implicit version. The total number of inference questions was 24. Textual questions were constructed from the experimental paragraphs, rather than from dummy paragraphs as in Materials Set I, to counterbalance questions of the first type; two textual questions were constructed for each paragraph, one true and one false. True textual questions simply expressed propositions that were explicit in both paragraph versions; false textual questions dealt with either the negation or reversal of causality expressed in propositions explicit in both versions. The total number of textual questions was 20 (10 true and 10 false).

Procedure. Due to the large number of paragraphs in each set of materials, the experiment was divided into two sessions. Materials Set I was presented in the first session, and Materials Set II in the second.

Short Paragraphs. All subjects were tested individually, with all paragraphs and questions presented on slides. The subject was seated about 3 m from a screen on which the slides were shown with a Kodak Carousel projector. The experimenter was seated behind the subject; he exposed a slide and simultaneously started a Hunter timer. In front of the subject was a control box with three labeled buttons: on the right side of the box an "Advance Slide" button and on top "True" and "False" buttons. The subject kept two fingers of his left hand on the True and False buttons and the index finger of his right hand on the Advance button. The subject was instructed to read the paragraph carefully and to press the Advance button when he was finished. This response brought the question slide into view, stopped the timer, and started a second Hunter timer. The subject was instructed to "read the sentence as quickly as possible and answer whether it is true or false based on the information which is either implied or stated by the paragraph." Depressing either the True or False button stopped the second timer and turned on an indicator light on the experimenter's console. The experimenter recorded the results for that question, gave the subject a "Ready" signal, and proceeded to the next paragraph.

Four warm-up problems preceded the experimental trials. New random orders for presentation of the slides were constructed for every four subjects. Instructions emphasized that the subject was to work as fast as he could but that "the most important thing is to understand what you read, not speed." Since the probability of processing implicit propositions during reading was considered to be dependent upon the subject's integrating the two sentences, the instructions stated that the paragraphs were short newspaper clippings and that the subject should view them as integrated stories.

As soon as the subject finished reading and answering questions for all 24 paragraphs, a cued recall test of the 12 experimental paragraphs was administered. The subject was given a sheet of paper with a short phrase from each paragraph; the phrase was the surface structure realization of the first proposition for each text. He was told "to write down as much of the paragraph as you remember; exact wording is not as important as the meaning of the paragraph." The subject was given as much time as he needed to complete this task; the average time required was approximately 5 minutes.

Long Paragraphs. The experimental session on Materials Set II took place approximately two weeks after the first session. The procedure was the same as in the first session, except that following each paragraph there were 4 to 6 questions instead of only one. As soon as the subject pressed the button for his answer to the first question, the experimenter recorded the results, reset the timer, and exposed the next question. When all the questions for the paragraph had been answered, the experimenter informed the subject that a new paragraph was about to be presented.

Three warm-up problems preceded the 10 experimental paragraphs. New random orders of presentation, for both the paragraphs and the questions following each paragraph, were constructed for every four subjects. No final recall test was administered on the longer paragraphs on Materials Set II.

Results

A summary of the principal results for both materials sets is given in Table 2. Table 3 presents the results for the short paragraphs (Materials Set I) analyzed according to the levels-of-processing variable. All analyses were performed on data that had been pooled across paragraphs.

Reading Time. Only the reading times of subjects who responded correctly to the inference question were considered in the analyses of short paragraphs. For the long paragraphs, however, all reading times were considered, since no subject gave evidence of not processing the paragraph, i.e., no subject responded incorrectly to over 50% of the questions for a particular paragraph.

Paragraph version was not a significant factor in reading short paragraphs, $t(38) < 1$. For the long paragraphs, however, the explicit version required a significantly longer amount of time to read than the implicit version, $t(38) = 2.84, p < .01$.

With respect to the reading times shown in Table 2, level of processing is a highly significant factor, $F(2,76) = 17.34, p < .01$. A test of the difference between the means for the three levels using the Newman-Keuls procedure showed that the mean reading time for Level-1 paragraphs is significantly faster ($p < .01$) than those for Level-2 or Level-3 paragraphs. The difference between Level-2 and Level-3 paragraphs was not significant.

TABLE 2

Average Reading Times and Response Latencies (in sec) with Standard Errors and Error Rates as a Function of Explicit and Implicit Presentation of the Test Statement in Experiment I

	Short paragraphs		Long paragraphs	
	Explicit	Implicit	Explicit	Implicit
Reading time:	7.8	7.7	27.9	24.1
S.E.	.4	.5	1.8	1.6
Response time:	3.8	4.2	4.3	4.8
S.E.	.2	.2	.2	.2
Per cent error:	4	6	6	14

TABLE 3

The Data Shown in Table 1 for Short Paragraphs Analyzed According to the Level of Processing Complexity

	Level 1		Level 2		Level 3	
	Explicit	Implicit	Explicit	Implicit	Explicit	Implicit
Reading time:	7.2	6.8	8.2	8.3	7.9	7.9
S.E.	.4	.4	.5	.6	.4	.4
Response time:	3.9	4.4	3.7	3.9	3.6	4.4
S.E.	.2	.3	.2	.3	.2	.4
Per cent error:	4	3	3	5	4	9

Errors. For the 11 short paragraphs combined with the 24 inference questions from the long paragraphs, error rates were significantly greater for implicit versions than for explicit versions, $t(34) = 2.86$, $p<.01$. Furthermore, as the data in Table 1 indicate, there were significantly more errors made on inference questions from long paragraphs than from short paragraphs, $t(39) = 6.57$, $p<.01$. This difference was tested by pooling across paragraphs and computing a long paragraph and a short paragraph error rate for each subject.

Response Times. Only correct responses were analyzed. The data from the short paragraphs were considered together with the 24 inference questions from the long paragraphs. For each subject two mean scores were obtained, the response times for short and long[2] paragraphs. Factorially combined with the paragraph-length factor was a between-group factor, paragraph version. Thus, variations due to paragraph idiosyncrasies were averaged in the data used for the analysis of variance. Both factors were significant and there was no interaction. Questions from the long paragraphs took longer to answer than those from short paragraphs, $F(1,38) = 10.63$, $p<.01$. Subjects who read the implicit version of each paragraph took longer to verify the implicit propositions than the subjects for whom these propositions had been explicit, $F(1, 38) = 4.03$, $p = .051$. Evidence that this difference between the two groups is indeed due to the paragraph version and not to some spurious factor is found in the data for the textual questions. There was no difference between the two groups on these questions. The mean question reaction time to textual questions was 4.44 sec for those who read explicit versions and 4.49 sec for those who read implicit versions, which compares well with the 4.34 sec observed for the explicitly presented experimental questions.

Recall. Free-recall protocols were collected on only the short paragraphs. Of interest here was the percent recall of the implicit propositions. Since the task was administered after the subject had already answered a question concerning the implicit proposition, the results are somewhat contaminated and are thus of minor importance. For all levels of processing complexity, recall was better for the group who actually read the proposition than for the group who had to derive it from the rest of the text. In light of the reading time data and error data, it would be difficult to interpret this result as meaning that the proposition was not always processed when it was implicit. Perhaps the result is due to the subjects' interpretation of the task. Some subjects may have been able to distinguish in memory explicit and implicit information. If so, they may have strived to render their protocols as true to the paragraph as possible, thus not including implicit information.

Level-2 propositions were recalled best. Recall of Level-3 propositions was slightly inferior, and very few subjects ever stated the Level-1 propositions in their protocols. To do so would have been to state, for example, "the dog is an animal . . . ." Most subjects who referred to the lexical item DOG twice used a pronoun for the second occurrence. This result demonstrates that rules of style are dominant in · producing protocols and may hinder investigation of memory structures by means of free recall.

[2]More than one question was asked for each long paragraph. An analysis was performed comparing first questions with later questions. No systematic order effect was found.

Discussion

The experimental predictions were clearly disconfirmed. When subjects were asked to identify as true or false test statements that either had been presented explicitly in a text or had to be inferred on the basis of this text, they made more errors and had longer reaction latencies for implicitly presented statements than for explicitly presented statements. Either one of the original assumptions may have been wrong. First, subjects may not have processed the implicit propositions during reading, but did so only when asked specifically on the test, which resulted in errors as well as long latencies. In other words, the processing assumptions about reading might have been in error. Secondly, it is possible that subjects did infer the implicit propositions during reading, but that the assumptions about memory may have been wrong. Inferred propositions may not be stored in the same way as explicitly presented sentences.

We believe that the latter explanation is more nearly the correct one, but before proceeding with it some evidence must be noted which appears to support the idea that implicit propositions were indeed inferred during reading. The reading time results for short paragraphs did not differ significantly for the explicit and implicit versions, though the latter contained one less proposition or 14% less information than the explicit version. Furthermore, reading times for both versions increased as a function of the level-of-processing complexity of the proposition left unrepresented in the implicit version. This argues that subjects reading the implicit version had the same sort of difficulty in inferring missing propositions as subjects reading the explicit version had in decoding it from the given text. Thus, both were apparently processing this information during reading, though in different ways. The reading time data are complicated, however, because reading time depends not merely upon the propositional structure, but also upon the number of words in a text, and its syntactic complexity. For the long paragraphs these factors contributed towards producing longer reading times for the explicit paragraphs.

If one assumes that subjects did infer the implicit propositions during reading, which is what the data discussed so far indicate, at least to some extent, how can one then explain the faster responses to explicit test sentences? It may be that the decision to disregard levels of memory other than the propositional one is responsible for the faulty prediction that explicit and implicit propositions should be equally accessible at the time of testing. Perhaps they are indeed equally accessible at the propositional level, but explicitly presented statements may have an advantage over implicitly presented statements because the former are also represented in memory in different ways, say as memory for the exact words used in the paragraph, or as memory for the phoneme strings produced during silent reading. For the long paragraphs used in this experiment, one could hardly claim that after reading such a paragraph, material 50 or 60 words back could still be in a short-term memory buffer. However, we know relatively little about memory for text, including short-term memory for text, which may have quite different properties from the short-term memory store encountered in list-learning experiments. Thus, let us simply accept as a working hypothesis that after reading even 100 to 120 word paragraphs, a surface representation of the paragraph is still available. Furthermore, we assume that this surface representation can be accessed more rapidly than propositional memory. If so, the results of the present experiment are easily explained. Test sentences referring to explicitly presented material could be rapidly identified on the basis of memory traces of the surface structure of the sentence. Test sentences referring to implicitly presented material, on the other hand, involved accessing propositional memory which may be a slower process. The higher error rates for the implicit paragraphs may merely reflect the fact that encoding a proposition is easier when it is explicitly represented in the surface structure than when it has to be inferred.

The explanation offered here has the merit of being testable: if the faster response times for explicit paragraphs are indeed caused by the possibility of accessing a surface memory representation, a delay between reading and test should be sufficient to produce the results originally expected. A 15 min delay interval, followed with reading other material, should be more than sufficient to interfere with memory for the surface features of a text and to force subjects to rely upon propositional memory. On that level, however, explicit and implicit propositions should be equally accessible.

EXPERIMENT II

Method

Design. Each subject read seven experimental paragraphs of which three were short and four were long. Twenty of the subjects read two of the short paragraphs in their explicit versions and one in its implicit version, as well as two of the long paragraphs in their explicit versions and two in their implicit versions. The other 20 subjects read the same paragraphs as the first 20, only in their complementary versions. This design is a $2 \times 2 \times 2$ factorial, where the independent variables of interest are two within-subject factors: paragraph version (Explicit vs. Implicit) and paragraph length (Short vs. Long), and one between-subject factor, which was the result of counterbalancing materials. As in Exp. I, the dependent variables are reading time and question reaction time.

Materials. A subset of the materials used in Exp. I was chosen for this experiment. Three pairs of paragraphs from Materials Set I were randomly selected with the restriction that no Level-1 paragraphs be chosen. The reasons for this restriction were: *(a)* reading times for Level-1 paragraphs were significantly less than those for Level-2 and -3 paragraphs, indicating that the processing of the implicit proposition was different for these paragraphs than for the others; and *(b)* subjects sometimes reported that the questions for these paragraphs, for example, "The dog is an animal," were strange and the subjects considered them to be "trick questions." Four pairs of paragraphs randomly selected from Materials Set II were also used. The same questions used for these paragraphs in Exp. I were used again. In addition, eight dummy paragraphs, each having one question, were constructed; all questions for the dummy paragraphs required a False answer. Thus, each subject read a total of 15 paragraphs—seven experimental, of which three were short and four were long, and eight dummies. For the seven experimental paragraphs, the subject read the explicit versions for half of them and implicit versions for the other half. Each subject also answered 30 questions, 14 of which were inference questions and required a True answer, the other 16 being equally divided between textual questions from experimental paragraphs and textual questions from dummy paragraphs. Of these latter 16, 12 required a False answer and 4 required a True answer.

Procedure. The procedure here differed from that of Exp. I only in the time interval between reading the paragraph and answering the questions. Instead of answering the questions immediately after the presentation of each paragraph, the subject first read all 15 paragraphs with the experimenter recording reading time for each paragraph. Instructions emphasized that the subject should "read quickly, but carefully, since after completing another task, you will be required to answer some questions concerning these 15 paragraphs." Following his reading of all the paragraphs, the subject was given an interpolated task—a sentence memory task that took an average of 15 minutes to complete. After this task the 30 questions were presented one at a time and in random order, with the restriction that no two questions from the same paragraph follow each other.

Subjects. Forty Introductory Psychology students served as subjects in partial fulfillment of a course requirement.

Results

A summary of the principal results is given in Table 4. Mean reading times for the short paragraphs are based only upon those subjects who responded correctly to the inference question, while for the long paragraphs all reading times were considered. Question reaction times are based only upon correct responses.

Reading Time. As Table 4 indicates, subjects required more time to read the explicit version of a paragraph than its implicit version. This difference was tested for significance by pooling over long and short paragraphs and computing for each

TABLE 4

Average Reading Times and Response Latencies (in sec) with Standard Errors and Error Rates as a Function of Explicit and Implicit Presentation of the Test Statement after a 20-min Delay in Experiment II

| | Short paragraphs | | | Long paragraphs | |
	Explicit	Implicit		Explicit	Implicit
Reading time:	8.4	7.8		21.1	17.7
S.E.	.4	.4		1.0	.9
Response time:	4.1	4.1		5.2	5.4
S.E.	.2	.2		.2	.2
Per cent error:	2	3		9	13

subject his mean explicit version reading time and his mean implicit version reading time. It was found that paragraph version is a highly significant factor in determining reading time, $F(1, 38) = 84.48$, $p < .01$.

Errors. The analysis of errors on the 14 inference questions was also performed by pooling over long and short paragraphs. We computed for each subject his total number of errors when the paragraphs he read were explicit and when they were implicit. The difference in number of errors between explicit and implicit versions did not reach significance, $t(30) = 1.59$, though there was a clear trend for subjects who read implicit versions to err more frequently than those who read explicit versions. It might also be noted that despite the interpolated task and 15-minute delay, error rates were approximately the same as in Exp. I. No real comparison can be made, however, since Exp. II involved different subjects and only a subset of the materials of Exp. I.

Response Time. Question reaction times were analyzed as a two-factor factorial design, with Paragraph Version and Paragraph Length as main effects. The effect of paragraph version, which was found to be significant when questions followed immediately after reading the paragraph (Exp. I), was no longer significant when the questions were delayed for 15 minutes. For the means presented in Table 4, the test of the difference in question reaction times between explicit and implicit versions yielded $F(1, 38) = 1.31$, $p > .25$. As in Exp. I, paragraph length was found to be a highly significant factor in question reaction times, $F(1, 38) - 52.25$, $p < .01$. Questions concerning long paragraphs result in longer response times than questions from short paragraphs. Response times, whether for long or short paragraphs, were generally longer in Exp. II than Exp. I. The average increase was .40 seconds, which may reflect the time needed to locate the paragraph to which the question referred after the delay interval.

Discussion

The results of this experiment support the interpretation of Exp. I. Since there was no difference in question reaction times for explicit and implicit information, we can conclude that the implicit propositions were indeed processed during reading. The effect of the 15-minute delay and interpolated task is to eliminate any memory for surface form; both explicit and implicit information are now represented only in propositional memory. This is also reflected in the error data. When explicit questions could be answered from a memory for surface form as in Exp. I, the difference in errors between explicit and implicit versions was highly significant. Now that questions concerning both kinds of information are answered by accessing propositional memory, the difference in errors is no longer significant. There still remains, however, a slight trend for implicit versions to have higher error rates. Presumably this is an encoding phenomenon: Deriving a proposition when it is implicit is less accurate than processing it when it is explicit.

In both Exp. I and II, question reaction times were slower when the question concerned a long paragraph than when it concerned a short paragraph. Unfortunately, this result is ambiguous due to a confounding in the number of words contained in the questions for the two paragraph lengths. The number of words in the questions ranged from 4 to 6 for short paragraphs, and from 3 to 20 for long paragraphs. Since question reaction time includes the time to read the question as well as respond, the slower response times for questions from long paragraphs may only reflect the larger number of words to be read. On the other hand, Monk (reported in Chapter 5) has controlled the number of words contained in questions and has still found response times to be longer for questions from long paragraphs than from short paragraphs. The whole question of the effects of paragraph length upon access speed will be investigated systematically in the next chapter. At this time, however, a study that is both a replication and extension of the experiments just reported must be discussed.

2. RESPONSE LATENCIES TO EXPLICIT AND IMPLICIT STATEMENTS AS A FUNCTION OF THE DELAY BETWEEN READING AND TEST[3]

The most important result of Exp. I and II is the question-delay effect: Explicit-version questions were answered faster than implicit-version questions when the questions were asked immediately but not when they were delayed by 15 min. Exp. III is an attempt to replicate and extend this finding.

To explain the question-delay effect, we hypothesized a surface structure memory for prose. This memory was short-term because it was lost before 20 min, but is it similar to the traditional short-term memory which is lost before 30 sec? To answer this question, a delay condition of 30 sec was included in the design with 0- and 20-min delays.

The fact that explicit-version and implicit-version questions were equally time consuming after 20 min was interpreted as evidence that both types of questions were answered from the same long-term memory representation. If the explicit and implicit information is indeed stored in the same memory representation then, with longer delays, explicit-version and implicit-version questions should continue to require equal amounts of time to answer. To test this prediction, the design included a 48-hour delay condition.

Experiment III was intended to extend the question-delay effect to new materials as well as to new time intervals. The paragraphs of Exp. I and II were all relatively short. If the assumed surface structure memory shared the limited-capacity characteristics of traditional short-term memory, then the immediate reaction time difference between explicit and implicit questions might disappear with longer materials. Experiment III paragraphs were therefore much longer than the paragraphs of the first two experiments.

The paragraphs of Exp. I and II were all similar to each other in style and construction. These paragraphs, labeled descriptive, formed listings of statements, each statement describing the topic. The sentences were related to each other mainly by conjunctions, so that sentence order was relatively unimportant. Experiment III included paragraphs with a different structure, which presented arguments in support

[3]By G. McKoon and J. Keenan.

of an idea or an explanation of a process. The sentences of these argumentative paragraphs were very strictly ordered by causation and implication, both with respect to each other and to the topic. Given the same number of surface structure words and the same number of base structure propositions, the more complex relationships of the argumentative paragraphs should require more encoding time than the simpler descriptive paragraphs. Will this increased amount of processing erase the surface structure memory and with it the question-delay effect, or is this effect a general characteristic of prose comprehension?

Method

Subjects. Forty undergraduates fulfilled a course requirement by participating in two one-hour sessions.

Design. Each subject read eight paragraphs, four descriptive and four argumentative. Concerning each of these paragraphs, the subject answered four questions: one true-explicit, one true-implicit, one false-explicit, and one false-implicit. The questions corresponding to a particular paragraph were either presented immediately after the subject read the paragraph, or after a delay of 30 sec, 20 min, or 48 hr. The dependent variables were response time per question and number of errors per question in a 2 × 2 × 2 × 4 completely within-subject factorial design. The factors were paragraph type (descriptive or argumentative), question representation (explicit or implicit), question truth (true or false), and paragraph-question interval (0, 30 sec, 20 min, or 48 hr). The false questions were included in the design for counterbalancing purposes only; no hypotheses about the process of answering false questions were proposed.

Materials. Unlike the first two experiments, the experimental paragraphs were chosen from literary sources, rather than constructed by the authors. The eight paragraphs discussed topics unfamiliar to the subjects. The four descriptive paragraphs were chosen from *American Heritage* and *Saturday Review*; these paragraphs described P. T. Barnum's midgets, a district of Athens, an early Arapahoe reservation, and the history of the piano. The number of base structure propositions in the descriptive paragraphs varied from 56 to 59 and the number of surface structure words varied from 116 to 155. The argumentative paragraphs, which represented base structure propositions in a more complex style than the descriptive paragraphs, were drawn from the writings of Bertrand Russell and from a scientific text. These paragraphs offered an argument that history cannot be viewed as a science, an argument that mathematics and logic are historically distinct disciplines, an explanation of Aristotle's claim that man is rational, and an explanation of a biochemical process. Number of underlying propositions varied from 55 to 60 and number of words from 147 to 160.

The paragraphs of this experiment differed from the paragraphs of the first and second experiments in one especially important respect: The explicit-implicit variable applied to questions and not to paragraphs. An explicit question concerned propositions explicitly stated in the surface structure while an implicit question concerned propositions of the base structure not explicitly stated in the surface structure. Both kinds of questions were obtained from the same version of each paragraph, so that the explicit questions concerned different propositions than the implicit questions. Thus in this experiment, a particular question must be always explicit or always implicit, whereas in the first two experiments the same question could be either explicit or implicit depending on which version the subject read. Note that every paragraph contained some implicit propositions; there were no paragraphs in which all base propositions were realized in the surface structure.

Four true-false questions were constructed for each paragraph. Explicit questions were copied directly from a sentence or clause of the paragraph, preserving meaning and word usage. An explicit question obtained in this manner was falsified by negation or by the substitution of some incorrect noun from the paragraph. The types of inferences represented in the implicit questions varied as in Exp. I and II, except that none were Level-1 inferences; no attempt was made at categorization, as opposed to Exp. I. In every case, the inference was required for understanding of the paragraph, but not explicitly stated in the surface structure. For example, one descriptive paragraph stated that "when the Arapahoe first settled on a reservation they knew little of the white men's culture" and that "stairsteps, built to take people up to a house on top of another house, amused them." The unstated but necessary inference is that the Arapahoe had never used stairsteps, and the resulting false-implicit question is "Arapahoes had used stairsteps before white men came." The questions of Exp. III were not limited to one proposition but contained 3 or 4 propositions. The questions varied from 7 to 11 words.

When the paragraph-question interval was 30 sec or 20 min, the interval was filled with a sentence unscrambling task. This task was chosen because it involves processing of linguistic information and thus should prevent rehearsal of the experimental paragraphs. One hundred sentences of 9 to 12 words were constructed and the word order of each sentence was randomized. The sentences did not deal with topics discussed in the experimental paragraphs. The subjects attempted to unscramble the words and form a sentence, completing as many such sentences as possible during the intervals.

Procedure. Except for introductory instructions read by the experimenter, all experimental materials were presented on the screen of a Uniscope keyboard/display unit, 100 model, controlled by a Sigma 3 computer. Slightly below and in front of this screen was a response box displaying three buttons labeled "true," "false," and "finish."

Subjects were tested for two one-hour sessions separated by 48 hr. The order of presentation of the experimental materials during these sessions was determined in the following manner for each subject. First each paragraph was assigned to a paragraph-question interval, one argumentative and one descriptive paragraph to each interval. The subject read the two paragraphs assigned to the 48-hr interval during the first session and answered the corresponding questions during the second session. One of the 30-sec interval paragraphs, one of the 20-min interval paragraphs, and one of the 0 interval paragraphs were also presented with their questions on the first day.

In the second session, the subject read the remaining three paragraphs, followed by questions, and answered questions for the two 48-hr interval paragraphs. The order of the 5 events on each day was randomized. When the paragraph-question interval was 20 min or 30 sec, the interval was filled by the sentence unscrambling task. Five minutes of the unscrambling task followed reading of the 48-hr interval paragraphs on the first day, and preceded answering of the corresponding questions on the second day. The assignment of paragraphs to intervals and subjects was completely counterbalanced. All possible combinations of paragraphs were chosen equally often.

The experimenter began the first session by reading instructions that described the several experimental tasks: reading paragraphs, unscrambling sentences, and answering questions. The subject was asked to read each paragraph carefully for understanding and to press the finish button when he reached the end. The finish button caused the reading time to be recorded and the next task to be presented on the screen. For unscrambling sentences, the instructions emphasized speed. The subject was required to write his solution sentences and then press the finish button; the next scrambled sentence then appeared, unless the sentence-unscrambling interval was over. The subject answered the true-false questions "quickly but accurately" with one index finger on the true button, the other index finger on the false button. When one of these buttons was pressed, response time was recorded and the next question was presented. Each experimental task was preceded by a short instruction which the subject read from the screen and which told him what to do next; for example, "Now unscramble the following sentence" or "Now read the following paragraph." The instruction for questions included one or two words (e.g., "piano paragraph questions") to indicate about which paragraph the subject was to be interrogated. The subject was never informed about the length of the delay interval.

The experimental materials of the first session were preceded by practice materials that included each kind of task. No practice materials preceded the experimental materials in the second session, but the instructions were reviewed.

Results

Reading Time. The mean descriptive paragraph reading time and the mean argumentative reading time were computed for each subject. A test of the average difference between these means showed that descriptive paragraphs were read faster than argumentative paragraphs, $t(39) = 4.88$, $p < .01$. The average reading time for a descriptive paragraph was 55.35 sec, and the average reading time for an argumentative paragraph was 62.90 sec. This difference cannot be accounted for by number of base structure propositions because this number was equivalent for the two types of paragraphs. The number of words for descriptive and argumentative paragraphs was equal for only three of the descriptive paragraphs (the fourth one was shorter than either the other descriptive paragraphs or the argumentative paragraphs), but reading times still differed when number of words was controlled. Thus, the finding that descriptive paragraphs are read faster than argumentative paragraphs can be attributed neither to differences in the number of propositions in the base structure of the paragraphs nor to differences in the number of words. It must be attributed to the more complex structure of the argumentative paragraphs which required more processing time.

Errors. Table 5 shows the percentage of error responses in each condition of the experiment. The table summarizes the data for those questions for which true was the correct answer. The data from questions for which false was the correct answer will not be analyzed here. No experimental hypotheses pertained to these data, since how subjects infer that a sentence is false in the present experiment is rather beyond speculation. Furthermore, the observed pattern of results did not prove to be particularly suggestive.

For each subject the mean number of explicit question errors and the mean number of implicit question errors was computed. The difference between these means was significant, $t(39) = 5.08$, $p < .01$; subjects averaged 1.35 implicit errors (on a total of eight questions), but only .40 explicit errors (also on eight questions). A similar t test on the error means of descriptive and argumentative paragraphs showed that this variable did not significantly affect the number of errors. Analysis of variance on the error means for each question delay interval also showed no significant differences; number of errors did not increase as the interval between paragraph and questions increased.

Question reaction times. Table 5 and Fig. 1 summarize the relevant results. The reaction times are based on correct responses only. Extreme reaction times were

TABLE 5

Error Rates, Mean Response Latencies, and Standard Errors for "True" Responses in Experiment III

Interval	Argumentative paragraphs		Descriptive paragraphs	
	Explicit	Implicit	Explicit	Implicit
0:				
Per cent error:	2	17	12	15
Response time:	4.7	5.4	3.3	3.6
S.E.	.4	.4	.2	.2
30 sec:				
Per cent error:	7	25	2	10
Response time:	4.6	5.8	3.2	4.2
S.E.	.4	.4	.2	.3
20 min:				
Per cent error:	5	17	2	12
Response time:	5.1	5.3	4.3	4.2
S.E.	.4	.4	.3	.2
48 hrs:				
Per cent error:	2	25	5	12
Response time:	5.3	6.6	4.4	4.3
S.E.	.4	.4	.4	.3

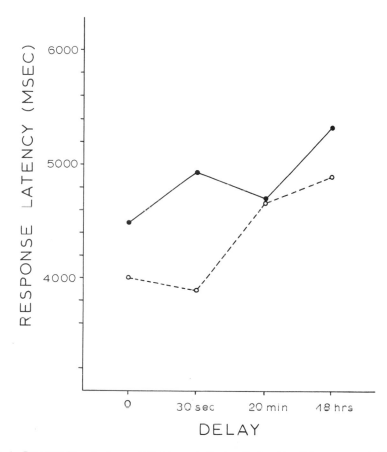

FIG. 1. Response latencies for explicit statements (broken line) and implicit statements (solid line).

discarded if they fell more than two standard deviations above a subject's mean, and a reaction time equal to the second standard deviation point was substituted. Response times lost because of error were replaced by substituting a value proportional to both the row and column mean.

Questions concerning argumentative paragraphs required more time to answer than questions concerning descriptive paragraphs, $F(1,554) = 59.75$, $p<.001$, equally for explicit and implicit questions. No interaction involving the paragraph type variable was significant. Descriptive and argumentative paragraphs involved the same number of base structure propositions and there were no differences in error rate. Hence, one can assume that the memory representations for both types of paragraphs were equally long and equally accurate. The differences in question reaction times must then be attributed to the greater structural complexity of the memory representation of the argumentative paragraphs. Apparently, access time to information in episodic memory depends not only upon the total size of the unit that contains the required information (as was suggested by the differences between long and short paragraphs in Exp. I and II, and as will be demonstrated more conclusively in Chapter 9) but also on the complexity of the base structure.

Question response time increased as the delay between reading and the test increased, $F(3,554) = 4.78$, $p<.005$. The effect of explicit presentation of a test statement was also significant; implicit questions required more time to answer than explicit questions, $F(1,554) = 9.44$, $p<.005$. The most interesting result, however, concerns the interaction between the delay interval and the presentation mode. It was hypothesized that at delays where a memory representation of the surface features of the paragraph is still available, explicitly presented statements will be answered more rapidly than implicitly presented statements, but that this difference will disappear with longer delays, because responses on the basis of memory for surface features are no longer possible. Specifically, this implies that performance on the immediate test and after a 30-sec delay should be equivalent, and that performance after a 20-min and 48-hr delay should be equivalent, but that the superiority of explicit questions should be restricted to the 0- and 30-sec delays. These predictions were tested by means of orthogonal comparisons. Because the paragraph type variable did not interact with any of the other experimental variables the data were averaged over argumentative and descriptive paragraphs. These averages are shown in Fig. 1. The comparison between the 0-interval condition and the 30-sec delay condition yielded a nonsignificant $F(1,554) = 1.95$. The difference between the 20-min delay and the 48-hr delay also failed to reach statistical significance, $F(1,554) < 1$. However, there was a statistically significant difference between explicit and implicit test statements for the 0- and 30-sec delay conditions, $F(1,554) = 11.40, p<.01$. For the 20-min and 48-hr delay conditions, the difference between explicit and implicit response times was not statistically significant, $F(1,554) = 1.54$. Thus, the question delay effects of Exp. I and II are fully replicated.

Even though it did not affect the statistical analyses very much, there is one deviant result, as can be seen from an inspection of Table 5. The mean response latency for implicit questions from argumentative paragraphs after 48-hr delay is quite a bit longer than any of the other times that have been obtained. Is this an indication of differential decay rates for explicit and implicit information, or is it merely a consequence of selecting a few particularly difficult test statements for that experimental condition? Although there is no way of deciding this question here, one must proceed with caution: Perhaps the data are more complex than the statistical analysis makes them appear.

Discussion

Sentences must often be regarded as incomplete in their coding of the intended content. In this sense, comprehension must always involve some processing of implicit information. Some implicit information that must be processed involves syntactic deletions of only a single case within a proposition. For example, (LARGE,BOX)&(RED,BOX) are not usually realized as *the box is large and the box is red* but rather as *the large red box*, where one occurrence of box is deleted. The question that the present studies were designed to answer is whether a reader will process implicit information when that information consists of *whole* propositions. The textual conditions under which the question was investigated were such that the processing of successive propositions depended upon the encoding of the implicit proposition.

The answer that Exp. II and III have provided to this question is unequivocally "yes." If subjects are given a paragraph in which one of the base structure propositions is not represented explicitly, this proposition will be inferred during reading and stored in memory if *(a)* the proposition is redundant in the sense that it is possible to infer it on the basis of general knowledge as well as the specific paragraph context, and *(b)* if such an inference is required in order to preserve the continuity of the text. The conclusion that subjects do infer redundant implicit propositions during reading is in agreement with results obtained by Frederiksen (1972), who studied subjects' recall of text, and in particular the kind of errors and distortions that occur during recall. On the basis of such data, Frederiksen concluded that inferences are made during reading, in addition to being formed during the reconstructive activity at the time of recall.

Error rates were higher for implicit material than for explicit material but did not increase with the delay interval in Exp. III. This result supports the interpretation of the data offered here that inferences are made during reading, rather than at the time of retrieval. Inferring a proposition during reading is more difficult than decoding one that is explicitly represented in the surface structure, but once that proposition is stored in memory it is treated like all other propositions.

The difference observed here between descriptive and argumentative paragraphs deserves some comment. These paragraphs were included because it seemed possible that memory for surface features might not be as good for the complex argumentative paragraphs as for the rather simple descriptive paragraphs. For example, surface memory for argumentative paragraphs might contain less information because argumentative encoding time was longer. Or, surface memory might contain only a listing of propositions and not the structure connecting those propositions. Such a listing would be adequate for answering descriptive explicit questions, but not for answering argumentative explicit questions. If this had been the case, the superiority of explicit questions at short delays would have been reduced or absent for the argumentative paragraphs. Instead, the question-delay effect was as great for these paragraphs as for descriptive paragraphs.

Both reading times and question response times were longer for argumentative paragraphs than for descriptive paragraphs. These results show that the argumentative paragraphs were indeed more complex semantically. If the two paragraph types had differed only in surface or syntactic complexity, then reading times would have differed as they did, but question response times would have been equal (see Chapter 5). In other words, if the two paragraph types had the same kind of memory structure, then times to access information in those structures should also be the same. But access time for argumentative paragraphs was longer than access time for descriptive paragraphs both in long-term memory and in surface memory.

How do the structures of the two paragraph types differ? They do not differ in the size of the memory representation, because number of surface words and number of base propositions were controlled. The difference must therefore lie within the memory representations. Either the argumentative propositions themselves are more complex (e.g., more abstract) or the argumentative organization is more complex. If the organization is more complex, then any single proposition would be more difficult to locate. Thus argumentative access times would be longer than descriptive access times. This same interpretation, that the propositions of an encoded paragraph are not content-addressable, described the paragraph length effect in Exp. I and II. Other interpretations are, of course, possible; for example, argumentative paragraphs are more abstract. But however the argumentative-descriptive differences are interpreted, the important result remains: The question-delay effect applies to both types of text.

The most interesting result of the studies reported here was an unexpected one: the failure to observe the predicted results in Exp. I, and for the short delays, in Exp. III, which we interpreted to be a consequence of the fact that memory for text is a multi-level phenomenon. Specifically, we have observed two different memory representations: a relatively stable propositional representation of the meaning of the paragraph, which was the same whether or not redundant propositions were explicitly expressed in the text, and a less stable memory for surface features of the text, perhaps for the actual words used, which was available only right after reading the paragraph or after a 30-sec delay. Twenty minutes of reading other material effectively interfered with this memory for surface features and forced subjects to rely upon the propositional memory. Access time to surface-type information was faster than access time for propositional-type information. The latter was approximately equal for explicitly presented propositions tested after a delay, and implicitly presented propositions, irrespective of delay. For the data in Fig. 1, the average response time for explicitly presented material with no (or 30-sec) delay was 3.9 sec, while for the same material a response time of 4.8 sec was observed after a delay, which is quite comparable to the 4.7 and 5.0-sec response times for implicit propositions, tested either without or with delay. There is, in addition, a suggestion in Fig. 1 that response times increase as a function of delay, even if one disregards the 0- and 30-sec tests of explicitly presented material. This would mean that access time to propositional memory itself becomes longer as a function of delay. There may be various explanations for this phenomenon. For example, it might mean that as the interval between reading and test increases, the time to access the right paragraph in memory becomes longer.

It is not easy to decide exactly what the relationship is between the memory for surface features of a text, as observed here, and the short-term memory identified in list-learning studies. Classical short-term memory is severely restricted in its capacity, and the type of memory that was observed here goes well beyond this capacity, even if one grants that exactly what constitutes a "chunk" of text is still a little puzzling. If one equates short-term memory with the contents of a subject's consciousness, as was suggested in Chapter 4, it is again obvious that 120-word paragraphs exceed the capacity of consciousness, though one would be hard put to state precisely what that capacity might be. Therefore, it appears that memory for surface features of a text is something else than the familiar short-term memory, a level intermediate between it and memory for meaning. Short-term memory proper has been demonstrated in studies concerned with speech and recall in the work of Jarvella (1970). Jarvella showed that when spoken discourse was interrupted and the listener was asked for immediate recall, subjects could, essentially, recall perfectly the current syntactic clause, but that verbatim recall dropped off sharply prior to that. The memory level identified by Jarvella may be much more like the acoustic short-term memory buffer that keeps reappearing in list-learning work than the memory for surface features that we were forced to postulate here. The latter has a much larger capacity and is not acoustic or phonemic but is at a deeper, perhaps verbal-linguistic level: It was not disrupted by the slight changes in the wording between text and question that were made in Experiment 1.

The alternative to a short-term memory explanation is a depth-of-processing hypothesis, as suggested by Craik and Lockhart (1972). Craik and Lockhart posit a limited-capacity central processor which may be deployed in a number of different ways. One type of processing involves deeper analysis of the stimulus. Memory is, thus, a continuum from the transient products of sensory analyses to the more stable products of semantic operations. Superimposed on this basic memory system, however, is a second way in which stimuli are retained—recirculating information at one level of processing. Whenever information is maintained at one level, the phenomenon of short-term memory appears. While limited capacity is a function of the processor itself, the number of items held depends upon the level at which the processor is operating. The deeper the level of processing, the greater its apparent capacity. Likewise, information is lost at a rate appropriate to the processing level: Deeper levels involve slower rates.

The observed phenomenon of a surface memory for prose can be easily derived from the processing assumptions of Craik and Lockhart. First of all, processing of the textual information used in our studies must proceed to deeper levels of analysis than processing of single words or word pairs in list-learning tasks. Short-term memory for prose should, therefore, exceed the capacity of short-term memory observed in list learning, since the level at which the central processor maintains the information is deeper. Furthermore, since rate of loss from short-term memory is a function of processing level, one should expect short-term textual information to be lost more slowly than the 20- to 30-sec temporal limit observed for single words. The only addition to Craik and Lockhart that is required to explain our results is that access time is a function of level. This additional assumption is necessary because reaction times to explicit propositions were significantly faster than those to implicit propositions when the surface representation was still available.

Summary

Comprehension consists in constructing a text base from whatever cues are available in a text. Usually, each proposition in the text base is explicitly cued by the text, but it happens quite frequently that a coherent text base can only be constructed if some propositions are included that are not directly represented in the surface structure of the text. The processing of such implicit propositions was studied in a series of experiments wherein subjects read paragraphs in which a given critical proposition either was or was not explicitly expressed. Immediately after reading, a test sentence based upon the critical proposition was shown to the subject who gave a true-false response. Subjects were very well able to recognize such sentences as true even when these sentences had not been explicitly a part of the paragraph, but they responded faster when they had actually just read the sentence. On the other hand, if the true-false test was delayed 20 minutes or more, reaction times to explicit and implicit sentences were equal. The latter finding was interpreted as support for the notion that whether or not critical sentences are explicitly given in a paragraph, the reader will infer the corresponding proposition and store it in memory as part of the text base that is his memory for the meaning of the paragraph. Therefore, when asked a question about it, he will answer it with equal ease whether or not the sentence had actually been read—except that if the test question is asked while he still has other information about the text (memory for the actual words used), he can answer on the basis of this auxiliary memory, speeding up his response time. Memory for surface features is, however, subject to strong interference and is quickly lost; hence, the initial superiority of explicit sentences is also lost and subjects must rely upon their propositional memory, which is, presumably, equal in the cases studied here for explicit and implicit test sentences.

9
MEMORY SEARCH I:
PARAGRAPH MEMORY AND THE
RETRIEVAL OF INFORMATION

Chapters 9 and 10 are concerned with the speed with which subjects can retrieve information from memory. Chapter 10 deals with the retrieval of general knowledge, that is, with semantic memory processes. The experimental paradigm to be studied in the present chapter involves first the presentation of some new information for the subject and then a demand to retrieve some of this information as fast as possible. The information presented here is in the form of paragraphs of natural language texts, and the test questions are simple sentences based on this text.

In list-learning studies, the speed with which subjects can retrieve information from memory has already provided some important clues about how information is accessed in memory. By now it is well-known that if subjects hold brief lists of words (digits, letters) in short-term memory and are asked whether a given test item is one of the target words, strong list-length effects are obtained. Each additional word in the target set adds about 40 msec to the response latencies obtained (Sternberg, 1969). There have been numerous replications and variations of Sternberg's original experiments, but although there are some inconsistencies in the data and some remaining gaps in our knowledge, the data are fairly clear on the list-length effects mentioned (Nickerson, 1972). What is not at all clear at this time is how the data should be interpreted. Sternberg (1969) proposed a model involving a serial and exhaustive search of short-term memory, which accounts well for the original data and with a few modifications (e.g., to handle serial-position effects) may still provide a satisfactory explanation of the data now available. Yet recently, it has become obvious that the data from these experiments do not constrain theories sufficiently and that there are alternative explanations of the data which are just as good, postulating entirely different processes (Theios, 1973; Townsend, 1971). Therefore, we shall for the moment defer the discussion of theories and concentrate upon the data themselves.

Atkinson and Juola (1973) extended Sternberg's memory search paradigm to longer lists that exceed the capacity of short-term memory. Their results are analogous to Sternberg's, except that the slope of the function relating list length and reaction time is drastically reduced and the intercept is raised. For lists of 16 to 32 words, each additional word in the list lengthens response latencies by only 4 msec. Furthermore, while the list-length – response-latency functions for positive and negative items (that is, items that are or are not members of the target set) are parallel when the lists are short enough to be held in short-term memory, Atkinson and Juola reported essentially flat functions for negative test words. (We shall not be concerned here with the data from the repeated presentations which are also included in the report.)

What happens when the subject is given not a list of words, but a paragraph to be remembered, and is then asked whether some simple statement was or was not part of that paragraph? Will the length of the paragraph have similar effects as the length of a word list, that is, will it take more time to recognize a test statement as old as the length of the paragraph increases? If recognition latencies in this situation do not depend upon paragraph length, one could conclude that the recognition process contacts relevant information directly, that is, the relevant trace was content addressable. If, on the other hand, recognition latencies turn out to be positively correlated with paragraph length, a variety of explanations, including some sort of a search process, become feasible.

When subjects read a paragraph and are then asked to recognize some information from it, there are two obvious ways to do so. One can evaluate the truth or falsity of the test question in the light of the paragraph read, or one can judge whether or not the test item was contained verbatim in the paragraph. The latter is what is usually meant by the term recognition and is, of course, the only thing subjects can do in list-learning experiments. However, when faced with a text rather than a word list, subjects are often not able to recognize a test sentence verbatim and respond on the basis of the meaning of the sentence. Thus, test sentences that are true, as judged by the information given, are "recognized" while sentences incompatible in meaning are rejected (Bransford & Franks, 1971; Sachs, 1967). We have, therefore, used two different experimental procedures. In Experiment I, subjects were given a paragraph of text followed by a test sentence and were asked to judge whether or not the test sentence was true with respect to the preceding paragraph. Experiment II followed a similar procedure, except that subjects were asked to decide whether or not the test sentence had been one of the actual sentences of the paragraph. That is, subjects were required to make a recognition response, rather than a true-false judgment. In both experiments, the length of the paragraph was the independent variable. Paragraphs between 20 and 120 words were used, and the latencies of the responses to the test sentences were plotted as a function of paragraph length.

The decision to measure paragraph length in terms of number of words needs justification. Number of propositions would appear to be a much more appropriate measure. However, number of propositions and number of words are highly correlated in normal text, and the latter is a much more convenient measure. More importantly, controlling number of propositions by itself is by no means sufficient, as the considerable differences in reading times and question answering times between argumentative and descriptive paragraphs (which did not differ in this measure) have shown in the previous chapter. Not only must the number of propositions in a text base be controlled, but also their structural complexity. We do not even know, as yet, precisely what is involved in structural complexity, or what other variables might be important. Lacking the ability to control our materials, we decided to select paragraphs at random, specified only as to number of words, from a set of experimental paragraphs recently constructed by Anderson, Sawyers, and Farkas (1972). These paragraphs are all on similar topics (American presidents) and written in a similar style and without obvious variations in complexity. Therefore, for such a homogeneous set of paragraphs, number of words is probably a good index of paragraph length.

1. EXPERIMENT I: LATENCIES OF TRUE-FALSE JUDGMENTS AS A FUNCTION OF THE LENGTH OF PARAGRAPHS[1]

Recognition memory for facts was investigated in this experiment. More specifically, the speed with which true-false judgments were made was studied as a function of the amount of material in which each fact had been embedded. Each subject read 16 paragraphs, four each of lengths 20, 40, 80, and 120 words. Half of the paragraphs (two of each length) were followed by a true statement, which was taken in only slightly modified form from the preceding text. The other paragraphs were followed by false statements. In order to avoid complications due to short-term memory, a 30-sec short-term memory suppression task (paraphrasing aloud an unrelated paragraph) was inserted between the original paragraph and the question about it.

Method

Subjects. The subjects were 34 undergraduate students at the University of Colorado who were participating in an experiment of their choice to fulfill a course requirement.

Materials. The 16 paragraphs for the factual recognition task, each concerning a different U.S. president, were adapted from the *President Paragraphs* of Anderson et al. (1972). For each paragraph a seven word test statement, either true or false, was constructed. Four paragraphs each of 20, 40, 80, and 120 words were used. The information targeted by the statements appeared approximately midway through each paragraph. All statements used words from the vocabulary of the corresponding paragraph, but the text was slightly modified from the way it occurred in the paragraph by simple word exchange, word substitution, word omission, or by an order rearrangement. In false statements the modification created an assertion clearly contrary to the facts of the paragraph. A frequently occurring change was the substitution in the question of the referent itself for a pronoun in the target clause of the paragraph. For example, the true statement *Hayes repaid favors by doling out*

---

[1]By D. Monk and W. Kintsch.

jobs targeted *He repaid these favors by doling out federal jobs.* Sample paragraphs, together with their test sentences, are shown in Table 1.

The materials for the 30-sec paraphrasing task were paragraphs of 50 words each on biological topics, such as agricultural practices and current developments in medicine. They were taken from daily newspapers, and only very minor alterations were made to achieve coherence in 50 words. Most of their content was semitechnical; all historical and political subjects were avoided. The experimental paragraphs and the paraphrase items were paired randomly, with a different presentation order for each subject.

Procedure. Each subject was told that the experiment concerned factual information processing. He was asked to perform two tasks consecutively: first, to read a factual paragraph (typed on a sheet of paper) silently at his own pace, trying to remember facts it contained, since he would be asked a question about it later; second, to paraphrase aloud another paragraph (also a typed sheet), retelling it in his own words as he read. He was told not to read the second paragraph through completely before speaking, but to paraphrase it a few words at a time, that the time for this second task was limited to 30 sec, and that he would probably not finish before the experimenter gave a stop signal. After this signal, the subject placed two fingers on a button box provided and pressed the appropriate button to respond "true" or "false" to a statement that appeared before him on a projection screen, taking as much time as needed to answer. It was made clear to the subject that the true-false statement was based solely on the one paragraph read silently just preceding his paraphrase, and that it was true or false without any ambiguity. He was told to base his responses only on the information he read and not on his own opinions; although the experimenter would be recording the time taken for the various tasks, time was limited only for the paraphrase, and accuracy was more important than speed. The subject was informed that all the material in the silently read paragraphs and the statements concerned U.S. presidents, that the paraphrased paragraphs were on biological topics, that there were 16 independent items of each of the two types plus two pairs for practice, and that feedback would be provided after he finished all items.

Results

Table 2 summarizes the principal results of the experiment. All numbers shown in Table 2 are the averages of the values obtained from two different paragraphs. Thus, at least to some small extent, variations between paragraphs are averaged out in the data shown. All latency data are for correct responses only.

Reading times for the paragraphs of different lengths increased as expected, but not quite in proportion to paragraph length. The reading time per word actually decreased somewhat as paragraph length increased.

The error rate was tolerably small for true sentences, and the existing differences between paragraph lengths were not significant statistically. This was not the case, however, for false sentences, where for four of the eight paragraphs error rates in excess of 20% were obtained. However, these differences may have been more a consequence of chance variations in the difficulty of the test sentences, rather than a

TABLE 1

Sample Paragraphs and Test Sentences for Experiment I

20 Words:

"Van Buren sought to avoid the entire slavery issue, making no promise to either faction except the pledge of noninvolvement."

Test Sentence: Van Buren promised to solve slavery issues. (FALSE)

40 Words:

"When Woodrew Wilson reached the Presidency, he carried into office a strictly Southern viewpoint on issues and policy, including social prejudices against the Negro. Although favoring social justice in other areas, Wilson failed badly in the matter of racial justice."

Test Sentence: Wilson had social prejudices against the Negro. (TRUE)

80 Words:

"When Grover Cleveland was President, a severe economic crisis gripped the nation. Against the warnings of his economic advisors, and contrary to the wishes of a large part of his party, President Cleveland proposed a repeal of the Silver Purchase Act. Cleveland was obstinate and, after a long fight in Congress, the repeal bill was finally passed. However, Cleveland's bill did not accomplish its purpose and the economy grew worse. Moreover, the controversy over the bill had divided the nation."

Test Sentence: President Cleveland proposed the Silver Purchase Act. (FALSE)

120 Words:

"Early in 1941, Senator Harry S. Truman was appointed chairman of an important Senate committee to investigate the procurement and construction of all supplies, munitions, vehicles, and facilities connected with war against Nazi Germany. Truman dedicated himself to this work and did an outstanding job. Through fair and comprehensive investigations, Truman exposed many costly acts of mismanagement and corruption. Through such actions, the Truman Committee soon developed a formidable reputation. In many cases all that was required to correct an abuse was Truman's announcement that he would investigate. It is estimated that the Truman Committee produced a direct saving of 15 billion dollars for the American taxpayer. In addition, the committee's reputation probably kept countless other problems from ever developing."

Test Sentence: Truman exposed many costly acts of mismanagement. (TRUE)

TABLE 2

Reading Time, Error Rates, and Response Latencies to the Test Sentences as a Function of Paragraph Length in Experiment I for True and False Test Sentences

	Paragraph length (words)				
	20	40	80	120	
Reading time (in sec):					
True	10.1	16.8	32.2	42.5	$F(3,96) = 228\ p<.001$
False	12.3	20.2	32.2	42.5	$F(3,95) = 213\ p<.001$
Error rates (in per cent):					
True	3	4	13	6	$F(3,96) = 1.69$ n.s.
False	6	13	36	25	$F(3,95) = 13.9\ p<.001$
Test sentence latencies (in sec):					
True	4.7	5.1	5.8	5.7	$F(3,96) = 7.07\ p<.001$
False	5.3	5.9	5.7	5.9	$F(3,95) = 1.24$ n.s.

function of paragraph length *per se*. The correlations between paragraph length and error rate, though positive, were not significant for either true or false test sentences. The trouble seems to lie in the way some of the false sentences were constructed. High error rates occurred when the test statement differed from the sentence actually appearing in the paragraph by only one word (the grammatical subject or a modifier). When the changes made in the test statement were more extensive, or when they involved the main verb of the sentence, error rates were low.

The results of primary interest are the response latencies to the test sentences. As Table 2 shows, differences between test latencies as a function of paragraph length were highly significant statistically for true test sentences, but not for false sentences. The exact nature of the relationship between test latencies and paragraph length is, however, obscured by the high error rates for some of the false test sentences. Therefore, for the purpose of further analyses, all test sentences for which the error rate was greater than 20% were deleted. Means, together with 95% confidence intervals, for the remaining paragraphs are plotted as a function of paragraph length in Fig. 1. For true sentences, no data were lost, and the results are fairly clear, in spite of the sometimes considerable variation between paragraphs of the same length. Reaction times for true statements increased as a function of list length, this increase being primarily a linear one ($F_{\text{linearity}}(1,96) = 11.34$, $p < .01$, no higher order trend significant).[2] The linear trend accounts for 79% of the paragraph-length sum of squares. The least-square line shown in Fig. 1 has the equation

$$t_{TRUE} = 4641 + 10.9W. \tag{1}$$

Each additional word in our paragraphs added about 11 msec to the response latency for true judgments. The results for false judgments are less clear, because of the high error rates for some of the false test statements. However, there are certainly no indications in the present data that paragraph length affects response latencies for false statements in the same way it affects true responses. If the paragraphs with high error rates are retained as in Table 2, no significant latency differences are obtained, and excluding the high-error items as in Fig. 1 does not alter this conclusion.

Discussion

Access times to episodic memory, when the episodes involved are derived from natural language text, exhibit quite similar properties to access times when the episodes involved are members of a word list. A comparison of Fig. 1 with the corresponding results of Atkinson and Juola (1973) for word lists clearly makes this point. In both cases there is a strong list length effect for positive items, though the slope of the present function is steeper (11 msec per word) than that for word lists (4 msec per word). Similarly, only insignificant increases due to list length were found for negative items (none for paragraphs, .5 msec for word lists). The differences between the two sets of results lie in the intercepts of the length – reaction-time

[2]See Footnote 2, Chapter 5, *Statistical Notes*, on page 111.

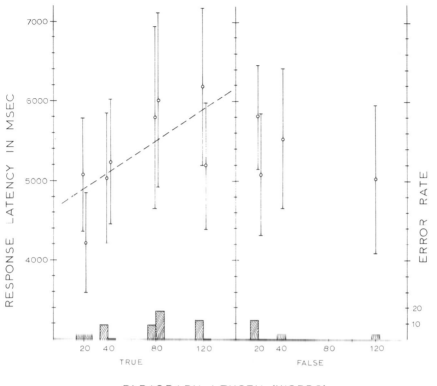

FIG. 1. Mean response times and error rates for true and false test statements as a function of paragraph length in Experiment I.

functions. Intercepts of about .75 sec for word lists contrast quite strikingly with the values of around 5 sec obtained in the present study. Some difference is undoubtedly due to longer reading times for statements than for single words, but this can only be a minor factor. Clearly, the fairly deep semantic processing that statement recognition required (both because of the delay between presentation and test and because of the nature of the false test sentences) must be primarily responsible for these very long decision times. A second difference between the results for word lists and paragraphs is the reversal in latencies for positive and negative items: For word lists, negative items were responded to much more rapidly than positive items, while false test statements actually produced longer latencies than true statements, as shown in Table 2. This result is probably due to the way in which new test statements were constructed. They contained mostly words that had appeared in the paragraph, but these words were combined so that a false assertion was made. Thus the subjects could not simply respond on the basis of word recognition, but had to work at a deeper, propositional level.

Before continuing with the discussion of the present results, however, a second experiment must be described in which yes-no recognition judgments were used to test sentences after subjects read paragraphs of varying lengths.

2. EXPERIMENT II: RECOGNITION LATENCIES AS A FUNCTION OF PARAGRAPH LENGTH[3]

Method

Subjects. Thirty-four University of Colorado students who responded to an advertisement served as subjects. They were paid for their participation in the experiment.

Materials. Twenty paragraphs not used in Exp. I were adapted from the *President Paragraphs* of Anderson et al. (1972). Four paragraphs each were 20, 40, 80, and 120 words long, and four were also 120 words long, but divided into three subparagraphs of 40 words each. The 3×40 paragraphs were included in order to gain some idea about the effects of subdividing a paragraph. The three subsections were all on a separate topic, though they concerned the same president. For example, the first 40 words in the Jackson paragraph dealt with Andrew Jackson's economic policies, the second with foreign policy, and the last third described his relationship with the Indians.

Paragraphs were rewritten so that *(a)* the number of words came out exactly as intended and *(b)* there was a seven-word sentence approximately in the middle of half of the paragraphs, which could be used as a test sentence. In this way, old test sentences appeared on the test exactly in the same way as in the paragraph. (It will be remembered that this was not the case in Exp. I.) New test sentences were constructed as in Exp. I, by using words from the paragraph but putting them together in a new way, except that care was taken that no distractor sentence differed from an actual sentence in the paragraph by less than two words. (Sentences differing by only one word produced too many false positive responses in the earlier experiment.) Note that the way in which distractor sentences were generated necessitated that subjects pay attention to the meaning of the whole sentence and not just to single words. "New" test sentences in the present experiment were also false, in the same sense as the distractor sentences of Exp. I.

Examples of paragraphs, together with their test sentences, are given in Table 3.

Procedure. The procedure and the experimental apparatus were identical to those of Exp. I, except for the change from true-false to yes-no recognition judgments. In particular, there were again two warm-up paragraphs that were not scored and a 30-sec paraphrasing task between reading a paragraph and the presentation of the test slide. Instructions to the subject emphasized the recognition aspects of the task and did not mention the words true or false at all: "The test statement appeared verbatim

[3]By D. Monk and W. Kintsch.

TABLE 3

Sample Paragraphs and Test Sentences for Experiment II

---

20 Words:

"President Tyler's administration was stormy. He made it clear who was boss. He would never consent to being dictated to."

Test Sentence: He made it clear who was boss. (YES)

40 Words:

"Shortly after Van Buren's election, the country's first economic panic began. The inactive Van Buren was not involved in causing the panic. He firmly believed in a passive federal government, and so did not attempt to interfere with the economy."

Test Sentence: Van Buren's active interference caused economic panic. (NO)

80 Words:

"As president, Benjamin Harrison promoted growth within the nation and peace abroad. Primarily due to his urging as chairman of the committee on territories, six new states were admitted to the Union, the greatest number of additions under any one President. Harrison avoided major conflict with foreign powers. His organization of the Bering Sea arbitration was important for relations with Great Britain. President Harrison also furthered harmony with the Latin American countries by convening the Pan American Congress in Washington."

Test Sentence: Harrison avoided major conflict with foreign powers. (YES)

120 Words:

"In his inaugural address, President Thomas Jefferson pledged that he would remove no one from government office for political purposes. However, he immediately began to do just that, thus beginning the spoils system in government. In one glaring example, Jefferson removed a competent employee from an important job and installed in his place an old man who was feeble in mind and body, with absolutely no qualifications for the office except that he belonged to Jefferson's political party. After successfully impeaching one district judge, Jefferson moved directly against a Supreme Court member. Jefferson was defeated in this attempt, however, and the judge was finally absolved of all Jefferson's charges. Throughout his administration Jefferson attempted to take away the court's powers."

Test Statement: Jefferson removed Supreme Court Justices from office. (NO)

3 × 40 Words:

President Andrew Jackson did a great deal to further the economy of the nation and to initiate internal improvements. After completely paying off the national debt, President Jackson distributed all the excess left in the treasury to the individual states.

The United States had a hostile interlude with France during the Jackson administration. Jackson demanded unreasonable damage payments from France. Fortunately, France had more sense than to go to war over such a trivial matter and made a token payment.

Andrew Jackson was an old Indian fighter and continued in this attitude when he became President. He had little regard for Indian rights. Most eastern tribes were forced to give up their lands and were shoved further and further west.

Test Statement: Jackson demanded unreasonable damage payments from France. (YES)

---

in the text or else it was not there at all. If the statement was not there, it is possible that some of the statement's words may have appeared in the paragraph, but we are only interested in the statement as a whole. Your task is to indicate whether the statement on the screen was present or absent. If the statement was present in the silently read text, press the 'yes' button; if the statement was not present, press the 'no' button." In all other respects, the instructions were similar to those of Exp. I.

Results

The data shown in Table 4 are the averages for the two paragraphs in each condition, based only upon trials on which a correct response occurred.

The reading time results show the same increase as in Exp. I, though they are slightly shorter. Error rates show that the response bias from Exp. I has been reversed: The true-false judgments showed a "true" bias, while in the present experiment many more errors occurred in the direction of "no" responses than in the direction of "yes" responses. Indeed, for new test statements, error rates were quite small and did not differ significantly between conditions, while for old sentences appreciable error rates were observed for the 80- and 3×40 word paragraphs. Error rates and paragraph lengths were uncorrelated. Test sentence latencies showed the same pattern of results as in Exp. I: There was a significant difference between paragraphs of different lengths for old sentences, but not for new sentences. The latter tended to be about as long as the longest means for old sentences.

A more detailed analysis of the test sentence latencies as a function of paragraph length is shown in Fig. 2. Again, as was done previously, paragraphs with an error rate greater than 20% were not included in the analysis, since such high error rates make the interpretation of the response latencies questionable. Only one mean was lost in this way (one of the 80-word paragraphs). The 3×40 paragraphs are not shown in Fig. 2. Figure 2 is very similar qualitatively to Fig. 1. In both cases, only the differences between positive instances are significant, and this significance can be traced to a linear increase in response latencies as a function of paragraph length $\left[F_{\text{linearity}}(1,127) = 3.94, p < .05, F_{\text{higher orders}}(2,127) = 1.54, \text{n.s.} \right]$. The least-square line for the "yes" responses in Fig. 2 is:

$$t_{YES} = 3237 + 4.3W. \tag{2}$$

TABLE 4

Reading Times, Error Rates, and Response Latencies to the Test Sentences as a Function of Paragraph Length in Experiment II for Old and New Test Sentences

	Paragraph length (words)					
	20	40	80	120	3 × 40	
Reading time (in sec):						
Yes	8.0	15.3	28.3	32.3	36.1	$F(4,127) = 234\, p < .001$
No	8.0	16.2	25.4	35.0	39.2	$F(4,129) = 187\, p < .001$
Error rates (in per cent):						
Yes	13	13	22	4	22	$F(4,132) = 3.00\, p < .05$
No	7	7	1	10	15	$F(4,132) = 2.06$ n.s.
Test sentence latencies (in sec):						
Yes	3.1	3.6	4.0	3.7	3.8	$F(4,127) = 3.52\, p < .05$
No	3.7	4.0	4.2	4.0	4.4	$F(4,129) = 2.14$ n.s.

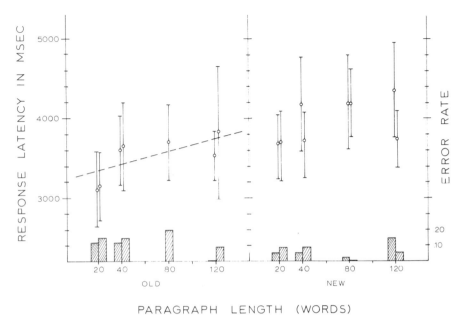

FIG. 2. Mean response time and error rates for old and new test statements as a function of paragraph length in Experiment II.

The 3×40-word paragraphs were included in the present experiment in order to determine whether such paragraphs behave more like 40-word paragraphs or more like 120-word paragraphs. Arguments for either possibility can be advanced, since one can consider these paragraphs either as three separate topical units or as one unit concerned with a single president. The data, unfortunately, do not permit a resolution of this question. For "yes" sentences the mean response latency for the two 3×40 paragraphs is 3.8 sec and falls within the confidence limits of both the 40-word and 120-word paragraphs. This conclusion remains unchanged even if one of the 3×40 paragraphs with a high error rate is excluded. A more powerful experiment than the present one would be required to answer this question, and it would involve a wider sampling of paragraphs in each condition.

A comparison of the results obtained for true-false and yes-no judgments reveals an over-all qualitative consistency, but some interesting quantitative differences. There is first of all the reversal in response biases, which favored "true" responses in Exp. I, but "no" responses in Exp. II. This is not very surprising: Instructions in Exp. II required subjects to respond "yes" only to sentences that repeated text sentences verbatim. Given that memory for the precise surface features of a text is not very reliable, subjects' reluctance to give "yes" responses in Exp. II is quite understandable. More interesting is a comparison of Eqs. (1) and (2). Both the slope (11 sec vs. 4 sec) and intercept (4.6 sec vs. 3.2 sec) were appreciably higher for "true" responses than for "yes" responses. Since the test statements were of equal length in the two experiments, differences in reading time for the test statements cannot explain these observations. In both cases, paragraph length had the same kind of effect (indeed, the same effect as list length in studies of word recognition), but processing times for true-false judgments are greater than for recognition judgments, and the effects of paragraph length were more pronounced for the former than for the latter.

3. DISCUSSION

Considering the two experiments jointly, the question posed at the beginning of this chapter can be answered with some confidence: When subjects read a paragraph and are then asked to access information contained in it, response times increase as the paragraphs become longer. This effect was clear in Exp. I where subjects had to indicate whether a test sentence was true or false with respect to the paragraph just read, and it reappeared in Exp. II when subjects merely had to recognize whether or not a test sentence had been presented before. This was true, however, only for positive test sentences. Response latencies to distractor sentences, which in these experiments were sentences that used some words from the paragraph but combined them in a new way so that the statement made was false with respect to the text, were not affected by paragraph length. Since the variability of the latencies was large and Exp. I was also subject to a relatively high error rate for distractor sentences, this conclusion must remain somewhat speculative. The finding that paragraph length determined access times is incompatible with a simple model of information storage in memory that claims that information is content addressable.

The differences between the true-false judgments in Exp. I and the recognition judgments in Exp. II may be due to several different sources. First of all, it may be the case that true-false judgments involve essentially different psychological processes than yes-no recognition judgments. For the latter, subjects presumably search their memory to determine whether the test item has been stored in the right context. True-false judgments, on the other hand, may not merely involve locating a particular memory trace in a particular context, but also testing its relationship to other memory traces in that context. The truth of a statement may not be determined simply by noting that the statement is stored in memory in the right kind of context, but by evaluating its connections with the other statements that comprise the memory for the particular text. Obviously, such a procedure must be followed if the test statement itself is not stored in memory but rather must be inferred on the basis of the information stored, as was the case in some of the other experiments reported here. It is possible, however, that even if the test statement has been presented explicitly and is presumably stored in memory, subjects nevertheless engage in the same kind of inferential behavior in determining its truth or falsity. In other words, the truth of a statement may lie in its connections to other items, and the fact that the statement itself is accessible in memory may not be decisive by itself.

Such an explanation accounts qualitatively for the observed differences between true-false and yes-no judgments. The former take longer over-all, because of the cross-checking involved, and paragraph length effects are more pronounced, because the larger the total unit in which a test sentence is contained, the greater the number of relationships to other memory traces that must be tested. However, this explanation is not the only one possible. Suppose, on the contrary, that determining the truth of a test statement in the present experiment merely involves accessing its propositional representation in the episodic memory trace that comprises the paragraph memory. If a corresponding proposition (or propositions) can be located, the sentence will be called true; if not, it will be called false. Also, assume that the yes-no recognition task used in Exp. II involves a quite similar process, except that what is being accessed is not the propositional representation of the paragraph but the memory for the surface form of the text, in accordance with the experimental instructions to determine whether a given test item had been presented verbatim in the text. Thus, the difference between the two experiments may be that two different levels of memory are involved: a propositional level, for determining the truth of test sentences (which did not correspond verbatim to any previously presented sentences), and a verbal surface memory, to test whether something is a verbatim repetition or not. That access to surface representations is faster than access to the base representation of a text has already been demonstrated in Chapter 8. It was shown there that access times to sentences that are stored in memory only at a propositional level are significantly longer than access times to sentences for which a surface memory for the actual verbal expressions used is also available. Thus a fairly simple explanation can be given for the data reported here. Both true-false and yes-no recognition judgments involve basically similar processes under the conditions of the present experiment: checking whether a certain memory trace is or is not available in memory. The difference arises because true-false judgments require accessing propositional memory, while yes-no recognition judgments have to rely upon the memory for the surface features of the text. The latter process, in agreement with the experiments reported in the previous chapter, is considerably faster. In both cases, however, response latencies are positively correlated with paragraph length when a positive test sentence is identified.

A rather simple model will be offered here, one that can account for the data by using, as basic operations, the pattern matching and pattern completion operations that have played such a central role in the theorizing about episodic memory in Chapter 4. Indeed, the model must be regarded as an application of that theory to the present experimental situation. Suppose that memory for a paragraph consists of a set of complex elements, as hypothesized in Chapter 4. Two kinds of elements are of special interest here: propositions, which constitute the memory for the meaning of the text, and verbatim memory for the actual words used in the text, that is, for the surface features of a text. Other elements of the memory representation, such as contextual and phonemic elements, can be disregarded for the moment. When the subject is given a test statement he attempts to match it with the information held in memory. It is assumed that this matching involves a two-stage process. The first stage selects the right paragraph out of the mass of traces in episodic memory. On the basis of common elements between the code of the test sentence and episodic memory codes, including contextual and temporal information, the right paragraph is singled out for further investigation. Note that given the experimental procedures used here, Stage 1 processing will always be successful, for even the negative test sentences share common elements (words, context, time) with episodic memory codes. Stage 2 processing involves matching the encoding of the test stimulus to the memory code located by the Stage 1 processing. Stage 2 processing is not merely a common element count; instead, a precise match with some of the components of the paragraph memory is required. Depending upon the experimental task, the subject encodes the test sentences either propositionally (for the true-false test) or verbatim (for the recognition test) and matches this test-item code to the components that make up the paragraph memory. It is assumed that this matching occurs in parallel. A paragraph-length effect arises because the time required for a match (or mismatch) is a random variable; the total matching process is finished only when the last of the subprocesses is finished. Thus, for a paragraph containing n components, the decision time will be given by the longest of n random matching times.

To create a testable model from this theory, we must add a few more specifications. First of all, we assume that the matching times are identically distributed exponential random variables with probability density functions

$$f(x) = \lambda e^{-\lambda x}. \tag{3}$$

Secondly, we assume that the number of components in the paragraph memory code that must be investigated is proportional to the number of words (W) in the paragraph. Number of propositions would probably give us a better measure, as was argued before, but since memory for surface features is involved in Exp. II, and since in any case neither our paragraphs nor our test sentences were controlled for number of propositions, the cruder measure of number of words must be used here. Somewhat arbitrarily, it was decided to use the number of words in the test sentences (seven) as a measure for the number of memory components in a paragraph. Thus, 20-word paragraphs are assumed to consist, for the purpose of the present analyses, of 3 seven-word components against which the test sentence must be matched. Similarly, the number of components for 40-, 80-, and 120-word paragraphs has been assumed to be 6, 12, and 18, respectively. This assumption is arbitrary, but not unreasonable, given the design of the present experiments. Some sort of a prior assumption is needed here, otherwise the number of parameters to be estimated would be excessive.

With these assumptions, the model can be formulated quite easily. The following equation for mean response latency is assumed, where k is an empirical constant (including Stage 1 processing and the motor component of the response times) and $f(W)$ is the mean decision time for deciding that a given test sentence is true (or was presented verbatim) for a paragraph W words long:

$$E(t_+) = k + f(W). \tag{4}$$

The term $f(W)$ is given by the expectation of the maximum of n identical, independent, random variables, each with density function (3):

$$f(W) = \frac{1}{\lambda} \sum_{i=1}^{n} \frac{1}{i} \tag{5}$$

Using an approximation for the sum in (5), we can rewrite (t_+) as

$$E(t_+) = k + 1/\lambda \, (C + \log h \, n + 1/2n) \tag{6}$$

where $C = .5772$ is the Euler constant. Since the value of n is determined by the assumptions made, two parameters k and λ remain to be estimated from the data. Figure 3 shows the mean response latencies for paragraphs 20, 40, 80, and 120 words long (the same data as in Figs. 1 and 2) together with predicted values on the basis of

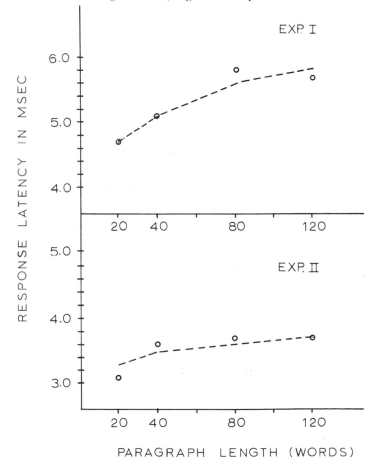

FIG. 3. Observed (circles) and predicted (broken lines) response times as a function of paragraph length.

Eq. (6). Estimates for k and λ were obtained by a modified method of moments, using the slope of the lines in Figs. 1 and 2 and the grand means. The prediction equations are

$$E(t_+) = 3.50 + .66\ (.5772 + \log h\ n + 1/2n) \tag{7}$$

for Exp. 1, and

$$E(t_+) = 2.83 + .26\ (.5772 + \log h\ n + 1/2n) \tag{8}$$

for Exp. 2. Thus the estimated processing rates for seven-word test components turn out to be about 1.5 per sec for true-false testing, and 3.9 per sec for recognition. The fit of the model to the data in Fig. 3 is reasonably good, but that means little since many other models could fit four data points that fall almost on a straight line with two estimated parameters. Only further work can decide how good the model described here really is. It was presented here merely to show that a simple model that is consistent with assumptions and results from various other chapters in this volume can provide a good account of the present data. Note that Eq. (6) is not linear in n, and hence not in W. Although the quadratic trends in Figs. 1 and 2 were not statistically significant, and only straight lines were required to fit the data, this property of the model is actually in good agreement with the obtained results. The prediction that latency-length functions should not increase linearly but logarithmically is, of course, open to empirical test with a wider range of paragraph lengths, and what is probably more important, a wider selection of different paragraphs of each length so that paragraph idiosyncrasies average out better than they did in the present studies.

The relationship between the present results and those obtained in comparable list-learning studies has already been discussed. The qualitative similarity between these sets of data is quite striking. It also seems possible to modify the two-stage model proposed here to account for word recognition latencies, as was suggested earlier (Chapter 4, Section 3.1.5). If one thinks of the first stage as an over-all similarity match on the basis of common elements, it is reasonable to assume that in word recognition studies, the subject may sometimes respond only on the basis of first-stage processing: ''Yes'' responses are given if the number of common elements is very high, ''no'' responses if it is very low. Only if the first-stage match produces an intermediate result is an extended search of memory performed. Such a model, if developed, would probably be very similar to one proposed by Atkinson and Juola (1973) and Atkinson, Herrmann, and Wescourt (1974) for exactly this experimental situation.

An interesting comparison can be made between the inference data discussed in Chapter 5 and the absolute values of the response times for the true-false recognitions and yes-no recognitions in Exp. I and II. Exact comparisons are meaningless because of numerous differences in materials and procedures, but it is nevertheless striking that the inference times are of about the same magnitude as the recognition times obtained in the present experiments. Comparing only over-all means (including errors and all experimental conditions), we have a mean of 5.76 sec for the true-false judgments and 4.04 sec for the yes-no recognitions, versus 4.40 sec for the inferences in Exp. I of Chapter 5 and 6.80 sec for those in Exp. IV (these two studies used paragraphs most comparable to those used here). It seems as if drawing inferences takes little time, relative to the time spent accessing the right information. Presumably, the information stored is in propositional form, and once the right propositions are located, the correct inferences are readily obtained. If one participates in one of these inference experiments (with their intentionally simple tasks), introspection confirms this account; the inferences themselves appear quite trivial, and the problem is to get the facts straight. Where the difference between inference times and recognition times becomes marked is in the variability of the scores: The standard deviation of the inference times is three times as large as that of the recognition times.

SUMMARY

If propositional memory is content addressable in the most direct sense of that term, then access times should not depend upon the length of the text base in which a given proposition is embedded. Experimental tests of this hypothesis were arranged by having subjects read texts varying in length between 20 and 120 words and then asking them to respond true or false to a test sentence from each paragraph. In other experiments, subjects were required instead to indicate whether or not they recognized the test sentence as having been included in the paragraph. The results for both types of tasks were qualitatively similar: It took subjects longer to positively identify a test sentence as paragraph length increased, the function relating response times to the number of words in the paragraph being approximately linear, with a slope of 11 msec per word for the true-false task, and 4 msec per word for the recognition task. Some interesting parallels between the present results and corresponding data from list-learning experiments were discussed. The data were interpreted as indicating some sort of memory search, rather than a content addressable memory. Two explanations were proposed. First, it is possible that propositions from longer texts require more evaluation time because more relationships to other propositions must be tested. Secondly, the pattern-match model described in Chapter 4 for list-learning data was extended to the present situation. It assumes that the test proposition is matched in parallel to all propositions in a base, and that a response occurs only after all matches have been completed.

10
MEMORY SEARCH II:
THE USE OF KNOWLEDGE IN THE
VERIFICATION OF STATEMENTS

Modern experimental psychology has only just touched upon the question of how knowledge becomes actualized. In prebehavioristic days this was one of the central problems for psychologists like Höffding (1891), James (1890), Müller (1913), and Selz (1922) some of whose work has entered into the discussion in Chapter 2. The concern with how knowledge is retrieved and how it is used reappeared in experimental psychology only quite recently and in a very restricted manner, primarily through papers by Landauer and Freedman (1968) and Collins and Quillian (1969). A burst of activity has followed these seminal papers, but it has stayed within the rather narrow limits of the original work. Modern psychology has as yet failed to consider the problem of knowledge actualization in its general form and has, instead, become embroiled in controversies that arose from too narrow formulations of the problem and corresponding restrictions in the scope of the experimental work. It is the purpose of this chapter to review this state of affairs and to present some data that demonstrate the need for a new, broader, and theoretically better motivated approach. Finally, a theoretical framework derived from the model presented in Chapter 2 will be outlined which accounts for the data presently available, and more importantly, which may serve as a guide for future experimental work directed towards the general problem of knowledge actualization.

1. REVIEW

In their paper published in 1969, Collins and Quillian derived experimental predictions from the semantic memory model of Quillian (1967, 1968, 1969). The relevant aspects of the model are illustrated in Fig. 1. Semantic memory is organized around a noun hierarchy: the nodes *oak, cedar, birch,* . . . are all connected to the

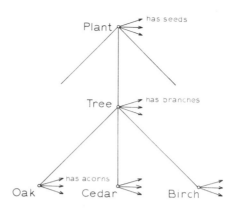

FIG. 1. A noun hierarchy in semantic memory according to the model of Collins and Quillian (1969).

superset node *tree*, which in turn is connected (together with *vegetable, grasses*, and others) to the superset *plant*. Properties are stored in an economical way, that is, at the highest level possible. Thus, for instance, the property *having branches* is stored with *tree*, rather than directly with *oak, cedar*, etc. A simple processing model is obtained by assuming that comprehending a sentence involves finding a path between the constituents of the sentence in this noun hierarchy. Thus, if a subject sees *A birch is a plant*, the connection between *birch* and *plant* is formed via *tree* (a Level-2 sentence), while for *A cedar is a tree*, there is a direct connection between the *cedar* and *tree* node (a Level-1 sentence), and *An oak is an oak* involves merely an identity match (Level-0 sentence). Similarly, we have for property sentences *An oak has acorns*, which is a Level-0 sentence and involves merely the look-up of a property stored at the *oak* node. *A cedar has branches*, on the other hand, first requires that a connection be made between the nodes *cedar* and *tree* (Level 1), while *A birch has seeds* requires a two-step connection between *birch* and *plant* before the property *has seeds* can be connected with *birch* (Level 2). If moving up (or down) levels in a hierarchy such as Fig. 1 requires time, quite straight-forward predictions can be made regarding the verification times for sentences as a function of level, that is, the degree of separation of subject and predicate in the noun hierarchy. Verification times should increase the farther apart they are.

The experimental task introduced by Collins and Quillian (1969) is a simple reaction time task: Subjects are shown a sentence and asked to press one button if they confirm the statement as true and another button if they reject it as false. The well-known result of their study was that verification times for sentences increased as a function of level, for both superset statements and property statements. In each case, a one-node difference added about 75 msec to the verification time. In addition, property sentences took considerably longer than superset sentences, which was interpreted by the authors as indicating that extra time was needed to retrieve a property from a noun node.

The levels that were the independent variable in Collins and Quillian's experiment were derived from an intuitively defined noun hierarchy. Later investigators showed that Collins and Quillian's levels were confounded with other variables, notably sentence frequency. Wilkins (1971) demonstrated that reaction times for superset sentences were a function of the conjoint frequency of subject and predicate on the Connecticut category norms (Cohen, Bousfield, & Whitmarsh, 1957). Responses were faster for *A robin is a bird (robin* is a high-frequency response for the category *bird)*, than for *A goose is a bird (goose* is a low-frequency response to *bird)*. Conrad (1972) obtained a similar result. She collected her own normative data by having subjects provide descriptions of words. The properties mentioned in these descriptions were ordered according to the number of subjects who used them, and high- and low-frequency sentences were constructed on the basis of these data. A levels factor, as defined by Collins and Quillian, was also included in this experiment. Conrad's results were quite clear. The levels effect of Collins and Quillian was replicated but was at least in part caused by confounding with sentence frequency. The frequency effect was very large: verification times were about 200 msec faster for the frequent sentences than for the infrequent sentences.

Thus, the interpretation of semantic distance as levels in a noun hierarchy must be questioned. Wilkins has shown that nouns within the same category vary in accessibility, and Conrad has shown that high-frequency sentences are verified faster than low-frequency sentences, irrespective of level. The problem was brought into clear focus by Rips, Shoben, and Smith (1973) who demonstrated that large within-category differences exist in verification times, and that Level-2 sentences are not necessarily slower than Level-1 sentences. Rips et al. used 12 bird names in sentences *(X is a bird* and *X is an animal)*, 12 mammal names in frames *(X is a mammal* and *X is an animal)*, and 12 names of cars in frames *(X is a car* and *X is a vehicle)*. Large within-category differences were obtained (for some inscrutable reason subjects decided very quickly that *cows* were *mammals*, but took over 200 msec longer to reach the same conclusion for *pigs*). Most importantly, while *bird* was always faster than *animal*, and *car* almost always faster than *vehicle*, as required by Collins and Quillian's model, the superset effect was reversed for *mammal* and *animal*: On the average, subjects were 88 msec faster in verifying *X is an animal* than *X is a mammal*! Rips et al. went on to show that their reaction time data could be reasonably well predicted by ratings of the semantic distance between the words. They obtained a correlation of $r = .63$ between the rated distance between word pairs and reaction times.

The conclusion then is inevitable that a model, as sketched in Fig. 1, cannot account for the sentence verification data. At the very least, it would need additional mechanisms for the observed frequency and within-category effects. That not all category members are equally accessible has also been demonstrated by other investigators with different experimental paradigms. A particularly definitive study is one by Loftus and Suppes (1972), who have observed the speed with which category items can be retrieved from semantic memory. They gave their subjects a noun category plus a restricting letter and required them to produce an instance of the category that began with the given letter. For example, a proper response for *fruit*-P might be *plum*. The observed reaction times were correlated with 12 structural variables that were regarded as possible influences on retrieval speed in this task, mostly various frequency, category size, and dominance measures. A multiple of R^2 of .61 was obtained, with the most important variables being dominance in the category (the highest rank position in the category of an available correct response, as determined from the Battig and Montague, 1969, norms), frequency of the stimulus category of children's vocabularies, and frequency of the most likely response in children's vocabularies. Although the significance of the two childhood frequency measures is of considerable importance in itself, the dominance variable is of particular interest in the present context. Dominance, as defined here, is closely related to the conjoint frequency of Wilkins (1971). Wilkins worked with a sentence verification paradigm while Loftus and Suppes used a restricted association paradigm, but the effects observed were quite similar in both cases: Words that were closely related normatively yielded faster reaction times.

The generalization that semantic distance, though it may be operationally defined in various ways, is an important determinant of reaction times holds for other experimental paradigms as well. Schaeffer and Wallace (1969) showed subjects two words and asked them to decide as quickly as possible whether the two words belonged to the same semantic category (e.g., were both *living things* or not). Faster reaction times were observed when the two words were similar semantically (e.g., *lion-zebra*) than when they were dissimilar semantically (e.g., *lion-tulip*). Meyer and Schvaneveldt (1971) observed a similar effect even though they merely required their subjects to respond whether the two letter strings presented were words or not, that is, no judgment of semantic distance was required by this task at all. Associated words were responded to more rapidly than semantically unrelated words.

When subjects are asked to evaluate false statements, semantic distance is just as important as in the case of true sentences, except that now the effects are reversed. If subjects are asked to determine if two words belong to the same category, reaction times are slower if the words are semantically similar but belong to different categories (Schaeffer & Wallace, 1970).[1] If the subject and predicate of a sentence are semantically related, judgments are slower than if they are unrelated (Collins & Quillian, 1972a; Rips et al., 1973). In the Collins and Quillian (1972a) study, semantic distance was varied in two ways: *(a)* whether or not the two concepts were related by an "extraneous path," e.g., *almond* and *fortune* are so related, via *cookie*, and *(b)* whether sentences were anomalous or not, where an anomalous property was defined as one that was not applicable to any instance within a three-level

---

[1]This result was obtained in Exp. I, III, and V of Schaeffer and Wallace (1970). No significant differences between semantically dissimilar different-judgments were observed in their Exp. II and IV. However, in both cases the differences were in the same direction as in Exp. I, though small, and not significant statistically. No statistics are given, but the power of the test used appears to have been exceedingly low. Though one cannot quite tell from their incomplete report, the appropriate error term for the analysis of variance seems to have had only seven degrees of freedom.

hierarchy such as Fig. 1 (e.g., *birch has acorns* is not anomalous by this definition, but *birch has a sparkplug* is). Reaction time effects were observed only for the presence or absence of an "extraneous path" but not for anomalous and non-anomalous sentences. In the Rips et al. study, semantic distance for false sentences was varied by violating the animate-inanimate distinction. For instance, the distance between *robin-mammal* is smaller (and the reaction time larger) than that between *robin-car*.

If one puts all of these studies together, a rather powerful empirical generalization emerges: Semantic distance plays a crucial role in various reaction time tasks involving sentence verification, same-different judgments, and word retrieval from semantic memory, both for positive and negative cases. Positive judgments are facilitated if the concepts involved are closely related semantically, while for negative judgments, relatedness acts as an inhibiting factor. Semantic distance has been defined operationally in various ways (as steps separating concepts in a hierarchy, category dominance, definitional frequency, associations among words, as well as rated distance), and we do not yet know which of these, if any, may be the true or most appropriate measure of semantic distance. Nevertheless, at a descriptive level, it is a sound empirical generalization that processing times in these experiments are strongly affected by semantic distance. There are surprisingly few exceptions to this rule. The only outright contradiction appears to be a study mentioned in Landauer and Meyer (1972) in which rated "closeness of meaning" had no effect on reaction times for judgments about test words not belonging to a stated category. However, Landauer and Meyer do not present their materials so one cannot evaluate the range of semantic distances involved. Furthermore, their ratings were based upon as few as ten subjects and, judging from the quoted concordance of .27, were quite unreliable.

In addition to the generalization about the role of semantic distance, there is another generalization that can be made, though with much less certainty. Landauer and Freedman (1968) have shown that verification times for superset statements depend upon the size of the semantic category involved. In later studies, tasks in which subjects had to recognize as well as produce members of familiar semantic categories have yielded further evidence that response times are inversely related to set size, though the effect is in general quite small. The reality of the category size effect has been questioned repeatedly, but one can probably go along with the conclusion reached by Landauer and Meyer (1972) that a category size effect exists independent of semantic relatedness.

In what way, then, do the data reviewed here extend our knowledge about how people search semantic memory and retrieve information? We have two empirical phenomena, the strongly supported semantic distance effect, and probably a category size effect. The processes that are implied by these phenomena are, however, far from clear. Collins and Quillian's original formulation is certainly discredited by now. There are too many results that are not in agreement with the simple model outlined in Fig. 1. The various frequency effects that have been observed by several experimenters contradict their 1969 model, as well as the variation in reaction times within semantic categories.

The 1969 model is simply "too logical" for the real world, as Rips et al. put it: *Sparrow-bird-animal* may, perhaps, be organized in a hierarchy as claimed, but *dog-mammal-animal* certainly are not.

Alternative explanations of the semantic distance effect assume that concepts are represented in semantic memory by sets of elements (attribute values of features), and that the tasks discussed here require a comparison between two sets. The overlap of elements between the two sets is considered a measure of semantic distance. The difference between a network model as advocated by Collins and Quillian (1969, 1972a, 1972b) and the set-comparison models is a very significant one. Unlike network models, the latter make no assumptions about the structure of memory. They are more parsimonious in that no complex assumptions about hierarchical structures in memory are required, and the data can be explained quite satisfactorily in a much simpler way, namely, by postulating comparisons between sets of memory elements. Meyer (1970) and Schaeffer and Wallace (1970) first proposed such models, but the most satisfactory statement of set-comparison models is that of Rips et al. (1973). The semantic distance between two concepts is given by the feature overlap between the two corresponding sets of features. Statements of the form *A (instance) is a (category)* are evaluated in a two-stage comparison process. The first stage consists simply in computing the overlap between the two sets of elements, i.e., their semantic distance. This provides an over-all measure of similarity. It is assumed that if this measure is either very high or very low, a response (positive or negative, respectively) will be given without stage-two processing. Thus, the quick acceptance of sentences containing strongly related concepts as well as the quick rejection of sentences containing disjoint concepts can be explained. For intermediate semantic distances, a stage-two comparison is made which does not involve all elements of the concept set, but only its defining features. Only if there is an agreement between the defining features of the two concepts will a positive response be made. Stage-two processing requires time, and thus the long reaction times for positive judgments of dissimilar concepts, as well as for negative judgments of similar concepts, may be explained. The finding that *A sparrow is a bird* is evaluated faster than *A sparrow is an animal* simply means that *sparrow* and *bird* have more elements in common than *sparrow* and *animal*, while the converse relationship holds for *dog-mammal* and *dog-animal*. Subjects just don't know much about *mammals*, and hence the element overlap between *dog* and *mammal* is relatively small.

A somewhat different but equally parsimonious model has been proposed by Landauer and Meyer (1972) for the category size effect. Their model is a true memory search model. Suppose a subject is asked to decide whether *collie* belongs to the category *dog*. It is assumed that the stored category members are compared with the test word, and if the test word is found during the search, a positive response is made. Clearly, the larger the category, the more time will be required to decide that a test word is not a member of the category; and, as long as the search is not strictly parallel, a similar prediction is obtained for positive responses. Thus, category size and superset effects can be explained, though the model makes no attempt to deal with semantic distance effects in general.

The set-comparison model of Rips et al. and the category search model of Landauer and Meyer account very well for the data for which they were proposed. Nevertheless, both are totally unsatisfactory and unacceptable. They would be great if the particular data sets with which their authors worked were of interest in themselves. But who wants to know about the category size effect *per se*? We are only interested in these phenomena insofar as they tell us something about how information is retrieved from semantic memory — what is involved in the process of knowledge actualization. Narrow theories that deal only with artificially limited data sets are of no interest, however parsimonious they might be, if it can be shown that they are insufficient to deal with the general problem. Somehow, by no means for the first time in the history of experimental psychology, a broad significant problem, that of knowledge actualization, has been narrowed down to a few research designs, and in fact, has been lost from sight: Explanations are proposed for particular experiments, not for the question that at one point had motivated the experiments. Landauer and Meyer (1972) are quite right when they claim that their model "requires less information to be stored in memory, and embodies fewer assumptions about memory organization and search processes. At the same time, we believe that the simpler model can explain results from the categorization task, and that more elaborate theoretical assumptions are not required at present [p. 544]." However, the elaborate theoretical assumptions are required not for the categorization task, but for other aspects of the more general problem of information retrieval. The real question is whether these elaborate theoretical assumptions, which have to be made for quite different reasons, can also account for the particular experimental results at hand, the category size effects, as well as the semantic distance effects, rather than the question of what is the most parsimonious explanation for either of these phenomena taken out of their broader context and considering only certain restricted experimental results.

The inadequacy of the models discussed here can best be shown by reexamining the set-comparison model of Rips et al. (the category search model is, if anything, even more restricted in its scope). Rips et al. arrive at a simple looking, parsimonious model by waving aside the difficult and most interesting questions. The crucial assumption in set-comparison models is that the distance between an instance and a category may be represented by the feature overlap between the two. But what is a feature? More specifically, should only "critical" or "definitional" features be counted, or all possible features? Rips et al. realize that neither of these possibilities will do. If only those features count that define category membership, all instances would be equidistant from the category name, which is clearly not the case. On the other hand, the set of all possible features is very large, especially when negative features are included (e.g., a *dog* cannot *sing*, is not a *desk*, etc.), and defining semantic distance in terms of all possible features would surely be nonsensical as well as unworkable. Therefore, Rips et al. (1973) introduce a new term, the set of functional features, which "include those that strictly define the category membership plus some others that characterize most instances of the category, for example, a determinate size or degree of predacity [p. 18]." In addition, these functional features must somehow be tagged as definitional or nondefinitional, because the second stage comparison process operates only upon the former set of features and excludes those features that are merely characteristics. If one grants Rips et al. their "functional feature sets," so defined, they have a nice, clean simple model, indeed. But all they have done is to hide the real problems under some well-chosen terms: functional, definitional, and characteristic features. The reason why other theories are so elaborate is that they are trying to explicate what Rips et al. merely name. By the time "feature," "functional," "definitional," and "characteristic" are defined in a serious way, rather than merely postulated in the hope that the reader's intuition will take care of the rest, set-comparison models may have lost most of their deceptive simplicity.

There are further problems with such models, however, which may be even more serious. Set-comparison models, as well as the category search model, deal only with superset statements. However, semantic distance effects are more general and have been demonstrated for property sentences by Collins and Quillian (1969, 1972a) as well as by Conrad (1972). Unfortunately, most of the research done in the last few years concentrated upon superset relationships to such an extent that other problems have been lost sight of. It is not clear that the set comparison model (or the category search model) can be extended to deal with property statements, not to mention more complex sentences. Perhaps one of its advocates will show how this can be done, but presumably the model will thereby lose a little more of its simplicity and parsimony

Actually, there is nothing wrong at all with the idea that sets of elements are being compared. In the present model too, such a process plays a very basic role in the pattern matching and pattern completion operations of Chapter 4. The objections being raised here have to do only with the view that the sets of elements that enter into these comparison processes can exist in a static, unstructured memory. Consider, for a moment, *Napoleon's toes*. Presumably, no reader has ever given much thought to them before. To assume that the "functional feature set" for *Napoleon* includes *toe*, or that in some other way memory contains the information that *Napoleon had toes* is preposterous; clearly such information cannot be stored in memory but must be derived from other knowledge about *Napoleon* and *toes*. What I am saying here is simply that a memory must have the capacity to make inferences. The fact that one can explain this or that experimental phenomenon without recourse to inferential processes merely means that one deals with data sets that are impoverished when taken out of context. There is probably no single experimental result that cannot be explained, in isolation, without the elaborate theoretical machinery of semantic memory models, but that elaborate structure is needed to explain the conjuction of the psychological and linguistic data. Single results are important insofar as they interact with and modify various aspects of the general theory.

Thus, far from regarding parsimony as a virtue, models that make no reference to inferential capacities can be discarded as irrelevant on *a priori* grounds. In order to push the problem back into proper perspective, an experiment will be reported below in which sentences that in all likelihood must involve inferences are evaluated. In addition, property sentences are used, as well as superset statements, in a further effort to broaden the data base for studies of information retrieval from semantic memory.

2. JUDGMENTS OF SEMANTIC ACCEPTABILITY[2]

The experiment to be reported here is a sentence evaluation experiment in the tradition of Collins and Quillian (1969). We want to compare reaction times for sentences that are stored in memory with reaction times for inferred sentences. We shall call sentences that may be stored in semantic memory as part of lexical descriptions *definitional* sentences, while sentences that, presumably, are not stored as units in semantic memory will be referred to as *inferred*[3] sentences. Definitional and inferred sentences together comprise the set of *semantically acceptable* sentences. A sentence is semantically acceptable if there exist circumstances under which this sentence could be true. The term semantically acceptable is used instead of true sentence because, in experiments like the present one, the truth of a sentence is usually indeterminate: *The lion growls* is true only if there is, indeed, a lion who growls, which is usually not the case under laboratory conditions. Therefore, asking subjects to respond to the semantic acceptability of sentences is less ambiguous than asking them to respond true or false to such sentences. Definitional and inferred sentences differ in terms of semantic distance. Since definitional sentences are, by assumption, part of the lexical description of a concept, the subject and predicate of such sentences are closely related semantically. For instance, we assume that *The shark swims* is part of the lexical description of SHARK: Therefore, SHARK and SWIM are closely related semantically. On the other hand, *The shark escapes* is probably not stored as part of our knowledge about sharks, though we can understand this sentence readily because we know that animals in general may escape from danger. Thus, the semantic acceptability of this sentence is determined by means of inferential processing, and, intuitively, the semantic distance between the lexical items SHARK and ESCAPE is greater than between SHARK and SWIM.[4]

Whether a sentence was judged to be stored in semantic memory or inferred was determined on the basis of the intuitions of the two authors. We have tried to select sufficiently extreme cases to avoid ambiguity, but we have, of course, no guarantee that sentences that were judged as definitional were indeed stored in the semantic memories of our subjects. The procedure used by Conrad (1972), of having subjects write down definitions of words and selecting high- and low-frequency sentences from these definitions, may be regarded as an objective counterpart to our subjective categorization. Conrad's high-frequency sentences were probably directly stored sentences, while her low-frequency sentences probably involved inference, though no guarantees are possible in this case either.

[2]This study, by W. Kintsch and E. J. Crothers, was originally reported as "The effects of some semantic and syntactic properties of simple sentences upon the latency of judgments of semantic acceptability," by W. Kintsch, E. J. Crothers, and L. N. Berman, Technical Report, University of Colorado, November, 1970. Part of the data have also been discussed in Kintsch (1972a). Several changes have been made in the present version to update the discussion.

[3]The term inferred sentence is used here instead of contingently true sentence, which was used in the original publication as well as in Kintsch (1972a).

[4]Note that in Collins and Quillian (1969), *The shark swims* would be a Level-1 sentence, hence requiring an inference. In the present model (as well as in Collins & Quillian, 1972b), it is assumed that such high-frequency characteristics are not inferred but definitional.

Unacceptable sentences are divided on the basis of semantic distance into *contradictory* and *nonsense* sentences. In contradictory sentences, the subject and predicate that are combined are relatively closely related; in nonsense sentences, they are totally unrelated. The distinction between nonsense sentences and contradictory sentences may be systematized in the following way. (Note, though, that many other similar procedures would serve equally well for our purposes.) In a contradictory sentence, something appropriate for an animate subject is predicated for animate subjects (though, of course, inappropriate for the particular one), and something appropriate for an inanimate subject is predicated for inanimate subjects. In nonsense sentences, the animate-inanimate distinction is violated, such that animate subjects are paired with predicates that require inanimate subjects, and vice versa. Rips et al. (1973) used the same criterion for varying semantic distance in false sentences.

The effects of semantic distance upon true-false reaction times have been reviewed in Section 1 of this chapter. True responses were faster the closer the subject and predicate of the sentences were related, while the opposite held for false responses. In the present experiment, subjects were instead asked to judge whether sentences were semantically acceptable, but the same kind of relationships between semantic distance and reaction times are expected to hold. The third variable investigated here is syntactic form class. Three types of sentences are used: *The (noun) is a (noun), The (noun) is (adjective)*, and *The (noun) (verb)*. Collins and Quillian (1969) reported that sentences stating a property (like the present verb and adjective sentences) were harder to process than sentences stating a set inclusion (like the present noun sentences): *A canary is a bird* required about 200 msec less processing time than *A canary can fly*. A main purpose of the present experiment is to investigate further whether syntactic form class influences judgment times when better controlled stimulus materials are used. Given the importance of set-inclusion for the structure of memory, and the Collins and Quillian results, we expected set-inclusion statements to be processed faster than noun-verb and noun-adjective sentences. No differences were expected between the latter two sentence forms because the distinction between verbs and adjectives does not appear to be essential in linguistic theory.

Three experiments were performed in order to investigate the importance of various surface structure features that present problems even with the simple sentences used here. In Exp. *a*, the indefinite article "a(n)" was used in all sentences *(A bird is an animal)*. Since subjects may interpret "a" as a universal quantifier, we substituted the definite article "the" for the intitial "a" in Exp. *b (The bird is an animal)*.

The second problem that we were concerned with is sentence length. The noun sentences were five words long, adjective sentences were four words, and verb sentences only three words, counting the articles. In Exp. *b*, we equated adjective and verb sentences in terms of number of words by using the progressive form for verb sentences *(The bird is flying)*. In Exp. *c*, we controlled the number of words by presenting only the two main words rather than complete sentences *(bird-fly)*, and instructing subjects to determine whether the words make an acceptable or unacceptable sentence when combined in a simple noun-noun, noun-verb, or noun-adjective sentence.

To achieve some comparability of the sentences in the various conditions, the same set of subject nouns was used in all conditions and only words of comparable frequency were employed as predicates.

Method

Materials. Eleven subject nouns were selected (3 human nouns, 3 animals, 3 utensils, and 2 natural formations) and 12 sentences were constructed with each subject noun according to a 3 × 4 factorial design. The first factor was form class (adjective, verb, noun) and the second was sentence type (definitional, inferred, contradictory, nonsensical). As an example, Table 1 shows the 12 sentences that were constructed with the subject noun SHARK. Only intransitive verbs were used. Morphological derivatives from another syntactic class were avoided, unless the derivative was definitely established in common usage (e.g., *actor*). With very few exceptions, only words within a middle frequency range were used (2 – 9 Thorndike-Lorge frequencies). Mean word frequencies of the content words in the four sentence types were 3.9, 3.8, 4.2, and 3.9, respectively. Mean word frequencies for the form classes were 3.8, 4.1, and 4.1 for adjectives, verbs, and nouns, respectively.[5]

Subjects. Subjects were college-age persons recruited at the University of Colorado who were paid $2.00 for their services. Twenty-one subjects participated in Exp. *a*, 15 in Exp. *b*, and 30 in Exp. *c*.

Procedure. The 132 test sentences were arranged in 11 blocks so that each subject-noun was represented in each block, and sentence types and forms were counterbalanced within each block. Within each block sentence order was random. All subjects were given the test sentences in the same order, preceded by 5 practice trials.

Sentences were printed by hand on plain 10 × 12.5 cm cards with letters 1.2 cm high. A trial started with the experimenter placing a card into the cardholder of a Scientific Prototype two-channel tachistoscope and saying "ok." He then depressed

TABLE 1

A Sample of the Experimental Material: the Subject Item "SHARK" and the 12 Predicates
with which It Was Paired

Sentence type	Syntactic form		
	verb	adjective	noun
Definitional	swims	is vicious	is a fish
Inferred	escapes	is eager	is a trophy
Contradictory	growls	is meek	is a frog
Nonsensical	ticks	is vacant	is a key

[5]The material for the three experiments was not precisely the same. A few changes were made after each experiment, in that sentences for which an especially high error rate was observed were replaced with less ambiguous sentences. Although only few changes were made, this complicates somewhat the comparison of the over-all error rates in the three studies.

a start button which turned on the tachistoscope light exposing the sentence and started a Hunter timer. The sentence was exposed for 3 sec in Exp. *a* and *b* and for 5 sec in Exp. *c*. Subjects were watching the tachistoscope with their index fingers on response keys labeled "TRUE" and "FALSE." They were asked to respond as quickly as possible but to avoid errors. Extensive explanations were given about a TRUE response signifying a semantically acceptable sentence and a FALSE response an unacceptable sentence. Subjects were told to disregard metaphorical or poetical uses of words. More detailed instructions were given in Exp. *c* to make certain subjects understood that their task was to judge whether the two words, noun-noun, noun-adjective, or noun-verb, made a meaningful simple sentence. Subjects were instructed to disregard more complex ways of combining the two words into a sentence, (e.g., LION-TELEPHONE can only be FALSE, because only *(The) lion (is a) telephone* may be considered, but not *(The) lion (bites the) telephone*).

Results

In accordance with our experimental hypothesis, verb and adjective sentences have been combined and will be referred to as property sentences. Figure 2 shows the percent error for the four sentence types for noun sentences and property sentences. In almost all cases, the largest number of errors occurs with the inferred sentences. Contradictory sentences come next, and sentences that are true by definition, as well as nonsense sentences, are most likely to be evaluated correctly. The only systematic difference between noun and property sentences was observed for unacceptable sentences, where more errors occurred for property sentences than for noun sentences.

The latency data that will be reported first are based upon correct responses only. For each subject his mean judgment time for each of the 12 sentence categories was determined. The means of three scores are shown in Fig. 3, where verbs and adjectives have been combined again as property sentences. Analyses of variance were performed using both subjects and sentences as random variables in order to be able to generalize over both populations. The F-statistics reported here are min F's after Clark (1973). The following factors were included in the analyses: Syntactic Form Class (noun, verb, and adjective sentences), Acceptability (acceptable and unacceptable sentences), Semantic Distance (related, i.e., definitionally true and contradictory sentences, and unrelated, i.e., inferred and nonsensical sentences), and Experiment (*a, b,* and *c*). The main effects, Experiment, Semantic Distance, and Acceptability, were all significant at the .001 level, with min F' of 12.75 (for 2,66 *df*), 11.59 (for 1,943 *df*), and 39.50 (for 1,655 *df*), respectively.

Times were slower in Exp. *c*, which was to be expected. Acceptable sentences were judged faster than unacceptable sentences, but a difference between the time to judge unacceptable sentences in Exp. *a* and Exp. *b* resulted in a significant interaction effect: Subjects could reject an unacceptable sentence more rapidly when it contained an *a* than when it contained a *the*. Presumably, the *a* was interpreted as *all* and, therefore, the unacceptability of a sentence could be more rapidly established.

The interaction between semantic distance and acceptability which is so obvious in Fig. 3 was highly significant, min F' (1,758) = 35.30, $p<.001$. Acceptable

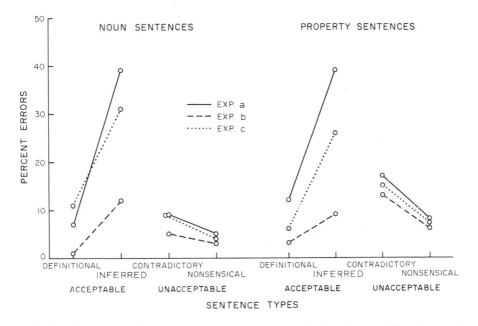

FIG. 2. Judgment errors for noun- and property-sentences as a function of acceptability and semantic distance.

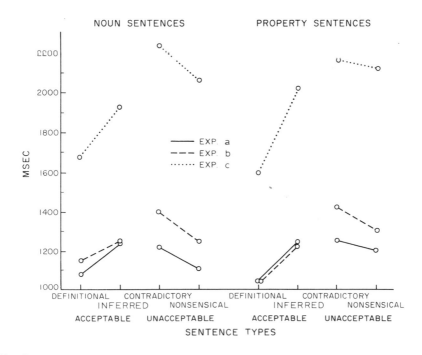

FIG. 3. Average latencies of true-false judgments of noun- and property-sentences as a function of acceptability and semantic distance.

sentences were judged faster when subject and predicate were closely related; unacceptable sentences were judged faster when subject and predicate were unrelated.

The effect of form class was not significant statistically over the three experiments ($F < 1$ in both the subject and sentence analysis), and none of the interactions of form class with other factors were significant. The Distance × Form Class interaction was marginally significant in the subject analysis, but not in the sentence analysis, and hence need not be considered further. No other significant effects were found in the analyses.

The latencies on trials with incorrect responses differed substantially from the pattern of results obtained for correct responses. Table 2 shows that the mean error latencies are always larger than the latencies of correct responses. This difference is small in Exp. a, which had a relatively large error rate, is bigger in Exp. b, where the error rate was much smaller, and is enormous in Exp. c, where a somewhat different procedure was used. Also shown in Table 2 is the fact that mean error latencies for unacceptable sentences are always higher than for acceptable sentences. This difference tends to be even larger for incorrect responses than for correct responses.

Like success latencies, error latencies do not differ systematically as a funciton of syntactic form class. However, unlike the results for success latencies shown in Fig. 3, there is no systematic difference as a function of semantic distance. A graph of error latencies corresponding to Fig. 3 duplicates the slope of the lines in Fig. 3 six times, but the slopes are reversed the other six times. Since the number of errors in the various conditions differs widely, the detailed pattern of these results cannot be taken seriously, but it seems clear that error latencies do not exhibit the same kind of regular dependency upon semantic distance that was observed for success latencies.

Discussion

The positive and negative results obtained in this study are equally significant. Judgment time is a function of the semantic distance between the subject and predicate of simple sentences, but it appears to be unaffected by syntactic form — verbs, adjectives, or nouns as predicates are processed equally fast.

TABLE 2

Mean Response Latencies (in msec) in Three Experiments as a Function of the Acceptability of the Test Sentences and the Correctness of the Response

Experiment	Response	All sentences	Acceptable sentences	Unacceptable sentences
a	Correct	1,186	1,161	1,212
	Incorrect	1,280	1,229	1,387
b	Correct	1,250	1,160	1,355
	Incorrect	1,493	1,376	1,665
c	Correct	1,977	1,811	2,143
	Incorrect	2,668	2,548	3,140

Semantic distance effects in the present study were in agreement with the results reported by other investigators and reviewed in Section 1 of this chapter. Definitional sentences, which may be presumed to be stored in memory, were more quickly judged to be semantically acceptable than sentences that must be inferred on the basis of other stored knowledge. Unacceptable sentences, on the other hand, were evaluated more rapidly when they were nonsense sentences, that is, not related semantically, than when they were merely contradictory, that is, where some kind of a semantic relationship between subject and predicate existed. A comparison of the present results with some sorting data reported by Steinberg (1970a, 1970b) is also of interest. Steinberg showed that subjects consistently classified sentences into the categories analytic, synthetic, contradictory, and amphigorous. Steinberg's amphigorous sentences correspond to our nonsense sentences. The analytic-synthetic distinction is not identical with our distinction between definitional and inferred sentences, but the semantic distance between the subject and predicate of analytic sentences must surely be less than for synthetic sentences, just as for definitional and inferred sentences. Thus, both sorting behavior and judgment times depend in a very regular manner upon how closely the words of simple sentences are related in the subjects' semantic memory.

Collins and Quillian found longer judgment times for sentences that stated a property than for sentences that stated a set-inclusion relation. We did not obtain this result, although at least Exp. c should have provided a fair test, because in this experiment the number of words that a subject had to read before he could make his judgment was the same for noun and property sentences. The words that were used for the noun, adjective, and verb sentences were equated in terms of the frequency of the words employed as predicates, and the same subject words were used in all three conditions. The stricter control exercised over sentences in the present study may be responsible for our failure to replicate the Collins and Quillian results. Note also that Collins and Quillian did not always find more rapid responding to property than to superset sentences (see Collins & Quillian, 1972a, p. 131).

It appears, therefore, that when comparable words are used to construct noun and property sentences, judgment times are the same for these two sentence types. At least in this experimental situation nominal and other types of predicates are equally accessible. Theories of sentence processing will have to take this result into account. However, in other experimental situations, form class nevertheless may be an effective variable. For instance, Zivian and Riegel (1969) have reported that logical and infralogical clues were differentially effective when used to identify a target word. This distinction corresponds at least in part to the noun vs. property distinction of the present study. Similarly, Loftus (1972) concluded that semantic memory was organized primarily into noun categories, on the basis of an experiment in which she had subjects generate category members of certain noun classes, and possessors of certain adjective properties. There is also impressive neurolinguistic evidence for the priority of nouns. Marshall and Newcombe (1966) have reported that dyslexic patients can sometimes read nouns quite well, but not adjectives or verbs (and never adverbs or prepositions). Gazzaniga (1970) also reported similar observations for the language capabilities of the right hemisphere. Finally, Weigl and Bierwisch (1970) found that dyslexic patients could read a sentence when they were told what it was, even when a semantically similar noun was substituted, but not if verb substitutions were made. Nevertheless, the present data strongly argue against a general noun priority in the subjective lexicon in that no evidence was obtained that nouns are more directly accessible than other word types.

The finding that acceptable sentences are judged significantly faster than unacceptable sentences might be attributed merely to a response bias, were it not for the fact that this relationship was observed for both correct and incorrect responses. Thus, this seems to be a genuine effect. To decide that a sentence is unacceptable requires even more processing time than to decide that it is true by inference (except in Exp. *a* where the article *a* was used, which brought the difficulty of the unacceptable sentences down to the level of inferred true sentences).

The error data that were obtained are interesting for several reasons. First, why should errors occur at all? The sentences were constructed so that if subjects were given enough time they would classify all or almost all sentences correctly.[6] However, in the experimental situation very substantial error rates were obtained, especially for inferred true sentences. A possible interpretation of this finding is that subjects did not always complete their sentence processing and responded prematurely because of the instructions "to respond as quickly as possible but to avoid errors." It appears that after a certain amount of processing there was an increasing tendency to terminate the sentence analysis with a guess response. Errors, therefore, would be mostly slow guesses, and furthermore, the likelihood of errors should be high for sentences that require much processing. This is, of course, exactly what was observed in the present study: Error latencies were higher on the average than success latencies, and the error rates and mean latencies for the various experimental conditions were highly correlated, as a comparison of Fig. 2 and 3 confirms.

3. THEORETICAL IMPLICATIONS

Semantic distance is a descriptive concept, not an explanatory one. Questions must be raised here concerning its theoretical foundation. Some existing proposals have already been criticized in Section 1 of this chapter. Collins and Quillian's (1969) attempt to identify semantic distance with the number of steps separating two concepts in a noun hierarchy was clearly too restrictive. Their more recent formulation (Collins & Quillian, 1972b), that semantic distance is a function of both the number of nodes along the path between two concepts and the accessibility of these links, modifies their model appropriately; but since "accessibility" is not further defined other than saying that "some properties are more important than others and may be reached more easily or quickly [p. 314]," this redefinition merely describes what is to be accounted for without explaining anything. The objections against equating the semantic distance between two concepts with the overlap between the

[6]The three experimenters plus several other associates judged the sentences as unambiguous, but we have not collected systematic data concerning this point.

sets of features that define the two concepts, as advocated by several authors, e.g., Rips et al. (1973), have already been stated, namely, that there are no fixed sets of elements that define the concepts. Concepts cannot be stricly defined in the subjective lexicon. One can only indicate how to use them properly in a loose and not necessarily logically consistent way, as was described in Chapter 2. Much of the information that people can generate about a given concept is not stored in memory as part of a feature set for the concept but instead must be inferred. Therefore, the meaning of a concept cannot be represented by some fixed set of elements, no matter what they might be, but depends upon how far the process of inferring additional information relevant to that concept is carried. We are repeating here a claim first made by Quillian (1967) that "a word's full concept is defined in the model of memory to be all the nodes that can be reached by an exhaustive tracing process, originating at its initial, patriarchal type node, together with the total sum of relationships among these nodes . . . [p. 413]." Thus, there is no single set of elements that can be regarded as the representation of a particular word. Word representations are dynamic, a nested set of elements whose dimensions depend upon how many inferential steps are considered. Surely, the full concept, which is arrived at only after all possible inferences have been performed, cannot underlie semantic distance calculations (and Rips et al. do not claim so, for good reasons, as has been discussed in Section 1). With equal assurance we can state that some inferences are made in calculating semantic distances. Subjects can frequently come up with a meaningful relationship between two words that at first sight appeared to them entirely unrelated.

The model for semantic memory, which was presented in Chapter 2, combines the virtues of network models (that is, their generative capacities) with those of set-comparison models (that is, their flexibility). The measure of semantic distance derived from the model is a function of both the amount of inferential processing that is performed in comparing two concepts and their element overlap. Let $S = \{S\}$ be the set of all propositions that are stored in memory at a given moment in time. Let ϕ be the set of all production rules in semantic memory. If the productions rules ϕ are used once to operate upon the set S of stored propositions, a new set of propositions P_1 is obtained:

$$\phi(S) = P_1$$

By applying the production rules repeatedly, nested sets of propositions P_1, P_2, . . . etc. can be generated:

$$\phi(P_1) = P_2 = \phi^2(S)$$
$$\phi(P_i) = P_{i+1} \tag{1}$$
$$\phi^k(S) = P, \text{ for } k \to \infty.$$

The set P is the set of all acceptable propositions, as argued previously in Kintsch (1972a, p. 279). Let x and y be two concepts and let X_0 and Y_0 be the sets of propositions in semantic memory in which x and y appear. Thus $X_0 \subset S$, $Y_0 \subset S$. Similarly, we define X_1 and Y_1 as the sets of propositions in which x and y appear, which are obtained by applying the production rules ϕ once to the set of propositions stored in semantic memory. Therefore, $X_1 \subset P_1$ *and* $Y_1 \subset P_1$. In general, we are concerned with proposition sets $X_i \subset P_i$ and $Y_i \subset P_i$, where the subscript i indicates the number of inferential steps used. A semantic distance measure for level i can then be defined as

$$D_{XY}(i) = N(X_i) + N(Y_i) - 2N(X_i \cap Y_i),\qquad(2)$$

where $N(X)$ is a function that assigns to a set X the number of its elements. It is easy to show that $D_{XY}(i)$ is a distance metric. It is assumed that in calculating an over-all semantic distance measure subjects combine overlap and inferential information so as to weigh inferred information less and less:

$$D_{XY} = \sum_{i=0}^{k} \frac{1}{i+1} D_{XY}(i).\qquad(3)$$

The value of k, that is, the amount of inferential processing, is assumed to depend upon task conditions and the available processing time. It does not seem possible at present to make more detailed processing assumptions, though a number of speculations appear quite reasonable. For instance, since inferences are being used here to detect semantic relationships between concepts that may not be apparent in the actually stored knowledge, it may be reasonable to expect that subjects would stop making further inferences as soon as the value of D_{XY} begins to decrease as k is increased, or even if there is no sufficiently large increment. However, to decide such a question one would need to have a workable computer simulation model of semantic memory and its production rules.

Given D_{XY} as a measure of semantic distance, the following model for latencies in sentence evaluation can be proposed. It is a two-stage model similar to those of Meyer (1970) and Rips et al. (1973), but it emphasizes the inferential nature of the stage-two processing.[7]

The model is outlined in Fig. 4. Stage 1 processing consists first of the parsing of the sentence, that is, translating from sentence into proposition. Next a check is made on whether the test proposition is already stored in semantic memory, in which case a fast "true" response occurs. This accounts for the results with definitional sentences in Fig. 3. If the proposition is not found in memory, the semantic distance between its arguments is computed. If this distance is zero or close to zero, a fast "false" response occurs, as in the case of the nonsense sentences in Fig. 3. If, however, the semantic distance is above a critical value, further processing is necessary. Since this may be very time consuming, the long latencies for inferred-true and contradictory-false sentences in Fig. 3 can be explained. In principle Stage-2 processing consists of determining whether or not the test proposition is semantically acceptable, that is,

---

[7]The present model is a generalization of one discussed earlier (Kintsch 1972a, Pp. 292–299). The procedure for evaluating sentences outlined there is a very efficient one for sentences of the type used in our experiments. It is quite possible that subjects may employ such a procedure under these particular circumstances. However, this could only be a task-dependent strategy, which would not be applicable in general. For instance, the semantic distance check employed in the earlier model would miss the type of relationship that holds between *cup* and *coffee*.

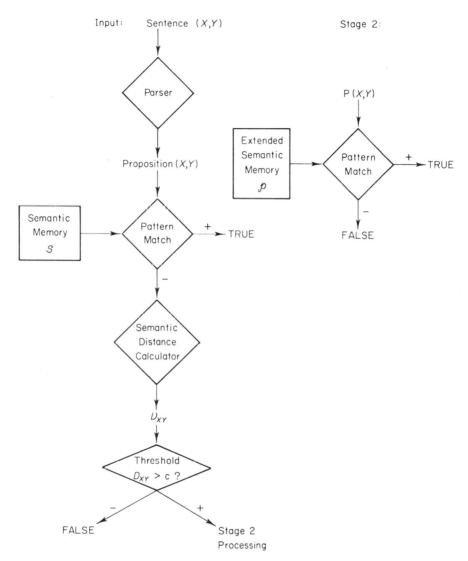

FIG. 4. An information-processing model for a sentence evaluation task.

whether or not $P(X,Y) \subset P$. The model is incomplete in that it does not fully specify how this is done; it merely claims that the production rules that are part of a person's semantic memory are used to generate inferences from the material directly stored in memory. Several examples of the operation of production rules have been given in Chapter 2, and at least inferences involving noun hierarchies have been explored in some detail. However, really systematic work on psychological inferences remains to be done.

It is interesting to speculate whether the two-stage processing that is necessary to account for the present sentence evaluation data may also be a characteristic of sentence comprehension in general. In the particular experimental situation with which Fig. 4 was concerned, a judgment of semantic relatedness was used to simplify the evaluation process. The parsing in this case was trivial, since the same sentence frames were used over and over again in this experiment. In general, however, translating a verbal expression into a propositional form is anything but trivial, and judgments of semantic relatedness may be used to simplify this process. It may be that sentence comprehension begins with a general process of determining semantic relationships among the concepts involved, prior to the detailed syntactic-semantic parsing itself. One of the observations that could be explained in this way is that though words in a sentence may have several different meanings, subjects are usually not aware of multiple meanings when reading or listening to a sentence. Ambiguity is perceived only as a result of reflection. This may be so because an initial semantic-relatedness test selects the most likely meaning of a word so that alternative interpretations never enter awareness. For instance, in *The tree's bark* and *The dog's bark,* entirely different meanings of *bark* will be selected on the basis of their semantic distance to the last word in the sentence. How this may be done has been described in Chapter 4 in discussing how subjects learn lists of words. It was assumed there that an input stimulus, say, for instance, a spoken word, is matched with the entries of the subjective lexicon in such a way that not only the particular input itself, but also other information which at that time is being held in short-term memory, is used. Thus, if short-term memory contains the concept *tree*, the phonemic stimulus /*bark*/ will be matched with the lexical entry BARK that is related to *tree*, rather than with the BARK of *dogs*. The task of the syntactic parser could thereby be significantly simplified. Needless to say, the parser must have the option of overriding this selection procedure if the most likely candidate, upon a more detailed analysis, does not fit, but such cases should be rare and accompanied by an awareness of the false processing start. Thus, to take care of lexical selection, one might add to a conventional syntactic parser a preprocessing of semantic distances, in this way combining the positive features of Quillian's (1969) Teachable Language Comprehender with those of more detailed linguistic analyses as exemplified for instance in Winograd's (1972) parser. Note that if two-stage processing is indeed a general feature of sentence comprehension, we have here a fairly remarkable instance of convergence between the information-processing mechanisms of list learning, true-false reaction times, and sentence comprehension.

In what way, then, does the present model differ from other proposals? From Collins and Quillian (1969), it differs mostly in that semantic memory is regarded as the product of a sometimes inconsistent development rather than a strict logical structure. It is not assumed that all category members are listed under each category name; as was described in Chapter 2, categories may not always be defined explicitly, either through listing of their members or through some defining characteristic. Instead, categories may merely be characterized through some typical members, and other members may be assigned to it on the basis of similarity. Furthermore, memory hierarchies may differ quite substantially from logical hierarchies, depending upon how they were learned. Collins and Quillian (1972b) make essentially the same points and clearly repudiate the oversimplified impression that they had given in their 1969 paper.

What sets the present model apart from the set-comparison models of Meyer (1970), Schaeffer and Wallace (1970), and Rips et al. (1973) is our insistence upon inferential processing. The fixed sets that are used to represent concept meanings in those models are nothing but illusions, the products of overly narrow theorizing.

The present approach also differs greatly from the category search model of Landauer and Meyer (1972), e.g., for the reason just mentioned, that categories are not always explicitly defined in the model. Category size effects may, however, arise because larger categories might have more atypical members and might be less well-defined themselves, thus requiring more processing time.

The model outlined here accounts, at least qualitatively, for sentence evaluation data, as well as for same-different judgments, semantic distance ratings, category size effects, and the category instance production data. There are, however, some further aspects of the data that have not yet been discussed, and that is the influence of the imagery value of sentences on evaluation latencies. Jorgensen and Kintsch (1973) have shown that if simple subject-verb-object sentences are rated according to the ease with which images can be formed, the resulting high-imagery sentences could be evaluated more rapidly as true or false than the low-imagery sentences. Table 3 gives examples of the sentence materials used in that experiment and also summarizes its main results. On the average, latencies for high-imagery sentences were 503 msec, that is, 30% shorter than the latencies for low-imagery sentences. This is a strong effect, but its interpretation in terms of the present model, or for that matter in terms of any model, is not clear. One's first reaction is to suspect some confounding, say that the associative connections between words in the high-imagery sentences as units were more frequent than the low-imagery sentences (frequency of isolated words was controlled). However, while this possibly may explain the results for true sentences, it cannot explain the results for false sentences, where the imagery effect was just as strong. For false sentences, both the high- and low-imagery sentences have essentially no associative relationship between their nouns, and approximately zero-frequency as a unit, as the examples in Table 3 illustrate.

TABLE 3

Sample Sentences and Mean Response Times as a Function of Truth Condition and Imagery Value (after Jorgensen & Kintsch, 1973)

Imagery	True	False
Low	*Truck has oil* *Ear produces wax* 1952 msec	*Carrot has stomach* *Calendar projects movies* 1908 msec
High	*Book has cover* *Knife cuts steak* 1278 msec	*Rock has hair* *Horse eats sand* 1432 msec

Such considerations leave two explanatory possibilities, as Jorgensen and Kintsch have suggested. Perhaps subjects use imagery in evaluating sentences, and since images are, by definition, easier to produce for high-imagery sentences than for low-imagery sentences, the results of Table 3 would follow. How forming an image of a horse eating sand can help one to decide that this sentence is false is not at all understood, though. The kind of research that may, perhaps, provide an answer to such questions is only in its infancy, and at present, further speculations along these lines would be premature. The second possibility suggested in the original paper is that imagery value may be closely related to some properties of the semantic structure that are relevant to sentence evaluation. Suppose that high-imagery, concrete words can be described in the subjective lexicon by a few strong relations, while low-imagery abstract words enter into more relations, and more diffuse ones, with other words. If learning (as in Chapter 4) is a matter of storing samples of cues from a word concept in episodic memory, then the easier learning for concrete words (say in a paired-associate task, as Paivio, 1969, has demonstrated) can be explained as an instance of encoding variability. The pool of cues from which samples are taken is smaller for concrete words than for abstract words, so that the same cues are more likely to be sampled and a more stable memory code will be formed, facilitating learning. A similar explanation could be given if sentences containing abstract words required more processing time in a true-false judgment task than sentences containing concrete words. A more extensive network of relationships must be checked in the former case than in the latter, leading to longer response times.

The assumption that low-imagery words differ from high-imagery words in terms of the diffuseness of the semantic network in which they are embedded can be tested in a fairly straight-forward way. If one assumes, e.g., with Clark (1970), that free or restricted associations mirror certain properties of the semantic network, it follows that associations given to high-imagery words should be fewer and have a greater commonality than associations given to low-imagery words. For instance, among the stimulus words used in the Michigan Restricted Association Norms (Riegel, 1965) there are eight nouns that have an imagery value of less than 4.0 on either the Paivio, Yuille, and Madigan (1968) or the Walker (1970) norms. They are the words *trouble, religion, music, memory, justice, fraud, controversy*, and *anger*, with a mean I-value of 3.43. To compare them with high-imagery words, eight nouns with I values greater than 6.0 were randomly selected from the norms (*window, river, insect, girl, cottage, child, butterfly, arm* — mean I-value of 6.51). Three association tasks were used for the comparison: *superset, verb*, and *adjective*. These tasks were selected because they are most similar to the experimental sentences used in Section 2 *(noun-is-noun, noun-verb*, and *noun-adjective)*. For each word, the number of subjects who gave a response that was common to 10 or more subjects (out of the 100 used in the Michigan Norms) was determined. Table 4 shows the results. The commonality for high-imagery words is, on the average, almost twice as large as that for low-imagery words. This difference was significant at the 5% level by the Wald-Wolfowitz runs test, in spite of the small word population for which data were available.

TABLE 4

Average Number of Subjects (out of 100) Who Gave a Common Response on Three
Restricted Association Tests for High- and Low-Imagery Words

	Task			
	Superordinates	Verbs	Adjectives	
Low imagery	35	40	16	30
High imagery	71	54	43	56

Though the results just reported clearly support the hypothesis that the nature of the semantic network may be different for high- and low-imagery words, they do not directly help us interpret the Jorgensen and Kintsch findings. In that experiment only high-imagery, concrete words (imagery and concreteness values above 6) were used. The imagery value of sentences was high or low because of the relationship that held between the nouns, not because of the imagery value of the nouns themselves. A recent study by Holyoak (1974) has, however, shed some light on this question. First, Holyoak had subjects rate the sentences used by Jorgensen and Kintsch (1973) for ease of comprehension. He found that high-imagery sentences were rated as easier to comprehend than low-imagery sentences, confirming the reaction time results reported above. However, he also obtained judgments as to the degree of relatedness between the subject and predicate words of the sentences. These judgments were, of course, much higher for true sentences than for false sentences, but there was also a significant interaction between imagery and truth: For true sentences, high-imagery sentences were judged to be more strongly related than low-imagery sentences, but the reverse was the case for false sentences. Thus, the Jorgensen and Kintsch data can be looked at as another instance of the by now familiar interaction between semantic distance and truth value. For true sentences, the more related the subject and predicate are, the faster the evaluation times (and the higher the comprehensibility ratings), but for false sentences the opposite relationship holds: Faster reaction times (and higher comprehensibility ratings) are obtained for sentences in which the subjects and predicates are unrelated semantically. It was probably not the imagery value of the sentences in the Jorgensen and Kintsch study that was affecting evaluation latencies, but their degree of semantic relatedness. This solves one puzzle, but creates another one. One can understand why true high-imagery sentences were rated as more closely related semantically, but why were low-imagery false sentences rated as more closely related than the high-imagery false sentences? Was it merely an accident of sentence selection in the original study, or does this result tell us something about the nature of imagery?

SUMMARY

The speed with which subjects can recognize as true or false statements expressing general items of knowledge has frequently been used as a source of information about how knowledge is stored in memory. A review of the literature reveals as the most significant variable in these studies semantic similarity, or its converse, semantic distance. Response times to true statements are generally positively related to the semantic distance between the subject and predicate of the statement, while an inverse relationship holds for false statements. An experiment is reported here that confirms this pattern of results. In addition, the syntactic form of the test sentences was also investigated, using nouns, verbs, or adjectives as predicates. No systematic differences due to this variable were observed, terminating speculations about a possible noun priority in semantic memory. The most interesting feature of the experiment, however, was the construction of the ''true'' test sentences. High levels of semantic similarity were achieved by constructing sentences that were, in the judgment of the experimenters, quite likely stored as such in semantic memory, e.g., *A shark swims*, while low levels of semantic similarity were achieved by combining words in accidental ways, as in *A dog yawns*. It seems most improbable that *yawn* should be part of what a person knows about *dog*, or *dog* part of the notion of *yawn*. Hence the truth of such sentences must be inferred. It was argued that current theories fail because they do not give sufficient attention to this inferential capacity of the memory system. A model was developed that stresses the role of inferences in sentence evaluation and provides a theoretical definition of the concept of semantic distance. The model is a two-stage model postulating an initial semantic distance check, followed in some cases by a more detailed evaluation that relies heavily upon inferential processes.

11
LEXICAL DECOMPOSITION: COMPREHENSION AND MEMORY

1. THE PROBLEM

How are word pairs such as *comprehend: comprehension, build: builder,* etc. stored in memory? Linguists have offered two hypotheses. The transformational hypothesis, also called the decomposition hypothesis, holds that only *comprehend* and *build* are proper lexical items, and that the abstract noun *comprehension* and the agent noun *builder* are transformationally derived from these source verbs. This hypothesis was originally advanced by Lees (1960), but it has been challenged by Chomsky (1965, Pp. 219 – 220, 1970) who proposed the lexicalist hypothesis, according to which both the source words and the derived nouns are lexical items. These item pairs are related because they share many or most semantic features, differing mainly in the features Verb and Noun. Chomsky's reasons for rejecting the transformationalist hypothesis are based upon a comparison of derived nouns with gerundive nouns, such as *comprehending*. Productivity is unrestricted for gerundive nominals, while there are many restrictions on the formation of derived nominals. For the gerundive nominal the meaning relation between the nominal and the source verb is quite regular, while derived nouns may stand in many different meaning relations to their source verbs. For instance, *comprehension* is the act of someone's *comprehending,* while *proof* is the result of someone's *proving,* to give only two examples of the varied relations between base forms and derived nouns. Finally, Chomsky notes that there are important differences between gerundive nominals and derived nominals in their syntactic behavior. Only the latter have the internal structure of noun phrases, so that one can, for instance, insert adjectives into derived nominals but not into gerundives. Thus we may have *John's brilliant proof of the theorem* but not *John's brilliant proving of the theorem.* For these reasons Chomsky prefers the lexicalist hypothesis over the transformationalist position and develops it in some detail in his 1970 paper.

The transformationalist hypothesis has not, however, been without supporters among linguists in recent years. Bowers (1969) and Chapin (1970) have worked out the transformation rules necessary and have demonstrated the feasibility of the transformational approach. Several generative semanticists have taken strong positions in favor of the transformational view (e.g., Lakoff, 1970a, 1970b), even to the extent of postulating nonoccurring source verbs such as *auth,* to underlie *author.* Lakoff has also extended the discussion beyond abstract nouns and agent nouns to complex verbs. He argues persuasively that complex words must be decomposed at the lexical level and that certain constructions can not be understood unless complex words are broken down into their elements.

The problem, then, is this. Everyone knows that

> *John persuaded Mary to hit Fred*   (1)

means that *John caused Mary to come about to intend to hit Fred.* But how is this knowledge represented in memory? According to the transformational hypothesis, the complex verb *persuade* is decomposed into its components, so that the base structure of (1) becomes (after Lakoff, 1970b):

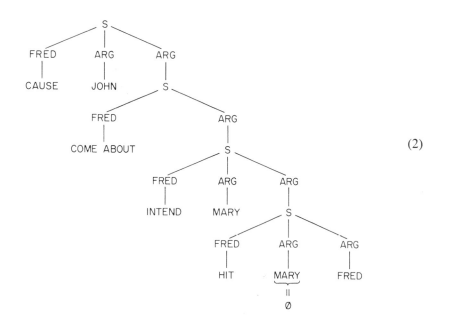

(2)

which after undergoing subject-raising and predicate-lifting transformations becomes

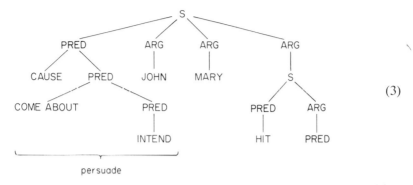

(3)

The alternative possibility is that *persuade* is a lexical item not decomposed into primitives, and that the necessary knowledge about the meaning of persuade is given by a meaning postulate as below (still in Lakoff's notation):

$$\forall x,y,z,(PERSUADE\ (x,y,z)\ ) = CAUSE\ (x, \qquad (4)$$
$$(COME\ ABOUT\ (INTEND\ (y,z,)))) \ .$$

In the present notation, the problem can be formulated as follows. Is the base structure of (1) the expression on the left side of (5) according to the lexicalist hypothesis, or is it the expression on the right hand side of (5) according to the decomposition hypothesis:

$$(PERSUADE,JOHN,MARY,(HIT,MARY,FRED)\ ) = \qquad (5)$$
$$= (CAUSE,JOHN,\alpha)\&(\ (COME\ ABOUT,\beta)=\alpha)\&$$
$$(\ (INTEND,MARY,\gamma)=\beta)\&(\ (HIT,MARY,FRED)=\gamma) \ .$$

It is clear that both expressions must be part of the lexicon, because the equivalence expressed by (5) must obviously be represented, but the question is whether the decomposition is the basic expression and the left side of (5) is derived by means of a lexical substitution rule as in (3), or whether on the contrary the complex word is itself a proper lexical entry and the right hand side of (5) is derived by means of an inference rule.

Linguists have provided good reasons for either choice but have failed to settle the issue conclusively. Chomsky (1970) maintained that "this is entirely an empirical issue," and one may take Chomsky at his word, admitting not only linguistic data (as Chomsky, and Lakoff, and others have already done) but also neurolinguistic and psycholinguistic observations. It is possible that considerations of performance might help one to decide between the alternatives.

However, there is not much to go on. Some neurological reports appear to favor the lexicalist hypothesis. Marshall and Newcombe (1966) and Marshall, Newcombe, and Marshall (1970) have consistently found that paralexic patients were able to read nouns much better than words from other form classes and were able to read derived nouns but not their source verbs. On the other hand, studies of language comprehension in patients with surgically severed connections between the two hemispheres of the brain have provided evidence more in agreement with the transformational view (Gazzaniga, 1970, Pp. 119–121). Comprehension of language in the right hemisphere is greatly reduced in these patients. Again, what can be understood with the right hemisphere alone is mostly nouns. However, not all nouns are present in the right hemisphere. Nouns derived from verbs can not be processed correctly by the right hemisphere. Patients did not understand *fall, hit,* or *jump* when used as nouns, and more interestingly, also failed with agent nouns such as *teller* and *locker*. At the same time simple nouns ending in *-er (flower, butter)* were easily recognized by the right hemisphere. These results indicate that agent nouns are not treated like other simple nouns, but more like their verb sources, and thus favor the transformational view over the lexicalist position.

As far as psycholinguistic research goes, no choice in favor of either decomposition or meaning postulates is possible at this time. We know, of course, that normal human subjects must be able to analyze lexically complex expressions if a task demands that; otherwise, a person could not be said to understand the language. However, this may be done either by means of decomposition or by inferences based upon meaning postulates. There exists a large body of research which is concerned with this question, and which, apart from being just about the most elegant work in psycholinguistics today, contributes immensely to our understanding of sentence comprehension in certain experimental tasks involving sentence comparisons or inferences. Contributions to this work have been made by several authors, primarily Clark (e.g. Clark, 1969, Clark & Chase, 1972). These are chronometric studies of sentence comprehension, based upon what Clark calls the "principle of congruence." This principle asserts that two semantic representations can be compared more quickly when they are congruent than when they are not. Therefore, in sentence comparison tasks or in sentence-picture comparisons, sentences are represented in memory in a canonical, decomposed form to facilitate the comparison. Thus, *John is absent* is represented as *false (present, John),* or *Peter is better than Paul* as *exceed (extent (good, Peter), extent (good, Paul))*. Response times in verification tasks can be accurately predicted from a model that assumes that each of the steps in the decomposition of a sentence to its canonical form requires a certain amount of time. There are two points to be noted, however. Time may be taken up by the transformations involved in decomposing a sentence, or equally by inferences via meaning postulates. Secondly, even if subjects decompose expressions in comparison tasks, where such a strategy is highly effective, they may not do so during normal comprehension where no comparison or inference response is required. When reading *John is absent*, do subjects store in memory (ABSENT, JOHN), or must this sentence necessarily be decomposed into the two-proposition expression (NOT, (PRESENT, JOHN))? If one asks the subject to make comparisons or inferences about presuppositions or implications, we know that subjects must and do, indeed, analyze these expressions (see, for example, Just & Clark, 1973, for inference experiments). But is this because the sentence itself is stored in its decomposed form, or because of the application of a meaning rule to a lexically complex expression? The Clark data can be accounted for either way. What is required are studies involving lexically complex words in which the task requirements do not force the comprehender to analyze these expressions into their components. Is there any evidence that lexical decomposition is used under such neutral task conditions?

There is only one psycholinguistic study of this type as yet available (Kintsch, 1972b), but it also fails to decide conclusively between the two competing interpretations, though it gives some support to the transformationalist position. Just as in the previous study, it demonstrates that under certain conditions in paired-associate learning, subjects treat lexically derived nouns more like their source verbs than like other nouns.

Kintsch (1972b) was concerned with the possibility that the results of paired-associate studies in which abstract nouns and concrete nouns were compared might have been confounded by lexical complexity effects. The concrete nouns used in these studies tended, in general, to be simple, nonderived nouns, while most abstract nouns may be derived from source verbs. It has been found regularly that concrete nouns are easier to learn than abstract nouns, and this effect has been attributed to the higher imagery value of the concrete nouns. However, it is possible that some or all of this effect may have been due to the lexical complexity of the abstract nouns, rather than to imagery value *per se*. Therefore, subjects were given paired-associate lists to learn with four kinds of stimulus terms: low-imagery – simple words *(interim)*, low-imagery–complex words *(ability)*, high-imagery–simple words *(comrade)*, and high-imagery–complex words *(speaker)*. The results are shown in Fig. 1. Both imagery effects and lexical complexity effects were highly significant statistically, and both added about equally to learning difficulty. Thus, in the usual imagery study where complex abstract nouns like *ability* and simple concrete nouns like *speaker* are compared, imagery effects are overestimated and confounded with lexical complexity effects.

Kintsch (1972b) reported some further studies of this phenomenon and employed the same kind of paired-associate design, which provided additional information concerning its generality and interpretation. First of all, high-frequency derived nouns are not different from corresponding (nonderived) control words. Such nouns appear to be treated like other nouns, that is, as proper lexical entries. Only nouns that are infrequently used in the language seem to be derived from source verbs. This result is reminiscent of the sentence evaluation data of the previous chapter. When dealing with frequently used words and sentences, subjects apparently do not take advantage of possible storage economies. Sentences like A shark swims appear to be directly stored in memory and are not inferred from A shark is a fish, and A fish swims. However, such inferences occur in similar cases with sentences that occur infrequently. Similarly, derived nouns like *teacher* and *marriage*, which for the subject population used were very high frequency words, were treated like nonderivable nouns, unlike *speaker* and *builder* which appeared to be derived from their

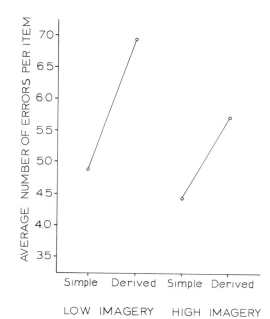

Fig. 1. Number of errors during learning as a function of lexical complexity for high- and low-imagery items.

source verbs. For high frequency words and sentences economy of processing is more important than economy of storage.

When a study was performed in which all derived nouns were replaced by their source verbs, almost identical results were obtained as with the derived nouns themselves. This result has important consequences for the interpretation of the data in Fig. 1. Apparently the slower learning with derived nouns in Fig. 1 was not caused by the difficulty of processing derived nouns because their source verbs were equally hard to learn. Instead, when subjects are given a paired-associate list with both nouns and verbs as stimuli, the nouns are learned faster than the verbs, and derived nouns are treated like their source verbs, not like ''real'' nouns. The source of such a bias is not clear, but the important point here is that there is, indeed, a psychological difference between derived and nonderived nouns.

The conclusion that performance differences between abstract and concrete words are often confounded by differences in lexical complexity is also supported by data reported by Weigl and Bierwisch (1970). In their study of the reading problems of an aphasic patient these authors obtained evidence that at first appeared to support the well-known thesis that aphasia primarily reduces the availability of abstract words. But upon further analysis this conclusion was shown to be at least in part dependent upon a confounding. The abstract words used tended to be lexically complex words, while the concrete words were, for the most part, lexically simple words. In fact abstract nouns without prefixes (that is, lexically simple abstract words) were read almost equally well as concrete nouns—the really hard words being the abstract, complex ones, much as in the paired-associate study just reported.

Where does all this leave us with respect to the lexicalist and transformational hypotheses? The observations on paralexic patients clearly support the former, while the split-brain study and the paired-associate experiments reported above argue for the latter. However, the paired-associate data are not at all clear with respect to their implications. They show one thing clearly: that there are psychological differences between derived and nonderived nouns, which is what the study was designed for. However, these data do not discriminate well among the transformational and lexicalist hypotheses. Psychologically, the lexicalist hypothesis emphasizes economy of processing, and the transformational hypothesis emphasizes economy of storage. If the differences observed by Kintsch (1972b) are not due to processing difficulties, the whole issue remains wide open as before.

The remainder of this chapter will report a series of experiments designed to permit a choice between the transformational and lexicalistic views on the basis of psycholinguistic data. First, the issue of processing difficulty will be further explored. If derived words are harder to process than nonderived control words, support for the transformational position will have been obtained. In the last two experiments, the way in which derived and nonderived words are stored in episodic memory will be explored.

Instead of using single words, the test words are embedded in simple sentences in the experiments to be reported. This procedure is followed in order to make sure that subjects really are dealing with the meaning of the words, which may not always be the case in list-learning studies.

2. EXPERIMENTS ON PROCESSING DIFFICULTY[1]

Experiment I

The measure of processing difficulty that was employed in the first two experiments was the sentence initiation time. Subjects were shown a word and asked to generate a sentence using that word. This measure has been employed in a number of studies as an indicator of the difficulty of the process of generating sentences (Murray, 1971). It correlates positively, though not very highly, with the length of pauses or hesitations during speech, which is also a widely used measure of processing difficulty (e.g., Goldman-Eisler, 1968). Taylor (1969) has shown that the latency measure is sensitive to content difficulty. Abstract words, as well as low-frequency words, required longer latencies than concrete words or high-frequency words, respectively.

Subjects. Twenty students from the University of Colorado participated in this experiment and were each paid $2.

Materials. Four groups of lexically decomposable words were used in this study: abstract nouns *(kindness, explanation, permission, ability),* agent nouns *(singer, juggler, attendant, performer, prosecutor),* verbs of saying *(deny, accuse, confess, commend),* and verbs of causation *(frighten, convince, persuade, liquefy).* In addition, there were lexically simple nouns *(mechanism, tuition, environment, majesty, frontage, orchestra)* and verbs *(relate, conform, inherit, mediate, save, generate,*

---

[1]The experiments reported here were performed by Steve Brunette.

announce) of comparable length, imagery value, and frequency. The average word frequency for decomposable words was 44, and for simple words 42 (Kučera & Francis, 1967).

Procedure. The experiment was performed in the Computer Laboratory for Instruction in Psychological Research (CLIPR) at the University of Colorado. Stimuli were presented on an oscilloscope. Presentation, timing, and recording were computer controlled. A cross appeared on the oscilloscope screen for three seconds, after which the test word was shown in the same place. The subject spoke each sentence into a microphone connected to a voice key. The latency between the appearance of the stimulus word and the beginning of speech was recorded.

Subjects were instructed to form a sentence, using the word shown on the screen, and were told:

> "The sentence can be about anything you want, as long as you use the word that is presented somewhere in the sentence.
> "Try not to use the same structure for every sentence; for example, don't say 'The tree is green,' 'The sky is blue,' 'The sun is red,' etc.
> "Also, try to avoid starting a sentence without knowing how to go on. Construct a sentence in your head before speaking it, and don't start by saying 'Uh' or 'Duh' or anything of the sort. In other words, don't say anything until you know what you're going to say."

Six warm-up trials preceded the experimental task. Words were shown in a different random order for each subject. The experimenter wrote down the sentence generated on each trial, and then started the next trial.

Results. Mean sentence initiation times were calculated for each stimulus word. The results did not confirm the experimental hypothesis, as shown in Table 1. The small differences between the means for simple and complex words were not significant by the Mann-Whitney U test, either for nouns or for verbs. Furthermore, there were no differences between abstract nouns and agent nouns, or between verbs of saying and verbs of causation. The only reliable difference observed was that responses to nouns were faster than responses to verbs.

Negative results like the present ones are difficult to interpret. It may mean that lexically complex and simple words are indeed comparable as far as the experimental task is concerned. On the other hand, it is not clear that the simple words that were used in this experiment as a control were indeed the proper controls. Therefore, a second experiment was performed in which new stimulus words were used. In

TABLE 1

Mean Sentence Initiation Times (sec) for Lexically Simple and Lexically Complex Nouns and Verbs in Experiment I

	Simple	Complex
Noun	2.4	2.6
Verb	3.0	3.2
Average	2.7	2.9

addition to comparing lexically complex words with simple words of the same form class matched in frequency, length, and imagery value, complex words were also compared with their own source words.

Experiment II

Subjects. Eighteen students from the University of Colorado participated in this experiment for a compensation of $2.

Materials and Design. As shown in Table 2, there were 10 groups of words used in this experiment. Each group contained four words, one of which is shown as an example in Table 2. The experimental words (groups 3, 6, 8, and 10) could be compared with their source verbs (2, 5, 7, and 9), and in addition the complex nouns could also be compared with matched control nouns (1 and 4) as in Exp. I. Because of the differences that were observed in Exp. I between nouns and verbs, such an additional control was judged necessary. The experimental verbs, however, can be directly compared with their source words, because no form class difference exists in this case.

Each subject received half of the 40 stimulus words, two from each word group. This was done in such a way that a given subject was never shown both a complex word and its respective source word. For example, Subject 1 in Group 1 was asked to form a sentence with *destruction,* and Subject 1 in Group 2 was given *destroy.*

Procedure. Each word was typed in the center of a 3″ x 5″ card. The experimenter, who was partially hidden from the subject by a wooden screen, presented each card by hand, at the same time starting an electronic timer that was stopped by means of a voice operated relay as soon as the subject started to speak.

The experimental instructions were like those of Exp. I except for the changes necessitated by the differences in the method of stimulus presentation.

Results. As in Exp. I, mean response latencies were computed for each stimulus word. Again, no differences were observed between abstract nouns and agent nouns, nor between verbs of saying and verbs of causation. There was, however, a sizable difference between the two groups of subjects. Therefore, the data are shown in Table 3 separately for the two groups, but summed over all nouns and verbs in each group.

TABLE 2

Experimental Materials Used in Experiment II

1. Abstract simple noun (idea)	2. Source verb (destroy)	3. Abstract complex noun (destruction)
4. Agent simple noun (soldier)	5. Source verb (preach)	6. Agent complex noun (preacher)
	7. Source verb (false)	8. Verb of saying (deny)
	9. Source verb (believe)	10. Verb of causation (convince)

TABLE 3

Mean Sentence Initiation Times (sec) for Lexically Simple and Complex Nouns and Verbs
for Two Groups of Subjects in Experiment II

	Simple	Complex
Nouns		
Group I	4.5	4.6
Group II	3.4	3.6
	3.9	4.1
Verbs		
Group I	5.0	4.8
Group II	3.0	3.2
	4.0	4.0
Total	4.0	4.1

As is apparent from inspection of the table, sentence initiation times for lexically simple and lexically complex words were about the same, as in Exp. I. This was true whether complex words were compared with simple control words (sentences 3 and 6 against 1 and 4), or whether the comparison was made between a complex word and its source word. Statistical analyses by means of the Mann-Whitney test confirmed this conclusion.

The difference in initiation times between verbs and nouns which had been observed in the previous experiment was not found here. The differences between the two groups of subjects appeared to be caused by one single unusually slow subject in Group I.

The lengths of the sentences that were generated by the subjects averaged about 7.5 words and were approximately the same for simple and complex stimulus words. The average sentence length for each stimulus word was correlated with the average response latency, which produced an $r = .37, p < .05$. Though this correlation is not very high, it does indicate that at least some aspect of the difficulty of generating a sentence from a given word is reflected in the sentence initiation time. On the other hand, no significant correlations were obtained between mean initiation times and frequency and length of the stimulus words. It must be remembered, however, that the frequency range of the words used here was very restricted: No really infrequent words were among the stimulus words. Taylor (1969) contrasted words occurring only once per million in the Thorndike-Lorge count with AA-words in a study wherein he observed a significant effect of word frequency upon sentence latencies. Taylor also reported that latencies for abstract words were longer than latencies for concrete words, but this effect was relatively small and it is not clear whether it was statistically significant or not. No indications of such an effect were observed in either of the present experiments.

In spite of the fairly clear negative results obtained with the method of sentence generation, the hypothesis that lexically complex words are harder to process than lexically simple words was further investigated by means of different experimental methods.

Experiment III

A method similar to the sentence generation method used above is the sentence completion method. It has been used successfully before, e.g., by MacKay (1966) who was able to show that ambiguous sentence fragments took more time to complete than nonambiguous control sentences. In the present application, sentence completion times for fragments containing lexically simple and complex words were compared.

Subjects. The 18 subjects who participated in the previous experiment also served as subjects in the present study. The sentence completion task followed the sentence generation task after only a brief rest interval.

Materials and Design. Eight sentence pairs were constructed. Each sentence was a four-word fragment with the critical word in the last position. Abstract nouns, agent nouns, and verbs of saying and causation were used as critical words, and each complex word was matched by a simple word embedded in a syntactically similar sentence fragment. Thus, *The rock's unexpected magnitude . . .* contrasted with *The boy's unusual ability . . . .* Each subject was given eight sentence fragments to complete, one from each pair, plus four warm-up trials.

Procedure. Apparatus and procedure were the same as in Exp. II. Instructions to the subjects merely asked them to complete the sentence fragments in any way they liked, so that an acceptable English sentence would result. They were warned not to make extraneous noises before speaking, which would set the voice key off prematurely, and to "try to know what you are going to say before you say anything."

Results. All responses were judged to be acceptable English sentences, meaningful though not necessarily entirely grammatical. Mean response latencies were computed for each sentence. Averages for nouns and verbs, separate for the two

TABLE 4

Mean Sentence Completion Times (sec) for Sentence Fragments Ending with Lexically Simple or Complex Nouns and Verbs for Two Groups of Subjects in Experiment III

	Simple	Complex
Nouns		
Group I	4.6	4.8
Group II	3.5	4.4
	4.0	4.6
Verbs		
Group I	4.6	3.9
Group II	3.2	3.6
	3.8	3.7
Total	4.0	4.2

groups of subjects, are shown in Table 4. As in Exp. II, the excessively long latencies of one subject in Group I make for between-group differences. The slight tendency in Table 4 towards higher latencies for the complex words was not significant statistically. Within-subject comparisons were made for each of the four sentence pairs for a total of 72 comparisons; of these, 34 times the sentence containing the complex word had a higher latency than the control sentence containing the simple word; latencies were reversed 37 times, and one score was missing. Thus, there is no statistical evidence in support of the experimental hypothesis.

Experiment IV

The phoneme monitoring method of Foss (1969) was chosen to assess the possibility that lexically complex words may be harder to process than lexically simple words in yet another way. The sensitivity of this method as a measure of processing difficulty has already been demonstrated, so that another negative result here would strengthen the conclusions reached above with the methods of sentence generation and completion.

In the method of phoneme monitoring, subjects are given two tasks concurrently: to comprehend an aurally presented sentence, and at the same time to monitor the occurrence of a critical phoneme. Reaction times to the phoneme are used as a measure of the difficulty of the concurrent sentence comprehension task. In Foss' study, the critical phoneme occurred either after a high-frequency word in the sentence, or after a low-frequency word. The phoneme detection times were longer after the infrequent words. Presumably, more of the subject's processing capacity

TABLE 5

Sample Sentences from Experiment IV

Abstract noun:

The boy's unusual *ability* Made him a successful participant in city wide competitions.
The girl's famous *ancestor* Made her an object of curiosity in the whole school.

Agent noun:

Mary talked to the *prosecutor* About lowering the fine.
John spoke with the *children* About the planned camping trip.

Verbs of Saying:

Many criminals *confess* THeir crimes because of a perverse pride.
Some students *commit* THeir worst mistakes on examinations because of nervosity.

Verb of Causation:

The doctor was *convinced* Only by his visitor's pallor.
The story was *believed* Only by the most gullible listeners.

Note.—The critical word in each sentence pair is italicized and the phoneme to be detected is capitalized.

was engaged in comprehending the lexically difficult words, so that they could not respond as quickly to the critical phoneme as they could after an easier word.

Subjects. Eighteen students from the University of Colorado were paid $2 each to participate in this experiment.

Material and Design. Abstract nouns, agent nouns, verbs of saying, and verbs of causation together with lexically simple control words were used as the critical words in this study. For each experimental word and its control word, sentences were constructed in such a way that the critical word was the third, fourth, or fifth word in the sentence, and the grammatical structure of the sentence was identical in each pair. The phoneme to be monitored always appeared right after the critical word. Examples of the four types of sentence pairs are shown in Table 5. There were four sentence pairs of each type, plus 24 filler sentences. Six filler sentences were used for warm-up trials. In the filler sentences the phoneme to be detected appeared either earlier or later than in the experimental sentences, or not at all. These sentences were included in the experiment in order to hide from the subjects the fact that in the experimental sentences the test phoneme always appeared in approximately the same place after 4–6 words. Experimental sentences had to be constructed in this way because Foss (1969) had shown that position in a sentence affected detection times (times were longer earlier in the sentence).

The word frequency of complex words and their controls could not be completely equalized. However, no really infrequent words were used (the lowest value on the Kučera and Francis norms is 2), and whatever frequency differences existed were in favor of the lexically simple control words. The average frequency for complex words was 21, but 61 for the simple controls, mostly because lexically simple agents tend to be very high frequency words *(man, children)*.

Procedure. The sentences were tape recorded by a male speaker with normal intonation. Filler items were interspersed with the experimental sentences. The two sentences of each pair always appeared in different halves of the presentation order. Two different presentation orders were recorded.

Subjects were seated in a sound proof booth in front of a small window. On each trial a letter card designating the phoneme to be detected on that trial was shown in the window. After the subject read the letter he placed his index finger on a photoelectric switch. The experimenter then started the tape recorder and the subject lifted his finger as fast as he could when he heard a word starting with the phoneme specified for that trial. After listening to the sentence the subject then had to generate a second sentence as a continuation of the sentence he had just heard. This procedure was used in order to insure that subjects were not merely concentrating on the phoneme detection task without processing the meaning of the sentence.

A signal on a second track of the tape recorder which coincided temporally with the test phoneme in the sentence on the first track started an electronic timer, which was stopped by the subject's response of lifting his finger from the photoelectric switch. A total of 56 trials were given in succession. After each trial the experimenter recorded the results (both the reaction time and the continuation sentence that the subject had generated), reset the timer, and presented the test phoneme for the next sentence in the window of the experimental booth, thereby starting the next trial.

Instructions to the subjects emphasized the importance of generating a plausible continuation of each test sentence as well as reliable and rapid responding to the phoneme monitoring task. Each of the two different presentation orders was used for half of the subjects.

Results. The sentences that subjects generated as continuations of the experimental sentences indicated that all subjects were trying to comply with the instructions and were indeed processing the meaning of the test sentences.

Subjects failed to detect the phoneme on 7% of the trials. Detection failures occurred somewhat more frequently after lexically complex words than after lexically simple words, 8.4% versus 5.7%. The probability of observing a difference of this magnitude or larger by chance is .03 on the basis of a sign test over subjects. The same probability value is obtained if the sign test is made over sentence pairs. Thus, there may have been a slight tendency towards more misses after complex than after simple words. An inspection of the detection times themselves, however, provides no evidence at all for the hypothesis that latencies are longer after complex words than after simple words. In fact, as Table 6 shows, average detection times are somewhat slower after simple words than after complex words. Two statistical analyses of the data were performed in which trials on which a detection occurred were combined with trials on which no response occurred. If no-detection trials are assigned a latency of ∞, each subject's performance on each sentence pair can be compared: If a simple sentence was faster than the complex sentence, the comparison was scored positively. Of 224 possible comparisons, 113 were positive, and 12 were ties. The probability of observing as many or more positive comparisons is greater than .30. Essentially the same conclusions were also reached by means of a different analysis. Each subject's detection times were ranked (again assigning ∞ to nondetection trials), and an analysis of variance was performed on the mean ranks for each subject for the eight different sentence types as shown in Table 5. The simple-complex comparison yielded an $F(1,98) = 1$, while the Abstract/ Agent/ Verb of Saying/ Verb of Causation comparison was statisticcally significant with an $F(3,98) = 4.90$, $p < .01$. Another main effect of Groups (which received two different presentation orders), and all interactions were not significant. As Table 6 shows, the significant main effect is mostly due to faster responses after nouns than after verbs.

TABLE 6

Mean Phoneme Detection Times (msec) for Four Sentence Types Containing Either a Lexically Simple or Complex Word before the Critical Phoneme (Experiment IV)

Sentence type	Simple	Complex	Mean
Abstract Nouns	758	598	678
Agent Nouns	627	625	626
Verbs of Saying	789	705	747
Verbs of Causation	694	724	709
Total	717	663	—

Discussion

In four experiments the hypothesis that lexically complex words are more difficult to process than lexically simple words has been investigated, and the results are quite clear: No differential processing difficulty has been observed. In addition, the original experimental study of lexical decomposition also failed to yield evidence of differential processing difficulty (Kintsch, 1972b). Thus, it seems fairly safe to conclude that lexical complexity has no effect upon processing difficulty. It is true that none of the experiments reported here are very powerful statistically, and one may question whether all the tasks used are indeed proper measures of processing difficulty. However, taken together the evidence is fairly strong. Surely, differential processing difficulty of simple and complex words must at best be a very insignificant factor compared with other variables affecting processing difficulty, or one of the experiments reported here would have registered its effects.

3. MEMORY EXPERIMENTS[2]

The remaining two experiments in this chapter are not concerned with the difficulty of processing lexically complex words but with the manner in which such words are stored in memory. Experiment V explores the hypothesis that, although complex words are not more difficult to comprehend and generate than simple words, they may require more storage space in memory; if so, subjects should be able to remember fewer sentences containing complex words than sentences containing simple words. In the final experiment of this series, the availability of the information contained in the decomposition of complex words will be investigated. Can source words serve as recall cues for lexically complex words, even though they are not morphologically similar and not associatively related?

Experiment V

Memory for sentences otherwise equal, but containing either a simple or a complex word, was investigated. For example, if a subject has to decompose the sentence *The performer receives his reward* into something like *Someone who performs receives his reward* in order to memorize it, and if this lexical transformation requires a significant portion of the subject's processing capacity, that sentence should be harder to remember than the control sentence *The seal receives his reward.*

Subjects. Forty students participated in the experiment as part of a course requirement. Half were males and half were females.

Materials. Forty experimental sentences were constructed. All sentences were five words long. There were five sentence pairs of each of four types: abstract nouns, agent nouns, verbs of saying, and verbs of causation. An example of each type, together with the propositional base of each sentence, is shown in Table 7. Word frequency was controlled as much as feasible within each sentence pair.

Procedure. The experimental procedure was patterned after Marks and Miller

---

[2]Experiments V and VI were performed by Sandra Barclay.

TABLE 7

Sample Sentences in Experiment V and their Propositional Base Forms, Both Incorporating and Disregarding the Lexical Decomposition Hypothesis

I. ABSTRACT NOUN:
Rapid advancement depends upon ability.   (DEPEND,(RAPID,ADVANCEMENT),(ABLE,$) or (DEPEND,(RAPID,ADVANCEMENT),ABILITY)
Rapid advancement depends upon events.   (DEPEND,(RAPID,ADVANCEMENT),EVENT)

II. AGENT NOUNS:
The performer receives his reward.   (RECEIVE,(PERFORM,$),REWARD) or (RECEIVE,PERFORMER,REWARD)
The seal receives his reward.   (RECEIVE,SEAL,REWARD)

III. VERBS OF SAYING:
John is accused of stealing.   (SAY,$,(GUILTY,JOHN,(STEAL,JOHN))) or (ACCUSED,JOHN,(STEAL,JOHN))
John is guilty of stealing.   (GUILTY,JOHN,(STEAL,JOHN))

IV. VERBS OF CAUSATION:
The dogs frightened the baby.   (CAUSE,DOG,(AFRAID,BABY)) or (FRIGHTEN,DOG,BABY)
The baby was afraid of dogs.   (AFRAID,BABY,DOG)

(1964). A trial consisted of the subject listening to five sentences and then attempting to recall these sentences immediately in writing. Before the subjects were presented with the experimental sentences, they experienced 20 warm-up sentences (i.e., 4 trials). The experimental sentences were recorded in two different orders. For half of the subjects, decomposable and control sentences were never mixed and all sentences of one type were presented together. For the other half of the subjects a semi-random order was used. The order of the five sentences within each trial was changed every five subjects.

The sentences were presented via a stereo tape recorder. They were spoken by a female voice, with a flat intonation, each sentence lasting 2.5 sec, with a 2-sec pause between sentences.

The subjects were seated at a table in a sound-controlled booth. After each trial the subject was given up to two minutes to write as accurately as possible the sentences he had just heard. Then, the same five sentences (in a new order) were played again, and the subject was again allowed two minutes for recall before proceeding to the next trial.

Results. The recall protocols were scored in two ways, strict (verbatim recall) and lenient (propositional recall). Neither analysis supported the experimental hypothesis that sentences containing a lexically complex word are harder to recall than control sentences with a lexically simple word. For the strict scoring, fewer subjects recalled the experimental sentences than the control sentences in 9 cases, but for the other 11 sentence pairs the relation was reversed. If lenient scoring is used, 9 pluses, 10 minuses, and one tie were obtained. In other words, there is no evidence whatever for the experimental hypothesis. These results are based upon total recall for each sentence, summed over both trials and all orders of presentation. However, more detailed analyses yield no additional information that would affect the conclusions drawn from this study. The data are shown in Table 8.

There are two subsidiary observations in this experiment that are of some interest. First, note that sentences with abstract nouns were recalled much worse than the other sentences in this study, in strong contrast to the results of Exp. I–IV. In the previous experiments processing difficulty was measured, and abstract-noun sentences did not differ from agent-noun sentences. Secondly, recall in the present experiment can be regarded as a function of the number of propositions in the base structure of the

TABLE 8

Percent of Sentences Correctly Recalled in Experiment V

Sentence type	Simple	Complex	Mean
Abstract Nouns:	56	56	56
Agent Nouns:	84	78	81
Verbs of Saying:	68	82	75
Verbs of Causation:	86	83	84
Mean	74	74	

sentences. Some sentences were based upon two propositions (e.g., the first and third sentence pairs in Table 7), while the majority (25) were based upon only one proposition (e.g., the second and fourth sentence pairs in Table 7). Recall for the two-proposition sentences was 63%, while 80% of the one-proposition sentences were recalled. This difference was significant statistically, $t(38) = 3.3$, $p < .01$. The data thus confirm results reported earlier in Chapter 7.

Discussion. No evidence has been obtained to indicate that sentences that contain a lexically complex word are harder to memorize than the same sentences with a lexically simple word substituted for the complex one. Thus, when the subjects remember sentences, decomposable words are treated just like simple lexical items. *John is accused of stealing* is remembered just as well as *John is guilty of stealing* — although, of course, the subjects can, upon demand, decompose the meaning of the former into *Someone says,* or *It is said that John is guilty of stealing.* However, in order to memorize the sentence either this decomposition is not performed, or such lexical transformations require no processing capacity, and complex sentences are just as easy to remember as simple ones. At present, the first hypothesis appears considerably more likely than its alternative.

The question about memory difficulty is therefore answered in the same way as the question of processing difficulty: Lexically complex, derived words are not different from simple, nonderived words.

Experiment VI

In Exp. VI the subject's ability to use base structure components as recall cues was explored. For example, if *accuse* appears in a sentence, which can be decomposed as *someone says that . . . is guilty,* how good is *guilty* as a retrieval cue? Embedded in a list of dummy sentences, a sentence containing a lexically decomposable word was presented to three groups of subjects. Only the critical sentence was tested for recall. For one group the crucial word itself was given as a recall cue, while for the other group a base structure component of that word served as a retrieval cue. For comparison, a third group of subjects received a strong associate of the critical word as a retrieval cue. One might expect, on the basis of linguistic intuitions and the earlier results of Kintsch (1972b), that base structure components would be fairly effective retrieval cues but not as effective as the original word. The latter prediction follows from the results of Exp. V: If lexically complex words are not decomposed for memory storage, the base structure component that is to serve as a retrieval cue is not stored together with the to-be-retrieved material, and hence, by the encoding specificity principle, should be less effective than a word actually stored as part of the to-be-retrieved sentence.

Subjects. Thirty undergraduates from the University of Colorado participated individually in the experiment. They were paid $2 each. The subjects were randomly assigned to the three experimental groups, 10 to each group. In addition, associative norms were collected from 102 subjects who were asked to fill out a prepared booklet on their own time.

Material. Twenty critical sentences were selected from those used in Exp. V. All were five words long and contained a critical word that was lexically complex. Four types of lexically complex words were used (in five sentences each): abstract nouns, agent nouns, verbs of saying, and verbs of causation. Examples for the four types, indicating the decomposition of the critical words, are:

Rapid advancement depends upon ability (someone is able).

The attendant (someone who attends) *closes the door.*

John was accused (someone says . . . is guilty) *of stealing.*

The student convinced (caused the . . . to believe) *the professor.*

The base structure of twelve of these critical sentences was formed by just one proposition (as in the second and last examples above), while the other eight sentences contained two propositions in the base structure (for instance, the first and third examples above).

Each critical sentence was embedded in a list of nine other unrelated sentences. The critical sentence always appeared in serial positions 3–6. All dummy sentences were five words long and followed no particular pattern, except that none of the words in the critical sentence were used in a dummy sentence. Thus, 20 blocks of 10 sentences, each containing a critical sentence, were obtained. In addition, seven more 10-sentence blocks consisting entirely of dummy sentences were constructed.

For each critical sentence three retrieval cues were used; the original (lexically complex) word itself (for the examples given, that would be *ability, attendant, accused,* and *convinced*); the base structure component of the original words (e.g., *able, attend, guilty,* and *believe*); and a high associate of the original words (e.g., *skill, gas station, blame,* and *persuade*). Since associative norms for the words used were not available, normative data were collected from 102 subjects. The subjects were given sheets of paper with the critical words and standard free-association instructions. From the data thus collected, the associate given most frequently was used as a retrieval cue. (In some cases the most frequent associate had to be rejected as a retrieval cue because it did not fit into the present sentence context, e.g., *black* was given as the most frequent associate to *segregate*, but that word was used here in the sense of *divide*.)

Procedure. The subjects listened to 10 sentences and then tried to recall one of them (the critical sentence) on the basis of a retrieval cue. Two 10-sentence blocks containing no critical sentences were used for warm-up. Five other dummy trials were interspersed between the experimental trials. This was necessary because experimental trials always contained the critical test sentence in the middle positions of the list, and therefore dummy trials on which either early or late serial positions were tested were needed to prevent the subjects from exploiting this regularity.

All sentences were tape recorded by a female voice with normal intonation. Two-second pauses separated the ten sentences of each block. After each block, the experimenter stopped the tape recorder and gave the subject the retrieval cue appropriate for this trial. Sentences that in one group received the original word as a retrieval cue were assigned to the base structure cue in the next group, and to the association cue in the third group. Thus, each sentence was paired with each cue. Upon hearing the retrieval cue, the subjects attempted to recall the corresponding sentence

TABLE 9

Percent Recall as a Function of Cuing Condition and Number of Propositions
in the Sentence's Base Structure

| | Cues: | | | |
	Original	Base component	Associate	Total
One Proposition	58	41	44	48
Two Propositions	50	31	26	36
Total	54	36	35	42

in writing without a time limit. They were instructed that "the cue word will be either an exact word from a sentence, or a related word." Examples of possible cues were discussed.

Results. A recall protocol was scored as correct if it expressed correctly the whole meaning of the propositions upon which the original sentence was based. Verb tenses were disregarded.

Table 9 shows the basic data obtained in this experiment. Overall, 55% of the critical sentences were recalled correctly if a word from a sentence was used as a recall cue. If either an associate of that word, or a component of the semantic decomposition of that word, was used as a cue, recall was reduced, but the subjects were still able to recall 37% of the sentences. Furthermore, sentences derived from a single proposition were recalled better (48%) than sentences derived from two propositions (36%). An analysis of variance of these data revealed that both type of cue and number of propositions were highly significant statistically, min $F'(2,174) = 6.04$ and min $F'(1,129) = 9.52$, respectively (both p's are less than .005). The interaction between these variables was not significant, min $F' < 1$.

While the same pattern of results held (approximately) for all sentence types, the overall difficulty differed. Sentences with abstract nouns were most difficult (33% correct recall), sentences with verbs of saying (37%) and verbs of causation (43%) were next in difficulty, while sentences with agent nouns (59%) were easiest.

Upon closer examination of the data, several other factors proved to be important in determining the effectiveness of an associate or base structure component as a recall cue. First of all, as would be expected, strength of association played a role. A correlation of .63 ($p < .01$) was observed between percent correct recall for each sentence and strength of association between the associate cue and the original sentence word that the associate replaced. Strength of association was measured by the percentage of the subjects who gave that particular word as a free associate. Secondly, form class also played a role in determining the effectiveness of a cue. If an associate and the original word belonged to the same form class (so that, to some extent, the associate could take on the same syntactic role in the sentence as the original word), the average differential in recall between original cue and associate cue was only 13%, while an associate was 24% less effective than an original word if the two belonged to different form classes. This effect was even more striking if one compares only those cases where the associate, when inserted in the original sentence, produced an acceptable paraphrase (e.g., *scared* for *frightened*): In that case, associates and the original words were equally effective as recall cues.

An interesting comparison can be made when base components are used as cues. In some cases (abstract nouns as well as agent nouns) the base component is morphologically related to the original word, e.g., *advance* for *advancement, attend* for *attendant*. In others (verbs of saying and causation), the two words are quite dissimilar in their surface form, such as *accuse-guilty, convince-believe*. The former kind of cues, not surprisingly, proved to be more effective: Relative to performance with the original words as cues, base component cues that had the same root as the original word were 77% effective, but cues that had a different root were still 54% effective.

Discussion. The question to which this experiment was addressed was whether or not people have knowledge of the decomposition of lexically complex words, and whether they can use this kind of knowledge if they are asked to do so. Quite clearly, the subjects did make good use of such knowledge in the present experiment, just as they did in the comparison and inference experiments of Clark and others mentioned earlier. In fact, base structure components were about as effective as strong associates in cuing recall in the present study. This effect can not be explained on the basis of mere formal similarity between the original word and the corresponding base component, because such cues were still quite effective even when there was no such similarity. Furthermore, the effectiveness of base components cannot be due to associative factors either. For 14 of the 20 words, the base component never was given as a response on the free association task, and in only one case was the base component also a strong associate. The average associative strength of the base components was .02, compared with .16 for the associative cues.

The results of the present experiment also confirm those of Exp. V, in that they, too, argue against the hypothesis that the subjects decompose lexically complex words for storage in memory. If that were the case, one might reasonably expect base components to be as good or better cues than original words—which was clearly not the case. Rather, it appears that subjects can decompose lexically complex words into their underlying expressions, but that they do so only when the task requires it.

There are at least two ways to explain the present results concerning the (partial) effectiveness of base structure components as retrieval cues. It is possible that at the time of presentation the subjects store sentences without decomposing a complex word. When given a base structure component as retrieval cue, that cue may elicit the original complex word via lexical transformation rules, and hence permit recall of the corresponding sentence. Such an explanation would be contrary to the model of retrieval processes in episodic memory, as developed in Chapter 4. According to that model a retrieval cue must be stored as part of a memory episode during learning if it is to be effective. If a subject is given the retrieval cue *guilty*, this cue may access the semantic memory item $S_{accused}$, but that will not retrieve the to-be-recalled sentence; the memory episode $M_{accused}$ is required for that, not merely a context-free lexical entry.

However, an explanation of the cuing results obtained here within the framework of Chapter 4 is readily available. According to the model, memory episodes are formed by selecting (with certain biases) cues from the perceptual stimulus as well as from the semantic memory representation that was matched by the perceptual stimulus. The semantic memory representation of, say, ACCUSE will include GUILTY, and hence with a certain likelihood the memory episode will contain GUILTY. Thus, the cue *guilty* on a test trial will match a component of the memory episode and thereby retrieve it. Note that this is not saying that lexically complex words are stored in decomposed form: What is stored is a code for *accused,* not for *someone says is guilty.* If the latter were the case, GUILTY would always be a component of the memory episode, and hence the retrieval cue *guilty* should be as good as an original word from the sentence. The effectiveness of source words as cues for lexically complex words is explained here in exactly the same way as the effectiveness of word associates as retrieval cues. What remains to be explained is why source words (at least for the sample of words used here) are not also given as associates on free-association tests, but that problem concerns performance on association tests in general (Clark, 1970), rather than lexical decomposition by itself.

As has also been observed in Experiment V, two-proposition sentences were harder to recall than one-proposition sentences. In the earlier study, with a completely different methodology, recall was 80% for one-proposition sentences and 63% for two-proposition sentences. In the present study the superiority of recall for one-proposition sentences was just as large (48% vs. 36%), and highly significant statistically. Such data are, of course, of great interest, because they confirm the results of Chapter 7, thereby providing further support for the claim that propositions are the basic building blocks from which semantic memory is constructed and form suitable units of measurement for psychological studies of memory.

CONCLUSION

The purpose of the series of studies presented here was to decide how derivable words are represented in episodic memory. The results were quite unambiguous; it appears that derived nouns (abstract nouns and agent nouns) as well as derived verbs (verbs of saying and verbs of causation) are stored in memory as lexical items in their own right, and are not necessarily decomposed either in comprehending or in memorizing sentences. The hypothesis that words are automatically decomposed in comprehension implies that derived words should be more difficult to process, because in addition to whatever else is involved, the derivation itself should require some of the available processing capacity. This prediction has been clearly contradicted for various measures of processing difficulty: Derived and nonderived words were found equally difficult in terms of generating a sentence from a given word (Exp. I and II), completing sentences (Exp. III), sentence comprehension (Exp. IV), and memory (Exp. V). A theory of memory in which both derived and nonderived words are represented in the same way as lists of propositions specifying their use agrees best with these results.

Experiment VI shows that if a task requires it, subjects can make use of the decomposition of lexically complex words. Again the data argue against automatic decomposition: If words were always decomposed during comprehension, an even larger cuing effect of the source words should have been observed, as was discussed above. Instead, the source appears to be simply part of the lexical description of derived words, so that subjects could use this information but did not have to use it in all cases.

It should be noted, however, that the present data have no implications with respect to the linguistic issues involved. It has merely been shown that in memory and comprehension a word is a unit, whether it is derivable or not. The lexicalist and transformational hypotheses, on the other hand, concern the form of the rules by means of which certain relationships among words are expressed; they do not concern sentence memory or comprehension. Either the transformational or the lexicalist hypothesis may describe the rules available as part of a subject's general knowledge of language. But it has been shown here that, even if words are decomposed in semantic memory, they are not automatically decomposed in comprehension and episodic memory. The implications of the present studies are, therefore, important for psychology and for artificial intelligence, in so far as such projects are conceived as simulations of human processes rather than as merely artificial computational devices, as will be further discussed in the next chapter.

In the beginning of this chapter some results were discussed that seemed to provide support for a transformational treatment of derived nouns. There was, for instance, the observation of Gazzaniga (1970) that derived nouns could not be processed in the right hemisphere, while other similar but nonderived nouns could be. In addition, there was the finding of Kintsch (1972b) that derived and nonderived nouns were treated differently in paired-associate learning. However, these data argue for a transformational view only in so far as it is assumed that the greater processing difficulty for derived nouns was responsible for the effects observed. The present results (and indeed the original data of Kintsch, 1972b, themselves) indicate that this was not the case. It is not claimed, however, that there are no psychologically important differences between the two classes of words. Even though a derivable word is stored as a separate unit in memory, just like its source word, it still differs from simple nonderivable words, because it can, upon demand, be decomposed into its elements by means of rules which must be part of its lexical description. Thus, instead of talking about derived and nonderived words, one should be speaking about derivable and nonderivable words.[3]

Rejecting the transformational hypothesis for the treatment of derivable words has an interesting implication for semantic memory models in general. Consider the original motivation for this hypothesis. On the one hand it was supposed to buy

[3]Note that we reject the transformational hypothesis only in so far as the decomposition of word concepts is concerned. Essentially linguistic surface transformations, such as the formation of gerundive nouns, are unaffected by these arguments. We also do not want to claim that every word in a language must have a corresponding unitary word concept; this is probably not the case for instances in languages that use many compound nouns as single words, such as in German.

storage economy at the coast of additional processing. But perhaps even more important for its supporters was the possibility of achieving a more general economy in the lexicon, of taking one step closer towards the ideal of constructing a lexicon from primitive semantic elements. This chapter has dealt a further blow to such hopes. If not even derivable words are in fact derived in semantic memory, why try to break down all words into primitive semantic elements? Such efforts have seemed rather hopeless before and they receive no encouragement from the present results.

SUMMARY

One of the first options confronting a theorist who is interested in formulating a system for the representation of meaning is whether he should decompose lexically complex word concepts into their semantic elements or admit simple as well as complex word concepts at an equal level. Some linguists and many computer scientists argue in favor of decomposition, though it hardly seems possible to resolve the issue on a purely linguistic level. For the psychologist, the question is an empirical one: Is there any evidence that lexically complex words are harder to process than lexically simple words? If so, this would mean that additional effort is required to decompose complex words into their elements, and it would strongly argue in favor of decomposition. Processing difficulty was measured in four experiments in various ways: by measuring sentence initiation times in experiments where subjects were instructed to generate a sentence using a given (lexically simple or complex) word, by measuring sentence completion times in similar experiments, or by using a phoneme monitoring method concurrently with reading sentences containing the critical words. No evidence whatever suggested that lexically complex words are more difficult to process than lexically simple words. A fifth experiment tested the prediction that if lexically complex words are decomposed, they should require more memory capacity than nondecomposable control words. Again, the results gave no indication that subjects stored words in decomposed form. On the other hand, a final study showed that the recall of complex words could be cued effectively with their source words. Obviously, subjects have available the information about the construction of lexically complex words, and they can use this information if required to do so. But there is no evidence whatever that they routinely decompose such words during comprehension and memory storage. Thus, the decision to use lexically complex word concepts as elements of propositions in the same way as lexically simple words is fully vindicated by the data reported here (as it was, in fact, influenced by the very same data in the first place).

12
INTERIM CONCLUSIONS

It remains to bring together the diverse material that was discussed here, and to provide some perspective as to how and where these studies fit into the larger picture. First of all, how does the experimental work reported here make contact with the theoretical work of Part I? The reader has surely realized by now that the experiments are not tests of strict deductions from the theory. The theory is not specified completely enough to permit such strict deductions. It merely sketches in the relevant logical-linguistic background, but lacks a detailed processing component. Linguistic-logical considerations are powerful enough to constrain our ideas about how knowledge can or must be represented in memory, but they fail to provide us with more than the most general notions about psychological processing. The experiments reported here are studies in search of a processing theory rather than tests of one. This is not a necessary approach; it is possible, especially if one radically restricts the scope of a model, to formulate explicit process models and proceed to test them experimentally. Every reader will be able to think of some outstanding examples of work of this kind. The present volume has different goals: With only some *a priori* constraints on the nature of memory representations, we have set out to explore models of processing. The model that we are after is very ambitious, because it should be able to deal with a wide variety of information-processing tasks. But its outlines are as yet indistinct and its development is a task for the future when sufficient experimental evidence has accumulated to permit greater precision in the formulation of our ideas about memorial processes.

In the meantime, what is the contribution of the experiments reported here towards the formation of such a processing model? Especially when the present results are considered together with relevant studies from other laboratories, some modest but nevertheless important generalizations begin to emerge. I shall organize this discussion under four headings. For the first one, which concerns the existence of an abstract representation of text in memory, the evidence appears firm and noncontroversial. The main contributions of the present work are to the second and third categories: what the nature of this abstract representation might be (viz., the propositional model explored here) and the role of inferences in comprehension and memory, respectively. Though hardly definitive, the evidence concerning these questions is quite suggestive. The fourth and last topic, the problem of memory search, for all its significance, remains the least well explored one.

1.

Much early work in psycholinguistics was concerned with demonstrating the psychological importance of such variables as the surface structure of sentences or their deep structure (for reviews see Kintsch, 1970b, or Fillenbaum, 1971). It became clear, however, that there must be a more abstract level of representation in memory which constitutes the sentence meaning and which is of the greatest significance psychologically. The seminal experimental work in this area is that of Sachs (1967). Sachs showed that subjects in a recognition experiment could detect only very poorly various syntactic changes in sentences, but they had no difficulties in spotting changes in the meanings of test sentences. If what subjects stored in memory was merely the deep structure of the sentences, Sachs' results would be difficult to explain. Such a hypothesis became fully untenable when the work of Bransford, Barclay, and Franks (1972) became public. These authors also used a recognition paradigm, but arranged their experimental conditions in such a way that linguistic deep structure explanations of their results were excluded and a more abstract conceptual representation of the sentence meaning was indicated. They showed their subjects sentences such as *Three turtles rested on a floating log and a fish swam beneath them.* Afterwards subjects failed to recognize as new the test sentence *Three turtles rested on a floating log and a fish swam beneath it,* which differs from the study sentence in deep structure, but has the same meaning: People know that if three turtles rest on a floating log, a fish swimming underneath must be both beneath *them* as well as *it.* Therefore, what these subjects remembered was some abstract representation of the sentence meaning, and they were basing their responses on it. The results reported in Chapter 5 make the same point, although a different methodological approach was used. We showed that subjects stored the same representation in memory for paragraphs that differed in the way they were expressed but not in meaning. The paragraph pairs we constructed were always based upon the same underlying propositions, but in one case they were expressed in a syntactically straightforward manner and in the other as a long, complex sentence. When given a test, after reading such paragraphs, that required them to make an inference on the basis of the material they had just read, subjects were able to respond as rapidly to correct statements coming from simple versions of the paragraphs as from complex versions. It took subjects longer to read, that is, to decode, the complex paragraphs than the simple paragraphs, but once they had stored the material in memory, the differences between the simple and complex versions disappeared. Apparently what was stored in memory was the meaning of the paragraph, independent of the syntactic complexity of the input.

An even more striking demonstration of this very same point has recently been reported by Honeck (1973). If memory for meaning rather than the actual verbal expression is so important, then quite dramatic effects can be achieved by using materials in which the meaning and the actual words used are discrepant, such as proverbs. In a memory experiment Honeck either repeated proverbs verbatim, with some slight changes in the word order, or as a paraphrase that expressed the meaning of the proverb but used different words. For example, the proverb *Industry is fortune's right hand and stinginess her left,* could be transformed to *Stinginess is fortune's left hand and industry her right,* or paraphrased as *You must work hard and spend money carefully to make a fortune.*[1] The transformation is similar to the original in the actual words used, while the paraphrase is not, though it expresses the meaning of the proverb. After listening to such sentences, subjects were given a cued recall test. The sentences that had been paraphrased were recalled best. Just as in the other experiments reviewed here, what was stored in memory (or more accurately, part of what was stored) must have been a representation of the meaning of the sentence, an abstract representation in the sense that it was something derived from the actual verbal expressions used but went well beyond them.

2.

The real problem is, of course, to determine the nature of that abstract representation. We know now that such a representation is needed (and the number of demonstrations of this intuitively obvious fact will undoubtedly multiply in the next few years), but this merely poses the much more difficult and much more important question as to *how* we should or could represent meaning. I have tried to approach this problem in two ways. In Part I, I have worked out a possible formalism for the representation of meaning. Chapter 2 was devoted to showing that this formalism works reasonably well and that it is relevant to a broad range of semantic problems. The propositional model was developed from logical and linguistic considerations, plus some rather general psychological notions and a good dose of intuition. Chapter 3 attempted to demonstrate that the model deserves to be taken seriously as a semantic theory, in that it is able to deal fairly well with several of the complex issues that traditionally been the proving grounds for theories of this sort. Treatments of definitivization, quantification, presupposition, tense, and time appear to be possible within the suggested framework. The experiments reported in Part II are supposed to help us take the giant step from the possible to the actual. It is unlikely that we have, as yet, enough or sufficiently powerful data to specify unambiguously the nature of the representation of meaning in memory, except to the most biased eye. Therefore, I do not wish to review the presently available evidence for the various theoretical proposals that have been made. Instead, I shall try to summarize the evidence relative

[1]See the discussion of metaphors in Chapter 2 for the theoretical representation of such expressions.

to the present propositional model, and to discuss its relationship to other theories only insofar as obvious alternatives are at hand. In other words, some of the data that are claimed here as evidence for the present model could also be claimed in favor of other similar theories.

2.1.

There is some direct evidence that is consistent with the case grammar format of the proposed theory. Kintsch (1972a) has shown that when subjects are given sentences that express a multi-argument proposition, but in which one of the arguments is missing, they can supply the missing argument easily and with considerable inter-subject agreement. Shafto (1973) had subjects learn to sort sentences into categories on the basis of the relationship between one of the sentence nouns (which was underlined) to the sentence as a whole. The nouns served in the roles of agent, experiencer, instrument, and object. Different rates of acquisition for these categories were observed, with agent the easiest and object the hardest. Furthermore, multidimensional scaling of the concept learning data revealed that the psychological space for the four cases used in this study could be described as two dimensional, with living-nonliving and active-passive as the underlying semantic features. In a second experiment, Shafto demonstrated that the nature of the verb frame determined confusability among simple sentences in a recognition experiment. These results are in nice agreement with the notion that something like case structure might be the basis for sentential memory.

2.2.

One of the most important characteristics of the propositional model as it is used here is that it does not decompose lexical items. Specifically, we write propositions as (KILL, TIGER, DEER) or (ACCUSE, SENATOR, PRESIDENT) instead of (CAUSE, TIGER, (BECOME, (DEAD, DEER))) and (SAY, SENATOR, (GUILTY, PRESIDENT)). The linguistic controversy that surrounds these alternative modes of description was discussed in Chapter 11. There is no reason to repeat these arguments, except for their conclusions: It appears that first, one *can* do it either way, and second, there are good arguments for both sides. If we look at other fields, the picture is not much clearer, though the preference seems to be for decomposition in artificial intelligence. A good example is the extensive and fruitful use of decomposition in the program of Rumelhart, Lindsay, and Norman (1972). This program comprehends a sentence by constructing a graph that represents the relations among the concepts that appear in the sentence. It is quite possible that the graphs of Rumelhart et al. may even be formally equivalent to the propositions used here, but the one real difference between the systems is that Rumelhart et al. decompose items into their constituents. Consider as an example the representation of the simple sentence.

Peter put the package on the table.   (1)

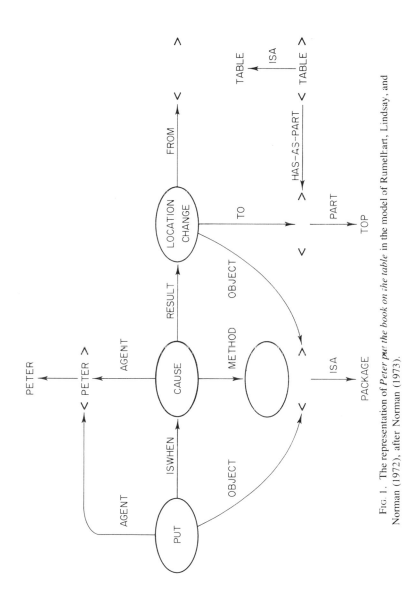

Fig. 1. The representation of *Peter put the book on the table* in the model of Rumelhart, Lindsay, and Norman (1972), after Norman (1973).

Figure 1 shows how Rumelhart et al. encode this sentence. The action underlying the sentence is specified explicitly. The word *put* is decomposed (by means of the IS WHEN relation) into something like "someone causes an object to change location from x to y by some method," and "on the table" is further analyzed as "on top of the table." Compare this with the analysis suggested by the present theory, which is to represent (1) as

$$\text{(PUT, AGENT:PETER, OBJECT:BOOK, GOAL:TABLE)} \tag{2}$$

which looks a lot simpler than Fig. 1. The simplicity is, however, illusory. What Rumelhart et al. assume to be explicit parts of the sentence encoding must be represented in the present model as meaning postulates, that is, as part of semantic memory. Thus, the verb frame for PUT must be listed as (PUT, AGENT, OBJECT, GOAL, SOURCE), with the obligatory arguments underlined, plus meaning postulates such as

$$\text{(IMPLY,(PUT,AGENT,OBJECT),(CAUSE,AGENT,}$$
$$\text{(CHANGE,OBJECT,LOCATION))),}$$

or

$$\text{(IMPLY,(LOC:ON,OBJ,TABLE),((HAS PART,TABLE,TOP)\&}$$
$$\text{(LOC:ON,OBJ,TOP)).}$$

In other words, the information about the structure of the action PUT, which Rumelhart et al. list as part of the encoding of the sentence, is conceived in the present theory as part of semantic memory. In the long run, therefore, neither way is really simpler: With a great deal of lexical decomposition the sentence encoding becomes complicated, but what one saves there is at least in part compensated for by the need for an extensive rule system in semantic memory if decomposition is not used. Indeed, it can be argued (Norman, 1973; Rumelhart et al., 1972) that decomposition provides substantial gains for artificial intelligence devices. Consider, once more, the decomposition of KILL. If the internal code for KILL in an artificial intelligence device is always "cause to become dead," then it does not matter whether one says, *The tiger caused the deer to become dead,* or *The tiger caused the deer to die,* or *The tiger killed the deer.* That is, lexical decomposition serves, in these instances, to solve the paraphrase problem. This is a very significant gain, and may be well worth the somewhat more cumbersome encodings. Nobody seems to have tried writing a computer simulation program using meaning postulates, however, so it is impossible to say how such an approach would compare in terms of efficiency with the decomposition technique.

In any case, whether decomposition or meaning postulates are used in comprehension and memory is an empirical psychological question. Linguistic arguments can make clear what the issue is, but they cannot decide it for us. Efficiency arguments from artificial intelligence are suggestive, but not more than that. What we need are psychological data.

The series of studies reported in Chapter 11 allows us to decide for the first time whether or not to use decomposition on the basis of psychological information. Previous psychological evidence, most of it coming from studies of patients with various kinds of neurological disorders, have not been decisive. These data are certainly fascinating and challenging, but their correct interpretation is not always clear. If anything, they argue for decomposition rather than against. Extensive psycholinguistic research by Clark and others (e.g. Clark and Chase, 1972) shows that if a task requires it, subjects can make use of decomposition, as was discussed in the beginning of Chapter 11. The present data, on the other hand, clearly contradict the notion of lexical decomposition as an obligatory psychological process in sentence comprehension and memory. In none of the studies reported in Chapter 11 was it possible to find systematic differences in ease of comprehension or memorization between sentences containing lexically decomposable words and control sentences with lexically simple words. As in all studies that yield no-difference results, there are problems of statistical interpretation. However, the best guard against overlooking a true difference in some experiment is to repeat the experiment with various methodological variations; if the no-difference result persists in all of them, one is probably justified in taking it seriously. That is what was done and what was observed in Chapter 11. There are certainly other ways of experimentally measuring the difficulty of comprehension of sentences than the ones used there, and there is no assurance that with one of those unexplored methods sentences with simple and complex words could not be differentiated. But this seems to be fairly unlikely, given the correspondence between our comprehension and memory results. Experimental tests of memory, unlike tests of comprehension difficulty, are well-defined, and we obtained no indication that sentences with simple words are easier to remember than sentences containing a lexically decomposable term. Thus, as far as psychological processes go, a word is a word, and the mere fact that it *can* be decomposed into more elementary concepts does not make it any harder to comprehend or remember. The rules that make it possible to decompose a complex word are available and can be used if the task requires it. But these rules have the same status as any other lexical information that relates a given item to other lexical items. They do not obligatorily replace the decomposable word in memory; that is, the person understands and remembers KILL, not its decomposed version.

Perhaps, this is not so very surprising after all, in spite of the efficiency arguments for artificial intelligence systems. Presumably, complex lexical items like KILL are employed in a language because of processing advantages over the longer original forms. It would be strange, then, if the system would not use the advantages gained from brief complex forms, but always return to the unwieldy explicit expressions.

The problem is a significant one because of the widespread, unquestioning acceptance of decomposition in computer simulation models of language processing. Part of the reason for this acceptance is a semantic metatheory that postulates the existence of a relatively small set of semantic elements (features, markers, etc.). Complex semantic concepts are then constructed through suitable combinations of these primitive elements. Such a view, either explicit or implicitly, is held by many. To give just two examples from linguistics, the well-known semantic markers of Katz and Fodor (1963) were conceived as semantic primitives, and the glossematics of Hjelmslev (1953), which are very influential in European circles, are thought of as an algebra of primitive semantic elements. In computer science, the goal of decomposing semantic expressions into a set of semantic primitives has been most clearly stated by Schank (1972). I have argued elsewhere (Kintsch 1972a) that too much emphasis on the search for semantic primitives may at present be a poor research strategy—they may not exist, after all. One should add that, in principle, an analysis into semantic primitives might co-exist with a processing theory involving decomposition as well as with a processing theory using meaning postulates. Thus, there is no need to let one's metatheoretical biases regarding semantic primitives enter into the question of whether or not decomposition is used in memory and comprehension.

2.3.

The results on lexical decomposition have provided a foundation for the further exploration of the processing of propositions. For instance, it has opened the way for studying reading rate as a function of the number of propositions in the base structure of texts. Once one has a psychological basis for deciding what to count as a proposition, material can be constructed in such a way that variations in the number of propositions are obtained while the length of the sentences measured in words is held constant. The free-reading data of Chapter 6 clearly indicate that reading time depended upon the number of propositions under these circumstances. It appeared that each additional proposition in a text required a certain amount of additional processing time. The amount of processing time required per proposition was found to correlate quite highly with the total length of the text, increasing from little more than a second for brief sentences to over 4 sec for the longest paragraphs used here (58 words). Thus, the reading data support the psychological reality of the theoretical entity "proposition." Number of propositions is, of course, a crude statistic, and it accounts for only about a fourth of the variance of the reading times. Much further research will be needed to explore which other attributes of propositions, in addition to their mere number, have significant influences on reading times. The number of arguments in a proposition can be expected to make a difference, and perhaps even more so the number of new arguments that each proposition introduces into a text. For instance, if the number of propositions is kept constant and the number of new arguments is varied, one would certainly expect effects upon both reading speed and recall. Clearly, a rich field of study is open for systematic research in this area.

2.4.

The recall data reviewed in Chapter 7 provide rather impressive support for the hierarchical relations that have been assumed to exist among propositions in a text. It will be remembered (Fig. 2, Chapter 7) that recall was best for the most superordinate propositions and declined rapidly the more deeply a proposition was embedded in a hierarchy. Again, this is no more than a beginning. There are many obvious questions that have not yet been asked, and even more importantly, the analyses performed were entirely *ad hoc,* in an experiment not really designed for that purpose. But at the very least, one can surely say that a deeper study of the role of hierarchical relations, as postulated by the present theory, in recall (and also in comprehension) seems promising.

2.5.

Somewhat more definitive are the data on part versus whole recall of sentences. Just as the results of Chapter 11 indicate that propositional representations are formed without decomposition of lexical units, the recall data of Chapter 7 provide some support for the notion that propositions form multi-argument units, in opposition to models that assume that propositions are binary units. Such models are derived from phrase-structure grammars and Chomsky's (1965) standard transformational theory, while the present theory is based upon generative semantic theories, in particular the case grammar of Fillmore (1968). The issue is an important one for the psychologist, because it is concerned with the question of what should be considered as a propositional unit, and hence the unit for the analysis of comprehension and memory. The problem can best be illustrated by comparing the proposed representations for simple subject-verb-object sentences. In the present theory such sentences are considered as propositional units (VERB,SUBJECT,OBJECT). The verb assumes a central role, and subject and object are both directly related to the verb. Their structural roles are comparable, although other factors may, and in general do, push one or the other, usually the subject, into the foreground. Phrase-structure grammars, on the other hand, first break down a sentence into noun phrase + verb phrase, and then further analyze the verb phrase into verb + object, arriving at the structure (SUBJECT,(VERB,OBJECT)). Thus, verb and object form a more closely related unit than either verb and subject, or subject and object. Again, this is not an issue that can be decided on the basis of purely linguistic arguments. For the psychologist, at least, the important question is whether there is any psychological evidence for the reality of verb-phrase units, or whether subject-verb-object sentences form units that are not to be further subdivided. The tendency within psychological research has been to follow phrase-structure grammars, and simply to assume the unitary nature of verb phrases. This is clearly evident in developmental research, where data have usually been analyzed in such a way that verb phrases were assigned a very important role in early language learning (e.g., McNeill, 1970). The relevance of these studies is, however, difficult to determine, because it is not clear to what extent the role that has been given to the verb phrase in early grammars represents a theoretical bias of the investigator, a kind of working assumption with which he approached his task. It is perhaps conceivable that semantically based grammars in which verb-phrase units do not appear may some day be just as successful in describing children's grammars as the present phrase-structure-derived grammars.

Within cognitive psychology proper, the most important attempt to restrict propositions to two terms, and hence to analyze sentences into noun-phrase–verb-phrase units, is the HAM model of Anderson and Bower (1973). Anderson and Bower attempt to show experimentally that verb-object units are more natural than verb-subject units (Chapter 10). They used a cued recall paradigm in which subjects were given sentences of the form subject-verb-object-location, and then one or more of these words as recall cues. The HAM model is a complete processing model and makes detailed predictions about recall under these conditions. In general, the data tend to confirm these predictions, but the effects observed are very small and hardly constitute definitive evidence as to the psychological reality of verb-phrase units. From the standpoint of the present theory, the data are impossible to interpret because much of their analysis depends upon combining subject and location into a "fact" node, which, of course, would be inadmissible in the present model because locatives are treated as separate propositions. Thus, we may conclude that at present there is no really convincing evidence for the psychological reality of verb phrases, while on the other hand, the data reported in Chapter 7 strongly argue in favor of treating multi-argument propositions as wholes. Certainly, the strong tendency to recall sentences with as many as three or four content words as wholes when they are derived from a single proposition, which is illustrated in Fig. 3 of Chapter 7, would be difficult to handle for HAM. Figure 3 is, of course, not just a demonstration that sentences tend to be recalled in all-or-nothing fashion, because control sentences derived from two or three propositions did not show this kind of wholistic recall pattern.

The use of multi-argument propositions with the verb as the central term suggests that in comprehending sentences the verb should play a special role. Whatever the details of a processing model might be, the identification of the verb frame must, if the present representation of propositions is correct, come early in the comprehension process and must be of central importance for the process as a whole. There is some evidence in the literature that agrees with this expectation. The view that the verb carries most of the information in a sentence, that it is processed with priority, and that its nature constrains the interpretation of the other sentence constituents is supported by several studies in which a variety of experimental approaches were used (e.g. Fodor, Garrett, & Bever, 1968; Garrod & Trabasso, 1973; Glucksberg, Trabasso & Wald, 1974; Wearing, 1970).[2]

3.

Some of the most interesting results in this work concern the role of inferences in the comprehension and memory of text. That memory for text is anything but verbatim, that it is reconstructive, making use of inferences in complex ways, has been known to experimental psychology at least since Bartlett analyzed his ghost story (Bartlett, 1932), but it has always been difficult to make much of this fact experimentally. The role of inferential processes in comprehension is equally obvious, but in either case we still have a long way to go before these matters become

---

[2]We know as yet very little about these questions. There is some neurological evidence (see p. 209) that has been interpreted as favoring noun priority. And what about the central role of the verb in sentence comprehension in a language such as German, where the verb tends to come at the end of long sentences?

clarified. Right now, not even the term ''comprehension'' itself is defined clearly, or used consistently. To quote from a recent paper by Bransford and McCarrell (in press), ''A person may have knowledge of a language and yet fail to comprehend an utterance because he is unable to make the necessary cognitive contributions.'' They demonstrate that people have difficulty understanding sentences, such as *If the balloon popped, the sound could not carry,* in isolation, but that the sentence is immediately understandable given a proper context (a loudspeaker suspended on a balloon, by means of which a guitarist plays for a woman looking out from a skyscraper window). But this is surely a curious use of the term ''comprehend.'' The uninitiated reader understands the critical sentence in some minimal way; he comprehends that if a certain (for him unspecified) balloon popped, ''the'' sound (again unspecified out of context) would not carry—the trouble is that in this instance he will probably be unable to construct a possible sentence context in which, according to his knowledge about balloons and sounds, this relationship would be likely to occur. This is only an extreme example of an entirely general phenomenon: that one cannot look at sentences in isolation. This is as true for *The child opened the door* as it is for the more extravagant example above, according to the arguments presented in Chapter 3. I am not sure that one should equate ''comprehension'' with ''full comprehension''; sentences out of context, or in a minimal context, are comprehended as well as possible, which in many cases may not be much, or may lead to ''wrong'' results, but it may be the best a listener can do with impoverished material. One is reminded of the discussion between Olson and Bever (see the footnote on page 15), about whether sentences can have meaning in isolation. Surely *The child opened the door* is meaningful, though not knowing what child or what door, it is an incomplete message and quite useless as a communication. Nevertheless, it specifics a perfectly meaningful relation between *child* and *door* (in the sense that *The coffee opened the door* does not).

3.1.

If we are going to work on processing models for sentence, or better yet, text comprehension, the term comprehension will need some conceptual clarification. But in any case, there can be no doubt about the involvement and importance of inferences in the process of comprehension. The contribution of the present data (Chapter 8) to the study of inferential processing during comprehension can be summarized quite briefly. We have observed that when subjects read a text in which some propositions are omitted, and these are crucial for the understanding of the text as a whole but are of such a nature that they can be inferred by the reader on the basis of his general knowledge and the remainder of the text, these propositions are in fact inferred during reading and stored in memory in the same form as propositions explicitly present in the text. There is an additional, highly interesting qualification that needs to be made concerning nonpropositional attributes of memory for text, but that does not concern the main point raised here and will be taken up below. The most important aspect of our results is that, as far as long-term memory for meaning is concerned, there appears to be no difference in the accessibility of information in memory when it was derived from explicit surface constructions in the text, as opposed to when it had to be inferred in the absence of explicit text cues. Throughout this book the view has been expounded that comprehension of a text consists of constructing an abstract representation of the meaning of a text from the cues provided by the actual physical stimuli (the spoken or written sentences). This view is entirely consistent with the results of Chapter 8. Whether a certain element of meaning is explicitly expressed or not should make no difference to the comprehender, as long as he is readily able to infer this element on the basis of the remaining text. In either case, what is stored in memory are the products of the subject's constructions, which he made on the basis of whatever cues were available to him: the actual speech pattern (or visual stimulus), the context of the message in the broadest sense of that term, and his own accumulated knowledge about language and about the world in which he lives. Thus, in a sense the meaning that a subject extracts from a message is always "inferred," and our terminology may be a bit misleading. Nevertheless, it seems quite reasonable to use the term inference as we did, and to make a distinction between meaning inferred from explicit verbal cues in the text and inferences made in the absence of such cues.

That inferences must be a part of comprehension is doubted by no one; the more interesting questions are how such inferences occur and how they are represented in memory. We have argued here that inferences are operations on propositions. By means of the rules available in semantic memory (say, about quantifiers, presuppositions, physical causality, psychological motivation, etc.) the comprehender supplements propositions directly inferred from the verbal text in such a way as to construct a coherent and consistent text base. Coherency and consistency are matters of degree. Usually the comprehender will have only minimal requirements, but if given the time and the motivation, very elaborate structures may be built upon very meager texts. As far as storage in memory is concerned, all this information is stored in propositional form, irrespective of the origin of particular propositions (but note the comments below on nonpropositional information in memory).

While there is good evidence to believe that something like that actually occurred in the experiments reported in Chapter 8, no claim is made that inferences must always be propositional, or, indeed, that meaning is always stored in propositional form. There is evidence in the literature that under some experimental conditions subjects employ abstract nonpropositional, probably analog, representations in memory (Barclay, 1973; Potts, 1972). In these experiments subjects were given several sentences of the form *A is greater than B, B is greater than C, C is smaller than D, . . . ,* where the relationship was always a transitive one. The sentences presented were sufficient to specify completely a linear ordering of the objects but were only a subset of all possible sentences describing this ordering. The results showed that the subjects successfully inferred the true ordering of the objects in question and stored it in memory. On later recognition tests they could discriminate very well between true and false test sentences, but not between the sentences they had actually seen during learning and new sentences that were also in agreement with the inferred ordering. In addition, Potts obtained latency data that tended to contradict propositional processing models of the kind we are assuming for the data in Chapter 8.

In comparing these experiments with our own, two things should be kept in mind. First, the inability of the subjects of Potts and Barclay to discriminate between true sentences actually presented and true sentences not presented contradicts our results. Our subjects indicated that they could discriminate quite well between sentences actually presented and inferential statements, by their faster responses to the former on immediate tests. Only when the tests were substantially delayed did this difference disappear. According to our interpretation, this indicates that right after reading a paragraph subjects had additional nonpropositional information available for the sentences actually presented, but not for the inferred ones. Why was this not the case in the experiments of Potts and Barclay? A look at the stimulus materials used explains the discrepancy: Potts and Barclay used high interference designs, presenting sentences all of the same format. Thus, any memory for the surface form of a study sentence was obliterated by interference from many other similar sentences presented, while in our case this interference was greatly reduced because a natural string of text was used. Secondly, Potts' arguments from his latency data, that his subjects employed an abstract but nonpropositional memory representation, can very well co-exist with the model proposed here. We have chosen to work here with propositional representations, but it has been stressed repeatedly that it would be pure folly to deny the existence of nonpropositional representations of meaning in memory. The linear arrays used in the studies discussed above probably invited the use of some kind of analog memory, just as the natural language texts employed in Chapter 8 invited a propositional representation.

Similar comments can be made about the well-known study of Bransford and Franks (1971). The learning material used there was somewhat more natural than sets of comparative statements, but again the experimental design assured that subjects were exposed to massive amounts of interference during the study period. The results showed that subjects stored in memory some abstract representation of the meaning of the input sentences, which enabled them to determine whether a test sentence was true or false with respect to the information received, but not to distinguish the particular true statements that they had experienced during learning from other true statements that they had not seen before. The first result is what would be expected; one may note that the abstractions that the subjects of Bransford and Franks formed were probably propositional in nature (rather than analog representations, or "images"). The second result, that subjects did not retain anything but meaning, and that there was no memory for particular instances, must be dismissed as procedural artifact, just as in the Barclay and Potts studies. Reitman and Bower (1973) have replicated Bransford and Franks and have shown that if memory is not overloaded, subjects were able to distinguish those items originally experienced from those items that were not. Further evidence that the abstraction of meaning does not necessarily imply that all memory for particular instances is lost comes from studies of memory for dot patterns (e.g., Posner & Keele, 1968; Posner & Warren, 1972). When subjects categorize dot patterns that were generated by distorting a few prototypes, they learn to abstract the prototype from the sample instances given (as evidenced by their ability to classify correctly new instances), but at the same time they retain information about the particular learning instances.

3.2.

Though one may conclude with considerable certainty that both abstract semantic information about the meaning of a text, as well as information about the physical attributes of it are usually stored in memory as a consequence of the act of comprehension, we have not yet answered the question about the nature of these memory traces. Following Bartlett (1932) and Oldfield (1954), it has become customary to refer to abstract representations of meaning as schemata. This is, of course, nothing more than a word, and we have every reason to suppose that the nature of a schema may vary widely, depending upon circumstances. Several examples have already been mentioned. The schema that subjects induce in classification experiments with dot patterns may be some kind of statistical average, while in the experiments in which subjects have to learn to order a series of objects according to some transitive relationship the schema may be an analog representation of the array. In the inference studies of Chapter 8, and also in those of Bransford and Franks (1971), the schema was probably propositional. As evidence for this claim, one may take the experiments reported in Chapters 6 and 7, which make a case for the argument that the meaning of a text is normally represented in memory as a list of propositions. The nonpropositional information that is also stored in memory along with the propositional information may be thought of as stimulus samples, as hypothesized in Chapter 4. It would seem that multiple traces are formed in memory during the comprehension of a text. On the one hand, there are memory traces that are the products of a relatively superficial analysis consisting of samples from the phonetic, graphemic, semantic, and contextual elements present in short-term memory as each sentence is being processed. On the other hand, as more information about the text accumulates, subjects perform a deeper semantic analysis of this material, relating propositions from various parts of the text, reorganizing the propositions into a reasonably coherent and consistent list, making whatever inferences are necessary in this process, and bringing to bear whatever knowledge and contextual information is available. Only this second, deeper analysis reveals the full meaning of a text. Unlike the first more superficial analysis, it relies primarily upon propositional information. The phonetic and graphemic attributes of the test, and indeed the actual words used, are not very important any more. Thus, memory for text becomes a two-level affair: a surface level, which might be viewed as the left-over from the initial processing of the text, which involves semantic, that is propositional, information as well as linguistic information and various stimulus attributes of the original message, and a second, deeper level, which is mainly propositional and can be considered as the meaning of the text as reconstructed during the comprehension process. There is one more observation to add: Our data imply that the rate at which forgetting occurs differs drastically for the two levels of memory. Surface memory is effectively blocked by 20 minutes of reading unrelated material, while propositional memory under the conditions of our experiments was unimpaired for up to two days.

The view that memory traces are multi-level (only two of which concern us here, though), with different forgetting rates associated with these levels is, of course, widely held today. Craik and Lockhart (1972) have explored the consequences of this assumption in the area of short-term memory, and Posner and Warren (1972) have advocated a multilevel, parallel processing theory of perception and memory. The theory of episodic memory, which was described at length in Chapter 4, incorporates multilevel views. There a basic distinction was made between a relatively raw record of experiences (sufficient for recognition in list-learning studies) and more elaborated retrieval schemes (which support free recall). It is clear that if the theory is extended to include an account of memory for text this distinction will again play a crucial role. We have, on the one hand, the superficial analysis of sentences, which includes a great many clues about the surface features of the text, but only an incomplete semantic analysis. It is not as well-interconnected with other memory episodes, and hence it is quickly forgotten. On the other hand, there is the deeper propositional analysis of the text, which is strongly interconnected and therefore remains retrievable. There is no point in elaborating this sketch, because important aspects of the sentence comprehension process are not sufficiently understood (we have not explored the crucial question of how a person extracts propositions from a verbal text). But there may be a basis here for further work.

In addition to the list-learning and perceptual studies mentioned above, which can be used to support the view that sentence memory involves two distinct memory levels, there are several other directly relevant reports in the literature. An early study by English, Welborn, and Killian (1934) provided rather striking evidence that memory for meaning resists forgetting much better than memory for verbatim phrases. The authors did a whole series of experiments on this problem. In their basic procedure subjects were given a fairly long paragraph of text to read (popularizations of psychological material), and were then given recognition tests with various types of items, among them verbatim statements from the paragraph and summaries of portions of the text. Subjects were asked to respond to each test statement in one of four ways: They could agree or disagree that the statement was true with respect to the paragraph, or they could respond that the test was irrelevent, i.e., not derived from the paragraph, or they could say that they did not remember. In a typical experiment, subjects were given tests prior to reading the paragraph to establish a baseline for the recognition scores. They were tested again right after reading, and then again after 47 days. The results were dramatic: Right after reading, performance was excellent for the verbatim items but little memory for verbatim items was detected after 47 days. For the summary items, in contrast, there was absolutely no decline in performance during this time. Indeed, in other studies that employed repeated tests, performance in fact increased for summary statements, while the typical Ebbinghaus forgetting curve was observed for verbatim items. In addition, the correlations between performance on the summary and verbatim items were very low, suggesting that there was little measurable commonality between the two memory systems.

Similar conclusions were reached in a study by Anderson and Hubert (1963), who quoted the English et al. work. Again, the conclusion was based mainly upon a lack of correlation between verbatim memory and memory for meaning, although the experimental situation was quite different. Their subjects read sets of six to eight personality adjectives and then rated their liking of the person so described. Later the subjects were asked to recall the adjectives. A comparison of the likelihood that a particular adjective was recalled with the importance of this adjective in determining the overall personality impression led Anderson and Hubert to claim that "the formation of the impression involves a memory process which is distinct from, and not dependent on, the immediate verbal memory for the adjectives."

Other studies, employing more conventional research designs, likewise support a multilevel view of memory for text. Sachs' much quoted experiment brought the difference between memory for meaning and verbatim memory to everyone's attention (Sachs, 1967). She showed that subjects could detect changes in the meaning of sentences on a recognition test, but not changes in the wording of sentences that did not affect meaning. The latter changes could be detected only if the test immediately followed the reading of the sentence. Thus, it appeared that one could equate verbatim memory with short-term memory as it is known from numerous list-learning studies, and memory for meaning with long-term memory. More recently, Garrod and Trabasso (1973) proposed a dual-memory model for sentence comprehension in which the classical short-term–long-term memory distinction plays a similar role. Their subjects read four-sentence paragraphs and then answered Yes or No to test questions concerning one of the study sentences. The voices (active-passive) of the sentences and questions were varied orthogonally, and the main response measures were response latencies. They concluded that surface information was available in short-term memory, while long-term memory contained a propositional representation of the meaning of the sentences plus some residual surface information. Note that the retention intervals used in this study were only of the order of a few seconds; thus, we are dealing here with classical short-term memory research, but not with a very long long-term memory. Anderson (1974), in a study that is similar in other respects, used longer paragraphs and asked more than one test question, so that the interval between reading a sentence and being asked a question could be as long as two minutes. His results resembled those of Garrod and Trabasso, but rather than interpreting them in terms of differences between short- and long-term memory stores, Anderson preferred to talk about two different memory levels. Immediately after reading, the sentence is represented as a "verbatim image" which includes visual and acoustic perceptual information as well as syntactic structure; after delays, the representation is both propositional and verbatim. This view is obviously closely related to the one advocated here, except that our experiments in Chapter 8 allow us to extend this picture considerably. Our immediate tests were comparable to Anderson's delayed tests (in both cases subjects were given a fairly long paragraph followed by a test question; Anderson's immediate tests involved interrupting the paragraph presentation with a question right after the critical sentence had been presented). At this point in time, according to both experiments, the text is represented in a manner that includes perceptual, linguistic, and semantic information. Our results show what happens with greater delays (20 minutes to 48 hours): The memory for surface features of the text, that is, the perceptual-linguistic information, is no longer available, but propositional information is unimpaired. We must, however, disagree with Anderson's use of the term "verbatim image," both on account of the image and the verbatim. It is not obvious what role images could play in our paragraphs (e.g., the rather abstract argumentative texts of Exp. II, Chapter 8); nor could the memory representation which facilitated responding on immediate tests in Exp. I have been verbatim. The test questions were not verbatim copies of sentences from the paragraphs, but involved minor paraphrases. Thus, it appears that we are not dealing with unanalyzed phonetic-orthographic copies of sentences (perhaps at a much earlier time we are), but already with the output of a superficial linguistic analysis. Our term "memory for the surface features of a sentence," however clumsy, is a more accurate approximation to this state of affairs than the term "verbatim image." One may expect to hear more about these questions from other researchers in the future.

4.

The last topic to be discussed here concerns the problem of how textual information is retrieved from memory, that is, the work reported in Chapters 9 and 10. The second of these chapters is concerned with retrieval from semantic memory, that is, with the retrieval of knowledge; the first deals with retrieval of textual information from episodic memory. A comparison of these two processes reveals some interesting similarities. There exists, of course, a rich literature on retrieval from episodic memory which is based upon list-learning experiments. These problems were explored in some detail in Chapter 4, but it is worthwhile to review some of the main features of retrieval processes as they appear in the free recall of word lists. With only the general experimental environment as a retrieval cue, the subject must recall a set of more or less unrelated words. This retrieval cue is too unspecific to yield much recall on the basis of pattern matches, and performance depends mostly upon the subject's ability to construct a retrieval scheme during learning, that is, some sort of interconnection between the to-be-learned words. The properties of such retrieval schemes were the main concern of Chapter 4. When we come to the retrieval of textual information from memory, the problem appears to be quite different. There is no need to construct a separate retrieval scheme because if comprehending a text means constructing a propositional text base from the given verbal text, the to-be-remembered items (propositions, in this case) are already sufficiently interconnected. Text bases are structured lists of propositions, with rich interconnections (e.g., Fig. 1 of Chapter 2). Access to a unit of text may be obtained on the basis of a pattern match: The retrieval cue, usually the title of a story or the like, shares a sufficient number of elements with the episodic memory representation of the text, and hence the match will be successful, as claimed in Chapter 4. In this way, access is obtained to the memory representation of the story as a whole, but how are the single propositions, the elements of this memory representation, retrieved? Since the propositions form an interconnected network, retrieval must be possible in principle, but many questions remain as to the details of the process. Is the proposition list processed serially or in parallel? Is the process self-terminating or exhaustive? The experiments on the effects of paragraph length upon retrieval speed were concerned with these questions (Chapter 9).

The paragraph-length effects obtained in these experiments very closely mirror the list-length effects reported by others. The longer the paragraph (or the list), the longer it takes to respond that a given item (a sentence or a list item, respectively) was or was not a member of the paragraph (or list). I don't believe that this is an accident, but that it results from a commonality of the processes involved. Assume that the model of Atkinson and Juola (1973) for list-length effects is essentially correct. It is a two-stage model where the first stage involves checking the familiarity value of an item (the overlap of elements as determined by a pattern match, in the terminology of Chapter 4). If the familiarity value is either high enough or low enough, a response occurs; if it is intermediate, a more detailed memory search is made, which introduces the list-length effects. The model that was suggested as an explanation of the paragraph-length effects is quite similar. Again, a pattern match is first made; however, in our experimental situation this does not provide the basis for a response, because it will always be successful. By means of this match the right paragraph unit is located in episodic memory. Next, a memory search is made: All propositions that are part of this memory unit are matched in parallel with the input sentence (or, more exactly, with a propositional representation of the input sentence), and a response is made on the basis of the outcome of this match. Again, paragraph-length effects occur because of the second-stage processing. The above interpretation was for true-false judgments; when yes-no recognition judgments are required, a different memory level is involved, but the process precisely parallels the one outlined above.

However speculative, these links between textual memory and list-learning results are interesting and potentially important. The tenuousness of the model proposed here has already been adequately emphasized in the discussion of Chapter 9: The two experiments merely open up a problem, but by no means adequately explore it. Alternative explanations must be followed up, as well as modifications of the present one. But, nevertheless, one should not lose sight of the intriguing possibility that the same theories may someday be able to explain both memory for texts and memory for lists.

Speculations need not stop here. Our results suggest that one may be able to integrate models of both episodic and semantic memory retrieval. The model for fact retrieval from semantic memory, which we arrived at in Chapter 10 as the best available description both for our data and the data of others, is strikingly similar to the processes assumed to be operating in episodic memory. It too is a two-stage model whose first stage is characterized by superficial processing and a quick response, and only if no decision occurs on the basis of this initial check is a detailed analysis of the sentence made. The initial check in this case is twofold: First, it determines whether the test proposition is already represented as a fact in semantic memory; if so, a yes response occurs. If not, the similarity (i.e., semantic distance) between the word concepts represented in the sentence is calculated. This can be done by means of a pattern match that determines the amount of element overlap between the concepts. If the semantic distance is too great, the sentence is rejected as anomalous without further processing. If, on the other hand, the concepts are semantically related an exact analysis of the sentence is performed. The outcome of this analysis may be either positive or negative, but in any case it requires additional time. It was even suggested in Chapter 10 that the two-stage process described here may be characteristic of sentence comprehension in general. That is, when given any kind of sentence to comprehend, the subject may perform semantic distance calculations between the major concepts involved and use the outcome of these calculations to guide the further analysis. If this is so, the possibility arises that the same basic cognitive operations can be identified in a wide range of performances, from the most mundane list-learning experiments to the esoteric topics of modern cognitive psychology.

*   *   *   *   *   *

This chapter has been called, not without reason, "Interim Conclusions"; it is all too obvious that we have nothing but interim conclusions. The study of memory for text, comprehension, knowledge retrieval, and the other topics in this book has only begun within experimental psychology. I have tried to show that the formal representation of meaning, which was offered in Part I, can serve as a useful basis for experimental investigations. The representation has many advantages: It is simple and easy to use, it can be extended from sentences to texts (unlike, say, a graph), and it is flexible. In spite of this flexibility, it is powerful enough to handle many of the intricate problems that are posed by the logical representation of sentences. Thus, it appears capable of providing the broad conceptual framework for the psychological study of memory and knowledge which the problem demands. The experiments reported here demonstrate that a broadly based approach is possible today, and even fruitful. It is true that some of the elegance and neatness of miniature models and miniature experiments are lost in such an approach, but I hope that the possibility of integrating formerly diffuse and separate subproblems is worth this loss. It is also true that what has been presented here is only a beginning. Obviously, these experiments raise many more questions than they answer, and even more obviously, the list of significant experimental problems that have been neglected is considerably longer than that of the topics considered. It is not unreasonable to expect a great deal of progress in cognitive psychology during the next decade, and it is hoped that this volume will contribute a small piece to its foundation.

REFERENCES

Abraham, W. Zur Linguistik der Metapher. *Linguistics Across* (Festschrift for P. A. Verburg). The Hague: Mouton, in press.

Anderson, J. R. A simulation model of free recall. In G. H. Bower (Ed.), *The psychology of learning and motivation*. Vol. 5. New York: Academic Press, 1972.

Anderson, J. R. Verbatim and propositional representation of sentences in immediate and long-term memory. *Journal of Verbal Learning and Verbal Behavior*, 1974, **13**, 149–162.

Anderson, J. R., & Bower, G. H. Recognition and retrieval processes in free recall. *Psychological Review*, 1972, **79**, 97–123.

Anderson, J. R., & Bower, G. H. *Human associative memory*. Washington, D.C.: Winston, 1973.

Anderson, N. H., & Hubert, S. Effects of concomitant verbal recall on order effects in personality impression formation. *Journal of Verbal Learning and Verbal Behavior*, 1963, **2**, 379–391.

Anderson, N. H., Sawyers, B. K., & Farkas, A. J. President paragraphs. *Behavior Research Methodology and Instrumentation*, 1972, **4**, 177–192.

Anisfeld, M. False recognition of adjective-noun phrases. *Journal of Experimental Psychology*, 1970, **86**, 120–122.

Atkinson, R. C., Herrmann, D. J., & Wescourt, K. T. Search processes in recognition memory. In R. L. Solso (Ed.), *Theories in Cognitive Psychology:* The Loyola Symposium. Potomac, Md.: Lawrence Erlbaum Associates, 1974.

Atkinson, R. C., & Juola, J. F. Search and decision processes in recognition memory. In R. C. Atkinson, D. Krantz, R. D. Luce, & P. Suppes (Eds.), *Contemporary developments in mathematical psychology*. San Francisco: Freeman, 1974.

Atkinson, R. C., & Shiffrin, R. M. Human memory: A proposed system and its control processes. In K. W. Spence & J. T. Spence (Eds.), *The psychology of learning and motivation*. Vol. 2. New York: Academic Press, 1969.

Bahrick, H. P. Measurement of memory by prompted recall. *Journal of Experimental Psychology*, 1969, **97**, 213–219.

Bahrick, H. P. Two-phase model for prompted recall. *Psychological Review*, 1970, **77**, 215–222.

Barclay, J. R. The role of comprehension in remembering sentences. *Cognitive Psychology*, 1973, **4**, 229–254.

Bartlett, F. C. *Remembering*. Cambridge, England: Cambridge University Press, 1932.

Battig, W. F., & Montague, W. E. Category norms for verbal items in 56 categories: A replication and extension of the Connecticut Norms. *Journal of Experimental Psychology*, 1969, **80**, (3, Pt. 2).

Becker, J. D. A model for the encoding of experiential information. In R. C. Schank & K. M. Colby (Eds.), *Computer models of thought and language*. San Francisco: Freeman, 1973.

Bickerton, D. Prolegomena to a linguistic theory of metaphor. *Foundations of Language*, 1969, **4**, 34–52.

Bierwisch, M. On certain problems of semantic representation. *Foundations of Language*, 1969, **5**, 153–184.

Bjork, R. A. Theoretical implications of directed forgetting. In. A. W. Melton & E. Martin (Eds.), *Coding processes in human memory*, Washington, D.C.: Winston, 1972.

Black, M. *Models and metaphors*. Ithaca, N.Y.: Cornell University Press, 1962.

Blumenthal, A. L. *Language and psychology*. New York: Wiley, 1970.

Bolinger, D. Semantic overloading: A restudy of the verb remind. *Language*, 1971, **47**, 522 – 547.

Borges M. A., & Sawyers, B. K. Common verbal quantifiers: Usage and interpretation. *Journal of Experimental Psychology*, 1974, **102**, 335 – 338.

Bower, G. H. A multicomponent theory of the memory trace. In K. W. Spence & J. T. Spence (Eds.), *The psychology of learning and motivation*. Vol. I. New York: Academic Press, 1967.

Bower, G. H. Stimulus sampling theory of encoding variability. In A. W. Melton & E. Martin (Eds.), *Coding processes in human memory*. Washington, D.C.: Winston, 1972.

Bowers, F. The deep structure of abstract nouns. *Foundations of Language*, 1969, **5**, 520 – 533.

Bransford, J. D., Barclay, J. R., & Franks, J. J. Sentence memory: A constructive versus interpretive approach. *Cognitive Psychology*, 1972, **3**, 193 – 209.

Bransford, J. D., & Franks, J. J. The abstraction of linguistic ideas. *Cognitive Psychology*, 1971, **2**, 331–350.

Bransford, J. D., & Johnson, M. K. Contextual prerequisites for understanding: Some investigations of comprehension and recall. *Journal of Verbal Learning and Verbal Behavior*, 1972, **11**, 717–726.

Bransford, J. D., & McCarrell, N. S. A sketch of a cognitive approach to comprehension: Some thoughts about understanding what it means to comprehend. In D. Palermo & W. Weimer (Eds.), *Cognition and the symbolic processes*. Potomac, Md.: Lawrence Erlbaum Associates, in press.

Carroll, J. B., & Freedle, R. O. *Language comprehension and the acquisition of knowledge*. Washington, D.C.: Winston, 1972.

Chafe, W. L. *Meaning and the structure of language*. Chicago: University of Chicago Press, 1970.

Chafe, W. L. Language and memory. *Language*, 1973, **49**, 261–281.

Chafe, W. L. Language and consciousness. *Language*, 1974, **50**, 111–133.

Chall, J. S. *Readability: an appraisal of research and application*. Columbus, Ohio: Ohio State University Press, 1958.

Chapin, P. G. On affixation in English. In M. Bierwisch & K. E. Heidolph (Eds.), *Progress in linguistics*. The Hague: Mouton, 1970.

Chomsky, N. *Syntactic structures*. The Hague: Mouton, 1957.

Chomsky, N. *Aspects of the theory of syntax*. Cambridge, Mass.: MIT Press, 1965.

Chomsky, N. Remarks on nominalization. In R. A. Jacobs & P. S. Rosenbaum (Eds.), *Readings in English transformational grammar*. Waltham, Mass.: Ginn & Co., 1970.

Clark, H. H. The prediction of recall patterns in simple active sentences. *Journal of Verbal Learning and Verbal Behavior*, 1966, **5**, 99 – 106.

Clark, H. H. Linguistic processes in deductive reasoning. *Psychological Review*, 1969, **76**, 387 – 404.

Clark, H. H. Word associations and linguistic theory. In J. Lyons (Ed.), *New horizons in linguistics*, Hammondsworth, Middlesex: Penguin Books, 1970.

Clark, H. H. The language-as-fixed-effect-fallacy: A critique of language statistics in psychological research. *Journal of Verbal Learning and Verbal Behavior*, 1973, **12**, 335 – 359.

Clark, H. H., & Card, S. K. The role of semantics in remembering comparative sentences. *Journal of Experimental Psychology*, 1969, **83**, 545 – 553.

Clark, H. H., & Chase, W. G. On the process of comparing sentences against pictures. *Cognitive Psychology,* 1972, **3**, 472–517.

Cofer, C. N., Bruce, D. R., & Reicher, G. M. Clustering in free recall as a function of certain methodological variations. *Journal of Experimental Psychology,* 1966, **71**, 858–866.

Cohen, B. H., Bousfield, W. A., & Whitmarsh, G. A. Cultural norms for verbal items in 43 categories. (Technical Report No. 22) Storrs, Conn.: University of Connecticut, 1957.

Collins, A. M., & Quillian, M. R. Retrieval times from semantic memory. *Journal of Verbal Learning and Verbal Behavior,* 1969, **8**, 240–247.

Collins, A. M., & Quillian, M. R. Experiments on semantic memory and language comprehension. In L. W. Gregg (Ed.), *Cognition in learning and memory.* New York: Wiley, 1972. (a)

Collins, A. M., & Quillian, M. R. How to make a language user. In E. Tulving & W. Donaldson (Eds.), *Organization of memory.* New York: Academic Press, 1972. (b)

Conrad, C. Cognitive economy in semantic memory. *Journal of Experimental Psychology,* 1972, **92**, 149–154.

Conrad, R. Acoustic confusion in short-term memory. *British Journal of Psychology,* 1964, **55**, 75–84.

Craik, F. I. M. A "levels of analysis" view of memory. In P. Pliner, L. Kramers, & T. M. Alloway (Eds.), *Communication and affect: Language and thought.* New York: Academic Press, 1973.

Craik, F. I. M., & Lockhart, R. S. Levels of processing: A framework for memory research. *Journal of Verbal Learning and Verbal Behavior,* 1972, **11**, 671–684.

Cramer, P. Magnitude and selectivity as independent factors in semantic generalization. *Journal of Verbal Learning and Verbal Behavior,* 1970, **9**, 509–524.

Crothers, E. J. Memory structure and the recall of discourse. In J. B. Carroll & R. O. Freedle (Eds.), *Language comprehension and the acquisition of knowledge.* Washington, D.C.: Winston, 1972.

van Dijk, T. A. *Some aspects of text grammars.* The Hague: Mouton, 1972.

van Dijk, T. A. Text grammar and text logic. In J. S. Petöfi & H. Rieser (Eds.), *Studies in text grammar.* Dodrecht: Reidel, 1973.

English, H. B., Welborn, E. L., & Killian, C. D. Studies in substance memorization. *Journal of General Psychology,* 1934, **11**, 233–260.

Estes, W. K. An associative basis for coding and organization in memory. In A. W. Melton & E. Martin (Eds.), *Coding processes in human memory.* Washington, D.C.: Winston, 1972.

Fillenbaum, S. Words as feature complexes: False recognition of antonyms and synonyms. *Journal of Experimental Psychology,* 1969, **82**, 400–402.

Fillenbaum, S. Psycholinguistics. *Annual Review of Psychology,* 1971, **22**, 251–308.

Fillenbaum, S. *Syntactic factors in memory?* The Hague: Mouton, 1973.

Fillmore, C. J. The case for case. In E. Bach & R. T. Harms (Eds.), *Universals in linguistic theory.* New York: Holt, Rinehart & Winston, 1968.

Fillmore, C. J. Types of lexical information. In D. D. Steinberg & L. A. Jakobovits (Eds.), *Semantics.* Cambridge: University Press, 1969.

Fillmore, C. J. Some problems for case grammar. In C. J Fillmore (Ed.), Working papers in Linguistics, No. 10, Department of Linguistics, The Ohio State University, 1971.

Fodor, J. A., Garrett, M., & Bever, T. G. Some syntactic determinants of complexity. II: Verb structure. *Perception & Psychophysics,* 1968, **3**, 453–461.

Foss, D. J. Decision processes during sentence comprehension: Effects of lexical item difficulty and position upon decision times. *Journal of Verbal Learning and Verbal Behavior,* 1969, **8**, 457–462.

Fredericksen, C. H. Effects of task-induced cognitive operations on comprehension and memory processes. In J. B. Carroll & R. O. Freedle (Eds.), *Language comprehension and the acquisition of knowledge.* Washington, D.C.: Winston, 1972.

Frege, G. Ueber Sinn und Bedeutung. *Zeitschrift für Philosophie und philosophische Kritik,* 1892, **100**, 25–50.

Frijda, N. H. Simulation of human long-term memory. *Psychological Bulletin,* 1972, **77**, 1–31.

Gabor, D. Associative holographic memories. *IBM Journal of Research and Development,* 1969, **13**, 156–159.

Garrod, S., & Trabasso, T. A dual-memory information-processing interpretation of sentence comprehension. *Journal of Verbal Learning and Verbal Behavior*, 1973, **12**, 155–167.

Gartman, L. M., & Johnson, N. F. Massed versus distributed repetition of homographs: A test of the differential-encoding hypothesis. *Journal of Verbal Learning and Verbal Behavior*, 1972, **11**, 800–808.

Gazzaniga, M. S. *The bisected brain*. New York: Appleton, 1970.

Glanzer, M. Distance between related words in free recall: Trace of the STS. *Journal of Verbal Learning and Verbal Behavior*, 1969, **8**, 105–111.

Glucksberg, S., Trabasso, T., & Wald, J. Linguistic structures and mental operations: An information-processing analysis of sentence comprehension. *Cognitive Psychology*, 1974, **5**, 338–370.

Goldman-Eisler, F. *Psycholinguistics: Experiments in spontaneous speech*. London: Academic Press, 1968.

Green, C. C., & Raphael, B. The use of theorem-proving techniques in question answering systems. *Proceedings of the 23rd National Conference, Association for Computing Machinery*. Princeton, N.J.: Brandon Systems Press, 1968.

Greeno, J. G. How associations are memorized. In D. A. Norman (Ed.), *Models of human memory*. New York: Academic Press, 1970.

Grossman, L., & Eagle, M. Synonymity, antonymity, and association in false recognition responses. *Journal of Experimental Psychology*, 1970, **32**, 244–248.

Halliday, M. A. K. Notes on transitivity and theme in English. *Journal of Linguistics*, 1967, **3**, 199–244.

Halliday, M. A. K. Language structure and language function. In J. Lyons (Ed.), *New horizons in linguistics*. Hamondsworth, Middlesex: Penguin Books, 1970.

Hamilton, W. *Lectures on metaphysics and logic*. Vol. 1. Boston: Gould & Lincoln, 1859.

Heider, E. R. Universals in color naming and memory. *Journal of Experimental Psychology*, 1972, **93**, 10–20.

Heider, E. R. On the internal structure of perceptual and semantic categories. In T. M. Moore (Ed.), *Cognitive development and acquisition of language*. New York: Academic Press, 1973.

Heider, E. R., & Olivier, D. C. The structure of the color space in naming and memory for two languages. *Cognitive Psychology*, 1972, **3**, 337–345.

Herbart, J. F. *Lehrbuch zur Psychologie*. Königsberg: Unzer, 1816.

Hilbert, D., & Ackermann, W. *Principles of mathematical logic*. New York: Chelsea, 1950.

Hjelmslev, L. *Prologomena to a theory of language*. Bloomington, Ind.: Indiana University Press, 1953.

Höffding, H. *Outlines of psychology*. London: Macmillan, 1891.

Hogan, R. M. Search patterns in memory. Unpublished doctoral dissertation, University of Colorado, 1972.

Hogan, R. M., & Kintsch, W. Differential effects of study and test trials on long-term recognition and recall. *Journal of Verbal Learning and Verbal Behavior*, 1971, **10**, 562–567.

Holyoak, K. The role of imagery in the evaluation of sentences: Imagery or semantic relatedness? *Journal of Verbal Learning and Verbal Behavior*, 1974, **13**, 163–166.

Honeck, R. P. Interpretive versus structural effects on semantic memory. *Journal of Verbal Learning and Verbal Behavior*, 1973, **12**, 448–455.

Horovitz, L. M., & Prytulak, L. S. Redintegrative memory. *Psychological Review*, 1969, **76**, 519–531.

Humphrey, G. *Thinking*. New York: Wiley, 1963.

Hunt, E. B., Marin, J., & Stone, P. J. *Experiments in induction*. New York: Academic Press, 1966.

Inhelder, B., & Piaget, J. *The early growth of logic in the child*. New York: Norton, 1964.

James, C. T. Theme and imagery in the recall of active and passive sentences. *Journal of Verbal Learning and Verbal Behavior*, 1972, **11**, 205–211.

James, C. T., Thompson J. G., & Baldwin, J. M. The reconstructive process in sentence memory. *Journal of Verbal Learning and Verbal Behavior*, 1973, **12**, 51–63.

James, W. *The principles of psychology*. New York: Holt, 1890.

Jarvella, R. J. Syntactic processing of connected speech. *Journal of Verbal Learning and Verbal Behavior*, 1970, **10**, 409–416.

Johnson, R. E. Recall of prose as a function of the structural importance of linguistic units. *Journal of Verbal Learning and Verbal Behavior,* 1970, **9**, 12 – 20.

Jorgensen, C. C., & Kintsch, W. The role of imagery in the evaluation of sentences. *Cognitive Psychology,* 1973, **4**, 110 – 116.

Just, M. A., & Clark, H. H. Drawing inferences from the presuppositions and implications of affirmative and negative sentences. *Journal of Verbal Learning and Verbal Behavior,* 1973, **11**, 21 – 31.

Kantor, J. R. *An objective psychology of grammar.* Bloomington: Indiana University Press, 1936.

Karttunen, L. Implication verbs. *Language,* 1971, **47**, 340 – 358.

Katz, J. J., & Fodor, J. A. The structure of semantic theory. *Language,* 1963, **39**, 170 – 210.

Keenan, E. L. A logical base for a transformational grammar of English. Unpublished doctoral dissertation, University of Pennsylvania, 1970.

Keenan, E. L. Quantifier structure in English. *Foundations of Language,* 1971, **7**, 255 – 284.

Kintsch, W. Recognition learning as a function of the length of the retention interval and changes in the retention interval. *Journal of Mathematical Psychology,* 1966, **3**, 412 – 433.

Kintsch, W. Models for free recall and recognition. In D. A. Norman (Ed.), *Models of human memory.* New York: Academic Press, 1970. (a)

Kintsch, W. *Learning, memory, and conceptual processes.* New York: Wiley, 1970. (b)

Kintsch, W. Notes on the structure of semantic memory. In E. Tulving & W. Donaldson (Eds.), *Organization of memory.* New York: Academic Press, 1972. (a)

Kintsch, W. Abstract nouns: Imagery versus lexical complexity. *Journal of Verbal Learning and Verbal Behavior,* 1972, **11**, 55 – 61. (b)

Kintsch, W., & Buschke, H. Homophones and synonyms in short-term memory. *Journal of Experimental Psychology,* 1969, **80**, 403 – 407.

Kintsch, W., Miller, R. F., & Hogan, R. M. Semantic structure and clustering in free recall. Technical Report, University of Colorado, 1970.

Kintsch, W., & Morris, C. J. Application of a Markov model to free recall and recognition. *Journal of Experimental Psychology,* 1965, **69**, 200 – 206.

Kiparsky, P., & Kiparsky, C. Fact. In D. D. Steinberg & L. A. Jacobovits (Eds.), *Semantics.* Cambridge: University Press, 1971.

Kučera H., & Francis, W. N. *Computational analysis of present day American English.* Providence, R.I.: Brown University Press, 1967.

Lakoff, G. *Irregularity in syntax.* New York: Holt, Rinehart & Winston, 1970. (a)

Lakoff, G. Linguistics and natural logic. *Synthese,* 1970, **22**, 151–271. (b)

Lakoff, G. Hedges: A study in measuring criteria and the logic of fuzzy concepts. Papers from the Eighth Regional Meeting, Chicago Linguistics Society. Chicago: University of Chicago Linguistics Department, 1973.

Landauer, T. K., & Freedman, J. L. Information retrieval from long-term memory: Category size and recognition time. *Journal of Verbal Learning and Verbal Behavior,* 1968, **7**, 291 – 295.

Landauer, T. K., & Meyer, D. E. Category size and semantic memory retrieval. *Journal of Verbal Learning and Verbal Behavior,* 1972, **11**, 539 – 549.

Lees, R. B. *The grammar of English nominalizations.* Bloomington: Indiana University Press, 1960.

Lehrer, A. Semantic cuisine. *Journal of Linguistics,* 1969, **5**, 39 – 55.

Loftus, E. F. Nouns, adjectives, and semantic memory. *Journal of Experimental Psychology,* 1972, **96**, 213 – 215.

Loftus, E. F., & Suppes, P. Structural variables that determine the speed of retrieving words from long-term memory. *Journal of Verbal Learning and Verbal Behavior,* 1972, **11**, 770 – 777.

Luce, R. D. A threshold theory for simple detection experiments. *Psychological Review,* 1963, **70**, 61 – 79.

Lyons, J. *Introduction to theoretical linguistics.* Cambridge: University Press, 1968.

MacKay, D. G. To end ambiguous sentences. *Perception & Psychophysics,* 1966, **1**, 426 – 436.

Mandler, G. Organization and recognition. In E. Tulving & W. Donaldson (Eds.), *Organization of memory.* New York: Academic Press, 1972.

Mandler, G., & Dean, P. J. Seriation: Development of serial order in free recall. *Journal of Experimental Psychology*, 1969, **81**, 207 – 215.

Marshall, J. C., & Newcombe, F. Syntactic and semantic errors in paralexia. *Neuropsychologia*, 1966, **4**, 169 – 176.

Marshall, M., Newcombe, F., & Marshall, J. C. The microstructure of word-finding difficulties in a dysphasic patient. In G. B. Flores d'Arcais & W. J. M. Levelt (Eds.), *Advances in psycholinguistics*. Amsterdam: North Holland, 1970.

Marks, L. E., & Miller, G. A. The role of semantic and syntactic constraints in the memorization of English sentences. *Journal of Verbal Learning and Verbal Behavior*, 1964, **3**, 1 – 5.

Martin, E. Stimulus meaningfulness and paired-associate transfer: An encoding variability hypothesis. *Psychological Review*, 1968, **75**, 421–441.

Martin, E. Stimulus encoding in learning and transfer. In A. W. Melton & E. Martin (Eds.), *Coding processes in human memory*. Washington, D.C.: Winston, 1972.

Matthews, R. J. Concerning a "linguistic theory" of metaphor. *Foundations of Language*, 1971, **7**, 413–426.

McCawley, J. D. Where do noun phrases come from? In R. A. Jacobs & P. S. Rosenbaum (Eds.), *Readings in English transformational grammar*. Waltham, Mass.: Ginn, 1970.

McCormack, P. D. Recognition memory: How complex a retrieval system? *Canadian Journal of Psychology*, 1972, **26**, 19 – 41.

McMahon, L. Grammatical analysis as part of understanding a sentence. Unpublished doctoral dissertation, Harvard University, 1963.

McNamara, T. Parsimony and the lexicon. *Language*, 1971, **47**, 359 – 374.

McNeill, D. *The acquisition of language*. New York: Harper, 1970.

Melton, A. W. The situation with respect to the spacing of repetitions in memory. *Journal of Verbal Learning and Verbal Behavior*, 1970, **9**, 546 – 606.

Meyer, D. E. On the representation and retrieval of stored semantic information. *Cognitive Psychology*, 1970, **1**, 242 – 300.

Meyer, D. E., & Schvaneveldt, R. W. Facilitation in recognizing pairs of words: Evidence of a dependence between retrieval operations. *Journal of Experimental Psychology*, 1971, **90**, 227–234.

Minsky, M., & Papert, S. *Perceptrons*. Cambridge, Mass.: MIT Press, 1969.

Moyer, R. S. Comparing objects in memory: Evidence suggesting an internal psychophysics. *Perception & Psychophysics*, 1973, **13**, 180 – 184.

Müller, G. E. Zur Analyse der Gedächtnistätigkeit und des Vorstellungsverlaufes. *Zeitschrift für Psychologie*, Ergänzungsband **5**, 1911.

Müller, G. E. Zur Analyse der Gedächtnistätigkeit und des Vorstellungsverlaufes, III. Teil. *Zeitschrift für Psychologie*, Erganzungsband **8**, 1913.

Murdock, B. B., Jr. *Human memory: Theory and data*. Potomac, Md.: Lawrence Erlbaum Associates, 1974.

Murray, D. C. Talk, silence, and anxiety. *Psychological Bulletin*, 1971, **75**, 244 – 260.

Nickerson, R. S. Binary-classification reaction time: A review of some studies of human information-processing capabilities. *Psychonomic Monograph Supplements*, 1972, **4**, (17, Whole No. 65).

Nilsson, N. J. *Learning machines*. New York: McGraw-Hill, 1965.

Norman, D. A. Memory, knowledge, and the answering of questions. In R. L. Solso (Ed.), *Contemporary issues in cognitive psychology: The Loyola symposium*. Washington, D.C.: Winston, 1973.

Norman, D. A., & Rumelhart, D. E. A system for perception and memory. In D. A. Norman (Ed.), *Models of human memory*. New York: Academic Press, 1970.

Oldfield, R. C. Memory mechanisms and the theory of schemata. *British Journal of Psychology*, 1954, **43**, 14 – 23.

Olson, D. R. Language use for communicating, instructing, and thinking. In J. B. Carroll & R. O. Freedle (Eds.), *Language comprehension and the acquisition of knowledge*. Washington, D.C.: Winston, 1972.

Osgood, C. E., Suci, G. J., & Tannenbaum, P. *The measurement of meaning.* Urbana, Ill.: University of Illinois Press, 1957.

Paivio, A. Mental imagery in associative learning and memory. *Psychological Review,* 1969, **76**, 241–263.

Paivio, A., Yuille, J. C., & Madigan, S. Concreteness, imagery, and meaningfulness values for 925 nouns. *Journal of Experimental Psychology,* 1968, **76**(1, Pt. 2).

Pellegrino, J., & Salzberg, P. Encoding specificity. Unpublished manuscript, University of Colorado, 1973.

Perfetti, C. A. Lexical density and phrase structure depth as variables in sentence retention. *Journal of Verbal Learning and Verbal Behavior,* 1969, **8**, 719–724.

Perfetti, C. A., & Goldman, S. R. Thematization and sentence retrieval. *Journal of Verbal Learning and Verbal Behavior,* 1974, **13**, 70–79.

Perlmutter, D. On the article in English. In M. Bierwisch & K. Heidolph (Eds.), *Progress in linguistics.* The Hague: Mouton, 1970.

Peterson, L. R. Search and judgment in memory. In B. Kleinmuntz (Ed.), *Concepts and the structure of memory.* New York: Wiley, 1967.

Peterson, L. R., Wampler, R., Kirkpatrick, M., & Saltzman, D. Effect of spacing repetitions on retention of paired-associates over short intervals. *Journal of Experimental Psychology,* 1963, **66**, 206–209.

Piaget, J. *Traité* de logique. Paris: Colin, 1949.

Posner, M. I., & Keele, S. W. On the genesis of abstract ideas. *Journal of Experimental Psychology,* 1968, **77**, 353–363.

Posner, M. I., & Warren, R. E. Traces, concepts, and conscious constructions. In A. W. Melton & E. Martin (Eds.), *Coding processes in human memory.* Washington, D.C.: Winston, 1972.

Potts, G. R. Information processing strategies used in the encoding of linear orderings. *Journal of Verbal Learning and Verbal Behavior,* 1972, **11**, 727–740.

Prytulak, L. S. Natural language mediation. *Cognitive Psychology,* 1971, **2**, 1–56.

Pylyshyn, Z. W. What the mind's eye tells the mind's brain: A critique of mental imagery. *Psychological Bulletin,* 1973, **80**, 1–24.

Quillian, M. R. Word concepts: A theory and simulation of some basic semantic capabilities. *Behavioral Science,* 1967, **12**, 410–43.

Quillian, M. R. Semantic memory. In M. Minsky (Ed.), *Semantic information processing.* Cambridge, Mass.: MIT Press, 1968.

Quillian, M. R. The teachable language comprehender. *Communications of the Association for Computing Machinery,* 1969, **12**, 459–476.

Quine, W. O. *Word and object.* Cambridge, Mass.: MIT Press, 1960.

Raser, G. A. Recoding of semantic and acoustic information in memory. *Journal of Verbal Learning and Verbal Behavior,* 1972, **11**, 692–697.

Reitman, J. S., & Bower, G. H. Storage and later recognition of exemplars of concepts. *Cognitive Psychology,* 1973, **4**, 194–206.

Rescher, N. *Introduction to logic.* New York: St. Martin's Press, 1964.

Rescher, N., & Urquhart, A. *Temporal logic.* Vienna: Springer Verlag, 1971.

Riegel, K. F. The Michigan Restricted Association Norms. Technical Report, April 10, 1965, University of Michigan.

Rips, L. J., Shoben, E. J., & Smith, E. E. Semantic distance and the verification of semantic relations. *Journal of Verbal Learning and Verbal Behavior,* 1973, **12**, 1–20.

Rivero, M. L. Remarks on operators and modalities. *Foundations of Language,* 1972, **9**, 209–241.

Rosch, E. H. Natural categories. *Cognitive Psychology,* 1973, **4**, 328–350.

Rosenberg, S. Association and phrase structure in sentence recall. *Journal of Verbal Learning and Verbal Behavior,* 1968, **7**, 1077–1081.

Ross, J. R. On declarative sentences. In R. A. Jacobs & P. S. Rosenbaum (Eds.), *Readings in English transformational grammar.* Waltham, Mass.: Ginn, 1970.

Rumelhart, D. E., Lindsay, P. H., & Norman, D. A. A process model for long-term memory. In E. Tulving & W. Donaldson (Eds.), *Organization of memory.* New York: Academic Press, 1972.

Rundus, D. Analysis of rehearsal processes in free recall. *Journal of Experimental Psychology,* 1971, **89**, 63 – 77.

Russell, B. The philosophy of logical atomism. In *Logic and knowledge: Essays 1901–1950.* New York: Macmillan, 1956.

Sachs, J. D. S. Recognition memory for syntactic and semantic aspects of connected discourse. *Perception & Psychophysics,* 1967, **2**, 437 – 442.

Schaeffer, B., & Wallace, R. Semantic similarity and the comparison of word meanings. *Journal of Experimental Psychology,* 1969, **82**, 343–346.

Schaeffer, B., & Wallace, R. The comparison of word meanings. *Journal of Experimental Psychology,* 1970, **86**, 144–152.

Schank, R. C. Conceptual dependency: A theory of natural language understanding. *Cognitive Psychology,* 1972, **3**, 552 – 631.

Schlesinger, I. M. *Sentence structure and the reading process.* The Hague: Mouton, 1968.

Schmidt, F. *Logik der Syntax.* Berlin: Deutscher Verlag der Wissenschaften, 1962.

Seebohm, H. B. Otto Selz: Ein Beitrag zur Geschichte der Psychologie. Inaugural dissertation, Universität Heidelberg, 1970.

Selz, O. *Über die Gesetze des geordneten Denkverlaufs.* Stuttgart: Spemann, 1913.

Selz, O. *Zur Psychologie des producktiven Denkens und Irrtums.* Bonn: Cohen, 1922.

Shafto, M. The space for case. *Journal of Verbal Learning and Verbal Behavior,* 1973, **12**, 551–562.

Shiffrin, R. M. Memory search. In D. A. Norman (Ed.), *Models of human memory.* New York: Academic Press, 1970.

Shulman, H. G. Encoding and retention of semantic and phonetic information in short-term memory. *Journal of Verbal Learning and Verbal Behavior,* 1970, **9**, 499 – 508.

Simmons, R. F. Some semantic structures for representing English meanings. In J. B. Carroll & R. O. Freedle (Eds.), *Language comprehension and the acquisition of knowledge.* Washington, D.C.: Winston, 1972.

Simmons, R. F. Semantic networks: Their computation and use for understanding English sentences. In R. C. Schank, & K. M. Colby (Eds.), *Computer models of thought and language.* San Francisco: Freeman, 1973.

Simmons, R. F., & Slocum J. Generating English discourse from semantic networks. *Communications of the ACM,* 1972, **15**, 891 – 905.

Skinner, B. F. *Verbal behavior.* New York: Appleton, 1957.

Slamecka, N. J. An examination of trace storage in free recall. *Journal of Experimental Psychology,* 1968, **76**, 504 – 513.

Slobin, D. I. Grammatical transformations and sentence comprehension in childhood and adulthood. *Journal of Verbal Learning and Verbal Behavior,* 1966, **5**, 219 – 227.

Sloman, A. Interactions between philosophy and artificial intelligence: The role of intuition and non-logical reasoning in intelligence. *Artificial Intelligence,* 1971, **2**, 209 – 225.

Steinberg, D. D. Analyticity, amphigory, and the semantic interpretation of sentences. *Journal of Verbal Learning and Verbal Behavior,* 1970, **9**, 37 – 51. (a)

Steinberg, D. D. Negation, analyticity, amphigory, and the semantic interpretation of sentences. *Journal of Experimental Psychology,* 1970, **84**, 417 – 423. (b)

Sternberg, S. Memory scanning: Mental processes revealed by reaction-time experiments. *American Scientist,* 1969, **57**, 421 – 457.

Suppes, P. Semantics of context-free fragments of natural languages. In K. J. Hintikka, J. Moravcsik, & P. Suppes (Eds.), *Approaches to natural language.* Dodrecht: Reidel, 1973.

Taylor, I. Content and structure in sentence production. *Journal of Verbal Learning and Verbal Behavior,* 1969, **8**, 170 – 175.

Theios, J. Reaction time measurements in the study of memory processes: Theory and data. In G. H. Bower (Ed.), *The psychology of learning and motivation.* Vol. 7. New York: Academic Press, 1973.

Thomson, D. M. Context effects in recognition memory. *Journal of Verbal Learning and Verbal Behavior,* 1972, **11**, 497 – 511.

Thomson, D. M., & Tulving, E. Associative encoding and retrieval: Weak and strong cues. *Journal of Experimental Psychology*, 1970, **86**, 255 – 262.

Thorne, J. P. On the notion "Definite." *Foundations of Language*, 1972, **8**, 562 – 568.

Townsend, J. P. A note on the identifiability of parallel and serial processes. *Perception & Psychophysics*, 1971, **10**, 161 – 163.

Tulving, E. Episodic and semantic memory. In E. Tulving & W. Donaldson (Eds.), *Organization of memory*. New York: Academic Press, 1972.

Tulving, E., & Madigan, S. A. Memory and verbal learning. *Annual Review of Psychology*, 1970, **21**, 437 – 484.

Tulving, E., & Osler, S. Effectiveness of retrieval cues in memory for words. *Journal of Experimental Psychology*, 1968, **77**, 593 – 601.

Tulving, E., & Thomson, D. M. Retrieval processes in recognition memory: Effects of associative context. *Journal of Experimental Psychology*, 1971, **87**, 116 – 124.

Tulving, E., & Thomson, D. M. Encoding specificity and retrieval processes in episodic memory. *Psychological Review*, 1973, **80**, 352 – 373.

Underwood, B. J. False recognition produced by implicit verbal response. *Journal of Experimental Psychology*, 1965, **70**, 122 – 129.

Underwood, B. J. Attributes of memory. *Psychological Review*, 1969, **76**, 559 – 573.

Underwood, B. J. Word recognition memory and frequency information. *Journal of Experimental Psychology*, 1972, **94**, 276 – 283.

Walker, H. J. Imagery ratings for 338 nouns. *Behavioral Research Methods and Instrumentation*, 1970, **21**, 165 – 167.

Walker, H. M., & Lev, J. *Statistical inference*. New York: Holt, 1953.

Waugh, N. C., & Norman, D. A. Primary memory. *Psychological Review*, 1965, **72**, 89 – 104.

Wearing, A. J. The storage of complex sentences. *Journal of Verbal Learning and Verbal Behavior*, 1970, **9**, 21 – 29.

Weigl, E., & Bierwisch, M. Neuropsychology and linguistics: Topics of common research. *Foundations of Language*, 1970, **6**, 1 – 18.

Weinreich, U. On the semantic structure of language. In J. H. Greenberg (Ed.), *Universals of language*. Cambridge, Mass.: MIT Press, 1963.

Weist, R. M. The role of rehearsal: Recopy or reconstruct. *Journal of Verbal Learning and Verbal Behavior*, 1972, **11**, 440 – 450.

Whitehead, A. N., & Russell, B. *Principia mathematica*. Vol. I. (2nd ed.) Cambridge: University Press, 1927.

Wilkins, A. T. Conjoint frequency, category size, and categorization time. *Journal of Verbal Learning and Verbal Behavior*, 1971, **10**, 382 – 385.

Winograd, T. Understanding natural language. *Cognitive Psychology*, 1972, **3**, 1 – 191.

Woods, W. A. Transition network grammars for natural language analysis. *Communications of the Association for Computing Machinery*, 1970, **13**, 591 – 606.

Wundt, W. *Logik*. Leipzig, 1880.

Zadeh, L. A. Fuzzy sets. *Information and Control*, 1965, **8**, 338 – 353.

Zadeh, L. A. Fuzzy languages and their relation to human and machine intelligence. In *Man and Computer, Proceedings of the International Conference at Bordeaux, 1970*. Basel: Karger, 1972.

Zadeh, L. A. A fuzzy set-theoretic interpretation of linguistic hedges. (Memorandum No. ERL– M 335), Berkeley, Cal.: Electronics Research Laboratory, 1972.

Zivian, M. T., & Riegel, K. F. Word identification as a function of semantic clues and associative frequency. *Journal of Experimental Psychology*, 1969, **79**, 336–341.

AUTHOR INDEX

Numbers in italics refer to the pages on which the complete references are listed.

A

Abraham, W., 38, *263*
Ackerman, W., 115, *266*
Anderson, J. R., 12, 39, 42, 46, 74, 77, 79, 147, 148, 252, 258, *263*
Anderson, N. H., 179, 184, 257, *263*
Anisfeld, M., 102, *263*
Atkinson, R. C., 93, 95, 178, 182, 192, 260, *263*

B

Bahrick, H. P., 74, 75, 97, *263*
Baldwin, J. M., 150, *266*
Barclay, J. R., 244, 254, *263, 264*
Bartlett, F. C., 252, 256, *264*
Battig, W. F., 198, *264*
Becker, J. D., 82, *264*
Bever, T. G., 252, *265*
Bickerton, D., 38, *264*
Bierwisch, M., 47, 210, 224, *264, 271*
Bjork, R. A., 75, *264*
Black, M., 38, *264*
Blumenthal, A. L., 42, *264*

Bolinger, D., 36, 72, *264*
Borges, M. A., 52, *264*
Bousfield, W. A., 197, *265*
Bower, G. H., 12, 39, 42, 46, 74, 77, 79, 80, 147, 148, 252, 255, *263, 264, 269*
Bowers, F., 220, *264*
Bransford, J. D., 49, 116, 178, 244, 253, 255, 256, *264*
Bruce, D. R., 95, *265*
Buschke, H., 99, *267*

C

Card, S. K., 149, *264*
Carroll, J. B., 15, *264*
Chafe, W. L., 64, 65, 67, *264*
Chall, J. S., 135, *264*
Chapin, P. G., 220, *264*
Chase, W. G., 222, 249, *265*
Chomsky, N., 1, 3, 38, 70, 219, 220, 221, 251, *264*
Clark, H. H., 111, 116, 117, 149, 206, 216, 222, 223, 240, 249, *264, 265, 267*
Cofer, C. N., 95, *265*

273

Cohen, B. H., 197, 265
Collins, A. M., 37, 46, 195, 196, 198, 199, 200, 202, 203, 204, 209, 210, 214, 215, 265
Conrad, C., 98, 197, 202, 203, 265
Craik, F. I. M., 66, 107, 175, 257, 265
Cramer, P., 92, 265
Crothers, E. J., 16, 140, 265

D

Dean, P. J., 95, 267

E

Eagle, M., 102, 266
English, H. B., 257, 265
Estes, W. K., 43, 265

F

Farkas, A. J., 179, 184, 263
Fillenbaum, S., 2, 102, 244, 265
Fillmore, C. J., 15, 24, 25, 53, 62, 63, 70, 251, 265
Fodor, J. A., 250, 252, 265, 267
Foss, D. J., 230, 231, 265
Francis, W. N., 226, 267
Franks, J. J., 116, 178, 244, 255, 256, 264
Fredericksen, C. H., 16, 173, 265
Freedle, R. O., 15, 264
Freedman, J. L., 195, 199, 267
Frege, G., 9, 265
Frijda, N. H., 23, 265

G

Gabor, D., 101, 265
Garrett, M., 252, 265
Garrod, S., 252, 258, 266
Gartman, L. M., 95, 266
Gazziniga, M. S., 209, 222, 241, 266
Glanzer, M., 95, 266
Glucksberg, S., 252, 266
Goldman, S. R., 150, 269
Goldman-Eisler, F., 225, 266
Green, C. C., 46, 266
Greeno, J. G., 94, 96, 266
Grossman, L., 102, 266

H

Halliday, M. A. K., 14, 141, 142, 266
Hamilton, W., 42, 266

Heider, E. R., 28, 266
Herbart, J. F., 4, 79, 266
Herrmann, D. J., 192, 263
Hilbert, D., 115, 266
Hjelmslev, L., 250, 266
Höffding, H., 42, 195, 266
Hogan, R. M., 75, 93, 96, 266, 267
Holyoak, K., 217, 266
Honeck, R. P., 245, 266
Horovitz, L. M., 150, 266
Hubert, S., 257, 263
Humphrey, G., 5, 266
Hunt, E. B., 31, 266

I

Inhelder, B., 46, 266

J

James, C. T., 149, 150, 266
James, W., 39, 40, 41, 66, 74, 86, 195, 266
Jarvella, R. J., 175, 266
Johnson, M. F., 95, 266
Johnson, M. K., 49, 264
Johnson, R. E., 140, 267
Jorgensen, C. C., 215, 217, 267
Juola, J. F., 93, 178, 182, 192, 260, 263
Just, M. A., 223, 267

K

Kantor, J. R., 5, 267
Karttunen, L., 57, 58, 267
Katz, J. J., 250, 267
Keele, S. W., 255, 269
Keenan, E. L., 45, 55, 59, 267
Killian, C. D., 257, 265
Kintsch, W., 16, 25, 28, 31, 36, 37, 42, 74, 75, 79, 80, 89, 93, 94, 96, 98, 99, 107, 108, 110, 116, 123, 137, 203, 211, 212, 215, 217, 223, 225, 233, 236, 241, 244, 246, 250, 266, 267
Kiparsky, C., 59, 267
Kiparsky, P., 59, 267
Kirkpatrick, M., 94, 269
Kučera, H., 226, 267

L

Lakoff, G., 28, 29, 31, 220, 267
Landauer, T. K., 195, 199, 200, 201, 215, 267
Lees, R. B., 219, 267

Lehrer, A., 34, 35, *267*
Lev, J., 111, *271*
Lindsay, P. H., 47, 246, 247, 248, *269*
Lockhart, R. S., 107, 175, 257, *265*
Loftus, E. F., 197, 209, *267*
Luce, R. D., 92, *267*
Lyons, J., 65, *267*

M

McCarrell, N. S., 253, *264*
McCawley, J. D., 16, *268*
McCormack, P. D., 75, 94, *268*
Mackay, D. G., 229, *267*
McMahon, L., 117, *268*
McNamara, T., 34, *268*
McNeill, D., 251, *268*
Madigan, S. A., 2, 216, *269*, *271*
Mandler, G., 76, 93, 95, *267*, *268*
Marin, J., 31, *266*
Marks, L. E., 233, 235, *268*
Marshall, J. C., 209, 221, *268*
Marshall, M., 222, *268*
Martin, E., 94, *268*
Matthews, P. J., 37, 38, *268*
Melton, A. W., 94, *268*
Meyer, D. E., 198, 199, 200, 201, 212, 215, *267*, *268*
Miller, G. A., 233, 235, *268*
Miller, R. F., 96, *267*
Minsky, M., 101, *268*
Montague, W. E., 198, *264*
Morris, C. J., 94, *267*
Moyer, R. S., 30, *268*
Müller, G. E., 39, 40, 43, 74, 195, *268*
Murdock, B. B., Jr., 93, *268*
Murray, D. C., 225, *268*

N

Newcombe, F., 209, 221, *268*
Nickerson, R. S., 177, *268*
Nilsson, N. J., 101, *268*
Norman, D. A., 23, 33, 47, 66, 80, 99, 246, 247, 248, *268*, *269*, *271*

O

Oldfield, R. C., 256, *268*
Olivier, D. C., 28, *266*
Olson, D. R., 15, *268*

Osgood, C. E., 24, *269*
Osler, S., 77, 96, *271*

P

Paivio, A., 216, *269*
Papert, S., 101, *268*
Pellegrino, J., 97, *269*
Perfetti, C. A., 150, *269*
Perlmutter, D., 48, *269*
Peterson, L. R., 93, 94, *269*
Piaget, J., 46, *266*, *269*
Posner, M. I., 255, 257, *269*
Potts, G. R., 254, *269*
Prytulak, L. S., 101, 150, *266*, *269*
Pylyshyn, Z. W., 6, 82, *269*

Q

Quillian, M. R., 37, 46, 47, 195, 196, 198, 199, 200, 202, 203, 204, 209, 210, 211, 214, 215, *265*, *269*
Quine, W. O., 9, 71, *269*

R

Raphael, B., 46, *266*
Raser, G. A., 98, 99, *269*
Reicher, G. M., 95, *265*
Reitman, J. S., 255, *269*
Rescher, N., 56, 68, *269*
Riegel, K. F., 209, 216, *269*
Rips, L. J., 197, 198, 200, 201, 204, 211, 212, 215, *269*
Rivero, M. L., 54, 56, *269*
Rosch, E. H., 28, 31, *269*
Rosenberg, S., 101, *269*
Ross, J. R., 56, *269*
Rumelhart, D. E., 46, 47, 80, 246, 247, 248, *268*, *269*
Rundus, D., 95, *270*
Russell, B., 48, 56, *270*, *271*

S

Sachs, J. D. S., 116, 178, 244, 258, *270*
Saltzman, D., 94, *269*
Salzberg, P., 94, 97, *269*
Sawyers, B. K., 52, 179, 184, *263*, *264*
Schaeffer, B., 198, 200, 215, *270*
Schank, R. C., 47, 250, *270*
Schlesinger, I. M., 117, 135, *270*

Schmidt, F., 47, *270*
Schvaneveldt, R. W., 198, *268*
Seebohm, H. B., 40, *270*
Selz, O., 41, 42, 81, 195, *270*
Shafto, M., 246, *270*
Shiffrin, R. M., 74, 95, *270*
Shoben, E. J., 197, 198, 200, 201, 204, 211, 212, 215, *269*
Shulman, H. G., 98, 99, *270*
Simmons, R. F., 15, 47, *270*
Skinner, B. F., 1, *270*
Slamecka, N. J., 96, *270*
Slocum, J., *270*
Slobin, D. I., 117, *270*
Sloman, A., 33, *270*
Smith, E. E., 197, 198, 200, 201, 204, 211, 212, 215, *269*
Steinberg, D. D., 209, *270*
Sternberg, S., 177, *270*
Stone, D. J., 31, *266*
Suci, G. J., 24, *269*
Suppes, P., 46, 197, *267, 270*

T

Tannenbaum, P., 24, *269*
Taylor, I., 225, 228, *270*
Theios, J., 177, *270*
Thompson, J. G., 150, *266*
Thomson, D. M., 75, 76, 77, 78, 96, *270, 271*
Thorne, J. P., 48, *271*
Townsend, J. P., 177, *271*
Trabasso, T. A., 252, 258, *266*
Tulving, E., 2, 4, 76, 77, 78, 80, 96, *271*

U

Underwood, B. J., 80, 92, 93, *271*

Urquhart, A., 68, *269*

V

van Dijk, T. A., 16, 45, 46, 48, *265*

W

Wald, J., 252, *266*
Walker, H. J., 216, *271*
Walker, H. M., 111, *271*
Wallace, R., 198, 200, 215, *270*
Wampler, R., 94, *269*
Warren, R. E., 255, 257, *269*
Waugh, N. C., 66, 99, *271*
Wearing, A. J., 150, 252, *271*
Weigl, E., 210, 224, *271*
Weinreich, U., 47, *271*
Weist, R. M., 95, *271*
Welborn, E. L., 257, *265*
Wescourt, K. T., 192, *263*
Whitehead, A. N., 48, *271*
Whitmarsh, G. A., 197, *265*
Wilkins, A. T., 197, 198, *271*
Winograd, T., 15, 23, 47, 214, *271*
Woods, W. A., 70, *271*
Wundt, W., 42, 72, *271*

Y

Yuille, J. C., 216, *269*

Z

Zadeh, L. A., 29, 31, *271*

SUBJECT INDEX

A

Adjectives, comparative, 29, 30
Adverbials, sentence, 54
Agent, 24, 34, 35, 141–150
Analog representations, 15, 33, 254, 255
Ambiguity, 11, 14, 71
Apperceptive mass, 4, 79
Associationism, 39–41
Augmented transition networks, 70

C

Case grammar, 23–25, 246
Competence-performance distinction, 3
Comprehension, 172, 253, 254
    two-stage model of sentence comprehension,
        105, 189–192, 212–214, 260, 261
Computer simulation models, 46, 47
Concept identification, 31
Conjunction, 13
Consciousness, 65, 86
Consequence operator, 32

D

Decomposition, 12, 104, 219–242, 246–250
Deductive reasoning, 31
Definite description, 47–50
Definitional sentences, 101, 203–210, 212
Derivability, *see* Decomposition

E

Encoding, 80, 82–90
    bias, 84, 214
    in short-term memory, 98–99
    propositional, 123
    specificity, 77–79, 97
Episodic memory, *see* Memory
Experiencer, 24, 34, 35

F

Familiarity tags, 77
Features, semantic, 35, 38, 249
Finite automata, 70
Fuzzy sets, 27–31

G

Generation-recognition models, 74–82
Gestalt psychology, 41
Goal, 24, 141–150

H

HAM, 148, 252
Hedges, 28–29

I

Identity of reference, *see* Repetition rule
Imagery
    and pre-propositional ideas, 6
    effects on sentence evaluation, 215, 217
    relation to lexical complexity, 223-224
    relation to semantic diffuseness, 216, 217
Implication, 32, 35, 56–62
Inference, 26, 31–34, 56–62, 67–70, 252
    as a function of syntactic complexity,
        108–122, 192
    during reading, 104, 153–175, 253, 254
    effects of irrelevant information, 117–121
Instrument, 24, 35, 141—150

K

Knowledge, 10, 78

L

Lexical description, 10, 34–36, 47, 83, 242
Lexicalist hypothesis, 221, 241
Levels of processing, 11, 43, 107, 108, 162,
        163, 174, 175, 256–259
Locative, 24, 62–64, 141, 142, 145–150
Logic
    natural, 45–47
    standard, 45–47, 56, 71, 109

M

Meaning, philosophical and psychological ap-
        proaches, 9
Meaning postulates, 221, 222, 241
Memory
    abstract memory representations for text,
        107, 120–122, 244, 245
    code, 83–91
    episodic memory, 73–102
    episodic-semantic distinction, 4, 77–81, 100
    long-term memory, organization of, 74
    reconstructive memory, 252
    semantic memory, 10, 23–36, 39, 47,
        195–217
    sentence memory, 140–150
Memory search, 104
    long-term memory, 178, 192
    paragraph memory, 177–193
    semantic memory, 195–217
    short-term memory, 177
Memory, short-term, 86, 97–100, 258
    limited capacity, 98
    acoustic coding, 98–99
Metaphors, 36–39
Mnemonics, 89
Modality, 53–56, 67, 68

N

Negation, 54
Nonsense syllables, 101
Noun hierarchy, 25, 26, 195–202
    production and deletion operators, 26
Noun priority, 209

O

Object, 24, 35, 141–150

P

Part operator, 32
Particular description, 50
Pattern completion, 42, 43, 83, 84, 101, 189
Pattern matching, 42, 43, 83, 84, 101, 102,
        189–192, 259, 260
Performatives, 56
Pragmatics, 14, 56, 72
Pre-propositional thought, 5
Presupposition, 59–62
Proposition, 12–15, 42, 82, 104
    implicit, 155–158, 165, 173, 174
    multi-element versus binary, 12, 104,
        141–150, 251, 252
    number of propositions in reading, 123–136,
        250
    recall, 140–150, 236, 238, 240
Proverbs, 245
Psycholinguistics, 2
Purpose operator, 32

Q

Quantification, 50–53

R

Rank of a proposition, 139
Readability, 135
Reading, inferences during, 104, 153–175, 253, 254
Reading time
  free reading, 111–117, 120, 124–130, 160, 164, 169
  model of, 131–134
  restricted reading, 112–115, 126, 128, 129, 138
Recall, 87–91, 257
  cued recall, 90, 96, 97, 236–240
  free, 90, 94–96
  learning, 94
  organizational effects, 95
  output order, 95, 96
  scoring procedures for text recall, 126
  spacing of repetitions, 94, 95
  test trials, 75
  two-stage model, 74–82
Recognition, 86, 87, 92–94, 257
  context effects, 75, 92, 93
  generation-recognition models, 74–82
  false recognition, 92
  frequency effects, 93
  latencies, 93
  organization of material, 75, 93, 94
  recall checks, 76
  recency effects, 93
  response bias, 92
  test trials, 75
  text recognition, 184–188
Repetition rule, 16, 49
Retrieval, 74, 88–90, 94–97, 239, 240, 257, 259
Rote learning, 89, 90

S

Semantic
  distance, 197-202, 204, 209, 212
  memory, see Memory
  relations in recall, 88, 89
Short-term memory, see Memory
Source, 24
Structure
  deep structure, 108, 244
  macro-structure, 17
  paragraph structure, 16–22
  paragraph structure in recall, 137–140, 250, 251
  structure-process distinction, 3, 23
  surface structure, 108, 244
Syntactic complexity, 108, 110, 116, 117, 134, 173
Syntactic transformation rules, 14
Syllogism, 114, 115

T

Tense, 64-70
Text base, 11, 12, 15–22
  uniqueness of, 20
  psychological reality, 123–151
Theme, 14, 149
Time, 24, 62–70, 141, 142, 145–150
Transformational hypothesis, 220, 241
Type-token distinction, 10

V

Verb frames, 34–36, 252
Verb recall, 150

W

Word concept, 11–13